THE OFFICIAL® PRICE GUIDE TO

CAMERAS

BY
THE HOUSE OF COLLECTIBLES, INC.

EDITOR
THOMAS E. HUDGEONS III

PUBLISHER'S NOTE: The camera information and pricing in this edition is derived from the *Price Guide To Antique and Classic Still Cameras,* 3rd Edition (1981-1982) by James M. & Joan C. McKeown. Most of the photographs are also from that book or from the *Collector's Guide to Kodak Cameras* by the same authors. The material is used under license from the authors and their publisher, Centennial Photo Service, P.O. Box 1125, Grantsburg, WI 54840.

FIRST EDITION
THE HOUSE OF COLLECTIBLES, INC., ORLANDO, FLORIDA 32809

IMPORTANT NOTICE. The format of **THE OFFICIAL PRICE GUIDE SERIES,** published by **THE HOUSE OF COLLECTIBLES, INC.,** is based on the following proprietary features: **ALL FACTS AND PRICES ARE COMPILED THRU A COMPUTERIZED PROCESS** which relies on a nationwide sampling of information obtained from noteworthy collectibles experts, auction houses and specialized dealers. **DETAILED "INDEXED" FORMAT** enables quick retrieval of information for positive identification. **ENCAPSULATED HISTORIES** precede each category to acquaint the collector with the specific traits that are peculiar to that area of collecting. **VALUABLE COLLECTING INFORMATION** is provided for both the novice as well as the seasoned collector: How to begin a collection; How to buy, sell, and trade; Care and storage techniques; Tips on restoration; Grading guidelines; Lists of periodicals, clubs, museums, auction houses, dealers, etc. **AN AVERAGE PRICE RANGE** takes geographic location and condition into consideration when reporting collector value. **A SPECIAL 3rd PRICE COLUMN** enables the collector to compare the current market values with the last's years average selling price... indicating which items have increased in value. **INVENTORY CHECKLISTS SYSTEM** is provided for cataloging a collection. **EACH TITLE IS ANNUALLY UP-DATED** to provide the most accurate information available in the rapidly changing collectors marketplace.

All of the information, including valuations, in this book has been compiled from the most reliable sources, and every effort has been made to eliminate errors and questionable data. Nevertheless the possibility of error, in a work of such immense scope, always exists. The publisher will not be held responsible for losses which may occur, in the purchase, sale, or other transaction of items, because of information contained herein. Readers who feel they have discovered errors are invited to WRITE and inform us, so they may be corrected in subsequent editions. Those seeking further information on the topics covered in this book, are advised to refer to the complete line of Official Price Guides published by The House of Collectibles.

©MCMLXXXIII JIM McKEOWN

All rights reserved. No part of this book may be reproduced or utilized in any form or by any means, electronic or mechanical, including photocopying, recording, or by any information storage and retrieval system, without permission in writing from the publisher.

Published by: The House of Collectibles, Inc.
Orlando Central Park
1900 Premier Row
Orlando, FL 32809
Phone: (305) 857-9095

Printed in the United States of America

Library of Congress Catalog Card Number: 82-84645

ISBN: 0-87637-383-X / Paperback

TABLE OF CONTENTS

Daguerre Started It All 1
Camera Collecting In Focus 5
Buying Collector Cameras 13
Selling Your Collector
   Cameras 25
Condition 30
Camera Hunting Abroad 32
Investing 33
Organizing A Museum Exhibit ... 36
First Aid For Old Leather Bellows 37
Camera Chronology 38
About The Prices In
   This Book 54
Clubs 56
Museums 56
How To Use This Book 56

ALPHABETICAL LISTINGS A-D . . 57
Acma — Avus 57
Balda-Werk — Butcher 70
Cadet — Cyclops 83
Daci — Durst S.A. 95

EASTMAN KODAK CO. 99
Autographic — Autographic
   Special 101
Bantam — Bulls-eye 104
Cartridge Kodak — Cirkut 116
Daylight — Duo-620 117
Eastman Plate — Eureka 119
Falcon — Folding Pocket
   Special 120
Gift — Girl Scout 124
Hawkette — Holiday 125
Jiffy Kodak 126
Kodak Junior — Kodet 127

Medalist — Motormatic 35 128
Nagel 129
Ordinary Kodak 130
Panoram — Pupille 130
Quick Focus Kodak 138
Recomar — Retinette 138
Screen Focus — Super Six-20 .. 142
Tourist 147
Vanity — Vollenda 148
World's Fair Flash — Zenith ... 150

ALPHABETICAL LISTINGS E-Z . 151
Ebner — Eyematic 151
Falcon — Futura Werk 156
Galileo Optical — Guthe 160
Kawee 174
Haking — Huttig 174
Ica A.G. — Iso 180
Japy & Cie — Juwella 187
Kalart — K.W. 188
Laack — Lyra 194
Mackenstein — Myracle 201
Nagel — Noviflex 208
Okam — Owla 211
P.D.Q. — Pygmee 213
Q.P. — Quick Focus Kodak 219
Raaco — Ruthine 219
Sabre 620 — Synchro 227
Taisei Koki — Tynar 239
UCA — Utility Manufacturing .. 243
Vag — Voss 246
Wabash — Wunsche 252
Xit 257
Zale — Zorki 257
Index 266

ACKNOWLEDGEMENTS

THE HOUSE OF COLLECTIBLES would like to thank Mr. Jim McKeown for his valuable assistance in pricing, identification, and supplying photographs used in this first edition.

PHOTOGRAPHIC RECOGNITION

Cover Photograph: Photographer — Marc Hudgeons, Orlando, FL 32809; Location — Courtesy of International Camera Corp., Casselberry, FL 32707.

Color Section: Photographer — Marc Hudgeons, Orlando FL 32809; Location — Courtesy of International Camera Corp., Casselberry, FL 32707.

Color Separations: World Color, Ormond Beach, FL 32074.

BECOME AN "OFFICIAL" CONTRIBUTOR TO THE WORLD'S LEADING PRICE GUIDES

Are you an experienced collector with access to information not covered in this guide? Do you possess knowledge, data, or ideas that should be included?

If so, The House of Collectibles invites you to **GET INVOLVED.**

The House of Collectibles continuously seeks to improve, expand, and update the material in the **OFFICIAL PRICE GUIDE SERIES.** The assistance and cooperation of numerous collectors, auction houses and dealers has added immeasurably to the success of the books in this series. If you think you qualify as a contributor, our editors would like to offer your expertise to the readers of the **OFFICIAL PRICE GUIDE SERIES.**

As the publishers of the most popular and authoritative Price Guides, The House of Collectibles can provide a far-reaching audience for your collecting accomplishments. *Help the hobby grow* by letting others benefit from the knowledge that you have discovered while building your collection.

If your contribution appears in the next edition, you'll become an **"OFFICIAL"** member of the world's largest hobby-publishing team. Your name will appear on the acknowledgement page, *plus you will receive a free complimentary copy.* Send a full outline of the type of material you wish to contribute. Please include your phone number. Write to: **THE HOUSE OF COLLECTIBLES, INC.,** Editorial Department, 1900 Premier Row, Orlando, Florida, 32809.

DAGUERRE STARTED IT ALL

Photography, for so long thought impossible, is now approaching its 150th birthday. Louis Daguerre of France developed the first successful photographic apparatus and made his invention known in 1839. He was certainly not the first to experiment along these lines, as efforts had been made as early as the 18th century to create "sun images." But he was the first to manufacture and demonstrate a workable camera. Daguerre's camera used copper plates coated with a thin silver wash and exposed to iodine vapor. The sunlight burnt images into these plates, which came to be called "daguerreotypes" after their developer. Faint and shadowy though they were, Daguerre's pictures became the marvel of the age. They not only ushered in a new industry in the making and selling of photographic equipment, but a new art form in photography; and the influence of Daguerre's invention went much further. Photography gave birth to the photo-illustrated book and magazine, and eventually to motion pictures (1897). Its effect on art was incalculable. Impressionism, post-impressionism, surrealism, cubism and other schools of modern art were all directly fostered by the camera, as artists found themselves in competition with photography and sought to create pictures beyond the camera's scope.

Daguerre almost instantly became a world figure and a household name. He published papers and books on photography, in addition to manufacturing equipment and running his own studio. In the minds of the public, Daguerre WAS photography for at least a decade following the announcement of his invention. But during this time others were making their own experiments, seeking to improve on his basic principles. In fact the earliest "competitor" of Daguerre appeared on the scene in that same year, 1839. Fox Talbot, an Englishman, brought out a patented process which he called "Photogenic Drawing." It used paper coated with chloride of silver, rather than a metallic plate, and thus produced the first negatives in the history of photography. Fox made a positive image by placing his negative against another sheet of paper and subjecting it to strong light. Whether the Daguerreotype or the Photogenic Drawing was a better picture was hard to say; but it hardly mattered. Talbot had millions of potential customers in Britain, just as Daguerre had millions on the continent, and there was no problem for either of getting in each other's way. In 1841 Talbot introduced the calotype, an improvement on his earlier technique, in which exposure time was shortened without interfering with image quality.

Though Fox Talbot may or may not have been a mechanical genius, his contributions to the development of photography were immense — as were his contributions to our record of social history. The earliest portrait photographs in England are Talbot's. Photos would not exist of most of the individuals who posed for Talbot, if it were not for him, and they included some of history's greats. But even more important than this, Talbot had the historical perception to photograph ordinary folk doing ordinary things — fishermen, washerwomen, people playing chess and loafing on benches. Thus his photos, very numerous in number, serve as a wonderful record of society in the 1840's, the early years of Queen Victoria's reign.

Most of the world was very excited about photography in that first historic decade from 1839 to 1849, though of course there were some who proclaimed it a passing novelty or money-making gimmick. Photography studios began opening up in the major cities of Europe, and almost everyone who could afford the photographer's services was curious enough (or vain enough) to go and have a portrait shot. This was quite expensive in the pioneer days, so those who could indulge were naturally limited. Having

2 / DAGUERRE STARTED IT ALL

a photo portrait became a status mark, and most of the early customers were just as proud of their pictures as of oil portraits by celebrated artists. Gradually advances were made which permitted photos of small size, known as *carte-de-visite* or C.D.V., capable of being mounted in handy cases or articles of jewelry and carried on the person. It was of course a much more sentimental age than our own, in which everyone wanted to carry a loved one's portrait. Shooting carte-de-visite photos became a booming trade, as did manufacturing and selling the cases to contain them. These were available in gold, silver, plated brass, plain brass or bronze, tortoiseshell, papier-mache, mother-of-pearl, and many other materials to suit every possible taste and budget. Sometimes one photo was contained in the case, with a velvet-lined lid; but many cases held two photos, generally of a husband and wife. The antiques shops of today bear testimony to the proliferation of carte-de-visite photos in the mid 19th century. They are still common, to the point where an ordinary specimen (not of a famous person) can often be bought for a dollar or two. Carte-de-visites were ambrotypes, made from wet plates and sometimes called "wet collodion process."

It took no great genius to recognize the profit potential in photography, nor its perfect suitability for the one-man entrepreneur. Here was a business anybody with a little cash could get into, without the need for a factory, employees, salesmen, or much of anything. There was no stock to carry, and you really didn't even need a studio — or even an address. Many of the early professional photographers just roamed around. They would park themselves at beaches, county fairs, railroad stations, parks, busy intersections of large cities. There were sure to be plenty of passers-by who could not resist getting a photo of themselves. At the same time there were other photographers out in the field, snapping landmarks and city views. These were sold for so much apiece, either on the spot or at a central location, just as Currier and Ives sold its lithographs. Why buy a lithograph of Niagara Falls when you could get a photo of it?

There was also another — though not quite so simple — way in which photography could be turned to a profitable business: manufacturing cameras commercially, and selling them to amateur photographers or those who had ambitions of becoming professionals.

Obviously, the rise of the camera industry was dependent upon amateur photographers, just as its success today is almost wholly thanks to the amateurs and hobbyists. If professional photographers were the only customers for cameras and gear, the trade would be a tiny fraction of its present size. Amateur photography took quite some time to get off the ground, however. Various factors were responsible for this. For one thing, the public as a whole in the 1840's, 1850's, and even into the 1860's considered photography too mysterious and complicated to be fooled with. You either devoted all your efforts to it, or left it alone: it was not rated as a suitable spare-time endeavor. For another, the early cameras were just too foreboding in appearance: big, bulky, cumbersome. The difficulty of making good prints, and the danger of physical harm (nitrate burns to the fingers), also proved discouraging. Clearly there was not going to be much amateur or hobby interest, with so many obstacles in the way.

Technical improvements such as the gelatin or dry plate brought about an upsurge in amateur photography during the 1870's. This was the first decade in which amateur photography became truly popular. Smaller, handier cameras were placed on the market, with corners cut in their case designs and materials to bring down the prices and attract a large potential audience. At the same time photography clubs and periodicals for amateur shutterbugs proliferated, not to mention photo contests with medals for the best pictures. This was the signal for more and more commercial manufacturers to get into the business, and to compete for the market. So the 1870's witnessed a great diversity of new brand names, new models, new styles. Each succeeding decade brought about further increase in the number of active amateur photographers, with a corresponding increase in the number of manufacturers and available cameras. A great boost was forthcoming in the 1880's with the rise of American mail order business, as cameras were stocked by all the mail order houses and sold to persons in rural areas, who would otherwise have had no contact with a supplier.

It did not take manufacturers long to realize that they must not only make good cameras, but do a good job of promoting and merchandising them. A potential buyer might not purchase a camera, if he could not find the right accessories to use with it; so the camera kit went on the market, in which you received not just a camera but everything needed to enjoy photography. Of course there was also an instructional book, explaining the workings of that particular camera and the art in general. As would be expected, these early booklets "talked up" photography much more than do their present-day counterparts. It was assumed that many people knew nothing about photography, and had no friends or relatives who owned a camera. Thus they needed to be indoctrinated into liking photography and wanting to own a camera. Magazine ads for cameras placed in the 1880's and even as late as the nineties did likewise, though by then the need for introducing the mass public to photography was really becoming obsolete. Another merchandising "must" was a colorful carton or box for the camera. Eastman Kodak accomplished more in this regard than any of its competitors. It made photography LOOK LIKE FUN, just from the zestiness of the boxes!

There were many problems to be solved and challenges to be met by the manufacturers — who were ever an inventive lot (there was perhaps more raw brain power in the early camera industry than in any other, including autos). You could not just keep feeding cameras to the public and expect them to keep buying. Some sales would be made, but many more were likely with improved models — smaller and handier in size, less prone to injury (people were always dropping them), more convenient to load and unload, capable of taking more pictures for the same money, and of course cameras that shot clearer pictures under less than perfect lighting conditions. The average amateur of that time (final quarter of the 19th century) was amateurish indeed. The 19th century amateur, like many of today's, made all sorts of goofs. He would shoot under the worst possible conditions, aiming directly into the sunlight or snapping in near darkness, then curse the manufacturer when he got an unsatisfactory print. Of course he was a source of bad publicity for amateur photography — he would say to a friend, "Find a different hobby — photography doesn't work." This is not to say that the old cameras were perfect by any means. They required more patience and skill to use, than those of today. But they were not nearly so bad, on the whole, as their all-thumbs users were led to conclude. So it remained for the manufacturers to try to educate people in how to use cameras, and at the same time try to create cameras as foolproof as possible — foolproof meaning just that, something that even a total fool couldn't blunder too badly with. Successful accomplishment of that task was somewhat beyond the capabilities of the 1800's, but great strides were taken toward cameras that almost operated themselves.

It became evident very early in the game that most amateur photographers were not going to try emulating Matthew Brady or the other titans of the art. They did not approach photography as an art form but as a pleasant diversion to accompany a picnic or Sunday at the zoo. Thus it was pointless shoving fancy equipment at them; the fine points of a fine camera were totally lost on 9 out of 10 amateurs. "Does it shoot a clear picture?" most people would ask. And if the answer was, "Yes, if you use it right," that was all the encouragement needed.

4 / DAGUERRE STARTED IT ALL

Another popular question was, "Can I get the film developed easily and inexpensively?"

In the early days of amateur photography, up to about 1880 (but in some parts of the country until later), film developing was done as a sideline business by profesional photographers. The cost was quite steep, for more reasons than one. Professional photographers did not really want to encourage the amateurs TOO much, as this might mean a loss of business for them. They would develop the amateur's film, but calculated their charges so that he'd end up paying just about as much as for a studio shot. This was bad for the camera makers, so they countered by setting up local developing studios or, where this was not practical, establishing agents who would do the job. As amateur photography grew, it became clear that even a large network of agent developers would not serve the purpose. They could not be scattered so abundantly as to be within easy reach of everyone. The solution was to entrust local merchants with receiving undeveloped film from the public and forwarding it on to developers. Pharmacists were selected for this duty, chiefly because every town had a pharmacy within easy reach. Though the pharmacists made only a few cents on each order for developing, the orders mounted up, and this became a worthwhile source of revenue for all involved.

It will be hard, perhaps, for anyone but a collector to think of the 19th century cameras as being physically handsome, though anyone would have to agree that they are rather awe-inspiring. One should realize that the manufacturers were not, in all but a few cases, trying to promote sales on the basis of looks. With all the other problems to worry about, they were not going to start thinking of whether their product was a thing of beauty. Certainly they could have made very fashionable-looking cameras — but for what purpose? If the camera was inferior, even gold lame would not make it a successful seller. If the camera was good, then the smartest merchandise tack was to sell it as cheaply as possible and create a huge potential audience for it. Anything that added to the price without adding to the quality of the pictures, or convenience of use, was just not smart business.

Nevertheless, some early cameras — quite a few of them, really — are appealing for their looks. They may not be attractive artistically, but appealing anyway. Sometimes you will find a leather-covered model from the eighties or nineties on which oxhide was used. It must have been fairly good-looking originally, but the passage of time has rendered it even more so, as the leather has mellowed to a rich chocolate brown with tinges of red. It is really a pity when specimens of this sort reflect obvious neglect by former owners, exhibiting cracks in the leather and powdering due to excessive dryness. It should be needless to point out that a camera with a good leather covering (not leatherette or imitation) ought to be "dressed" periodically by rubbing it over with a good oil. The best preparation for this purpose is called British Museum Leather Dressing, an English product which is generally available in the U.S. (but expensive). Sporting goods shops often have it, as gun hobbyists use it. Another type of early camera which some hobbyists will find physically attractive is that having a wood frame body, of which there are many examples. Wood meant low production cost. Unlike wood used for furniture, camera wood did not need to be turned or carved or specially treated, nor even seasoned as there was not likely to be any problem with shrinkage. It could be finished merely with a good machine sanding and several coats of hand-rubbed oil. The original buyers might have thought of this as pretty drab, but today these old wood frame cameras have a distinct charm. The wood has acquired a patina with age and handling.

If competition among manufacturers did not provoke artistic designs, it certainly did lead to novelty designs. Here it was not just a matter of appealing to the eye, but grasping the potential buyer's attention and drawing him to a particular model because it was so much out of the ordinary. Cameras of novelty design started coming out in large quantity by 1890 and increased in output for the remainder of that decade and into the 20th century. There was a pretty steady market for them, though the buyers were probably a slightly different class of amateur photographers than those who bought standard models. Of all the novelty types, the hidden camera received the most play and was certainly the all-around best seller, even though from a technical point of view (the quality of pictures it yielded), it was often quite inferior to ordinary standard cameras and to models costing much less. Being able to take a photo without being observed had an attraction in itself, and apparently there were many people who would settle for second-rate prints, for the sake of snapping them in secret. Collecting hidden cameras or camouflaged cameras has become a major branch of the hobby, and you will not find many interspersed throughout the listings section of this book. They reflect the approaches taken to merchandising by the camera companies and also provide something of a psychology lesson. One maker, Expo of New York, designed a hidden camera in miniature size to resemble a pocket watch. Carrying an exposed pocket watch was the most natural thing in the world — who would suspect that it was really a camera? The Expo Watch Camera was very successful commercially. Placed on the market around 1905, it remained in production about 30 years. It might have even gone on longer, except that the fashion for wearing pocket watches came to an end. (But what did the owner of an Expo Camera Watch do when someone asked him for the time?) Kemper's Kombi was not really a hidden camera, but at 4 ounces this 1890's creation could be concealed without too much effort.

CAMERA COLLECTING IN FOCUS

The amateur photographer — not to mention the professional — wants the very latest in equipment, and the best that his budget permits. He wants to create the best pictures he possibly can, and the equipment is simply a means to that end. Who cares about a camera's looks or aesthetic qualities if it takes great pictures? Who cares about the country of origin, or the maker's name, or what the world might think of that maker 50 years from now?

But deep in the psyche of many photographers — amateur and professional — lurks a bit of that special something of which collectors are made.

It's all very understandable. You can hardly be a serious shutterbug for any length of time without making comparisons between cameras, looking at the improvements made in different models and the way they've evolved step by step. You want to know precisely how they work... why they do what they do... and how they got that way. Obviously, Matthew Brady was not snapping instant pictures. A tremendous amount of technical advancement has occurred with the camera between then and now. How did it occur? How was it reflected, model by model, year by year? What were the ancestors of today's high-speed cameras REALLY like?

OK, maybe this is just of elementary interest to you, like strolling through a museum and looking at the fossil ancestors of today's animals. But the historical side of photography has a way of taking hold, sooner or later. You might start by casually picking up a portfolio of old ambrotype reproductions at the library. "Well, isn't that interesting?" you muse in a half-hearted way. But you pick up a few more and a few more, and then you might see an exhibit of antique photographic gear. Still, you have no intention of ever spending a cent on an OLD camera. What a foolish idea, when the old camera certainly isn't going to take satisfying pictures (if it takes any at all).

6 / CAMERA COLLECTING IN FOCUS

In time, the foolish idea doesn't seem so foolish any longer. You found a Vest Pocket Ansco at the local antiques shop. It was a little scratched up, but at $17.50 it wasn't going to hurt your photography budget TOO much, and, well, it was an interesting little conversation piece. Of course you're not going to become a COLLECTOR... you're going to buy just this one... just this once.

Oh, really?

Turn the calendar ahead a year. You now have a dozen antique cameras. You're a member of a camera collecting club. Your Saturdays are spent searching the local auctions, antiques shops and pawnbrokers for old cameras. You subscribe to a whole sheaf of hobbyist periodicals, which fill your mailbox to the bursting point. You're spending money not only on antique cameras but on reference books about them, and on miscellaneous old photographic equipment. You might even be buying some early photo prints or negatives, too, to see just what those vintage cameras were capable of doing, and to round out your collection.

Meanwhile, what's happened to your photography hobby? You're still taking pictures. In fact, you get a bigger thrill from photography than ever before. No longer are you just a guy who snaps a shutter. You're a photo historian, a collector, a connoisseur. You now know the evolution and the anatomy of cameras. You know their family tree up and down and sidewise. You know which are the best cameras because you can see, at first hand, how they BECAME the best. And even those which are far from the best have their appeal. They're all part and parcel of the grand panorama called the history and development of the camera.

For anybody who's enthusiastic about cameras, what could be more spine tingling?

If anybody ever tries to tell you that it's silly buying old models of something on which so many improvements have been made (which is unlikely in this enlightened age), you can point to plenty of things which are bought for reasons other than their usefulness. Classic autos don't have power steering or gas saving features or pollution controls, but certain Deusenbergs still fetch over $100,000 when they cross the auction block. And if you tried to mail a letter with the 5¢ 1847 Ben Franklin postage stamp, it would be short 15¢ and arrive marked "Postage Due." Yet that stamp is worth hundreds of cool dollars. What something is capable of DOING is not of the least concern to the hobbyist or collector. What it IS, where it came from and what it's all about are the telling points. With old cameras, you have all the intriguing qualities of other collectibles and some others besides. Scarcity, physical charm and historical lure are there in abundance. Even John Q. Public stops in his tracks at the sight of something like a Kodak camera from the Gay Nineties. He might know absolutely zilch about photography or cameras, but somewhere in the back of his brain is a dim recollection of having SEEN an 1890's ordinary Kodak camera somewhere, sometime... or maybe a model similar to it. Was it the old trusty box camera that Great Aunt Julia lugged to picnics? Gosh, that was a LONG time ago... I never realized how much cameras have CHANGED since then.

Of course you didn't. The changes came imperceptibly, just like in everything else. And that's one of the things that makes camera collecting so fascinating. You can bring 'em all back, right before your eyes; and you can even include models that were obsolete long before anyone alive today had been born.

Camera collecting has made enormous strides in the past 20 years. It really wasn't a huge hobby in the early or mid sixties, though it did have its followers — as it has always seemed to. It was more specialized and most of the antique camera collectors were "closet collectors." That is, they cut their own path like Mungo Park in darkest Africa. There were no decent reference books, no clubs, no periodicals with page after page of buy/sell/swap ads. There were no fellow hobbyists within a ten-mile radius, either, unless you happened to be awfully lucky. As far as acquisitions went, you had little choice but to scour the local sources of secondhand merchandise — picking among bric-a-brac and faded lace doilies and backdate copies of "National Geographic." There were NO specialist dealers who stood ready to assist you, and the auction sales presented no more rosy a picture either. In those days, when vintage cameras made an appearance in the sales rooms, it was invariably as a random lot in a big mixed estate sale. And the catalogue description usually said something very brilliant, such as "Lot 32, One Old Camera..."

Most of the pioneer camera hobbyists shunned publicity, and for a very sensible reason. With the hobby not yet in vogue, you were very 'iable to get a reputation as an eccentric if the neighbors knew that you spent $50 on a Verascope Stereo camera (but try to get one for twice that price today!). It was fine to spend hard-earned money on stamps or coins or some kind of LEGITIMATE hobby material...but cameras? In the early sixties we were still in the Age of Repression, so far as collector's items were concerned. You either collected what everybody else was collecting, or, if you collected something else, you at least had the decency to keep the matter private.

This problem — ridicule or sidewise glances from society — kept camera collecting from growing as rapidly as it could have. But that's all behind us now. Today, if your proudest possession is a Guthe and Thorsch Pilot, or a Zeiss Ikon Ikoflex, you can shout it from the rooftops. Not only will you have plenty of company, but plenty of envy directed your way. The number of active collectors is only slightly larger than the number of would-be collectors. This book is intended for them, too, and for ANYBODY who's ever looked at an old camera and wondered, "Gee, how old could it be?" or, "I wonder how much it could be worth?"

The research and discovery potential in camera collecting is beyond measure. When that kind of activity can be combined with a little personal nostalgia, you have an unbeatable one-two punch. Nostalgia? Well, it comes in all sizes and shapes. As a youngster, your parents might have taken you to the Hayden Planetarium in New York, to see the big "sky show." In the middle of the auditorium sat a huge instrument of gleaming steel, with thousands of little buttons and levers and devices all over it. This was the machine that "made" the sky show. It threw stars and planets and constellations on the ceiling. If you were five or six years old, you sat in open-mouthed amazement at the proceedings. But chances are you paid enough attention to the announcer's commentary to catch the word ZEISS. That big monster of a machine was made by Zeiss...it came from Germany...there were only two or three others in the whole country. Zeiss? Who were they? Camera people! In fact, the makers of some of the most advanced cameras of their time, in the 1930's and 1940's.

Of course, there are many possible approaches to camera collecting. The products of a single manufacturer may appeal to you, and in that event you'll want to hunt down (or try to) every model ever produced by that firm. Or you may want to narrow things further and zero in exclusively on folding cameras made by that particular company. If company collecting is not for you, your approach may instead be to collect certain specific types of cameras, such as spy or police models, or novelty cameras. You might want to limit your collecting by time period, drawing the line at 1900 and admitting nothing later into your collection. If you can afford it, the line can be drawn at 1890 or 1880 — but of course the farther back you go, the more limiting the selection becomes, and the higher the prices. If none of the above seem specially suited to you, you may want to specialize by country of origin, or even by the UNPOPULARITY of the brand — limiting yourself to cameras of manufacturers who only produced one or two models!

8 / CAMERA COLLECTING IN FOCUS

Generally speaking it's not too profitable for the beginner to draw up a long list of guidelines on what he WILL or WON'T buy. If your initial purchase is a Krauss Polyscop, you're apt to resolve then and there to collect nothing but Krauss. But more exposure to antique cameras (no pun, really) will soon convince you that other brands and types have much to offer, too. You will encounter models with certain features or physical characteristics that are extremely appealing to you ... irresistible, probably ... even though they bear no direct relation to the specimens already in your collection. And what's wrong with that? By acquiring cameras of various different makers, made in various different countries at different time-periods, you're building up a collection that reflects the development and progress of the camera. This is a "general" collection, a word that grates on the ears of some hobbyists. But do not automatically knock the general collection. It has much to be said for it. One major plus in its favor is that the owner of a general collection is never in a position of having to say "no" to a fabulous find or a camera that appeals strongly to him, just because it fails to fit into his line of specialization. If the whole realm of old and antique cameras is within your collecting sphere, you can take advantage of whatever opportunities fate places in your path.

Of course, your goals and ambitions are going to be different with a general collection than with a specialized one. The specialized hobbyist might for example be working toward "completion." He might have the goal of owning all the Conley box cameras that were produced, or all the Kodak Brownie Stereos. Whether or not these are reasonably obtainable goals would depend on his budgetary circumstances and the amount of time he can devote to the hobby. It all boils down to the fact that some people are happier having a definite goal they can work toward, like climbing a mountain and getting closer and closer to the summit. Completing a specialized collection is, for these individuals, comparable to planting a flag on the mountain's peak. It's the consummation of their work and time and expenditures as a hobbyist and they feel very rewarded about it. For others, however, there is absolutely no need to have a clear cut goal. They are just as satisfied building upon a general collection, or even a specialized collection which their common sense and the size of their bank account tells them cannot possibly be developed to completion. Who cares? If your collection is giving you enjoyment, you aren't too likely to bother about such considerations. Look at it this way. Museum collections, which are usually much larger and more spectacular than any private individual could put together, are very seldom complete. No museum has all the Rembrandts in the world, or all the Graeco-Roman marble busts. It is likewise true that no complete camera collection has ever been assembled, either, even by the museums. So you may very well want to give general of semi-specialized collection some serious consideration, before making any commitment to becoming a specialist. If your own instincts do not point you in any particular direction, some time spent in the hobby almost certainly will. And this book probably will, too.

Of course, anybody intent on being a serious collector does not want to become a mere packrat accumulator. Hobbyists call this the Jackdaw Syndrome. The jackdaw is a crow-like bird who picks up any loose bits of string or lint or miscellaneous junk and takes them to his nest. Some camera collectors, as well as collectors from other hobbies, behave in a fashion very similar to the jackdaw. If they're collecting stamps, they'll buy ANY stamp. If they're collecting cameras, they'll buy ANY camera. This is wrong. Not that we mean to trample on anybody's idea of self expression, but buying whatever comes along goes against the grain of sound, smart collecting. You will probably lose some money doing this but, even if you survive financially, you are likely to give yourself headaches in other ways. For one thing, the "buy 'em as you see 'em" collector lets his

CAMERA COLLECTING IN FOCUS / 9

hobby get out of hand. Unless he's awfully wealthy and has boundless storage and display space at his disposal, his collection grows too fast. Also, the quality of such a collection is not very well regulated. If you buy whatever you have the opportunity to buy, some of it just isn't going to be worth buying. You will come into possession of a really nice specimen here and there, just by law of averages...but plenty of weeds are going to come along with the flowers. It is entirely understandable for a beginner, and especially one with a burning enthusiasm for his hobby, to want to acquire every antique camera that he sees. This is simply an urge that has to be brought under control, if you're going to have a respectable collection. One cause of the "I have to have it" approach is the very mistaken belief, on the part of beginners, that antique cameras are rather scarce on the market and that a missed opportunity will become an albatross-like source of lifetime regret. Not so! Just the opposite is true, in fact. You will end up regretting your bad buys, and will say, "Why did I have to spend money on THAT one, when I could have used it for THIS one?" Selectivity is the key, and the big ingredients in selectivity are patience and connoisseurship. The word "connoisseur" is generally heard in reference to buyers of Dresden china and Chippendale furniture and other traditional antiques. But it's just as fitting to the camera hobby. The connoisseur knows what he's buying. He knows the hobby, knows what's available, and puts a restraint on his "must have" passions when that's the appropriate thing to do. Admittedly this takes some self-training, and there will be the occasional borderline situation where you could go either way and not be guilty of a clearcut blunder.

For example, you might come face-to-face with an Auto Graflex Jr. that's priced about 30% higher than the normal market value. The Auto Graflex is not, perhaps, your favorite antique camera, but you've read about them, and thought about them, and you really WOULD like to have one. This happens to be the first one you've actually seen in the flesh, and suddenly it hits you that the old Auto Graflex is much more charismatic in person than in those reference books on your library shelf. At this point, you begin being torn between those two voices in your head, one saying BUY, the other saying HOLD BACK.

It's a tough one to call. The Auto Graflex is not a really rare item. The fact that you haven't personally seen one before is not an indication of scarcity. It's just a matter of circumstances. There are some antique cameras worth $35 or $40 which you might not see in five years. It all depends on where you are, who you're dealing with, and that intangible thing called luck. But you can be pretty sure, with the Auto Graflex, that a missed opportunity does not mean the end of the line in your ambition to own a specimen. It invariably happens (or seems to, at any rate) that when you knowingly overspend for a camera, thinking that you're seizing a rare opportunity, the next week or next month brings an opportunity to buy the exact same camera for a more reasonable price. Now if the camera involved in this emotional tug-of-war was a Kodak satchel-box folding model, dating from around 1890, it might be another kettle of stew. That's a scarcer camera than the Auto Graflex, more desirable to collectors, and more valuable all the way around. If the specimen is in well preserved condition and everything is "go" except for a pricetag reading 30% above the normal market average, that would definitely be cause for pause. You don't want to make anybody a gift of $100 or so, no matter how much you want the camera. But, on the other hand, you have no really reliable way of knowing how much the NEXT specimen is going to cost. Will it be selling at a public auction, and possibly become the center of attention among five or six diehard hobbyists who want it "at any price?" Will it draw a bid of up to 50% or 75% above the book price? This is always a possibility — just as the possibility exists for you to luck out, and find a specimen selling for LESS than the usual market value. You are not going to be able to look into the future, so the only way to arrive at a decision is to weigh the possibilities against each other. What are your REAL chances of finding another specimen in THIS CONDITION, for a lower price than this?

Before coming up with an answer to that one, let's take a critical look at the main ingredient in this book — established market values.

If you're going to do any serious camera collecting, you need to know the established market values. You also need to know what they really mean to you as a hobbyist. How firm are they? Should you use them just for reference, or as laws to live by? How do OTHER people use the established market prices? In short, what effect do they have on the camera hobby as a whole?

One thing you need to realize (which you already do, unless you're very new to this hobby) is that a price or a value means different things to different people. Just as the sunset looks different depending on where you're standing, so does an established market price. If you're a professional dealer in antique cameras, you do not buy cameras by the established market prices. You do not pay $100 for a $100 camera, just as the grocer does not pay 59¢ for a can of tuna fish that he sells for 59¢. To a dealer, the value of any camera — even a beautiful Leica IIIc that would make any hobbyist's head swim — is LESS than the established market price. Quite a bit less in fact. When he buys, he pays a price that might have been equivalent to retail in 1973 or 1974. Even though prices have risen dramatically since then, this is all the camera is worth to HIM, because he must resell it. There must be a margin for his overhead and profit, because without profit involved he would not be selling antique cameras.

To a general collector, who has no intention of selling or making a profit on the cameras he buys, a $100 camera may be worth precisely $100. If he buys at this price — in other words, right at the established market average — he will probably feel he's gotten a fair or reasonable deal, and in most cases he will be correct. But if we turn the price up or down slightly, if we let it deviate a little in one direction or other from the established market average, then a number of "ifs" enter the picture.

Say you've found a camera with a book price of $100 selling for $85 — and this WILL happen sometimes. You weren't really looking for a specimen of that particular camera, and if the price was $100 you might automatically pass it by. But at $85 it IS a buy of sorts, and you might decide to purchase it if it falls within your sphere of collecting activity. Saving some money is an incentive in itself, though of course you would not buy a specimen in poor condition or one which does not suit your collection, just because the price happens to be low.

But just the reverse can occur, too, and provides us with a perfect illustration of "value." To someone who really wants a particular camera badly, it may be worth more — MUCH more — than the established market value. He does not think in terms of the prices that other collectors have paid, or that dealers are customarily in the practice of charging. He simply WANTS the camera, and he will not have any pangs of guilt about paying $150 for a $100 camera. It all depends on the collector, his level of enthusiasm, and the problems he might have encountered in locating a camera of that type or model. Frustration can play a big role, make no mistake about it! Let's say that our mythical collector had been trying for about two years to lay hands on a Challenge Deluxe. He's checked with other local collectors to see if anybody has one for trade. Harry across town has one, but wouldn't part with it for your right arm and right leg. After all, HE had trouble finding one, too! His brother Ben in Toledo used to have one — why not drop him a note? You write to Ben. Ben sold his Challenge Deluxe last week. Sorry! Then you pick up a dealer's catalogue. There, illustrated on the front cover, is — you guessed it — a gleaming, eye-popping Challenge Deluxe. With pulse beating fast, you dash off a check, even though the price IS slightly higher than you intended to pay. After two weeks of fidgety waiting, the mailman delivers the crusher: your check is back, the Challenge Deluxe was grabbed up by a little old lady in Pasadena. More weeks pass. You place an auction bid on a Challenge Deluxe. Once again the dice fail to roll in your favor. Are you beginning to get the picture? After going through this for a while (and this is not a unique little drama, in the world of collecting), getting a Challenge Deluxe starts to become an obsession, and gradually you don't even think about how much you'll need to pay. If one comes up for 50% more than the established market value, are you going to adopt a stoic attitude and bypass it? Not very likely. The value of a Challenge Deluxe has become, to YOU, more than established market value. Because, in your case, established market value has to be combined with the value of satisfying that dream of ownership. How much the dream is worth is a question only you can answer. But we can tell you pretty candidly that there are collectors who have knowingly paid twice the market value for a camera they especially wanted, or which proved especially elusive to them. Whether or not this is wise isn't even worth discussing, because the human element takes over and reason is banished from the scene. All we can say is that it would be a poor practice to HABITUALLY pay more than the market values for cameras you buy. If you occasionally get a deal on a camera and save $10 or $20, you're certainly allowed to consider yourself ahead of the game ... and allowed to "spend" your savings by over-reaching for a camera that means a lot to you. By and by, it will probably all even up if you put some thought and care into your collecting approach.

There are going to be some cameras which particularly dazzle you. They may be ones which are hardly ever pictured or talked about in the reference books, but which hit you squarely between the eyes when you come into contact with them. Don't be too surprised if you fall head-over-heels for a type (or types) of camera which are outside your normal sphere of collecting interest. Many are the Leica collectors who find love at first sight with a Polyscop or Speed Graphic or Anschutz Stereo. Why? Because opposites attract? No, more likely because the specialist — and particularly the arch-specialist who THINKS he wants to confine himself to a certain brand — often develops a myopic view of cameras. He spends so much time studying the small restrictive group of types and models that comprise his special sphere of interest, that he does not see the forest for the trees. The mere originality of another type — older, of a different function, made by a different company, or in some way DIFFERENT — gives it an immense appeal. It tells another chapter in the story of camera development and history, which his restrictive collection (even if enormously valuable from a monetary standpoint) is not telling.

Let's say you've got a Simplex collection. Nobody in the world is going to knock you for collecting Simplexes. If you have the funds to buy them, you're going to be the envy of numerous fellow collectors, and you're probably going to have an extremely sound investment with them as well. But in pursuing your Simplex collection, the odds are quite good that, sooner or later, you're going to be offered a wet plate camera. If you can afford the pioneer Simplexes, you can afford the average wet plate camera, and you will need super resistance to say "no." The wet plate will not really compliment your collection of Simplexes. It's a different animal. But that's just the point. It IS different. It harkens back to a more primitive era of photography, when the Simplex was not even on the drawing board. It serves as a link from the golden shadowy days to the Simplex, a span of three quarters of a century. You don't really NEED a wet plate camera ... but the "museum curator" in you (as in most true collectors) is probably going to take over. And you're probably going to buy it.

12 / CAMERA COLLECTING IN FOCUS

By the same token, if the thrust of your collecting interest is centered upon VERY antique models, you will probably end up buying some 20th century cameras just as evolutionary evidence of the camera's history. When you start piecing together the history of anything, big gaps have a way of becoming eyesores. At the moment you might not be as interested in the history of cameras, as in owning old cameras. It is a very good bet that more weeks and months of collecting will find your attentions turning to the historical angles of the hobby. You may even think you're the sort who hates research, but some of these research haters have proven to be the outstanding historians of photography, once they got going.

With antique cameras, the age is not the deciding factor in the price, and that may be all to the benefit of everyone concerned. If age were of paramount importance in setting values, those on limited budgets would be boxed in to the 20th century. Of course, prices on the whole tend to be higher for the very old cameras than for those half their age, because of scarcity and collector demand. This does not mean you cannot find inexpensive specimens among 19th century models, and it CERTAINLY does not mean that everything from the 20th century — or even everything from 1950 onward — is inexpensive. The trusty old Magazine Cyclone goes back to the nineties, and is available in various models for less than a hundred dollars (far less than you would pay for one of the more popular cameras of the 1960's, 1970's or 1980's). The Chase Magazine Camera, which is quite old and quite eye-appealing, can often be had for less than $100. The Kodak line includes NUMEROUS 19th century models that sell on the antique camera market for less than $100, so many in fact that you could probably spend a few years making a collection of them. Do not let the price fool you into believing that these models are less significant to the history of photography or less worthy of being collected and admired. If anything, they are MORE significant than many cameras costing $500 or $1,000. They were popular in their time, widely used and widely accepted. They brought the art and hobby of photography to the masses and did wonders to popularize it, whereas many of the rare, costly brands were virtually unknown to the public of their time. This is why their prices are low today. They were manufactured in much larger numbers than the lesser-known cameras of the 1880's and 1890's. Kodak cameras were not only retailed in department and specialty shops, but by the thousands through mail-order. Glance through a Sears Roebuck or Montgomery Ward catalogue of the 1890's and what do you see? Nothing esoteric, nothing for which today's collector pays a thousand dollars or more. You see, instead, pages and pages of Kodak cameras! If there were no Kodak cameras to get people started on photography, there would have been no market for (for example) a Mentor Folding Reflex.

The thing that appeals to you about one camera may be wholly different than what appeals to you about another. With one it may be the extreme antiqueness — not only of the camera, but of its APPEARANCE, which can be two different things. There are 1880's models which look like 1900 models; and there are 1880's models which have a Matthew Brady appearance about them. If you get deeply into the hobby you will undoubtedly buy some cameras just because of their charming "period piece" design and appearance. There is nothing unscholarly about this and you need make no apologies. Certainly the physical attraction of an old camera could be a point in its collector appeal.

Attraction is not just a matter of beauty. A wooden frame or partial wooden frame camera may have the look of hand-wrought craftsmanship, with a delicate patina to the wooden components. Immediately such a quality sets the camera apart as a specimen to be admired; even the non-enthusiast, if he has any kind of interest in antiques in general, will be attracted to such a camera. It seems to say "museum piece" and of course it is, even if the pricetag is only in the $75 range.

Attraction can also derive from unusualness. Far more gimmicky and queer types of cameras were made in the early days of photography than are made now. By and large they did not take very impressive pictures, but nobody is going to concern themselves about that. Stirn's Vest Pocket Camera is typical of that breed, a camera that looks like a flying saucer and seems oh-so-modern for the 1880's. This is an expensive one, but if you're into antique novelty cameras a Stirn will probably be high on your list of desirables. Much more expensive, but really striking, is the historic Jumelle de Nicour of the 1860's, which you could easily mistake for a ship's compass. The Photake and Photoret were other novelty types, these two from the nineties. You can find plenty of interesting novelty types from the early years of the 20th century, too. Novelty collecting has many, many followers. It is not only the appeal of novelty cameras that brings them popularity among collectors, but their obvious scarcity. Most of them were manufactured in small numbers as experimental jobs; and since few of them sold well, only the initial quantity reached the market. In many cases they are much, much scarcer than the more standard models of their time, and if scarcity were the only yardstick in determining value they would probably be selling for ten times as much as "ordinary" antique cameras.

BUYING COLLECTOR CAMERAS

Most of the basic principles of buying collector cameras are those applied in general to other "collectibles" bought by hobbyists. The usual suggestions on caution, perseverence, skepticism of unknown or little-known sellers, examination of physical condition and the like are all valid in relation to cameras. For camera collecting, when one boils it down, is not so very different than collecting antiques or historical documents. The objects are old, and one needs to have some respect for age; that is, not expect them to be in absolutely mint condition as if just leaving the factory. On the other hand, noticeably poor condition is a detraction to the camera's appeal and value, and such specimens are generally best avoided unless very rare (or unless they may yield parts which can be used in the restoration of another specimen). In other words, being a smart collector and a good buyer is largely a matter of knowing what is available, not expecting the impossible and yet not being guiled into purchasing junk as gems. You will not become an expert buyer instantaneously, though this book should put any beginner on the path to reaching that level. Real expertise comes mostly from experience. There is no substitute for handling a great number of old cameras of different types, talking with fellow collectors, reading the lists and catalogues of dealers, attending historical society photographic exhibits, and in other ways sharpening your knowledge. Those who want to learn it all immediately ought to realize that learning never stops; even the experts continue to learn, as no one has ever personally seen or handled every camera in the world.

The objective in buying is of course to get your money's worth, possibly even a bit more than your money's worth when the occasion permits. But simply to get one's money's worth is no assurance of building a good collection, or acquiring cameras that will give you satisfaction. In buying a badly defective specimen of a $400 camera for $100 you may be getting your money's worth, in the sense that you have not paid above the usual fair market value. Money's worth and quality do not necessarily go hand in hand. By the same token it is entirely possible to overpay for a camera and still receive

14 / BUYING COLLECTOR CAMERAS

one which is not really collector worthy. So the price becomes one consideration, in line with other considerations. It is not the controlling factor in arriving at a decision of whether or not to buy. The camera must be right, and it must naturally be appealing to you personally; when those two qualifications have been met, the seller's asking price can be weighed and judged.

Appealing to you personally? Perhaps it would be better to say, an appealing addition to your collection. You will have the opportunity to buy many excellent, desirable cameras, and these opportunities will increase as your acquaintance of dealers and fellow hobbyists increases. The chances to buy will be far more than anyone could possibly accept; so it becomes a case of using discrimination, and thinking not only in terms of whether the camera is good and the price fair, but whether it deserves to be in your collection. After a while you will probably find yourself taking a harder line on that matter than you do as a beginner. You will no longer be awed by the mere fact that a camera was made in 1880 or 1890, as you will encounter many, many such specimens. The styles and characteristics which now seem so bizarre to you, as a newcomer to the hobby, will eventually seem more commonplace. At this point the collector's judgment becomes more finely honed, and he makes much better selections. It is also at this point, usually, that he takes a look at the specimens already purchased and begins wishing he had not bought half of them! If it's of any comfort, you may care to know that all collectors make some purchases of which they are not too proud the following year or at some point in the future. In a way this is all for the best, as it creates a greater circulation of antique cameras within the market. If everyone bought intelligently from the outset, and remained firmly convinced that their purchases were good, not too many cameras would return to the market! The selections would be thinner and the prices obviously higher. Collectors deciding that they have bought wrong are responsible for many cameras finding their way back to the shops.

We wish we could tell you how to avoid every possible blunder or disappointment in buying. Unfortunately this is impossible because the human factor is involved when a collector buys a camera, just as in falling in love or deciding to go cave-exploring. Much of what you buy in the way of antique cameras will be bought because it fascinates or dazzles you at the moment. But human beings are not unchanging in what fascinates or dazzles them; yesterday's fascination could be today's bore, and that is why advice is useless. You can learn to inspect a camera for its condition, and you can become knowledgable about values, but you may not be able to prevent yourself falling in love with a camera that you fall OUT of love with later. You can, however, slant things somewhat in your favor by not buying very costly cameras at the outset of your collecting activities. Unless one is working with a really liberal budget, we would go so far as to suggest that $50 be the limit spent on any camera during the first year of collecting. The first year is really a time of learning, and one shouldn't mind serving an apprenticeship and restraining himself a bit; if some cash can be accumulated for future purchases, the time will truly be well spent. Regardless of what sort of approach you make, some of the cameras you buy at the outset of your collecting are not going to suit you two, three or five years from now. By then you will either have become a specialist in one particular kind of camera, or shifted your interests in such a way that some of these early purchases are no longer appealing, even if they are genuinely good cameras. You are apt to be reselling them, or trading them, and possibly you may (if enough time has passed, and the cameras are popular ones) you could realize a profit on them. Yet the possibility exists of suffering a loss, so it pays to take minimal risk and keep your potential loss low.

We will assume you have a certain budget available for your hobby, rather than limitless funds, which is the case with the vast majority of collectors. How can it be put to its best use? This is mostly up to the individual. Some hobbyists prefer to save up and buy cameras which would otherwise be outside their financial reach. Others do not care to go for long spells without buying; they want to see their collection grow more rapidly. They would rather spend $50 regularly and build up a large collection, even if this means never owning a camera in the $200, $300 or higher value range. It's your choice. There is certainly nothing wrong with a large collection of low-to-medium value cameras, nor with a small select collection comprising mostly specimens in the higher price area. What appeals to you is what counts, not how the collection might be judged by someone else. We would say, though, that the collector who goes out and buys every time he has accumulated $50 might sometimes be putting himself at a disadvantage. The time might come when he encounters a $300 or $400 specimen that absolutely delights him, and is left short on cash. If you take the opposite approach, if you save up a bit and go shopping with $300 or $400, you have that much more flexibility. You can still buy a $50 camera, if you have $400 in your pocket! So perhaps the smartest tack is not to restrict yourself in price range at all, but to do some savings between purchases and leave the door open to a possible large purchase.

Where should you buy?

This is a much more important question than it might seem to the beginner. There are many possible sources for old cameras, some of them probably right in your neighborhood. It is always convenient to buy locally, but this is not necessarily the best procedure in all cases. Much depends on where you live and what kind of local selection is offered. In a city such as Los Angeles, New York, Chicago or any major metropolitan area, there are many shops offering antique cameras and many knowledgeable dealers who are fully informed on values. In a smaller town the local sources may consist of the general antiques shops and pawnbrokers' shops, supplemented by thrift and bazaar outlets and of course the offerings of private owners. These are not really the favorite places to buy, for the experienced serious collector. Antiques shops and pawnshops hold out the possibility of bargains, and on occasion a real "find" is made, a camera listing at $500 or $600 which the proprietor, in his total ignorance of camera values, has given a pricetag of $50 or $60. The chance to make such finds has given antiques shops and pawnshops a kind of glamor for the beginning collector, out of all proportion (really) to what they really deserve. Serious camera collecting is not just a hunt after bargains, or a sounding-out for buried treasure. Rummaging in the antiques shops is great fun at first, and if you DO make an occasional "find" this will fuel your enthusiasm to do more hunting in more shops. Generally, however, the results are meager compared to the time and effort contributed. Many antiques shops have no cameras at all: good ones, bad ones, or indifferent ones. Those which have a camera or two will usually just have someone's secondhand Polaroid or perhaps a late-model Brownie worth $10 or $15 — and in bad shape to boot. If a collector's specimen does turn up in an antiques shop, it may not only be fully priced (in relation to the established market value) but OVERPRICED. Overpricing occurs for the same reason as underpricing. The shop proprietor has no real knowledge of cameras or their values, and is making an estimate. Who knows what his estimate is based on? The size of the camera? How old it looks to him? Whether the brand name is American or foreign? If he does not know camera values, his guess about the value will obviously be wrong, and it is just a matter of your luck whether it is wrong high or wrong low. More likely it will be too high, since he will probably tack a stiff percentage onto his guess to protect himself against guessing low.

16 / BUYING COLLECTOR CAMERAS

If he estimates a camera to be worth $60, he is likely to price it at $100 just to see "what happens." As a dealer in antiques, he knows from experience that some merchandise will sell, even if overpriced. He would much rather aim high and then reduce his asking price after three or four months if the camera is still in stock by then. You may be able to negotiate a better price with him, if the camera is worthwhile and his price is not outrageous.

You will get a clearer picture of the opportunities, or lack of them, awaiting you in antique shops by considering the source of antiques shops' merchandise. How is a really good collectible camera to find its way to a neighborhood antiques shop, which does the bulk of its trade in Edwardian oak furniture, glassware and household ornaments? Certainly not as the result of a camera collector selling it there. It would be inconceivable for an informed collector to sell a good antique camera to an antiques dealer; he would not get as much as selling it to a camera dealer, not to mention the frustration involved. Can you picture the scene?

"Sir, I have a Graphic Twin Lens Special for sale."
"What's that?"
"A very scarce early camera, it happens to be worth..."
"Never heard of it."

This is not a winning proposition, no matter how you cut it. And if you talk in terms of a COLLECTION of fine antique cameras, the thought becomes even more absurd. Nobody will consider selling to an antiques dealer, unless he must raise cash within the next 10 minutes.

So the antiques shop, if it has any cameras at all, will have gotten them in miscellaneous ways. They will have arrived in a cardboard carton containing the remnants of someone's attic trash. Or perhaps the dealer made a "bulk" purchase at one of the local estate sales, a lot consisting of a dozen or more jumbled items which happened (by pure chance) to include an old camera. The dealer is not a specialist in cameras. He does not even like cameras, and the chances are very good that he has no customers whatsoever for cameras. A camera is just another item for his stock, lost in the shuffle of the bric-a-brac and mangled typewriters and floral lampshades.

Obviously you cannot really BUILD A COLLECTION from antiques shops purchases, unless you live within easy reach of a great number of antiques shops. Even then, a collection formed exclusively from antiques shops purchases is going to show it. It will not have the kind of quality, in terms of condition, that one would expect of a collection assembled through purchases from camera dealers and fellow hobbyists.

Antiques shops are worth visiting as a kind of sub-hobby for the camera collector. There *is* the slim chance of making a find, and if you do not succeed in getting a Photoret Watch Camera for $75 you might possibly unearth some early photographic accessories or publications. But by and large they should be considered mainly as sources of entertainment rather than potential sources of good collectible cameras.

When you do scout in antiques shops, learn to look before leaping. The chances of making a regrettable buy are quite high, partly because of psychological and emotional factors. After going in and out of half a dozen shops in the course of a day, finding nothing that even remotely resembles a camera, there is a tendency to seize any opportunity to buy. If the outer body is in fairly good condition, the temptation will be even greater. But DO look inside, and satisfy yourself that the asking price is in line with the kind of sum that a camera dealer would be charging. In antiques shops you may sometimes find an old camera in its original storage or carrying case, or possibly the paperboard case in which it was retailed. The presence of the case adds to its appeal and of course it does add somewhat to the value, but keep in mind that the camera's condition is a more important consideration. A badly damaged or defective camera in its original case is not likely to be an attractive buy. Also, do not simply take the case at face value. The case could appear to be contemporary in age with the camera, and very possibly is, but is still not the ORIGINAL case supplied by the manufacturer. If the case was homemade, or switched from another camera, it adds practically nothing to the value. Look for markings on the case, which should be on the inner side of the lid, or possibly on the floor of the case. If the case was not homemade it will almost certainly be marked in an identifiable manner. It may even identify the model name or number of the camera, in addition to giving the manufacturer's name. Slight damage to the case is not a cause for concern. These remarks apply equally to printed paperboard cases or cartons in which the cheaper cameras of their day were retailed, such as the Kodak Brownie of the 1890's and early 1900's. Of course the printed cases are more easily identified, and are likely to be in poorer condition — stained even if not torn or crushed.

Pawnshops are often mentioned in the same breath as antiques shops, as potential sources of supply for collectible cameras. Truthfully speaking the pawnshops are probably on a somewhat higher level. Merchandise coming into pawnshops is subjected to a closer scrutiny than in most antiques shops, and the obviously damaged item is seldom seen. A pawnshop will not acquire merchandise by the carton-load, and it will not buy at auction. It inspects everything it buys individually and will not purchase anything which does not appear to have a reasonable resale potential. Pawnshops seldom buy anything of an antique nature, unless they are especially set up to deal in collector's items or unless the object is made of precious metal. Nevertheless, most pawnshops do buy and sell cameras which are in the "collectible" category even though they are not antique. You will find 1950's Minoltas in the pawnshops and occasionally even a Zeiss from the 1940's, and certainly Leicas from the past 20 or 30 years. They have been bought by the pawnshops as cameras, not as collector's items, and are being sold as cameras. This does not mean they will be selling for a song, but the philosophy among the pawnbrokers (unless they know they have a collector's item) is to give the buyer a somewhat better deal than he could obtain on new merchandise. Generally speaking the pawnbrokers are very fair in their pricing, simply because they could not generate business if they failed to undercut the shops selling new merchandise. As a collector you may find some good buys in pawnshops. You will not find a huge selection and if your interest is old Premos or Roussels, you can forget it. But if you want collectible cameras from the 1950's through the 1960's, the pawnshops are certainly worth looking into. You will find that their cameras are clean and, on the whole, in very good condition, though it pays never to make this assumption without taking the time to actually inspect them.

Of course you may very logically ask the question, "If an antiques shop cannot get its hands on good cameras, how does the pawnbroker accomplish this?"

It is really quite a different situation. We are not assuming that the COLLECTOR disposes of his fine cameras through pawnshops. But many people who are not collectors own Minoltas and Leicas made in the 1950's, and other cameras which they acquired strictly for purposes of amateur photography. Whether or not they are aware of the collector values is a moot point. In many instances they probably are not. In any event, when an occasion arises in which cash is needed quickly, this individual is not too likely to turn to a dealer in collectible cameras unless one is located nearby. If he is not a collector he may be unaware of the presence of such dealers in his locality, and instead he is more apt to approach the pawnbroker. He will certainly choose the pawnbroker rather than the antiques dealer, whom he would probably not trust to appreciate the camera's value either as a camera or collector's item.

18 / BUYING COLLECTOR CAMERAS

Many a good, valuable camera has been found in pawnshops, and when found they often have the original case and accessories, so we would certainly suggest that pawnshops not be overlooked. But as stated with regard to antiques shops, this can be considered only as a supplemental source in your collecting. You could not logically build an entire collection via pawnshop finds.

This takes us now to other possible sources of supply, which include the private owner, the camera shop, the specialist dealer in antique cameras, and the auction sale. All of these can be fruitful sources, and will be the primary sources of fine cameras for most collectors.

Buying directly from private owners is the ambition of many collectors. There is no arguing that this is, indeed, the best way to buy, though it is not so ideal or without pitfalls as one might imagine. The motive of most collectors, in buying from private parties or seeking to, is to "beat the dealer." Though this may not be a very noble goal, its causes are understandable. We all know — even as rank beginners — that dealers clear a healthy profit on the cameras passing through their hands. They do not buy for $60 and sell for $70. More often they buy for $50 and sell for $100, or buy for $200 and sell for $375. Though the collector cannot very well feel cheated if the ultimate price is in line with current market values, the thought of all that profit going to the dealer is unsettling. Why should he get it? Why shouldn't I be able to buy at the same prices he buys? Isn't my money just as good? If someone is willing to sell a $375 camera to a dealer for $200, why wouldn't they sell it to me for $200?

This line of reasoning is not 100% sound but it does have some merit.

You cannot, as a private collector, put yourself on the level with a dealer. You can occasionally buy cameras from the public at one-half their market value, or thereabout, but you cannot do it as consistently as the dealers. The dealer, you must remember, has a large operation from which he works. He does not simply insert a small classified notice in the newspapers and sit back to await results. If he has a shop, which most of the dealers do, he has "street traffic" coming into the shop. His name and address are known, and quite likely he has some kind of reputation in the business which draws both sellers and buyers to him. You do not have a shop or a name or a reputation. The dealer has many, many cameras offered to him, singly and in collections. The volume of offerings may be so heavy, at times, that he can afford to be choosy about who he buys from and how much he pays. If his top offer is $80 and the seller refuses to accept anything under $100, the dealer can stand firm, knowing (or at least suspecting) that tomorrow somebody will want to sell that exact camera for $80. In other words, the dealer has leeway. He has a fair amount of cash capital behind him, and can take advantage of the opportunity to make a large purchase. Also he has confidence in what he's doing, which the private party buying from a private party may not. But ABOVE IT ALL, the dealer is buying merchandise for the purpose of reselling it and making a livelihood out of it, which is totally different than buying something to derive pleasure and satisfaction from it. If the dealer was in a situation where his own tastes, his own likes and dislikes, came into the picture, he would probably not be nearly as successful in buying.

You CAN buy from the public, but you cannot do it on the same scale as a professional dealer, and you cannot expect to get the same margin of discount as a dealer. For one thing, if there is a dealer in the community, you are in competition with him when you buy from private owners — and a dealer is stiff competition. Given the choice between selling to a dealer or selling to you, the private owner will invariably choose the dealer — unless you make it worth his while to choose you. If he's going to obtain the same price from you or the dealer, he will sell to the dealer; the dealer has regular shop hours and can be visited without an appointment, the dealer pays with a check that stands no risk of bouncing, and so forth. So to lure the private owner away from the dealer, you must be willing to pay a higher price, and generally you must be prepared to make settlement in cash. How much higher? That's a hard one to answer. Most dealers will pay at least 50% of the market value for most collectible cameras, so you can use that as a starting point. If the camera is rare or especially popular with collectors (such as almost any Leica), the dealer may normally pay 60% of market value for an intact specimen. You would then need to go to around 70% or better to get the ball on your side of the court. But it isn't even as simple as this (if this sounds simple!). Private owners are not the automatons they're often cracked up to be. Some of them are extremely shrewd when driving a bargain. Any dealer can tell you that! They will be even more intent on milking you, feeling that as a private party you're a weaker opponent than a dealer. For example, if you offer 70% of the current established markt value for a $1500 Leica, confident that you're offering more than a dealer would, the owner might say: "Well, I just visited two dealers yesterday. Both of them offered me MORE than that, and I turned them down because I didn't feel it was enough." Did he visit two dealers? Did they offer him more? Probably not, but the die is cast and you're now seated directly on the old picket fence. If you proclaim flatly that 70% is the highest you can go, the negotiations may break off then and there. On the other hand, if you swallow the bait, figuring that 80% would still be a savings of 20% to you, you might be paying $150 more than you need to. A dealer doesn't do this. He never wraps up a purchase (buying something from the public) with doubt in his mind as to whether he gave the seller a "gift." He knows just how much he can safely afford to pay, and the line is drawn there regardless of the bargaining powers or histrionics of the seller. He would rather see that camera walk out of his shop and out of his life, than pay even $10 more than necessary for it.

    The best way and really only productive way of buying from the public is to run classified advertisements in your local daily newspaper. Most newspapers have a camera section among their classified merchandise ads — if not, you can use the antiques heading (or quite possibly the newspaper will create a camera heading for you). There will probably be half a dozen or so other ads under "cameras," some of which have been running for a good long while. If the ad just gives a phone number, it is impossible to know whether the party placing it is a dealer or private individual. Even if the ad reads, "Call after 6," this is not an assurance that the person is a private individual, as it could be a dealer using his home phone number. Generally speaking, it is best for a private buyer to let readers know that he is, indeed, a private buyer, but this is a point on which you will find differences of opinion. It is not necessary to use excessive words. An ad can state simply, "Antique Cameras Wanted," and still be very effective. If you are seeking only certain types, this ought to be spelled out, to save you from answering numerous unproductive phone calls. Even so, you will still get some calls from persons who have a Beau Brownie for sale, when your ad calls for a Beil and Freund. These are the "might as well give it a try" folks and you must put up with them — the dealers are stampeded by them!

    There are certain other matters to be thought out in advance. Do you want to go to the homes of prospective sellers, or have them come to you? If the distance between you is great, would it be worthwhile for either party to make the trip for a transaction in the $30 or $40 range? Is there a way you could meet more conveniently? Perhaps, even though you live distantly, both of you work in the same neighborhood and could rendezvous during the daytime. Keep in mind also that when a transaction falls through, it is not quite the same as a dealer saying "no, thank you." The prospective seller might not have gone more than a few steps out of his way to visit the dealer. If he has gone to any trouble in coming to you, not to mention expense, a "no sale" registers somewhat more disappointment. Of course this does not mean you should buy cameras that you do not think are fit buying, just to avoid disappointing anyone. But do try to elicit as much information as possible on the phone, so that you can form a fairly positive picture of whether or not the camera will be useful to you. If the seller is willing to discuss price on the phone, this should certainly be done. The camera may be excellent, but a sale might be out of the question because of the owner's inflated notion of its value. If he wants to receive the full established market value, and is firm in his desire to do so, there is really not much point in seeing him — unless this happens to be a camera that you very badly want and have been unable to find elsewhere.

Buying from dealers essentially means camera shops having a department devoted to "classics," and the specialist dealers who sell nothing but collector cameras. The attention now given to camera collecting has prompted many camera shops to devote some space to scarce and unusual types. It is certainly nothing new for camera shops to sell secondhand cameras, and in a way the ordinary traffic of secondhand cameras in these shops gave the hobby an important boost during the formative years of the 1960's. In addition to the recent secondhand types, some from the 1940's and even earlier would turn up, though in those days there were few camera shops which would accept VERY old models for their secondhand departments, a little fearful of their selling potential. When it seemed evident that the older models were drawing added attention because of their age and historical interest, that attitude softened a bit and the buyers for these camera shops began looking more receptively at the "oldies." Today there is hardly a good camera shop in the country, with a secondhand department, which does not think just as much about the collector as the photographer who wants secondhand equipment. Of course there is no real way of drawing a line between the two groups of customers; many cameras are bought for collecting AND photography purposes.

Selection in the camera shops may not be overwhelming in any given shop, though some of them do present very extensive offerings. Mostly the selections will be stronger in recent and semi-antique models than in those dating to the early 1900's or pre-1900, with emphasis on models from the 1940's, 1950's and 1960's. This is simply because the camera shops do a great deal of buying from persons who are not collectors but are in possession of cameras bought a number of years ago, which have acquired a collector status. Of course much depends on the focus of the shop in terms of the attention it gives to the collector angle of photography, and, also very importantly, whether there is a sizable clientele of active collectors in the area. A fairly recent camera will have double-threat sales appeal in a shop's secondhand department, for photography and its collectible status. Hence the average camera shop, especially in a small town where there may not be many collectors, would be more anxious to offer a $50 camera from 1950 than a $500 model from 1920. The $500 1920 model is probably a very appealing collector's item, but the shopkeeper (or the manager of the secondhand department) might have doubts about HIS ability to sell it. Naturally this is even truer of, say, an early novelty camera or something in the bizarre category. The average camera shop will rate this as an "exotic" piece and may be hesitant to handle it. On the other hand the $50 camera from 1950 is not only a collector's item, but might be equal in photographic usefulness to a 1980's camera selling for $100 or $150. If it does not sell to a collector, it could sell to someone who merely wants a good camera at a good price.

The prices in camera shops' secondhand departments are not always firm. For its new merchandise, the shop has undoubtedly paid standard wholesale prices, which are likely to vary ONLY accordingly to the quantities ordered. Thus it is not in a position to bargain on its prices, which will be set in direct competition with those of other retailers. For its secondhand cameras it does not pay standard prices, as the buying is done mainly from private individuals. On some of its secondhand or collector models, you can be sure that the shop bought for a favorable price, perhaps for one-third of the market value or even less. On others, it may have paid a much higher percentage of retail value, leaving little or no room for negotiation. Of course you will not know which cameras were its bargain buys, since all (or most) of them will be priced at approximately the ordinary retail range. The only possible approach is to "probe" it out by means of discussion with the manager. You might get some clues on which cameras are possible targets for negotiation, if you visit the shop periodically. Any camera which has just arrived in stock within the past week or two is not a good candidate for a price reduction. This is too brief a length of time for all the shop's steady customers to have seen the camera. Until it has been seen by the "regulars," the shop's manager will not care to entertain any suggestions of a lower price. But if you know that a certain camera has been in stock for more than a month, you might have luck in obtaining it for a lower price. The camera shops, like all businesses, want to turn over their stock regularly. Any item which does not move gradually becomes a black sheep for that shop, even though it may be an excellent camera. The fact that a camera has not found a buyer in a month, or even longer, is not necessarily a sign that something is wrong with it, though of course you would want to consider that possibility and inspect it thoroughly. Its failure to sell could result merely from the fact that no collectors of that particular type of camera have visited the shop. It may even represent a bargain at the marked price, and still not sell. You can be sure that the manager wants to move these long-stocked items, and if a reduction of MODEST size, in the 10% to 15% range, will succeed in accomplishing that, he will probably agree to it. You may sometimes obtain a larger reduction, all depending on circumstances. If the shop has put a large sum of money into an "exotic" camera and had it in stock for six months, the manager may be very anxious to "talk turkey" with you.

If you buy two cameras at the same time, your chances for obtaining a reduction are better. This gives you a bargaining edge. You would likewise have a bargaining edge by being a steady customer in that shop, but it is wise not to get into the practice of always seeking discounts, no matter how much business you do in a shop.

Get to know the manager of your camera shop's secondhand department. Let him see that you are not just an amateur photographer or a fan of old cameras, but are knowledgable about the history and values of cameras. Any camera shop that knows it has a collector in its midst will value him as a customer, presuming he will be making many future purchases.

Buying from the specialist dealers has a somewhat different complexion. These individuals, some of whom operate shops and some of whom deal through postal box addresses, are of course much fewer in number than camera shops. They are catering exclusively to collectors, and the number of collectors is a fraction of the number of amateur and professional photographers. For the more advanced serious collector they provide an invaluable service. They buy and sell rare and unusual models which would be difficult to find in any other way, handling the "cream" of collector cameras passing through the market. At the same time they normally also handle cameras in the more moderate value range, for beginning collectors or those on restricted budgets. But even their moderate value specimens will usually not be the sort of item to appear in ordinary camera shops. They will consist of obsolete models that are not sought for photography purposes, but are strictly in the hobbyist and historian realm.

Most of the dealers who specialize in collector cameras work through printed lists, if they do not have a shop. Each month, or on alternate months, a list is published of the cameras recently acquired, and copies are sent to persons on their mailing list. The lists of course are seldom very lengthy, as it is difficult for any single dealer to buy antique cameras in great volume. Also, the dealers are generally very meticulous and want to devote ample attention to examining every specimen they buy, and this limits the volume of business they can do. Nevertheless if you total up the values of the cameras offered on any given list, you will see that the dealer is not running a small operation by any means! Dealers' lists are voraciously read by active, serious collectors, for whom they constitute the "hotline" of the hobby — the link between interested buyer and the best collector cameras currently available. A dealer's mailing list may consist of only 50 to 100 active customers, but these individuals are ACTIVE in the true sense of the word. They will rush to the phone and call in their order, as soon as a list arrives containing a camera they want to buy. Real effort occurs between the customers to "get there first," since the dealer usually has only one specimen of each camera in stock and may not get another for months. You have to be prepared for occasional disappointment in this regard, as the lists do not reach every customer at the same time. Even if mailed simultaneously, they will arrive on different days, and it could be your bad luck that half the list is already sold out by the time the list reaches your mailbox. A call is of course necessary for any camera you're intent on purchasing, as an order sent by letter will take several more days of precious time. You may feel bad about ordering a camera and discover that someone else already bought it, but look at things this way: if nothing else, this at least indicates that the dealer is using fair prices and has good cameras on his list! Luck evens up eventually, and you will score many hits in your efforts to buy desirable cameras. It is simply a matter of persistence. Also, after a while you will discover which dealers tend to have the type of cameras which appeal most to you. Chances are you will become a steady customer of one or possibly two dealers.

The specialist dealers are, on the whole, careful about describing their merchandise in full detail and mentioning any faults or defects which may be a cause of concern to the buyer. For your own protection, however, you should read the introductory matter to each list, in which the dealer states his terms of doing business. This will indicate whether you have the privilege of returning a camera which does not meet your approval, and, if so, the length of time it can be held for examination before the sale is considered binding. If a dealer permits only 7 or 10 days for making a return, this may seem unfair, but you must consider the dealer's position. In the meantime he may receive other orders for the camera, and will be losing opportunities to sell it to someone else. Also, some customers (not many, thankfully) take advantage of the dealers by ordering a camera in the hope of selling it to someone else. If they cannot sell it, they return it to the dealer, and this of course is very unfair. In order to remain in business and keep their prices reasonable, the dealers must protect themselves. Without these safeguards, their costs of operating would be higher, and would be reflected in the prices they charge.

Since thousands upon thousands of collector cameras exist, only a fraction of them can appear on any given list of any dealer. Some cameras are so scarce that a dealer might handle only two or three specimens within his whole career in the business; with others, he might have them in stock regularly. You can't expect to pick up a dealer's list and find it as comprehensive as, say, the listings in this book. If there is a particular make or model for which you're searching, it might be necessary to check the lists of a number of dealers before locating it. Even better would be to drop the dealers a note, informing them of your interest in that camera. quite often the dealers have cameras in stock which do not appear on their lists, as they sell out too quickly. Some dealers actually have a great deal more cameras on hand than their lists would indicate. If you write to a dealer, you may have the opportunity to buy that special camera before it does appear on his list. The dealers like to do business this way. Any time they can sell a camera without listing it, it saves them some time and expense. They woud prefer selling all their cameras without putting out a list, if that were possible!

When you order from a list, make sure you know what you're ordering. Two cameras carrying the same model name, but different model numbers, could be quite different in style, function, and value. They may also be far apart in date of manufacture, too, one dating to 1910 and the other to 1925! Some model names, like Brownie, were kept in use eternally, but changes were made in the camera along the way. Beginners are sometimes disappointed with the camera they receive because they thought they were ordering something else. Occasionally it's the dealer's fault; if a camera is misdescribed, it will be taken back for a refund or credit with no problem.

Because of space considerations, the notes or other information on a dealer's list may be abbreviated. Printing is expensive, and the more compact a list is, the less costly it is to print and mail. This is also why illustrations on a list are either eliminated or kept to a minimum. They add to the dealer's overhead costs, and anything that adds to the dealer's cost will naturally be reflected in the prices he charges. Most collectors would rather have a no-frills list with prices as low as they can possibly be. If the dealer has used abbreviations with which you are unfamiliar, refer to the first page of the list for an explanation. If there is none, you are probably safer not to order that camera without first checking with the dealer and getting a clearer description. The dealers are very cooperative so far as this sort of thing is concerned. They welcome business from beginners and try their best to answer beginners' questions.

Cameras ordered from mail dealers will arrive well packed. If you should want to return any camera, be certain to pack it as carefully as when it arrived. Insure it for the full value as charged by the dealer. Any camera worth more than $200 should be sent by registered mail.

Buying at auction sales is another possible method of acquiring collector cameras. Sales devoted exclusively to cameras are infrequent, but collector cameras and accessories are often included in the "photographica" sales staged periodically by large auction galleries. The leaders in this field are Sotheby Parke-Bernet and Christie's, both of New York. Advertisements in collector periodicals will alert you to upcoming sales. A typical photographica sale will consist chiefly of important photographic prints, along with books and periodicals on photography and then a selection of cameras and equipment. There is no uniform approach as the contents of a sale will depend on the contents of the collection being sold. Occasionally, cameras will be found in miscellaneous sales, on which the catalogue cover reads "Victoria" or simply "Collectibles." The only time an auction house can stage a big sale of cameras is when a private collector having such a collection decides to sell it; or when he dies, and the executors of the estate place it for sale. Such collections have been relatively few in the past, compared to the large valuable collections made of coins, stamps, autographs and other collectibles; but this will certainly change. European auction sales are good sources for collector cameras, but then of course one has the long waiting period involved and the 10% buyers' premium to pay. At European sales, the final price is not the price at which an item is sold, but the sale price plus 10% — in other words, $550 on a lot sold for $500. This is done at some U.S. sales, too, and is becoming a growing practice in this country.

24 / BUYING COLLECTOR CAMERAS

Auction buying has a certain excitement attached to it, and the chance always exists for buying below the actual value. It is untrue that auction prices are habitually lower than dealer prices. Many cameras sold at auction bring just as much as the full established retail price, and some even sell in excess of it. This should really not be surprising, as the established retail value is only a barometer or guide to values. Just because a camera has a book value of (say) $500, this does not mean you can find one selling for $500. There may be none at all available at the present time. If several collectors are seeking a specimen of that camera, they might battle it out in the auction room and send the price up far beyond $500. Whether it's smart to pay more than the established value, for any camera, is a hard question to answer. You could pay $750 for a $500 camera and find another specimen of the same camera at $500 next week. On the other hand, none might show up on the market for six months, and by then the price could be $1,000. If the camera is scarce and desirable, there may be no other choice in obtaining one, but to pay more than the book value. It's partly a matter of luck, partly a matter of how badly or quickly you want the camera. Some people who go to an auction are determined to get bargains, and they will automatically stop bidding when the price gets up to 75% or 80% of book value. Others are resolved to get a particular camera and are not too concerned about the price. It does make sense, though, to establish maximum bids beforehand, on the cameras you're going to bid on. Bidding without any idea of how much you're going to spend is not too wise, especially if there are a number of cameras in the sale which interest you. You might miss out on a "buy" that occurs near the end of the sale, by spending all your money at the beginning of the sale. Always inspect the cameras on which you intend to bid. There will be a description in the auctioneer's catalogue, but this does not substitute for seeing the camera yourself and judging how much it appeals to you. Some cameras can have a number of faults and "sound bad" in a description, but are actually very appealing when you see them; and it can happen in reverse, too. The cameras will probably be under lock and key, but do not be shy about asking the attendant to take them out for you. The auctioneer wants you to be fully satisfied with your purchases. Of course you will handle them carefully. Catalogues for the sale will be available at the door, or at a "catalogue desk" in a large auction house. Here you can purchase the catalogue, if you have not already received a copy in the mail. Price for the catalogue will range anywhere from about $3 to $10, depending on the size of the sale and the number of color illustrations in the catalogue. You do NOT receive the list of prices realized by buying the catalogue (this is sent only to subscribers). However, if you attend the sale, it's a simple matter to jot down the price of each lot as it's sold. Auction catalogues are excellent for reference and should never be discarded.

At the larger sales, every lot will have a reserve price — that is, a preset figure representing the minimum selling price. These reserve prices are not divulged, in the theory that it would tend to cheapen the merchandise. You can usually assume that a reserve price will be about one-half the current market value, or slightly more. The reserves are used to prevent a disastrous sale, such as a $750 camera selling for $100. In a "reserved sale," there are no great bargains. Everything either brings at least one-half of its value, or goes back where it came from. Still, paying one-half the value for a fine scarce camera is not exactly a piece of bad luck. At almost any sale, there will be at least a few cameras which get just a shade above their reserve price before the bidding stops. There will also be some which fail to reach the reserve. Occasionally, a camera will come up which nobody places a bid on — the auctioneer cannot even get the bidding started. It's tempting in these cases to make a bid, just for the sake of getting

a bargain, but you should stop to consider the possibility that other bidders have inspected the camera and found it undesirable.
Generally speaking, auction sales are final. Items bought at an auction cannot be returned for any reason. There may be a provision for returning items that prove to be fakes or forgeries, but this would usually not apply in the case of cameras. If a buyer wanted to return a camera, it would probably be because some damage or defect was discovered, that had not been mentioned in the auctioneer's catalogue. This would not be considered grounds for making a return, as the merchandise in an auction is subject to inspection by the bidders and is offered "as is." It is presumed that someone would not be bidding unless he had thoroughly examined the item and satisfied himself of its condition and desirability.

SELLING YOUR COLLECTOR CAMERAS

Anyone who owns collector cameras, or even ordinary secondhand cameras in operable condition, need never be concerned about their potential for resale. Every working camera is a salable commodity. It can be turned into cash easily, and in most localities this can be done at a moment's notice. However there may be a vast difference between simply turning a camera into cash, and getting the best obtainable price for it.

The possible outlets for selling cameras are the same as the sources for buying them: camera shops; specialist dealers; other collectors; pawnbrokers. We will rule out the antiques shop from any part in this discussion. While it might be possible to occasionally buy a collector camera in an antiques shop, selling in antiques shops should not even be considered. The antiques dealers are not in a position to recognize or appreciate the value of a camera, and do not have a clientele of camera buyers; thus, they will pay only a small fraction of the value.

PAWNBROKERS

Pawnbrokers will buy most 35 mm. cameras in operating condition. They will usually not buy instant-picture models, regardless of the condition, as the resale value is not high enough. They will buy expensive models and in fact are anxious to do so — the problem is that prices paid by pawnbrokers are usually a bit lower than those paid by the secondhand departments of camera shops. The average pawnbroker wants to undercut the mainstream of his competition; it would be poor business for him to do otherwise. He knows very well that the local camera shop's secondhand department offers more cameras than he does. He knows that most people looking for a secondhand camera will think first in terms of the camera shop. Thus, to be competitive and draw potential customers into his shop, he must offer slightly better prices. This means he must spend less when he buys. Of course this does not apply in every single instance, nor with every pawnbroker in the country. Some pawnshops are very lavish operations and ARE very well stocked on cameras. They have a local reputation for cameras and do not need to undercut anybody, in order to attract customers. It is usually safe to assume that if you see just a few cameras in a pawnshop, the proprietor does little trade in them, and may not even be fully informed on values. He will almost certainly not be well informed on the value of "exotics."

26 / SELLING YOUR COLLECTOR CAMERAS

Mostly, the cameras bought and sold by pawnshops are of recent vintage, since the average pawnshop does not have collectors of old and rare cameras among its clients. It buys what it feels it has the best chance of selling. You will find some pawnbrokers who have an understanding of antique cameras and a willingness to take them do, but they are few and far between. Generally speaking, we would say that if you have an operable non-instant camera dating from the 1950's or later, you will find a willing buyer in the pawnbroker, though the price he offers may not be satisfactory.

The price obtained from a pawnbroker will be slightly higher if you sell outright, than if you pledge the item against a loan. When buying an item outright, the pawnbroker can place it on sale much sooner and get a fast return on his investment. A pledged item may remain on his hands, "frozen," for quite some time before it can be offered for sale.

Laws governing the operations of pawnbrokers vary from state to state. Generally, however, the term of pledge is 30 days. To redeem the item, it must be called for within 30 days, and the sum of the loan PLUS a small service fee paid. You have an option of extending the time beyond 30 days, by paying a storage fee at the end of each 30 day period, amounting usually to one-tenth the sum of the loan. The redemption period can usually be extended as long as six months in this fashion. If a 30 day period passes and the owner is not heard from, the pawnbroker acquires all rights to the property and is entitled to sell it, at whatever price he sees fit.

When selling to a pawnbroker, it is necessary in most localities to produce photographic identification, and have a fingerprint taken from the right thumb. These prints are automatically forwarded to local authorities, even if there is no reason to suspect the merchandise is stolen.

CAMERA SHOPS

Most camera shops will buy secondhand cameras for cash, though in the case of cameras with relatively low resale values they would much prefer to accept them as trade-ins. You will find that some camera shops are collector-oriented, buying and selling models that are too early to be of value for photographic purposes. Others, while maintaining a secondhand department, avoid any models with collector connotations and stay entirely to recent cameras that can be sold at a discount from the price of new models.

Camera shops that cater to collectors are good sources for selling your antique, unusual, or fine cameras. In most cases they will pay very fair prices. They will recognize the quality and value of the cameras you have for sale, however they will not necessarily be willing to *buy* any camera presented to them, even if the condition is operable. Some of them prefer not to stock certain types or makes of cameras, such as little-known foreign manufacturers dating before 1920. Their feeling is that the local collector demand for these more esoteric types is minimal, and that they would be tying up capital without any assurance of making an eventual sale. (As a hobbyist, however, you should not interpret this to mean that such cameras are any less worthy to collect. Worthiness is really in the eye of the beholder, especially when your primary interest in a camera is collecting rather than taking pictures.)

You can get a very good line on the type of cameras in which any particular shop is most interested, by the type it has displayed for sale. Classic early models by the major American manufacturers are salable in just about any camera shop having a collector or secondhand department, and you should have no trouble with an early Zeiss, Minolta or other top foreign makes either. If a camera is very rare, in the $1,000 and higher category, there may be some hesitancy on the part of the shop's manager to purchase it. Of course if the shop does a bustling collector business, this will be just the sort of camera it WANTS to buy, and perhaps the manager has been actively seeking just that make and model for a special client. The smaller shops with limited secondhand departments may feel that they do not stand a good chance of finding a customer who will spend $1,000 or $1,500 for ANY camera — even one studded with diamonds. If they do make an offer for such a specimen, the offer is likely to be calculated rather low. This gives them the option of putting the camera on sales in their shop for somewhat less than the usual retail price, or, if necessary, reselling it to another dealer and clearing a small margin of profit. For example they may offer you 40% of the book value on a $1,000 camera ($400), knowing or feeling fairly confident that a larger dealer would pay them 50-55% ($500-550). Obviously you can do better selling to the larger dealer yourself, as he will pay you the same price as he would pay to another dealer selling to him.

The camera shops want to do a fast turnover and will be more anxious of willing to buy models that have a reputation for selling quickly. If the shop has had six specimens of the camera within the past few months, and every one was sold within two weeks of acquiring it, it will not hesitate to buy yours and pay a good price for it. On the other hand, if several specimens of that very same camera are already on its shelves, it may not want to take on another one. "Overstocking" can be a problem in the camera business. A dealer will not go overboard on any particular make or model unless the price is so low that he can't say no. The dealer does not think in terms of making an investment for future growth, as a collector might, but of selling his cameras as he buys them and using a portion of the proceeds to buy additional stock. This is known as "cash flow." If cash flows out for the purchase of cameras for stock, and does not flow in through sales, the shop is in trouble.

The camera shops will purchase collections, just as they will purchase individual cameras. However, there may be certain cameras included in a large collection which are not appealing to them for one reason or another. They may either reject these or, if they agree to buy the whole collection intact, calculate these cameras at a very low price. Once again it becomes a matter of the proprietor leaving himself a reasonable safety margin to work with. He knows he can turn over the popular cameras in the collection rather quickly, and he wants to be sure that he can recover his cost PLUS a margin of profit on the popular cameras. Whatever he can make on the less popular specimens then becomes icing on the cake. If he cannot sell them himself, he will turn them over to another dealer or possibly to an auction house. At that point he is not terribly concerned, as he's already shown a profit on the collection.

Price offerings vary throughout the trade, just as retail prices vary. You may be able to form a fairly accurate idea of the prices you would receive for your cameras, in any given shop, by examining its stock of collector cameras and noting the prices being asked. Do the prices appear to be more or less in line with established market averages as listed in this book? (Do not expect total uniformity to established averages.) If so, the shop has probably been buying very competitively from collectors in the area, and paying anywhere from 50% to 60% of the book values. This is considered the fair average in most situations, though collectors (or anyone selling cameras to a dealer) tend to believe that 50% to 60% is unreasonably low. They expect to sell a camera to a dealer for almost as much as the dealer sells it, but of course in reality this would be impossible. The camera shop has rent to pay, a utility bill, advertising, employee salaries and additional expenses. It cannot buy a camera for $200 and sell it for $250, as much as it would like to. The shops would love nothing better than to be able to pay higher prices when they buy! This would draw many more top-quality cameras into their shops, which in turn would draw in more and more potential buyers. But if the profit margin is too small, all the business in the world would still end up unprofitable.

Do not go to the camera shop's secondhand department and ask if it would be interested in buying such-and-such type of camera. Bring in the camera; present it for inspection at the same time you discuss selling it. A query will often be answered with a "no," simply because the manager has some doubts about being able to use the camera and wants to save you what might be a wasted trip. If you already have the camera with you, your odds of selling it are better — and they improve even more if you seem truly anxious to sell it. Some people bring in cameras just for the sake of feeling out the proprietor or manager and obtaining what amounts to a free appraisal. Or they may go around to a number of shops and get comparison offers before deciding where to sell. If you appear to be ready to sell RIGHT NOW, ON THE SPOT, this will count in your favor. Of course it is not wise to appear DESPERATE to sell, as this suggests that you are badly in need of money and will agree to any offer.

Dust off the camera and clean the lens(es) before taking it in for sale. Do the same to the case and accessories, if you have them. If minor restoration is needed and you can do this yourself, it is certainly worthwhile to do so before attempting to sell the camera. You might succeed in raising the camera into the next higher condition grade, which would mean a difference in the price. The dealers can perform restoration work themselves, but if you can save them a little time and work you will also be saving them money and they appreciate this.

If you have more than just one or two cameras for sale, time your visit to the shop so that you arrive when it's not crowded. It is impossible for the manager of the secondhand department to devote proper attention to you, when there are numerous other buyers and sellers present. Saturdays are bad for seling, and so are lunch hours, as these are the most crowded times. Early in the morning and late in the afternoon on weekdays are generally the least crowded for most shops. If the manager of the secondhand department is not present, do not attempt to negotiate a transaction with anyone else, as other employees (who are probably not authorized to buy collector cameras anyway) are not in a position to recognize value or desirability.

SPECIALIST DEALERS

These are dealers who make a specialty of buying and selling collector cameras, rather than dealers who primarily sell new cameras and do only a sideline trade in collector specimens. As there are not many fulltime specialists, and as some of them deal out of box numbers rather than retail shops, it is usually necessary to conduct business with them by mail or phone. The specialist dealers are very anxious to buy good collector cameras, particularly early and scarce types. They are much more interested in the early and unusual types than in "borderline" cameras — those which have some collector status but are also still being used for photography purposes. They would rather leave the trade in borderline models to the secondhand departments of camera shops, just as most of the camera shops would prefer leaving the trade in bizarre, rare, and antique cameras to the specialists. The word specialist means precisely that. These individuals are collectors or ex-collectors and have an extensive knowledge of antique cameras, of their operation, history, and cash value. They will not make any mistakes about the value. Also, they will not fail to see the collector interest in a camera which may not be popular at the moment but is nevertheless historic or scarce. For what they can use, they will pay you fair prices, and they can use almost anything that would be of appeal to serious camera collectors. These are the people to turn to, when you want to sell a particularly rare camera or something that rates as a museum piece. They will buy the early wetplate, ambrotype, tintype, calotype and other primitive cameras. Of course they will also buy much more than this — it would be impossible for them to stay in business buying and selling nothing but "historics." In approaching specialist dealers it is normally best to make a listing of the cameras you have for sale, describing them in detail and sending along a photo of each one. Do not state an asking price but leave this as a matter for later discussion. The dealer may ask to have some or all of the cameras forwarded for his inspection, before entering into price negotiations or even making a firm commitment to buy. You can be quite certain however that if a dealer asks to see your cameras, he is interested in buying them. The only thing then which may stand in the way of a sale is whether his price offer is satisfactory to you.

If you have done regular business with a particular dealer, this should probably be the individual to whom you sell. He will not object to getting some of his cameras back again. Since he's already handled them, he need have no suspicions about hidden defects. A dealer does not mind selling the same cameras over and over again, so long as he makes a profit each time. Also, this dealer knows exactly how much you've paid for your cameras and will have a respect for your investment in them, though of course he cannot save you from taking a loss on them if his standard buying prices on those cameras would represent a loss. Whether you make a profit or sustain a loss on your cameras will depend to some extent on the length of time they've been in your possession. Someone who bought collector cameras in the early 1970's and went out to sell them today would almost certainly make a profit, and a good one, regardless of the makes or models. On the other hand, cameras sold within a year or two of being purchased will usually bring a financial loss to the seller. The market simply does not advance rapidly enough for cameras to be sold at a profit that quickly.

OTHER COLLECTORS

You can try selling to other collectors by running advertisements in your local daily newspaper or in the hobbyist periodicals. By selling to collectors you can usually obtain a higher price than selling to a dealer, since the collector does not have to work on a profit margin. He buys the cameras because he wants to own them, not because he makes a livelihood by doing so. Nevertheless, you should not expect to receive the FULL retail market values when selling to a fellow collector. Charging full retail values places you in direct competition with the dealers, and you just aren't in a position to compete against them. You want to offer a little something they can't, to draw potential customers, and of course the thing to offer is slightly better prices.

AUCTIONS

Auction selling should be considered only if you have valuable cameras of strong collector interest, or a large collection. In that case you may want to use the services of one of the major art/antiques/collectibles auction houses. Auction selling is uncertain as there is no way of predetermining the sales results. Some auctioneers will permit the use of a "reserve" or minimum selling price, but, even in that case, the allowable reserve will only be about one-half of the market value. For very valuable cameras, sales at one-half the market value would be considered disappointing. However in most cases the results at an auction are more favorable than this, occasionally reaching the full retail market value or even exceeding it.

CONDITION

As with all collector's items, the physical condition of a camera influences its value. One rule the hobbyist must learn is that an apparent bargain is not a bargain if the camera is in poor condition. In fact any camera being offered for less than the established market value should be suspect, and examined carefully to determine whether the low price has been prompted by some defect or damage. By the same token, a price in excess of the established market value is not necessarily too high, if the camera is perfectly preserved. Collectors will usually willingly pay a premium sum for outstanding condition, particularly in the case of a very old or scarce model which is normally found in less than the best condition.

Prices given in this book are for cameras in Excellent to Mint condition. While these are high grades of condition, they do not represent the absolute highest condition grade, which is New or Like New. The generally accepted grades of condition applied to collector cameras, and their definitions, are as follows:

NEW or LIKE NEW. Perfect in every respect, showing no signs of wear or use; exactly as the camera came from the factory, though it may no longer be in the original case or box, or have all of the accessories originally supplied with it. Very early cameras are hardly ever found in this grade of condition. The usual price for New or Like New cameras is 125% to 150% of the prices shown in this book. Example: for a camera listed at $200, the price for a New or Like New specimen woud be approximately $250 to $300. The age of the camera has a bearing on the amount of premium involved. It might be more than 150% on a New or Like New camera of 1890, and less than 125% on one dating from the 1960's.

MINT. Though in the collector parlance of most other hobbies, Mint is synonymous with new or perfect, in camera collecting it forms a category beneath New or Like New. This is important to remember; you may find the term Mint in a list or advertisement, and mistakenly assume that this is a camera to which a maximum premium should be attached. A Mint condition camera shows no signs of wear, but very minor indications of having been handled and used; it does not have that "straight from the distributor" appearance. It is certainly not defective in any way, and is so close to New or Like New that there may be some doubt, even among expert, about the category into which it should fall. The usual premium for a Mint camera is 110% to 140%; thus, for a camera listed here at $200, you could anticipate spending $220 to $280. As you can see this is very close to the premium for New or Like New, which shows that there is scarcely any difference in actual condition between the two grades.

EXCELLENT. As impressive as the word Excellent is, it constitutes not the first or even second grade of condition, but the third. An Excellent camera has obviously been used, but is not damaged or defective in any way. It is completely operable with no missing parts. It may be slightly scuffed. The great majority of ordinary secondhand cameras on the market, from the 1960's to the present day, fall into the Excellent category. In earlier cameras, the percentage of Excellent cameras is somewhat lower, and in very early antiques of the 1800's it is by no means an easy grade of condition to obtain. If a used camera has had only one owner, and he has taken reasonable care of it, it will most likely be in Excellent condition. For an early camera to be in Excellent condition, it must have had the good fortune to pass through the hands of several (or more) owners who were careful in their treatment of it. The more changing hands a camera does, from private owner to dealer to private owner, the more it will deteriorate. Don't forget that most of the early cameras did not change hands as gingerly-handled collector's items, but simply as "merchandise." They got tossed around in pawnbrokers' shops and maybe even served some time in a thrift shop. The usually accepted standard for Excellent condition, in terms of price, is 100% to 125% of the prices indicated in this book. More than anything else, the camera's age will determine whether any premium should be attached in the event of an Excellent grading and, if so, the size of the premium. It would be unusual for any post-1960 camera to carry a premium value because of Excellent condition, and this would be true of most cameras from the 1950's as well. Cameras of the past 25 or 30 years are expected to be in Excellent condition, and will not merit a premium value because of it. On the other hand an 1890 camera in Excellent condition is the exception rather than the rule, and if the usual value is $100, a price of $125 would normally be considered justified.

VERY GOOD. This category represents the middle range on the condition scale, quite a bit beneath the top but still very presentable. A very high proportion of the older model cameras, dating from the early 1900's up to the 1940's, are found in Very Good condition. A camera in Very Good condition is operable and has no missing parts, but needs minor refinishing to correct scuff marks, scratches, gouges in the leather and defects of that nature. A fairly modern camera should not, under normal circumstances, have been treated so roughly as to fall into the Very Good grade of condition. Hence such a camera will be considered a slightly inferior specimen, and will sell for about 10% less than the prices shown in this book. On the other a very early camera could possibly be hard to get even in Very Good condition, and merit a premium of 10% ABOVE the prices listed here. A camera which is not especially scarce, and dates anywhere from about 1910 to the 1940's, should sell right about at the indicated prices, when the condition is Very Good.

GOOD. This is the highest grade of condition into which a camera can fall if any parts (even minor ones) are missing or broken. For such a camera to be rated Good, the missing or broken parts cannot be integral ones, and the camera must have good potential for restoration. If it is questionable or doubtful whether the camera could be successfully restored, it does not merit a Good rating. Some refinishing will inevitably be necessary for a camera in Good condition." In evaluating a Good condition camera, it will generally be safe to figure a 20% discount from the prices shown in this book, if the camera is not very early or very scarce. Otherwise, the full price indicated may be justified; this would be true of most 19th century cameras, and certainly of all 19th century cameras listing at $200 or higher. It may surprise the beginner, but even so modest a condition grade as Good can be elusive in very old, scarce cameras.

FAIR. An inferior grade of condition, regardless of the age or scarcity of the camera, but counting much more seriously against its cash value if the camera is fairly recent or common. A Fair condition camera has broken or missing major parts, yet can be restored with some expense and effort by a skilled person. The discount in price will be anywhere from 30% to 70%, depending on the age and scarcity. For a camera to suffer only a 30% reduction in value when in Fair condition, it would need to be quite old and quite scarce.

POOR. A camera whose usefulness is limited to parts that can be salvaged from it, to use in restoring a specimen in better condition. Poor condition specimens cannot be restored in themselves as they have suffered too much damage. Their value is 10% to 30% of the prices shown in this book.

CAMERA HUNTING ABROAD

Almost every tourist magazine has carried, at one time or another, an article entitle "Hunting with a Camera in Europe" or "Hunting with a Camera in the Far East."

But what about hunting FOR cameras overseas?

Any camera collector taking a foreign holiday cannot help but wonder what sort of opportunities await him. Will he find rare exotic makes not available on the domestic market? Will he wander into a quaint Parisian shop and discover a genuine original daguerreotype camera that nestled in the attic of some local resident for 100 or more years?

It's natural to build castles in Spain when thinking about the cameras to be found abroad. After all, Europe was the birthplace of photography, and until about 1845 the number of cameras made there outnumbered those made anywhere else by a dozen or more to one. And we've all heard about the marvelous discoveries of valuable antiques of various kinds made in the antiques shops of London, Paris, Amsterdam and other European cities. So . . . isn't there good reason for the foreign traveler's pulse to beat fast?

Yes and no. To sum it up, you will find a greater selection of the very early pioneer cameras and equipment offered in Europe than on the American market. But it will not be inexpensive, and in fact you are apt to pay more for any given camera on the mainstream European market (that is, buying from specialist dealers) than for the identical camera bought in New York or Los Angeles. The exchange rate (the cost of converting American dollars to foreign currency) is partly responsible for this, but essentially the high European prices are the result of very strong collector activity. There are more camera collectors in Europe than in America, not just by a small margin but probably twice or three times as many.

Not only that, but investment in all "collectibles" is also stronger in Europe. Additionally, the European dealers in antique cameras do a great deal of business with museums. Unlike most American museums, which are short of funds and acquire only what is given to them, those of Europe go out and buy and are a very potent force in the trade.

With all these potential ways of making a sale, there is no reason for the dealers to discount their prices. Shopping in Europe you may, however, find a camera that you have long searched for without success. The condition of cameras in the stocks of European specialist dealers is usually quite good as they tend to adopt an "investor standard" so far as condition is concerned. The dealers on the whole are well informed and can usually provide a good deal of background information about their cameras. In a word they lean toward the scholarly side and are very satisfactory to do business with, if you can take the high prices.

As far as making finds in European antiques or bric-a-brac shops goes, this may not be an impossibility but the odds are very much against you. The local collectors (who are very well informed) scour these shops regularly and anything really worthwhile disappears almost as fast as it arrives. As is the case here in America, not many European antiques dealers choose to stock cameras because of the special knowledge required in evaluating them.

INVESTING

With all the enjoyment to be had from collecting cameras, does anyone have the right to expect a financial gain as well?

Before trying to answer that question, we must at least acknowledge the fact that investment interest has become a major force within most collecting hobbies. Today, any sort of "collectible" with an impressive track record of price increases will automatically draw attention as an "investible," too. Certainly, cameras have much to recommend them from an investment point of view compared to many other varieties of hobbyist items and art objects. They possess far stronger historical and cultural appeal than many groups of collector objects, and — very significantly — their buyers comprise a very broad range in terms of age, geographical locale, and personal income. In fact the "typical" camera collector is no more typical than the "typical" coin or stamp hobbyist.

The Official Price Guide to Antique Cameras takes no position pro or con on investment. The simple fact is that some people will want to invest and others will not, regardless of the advice they find in books or magazines; and this is certainly their prerogative. It seems more logical, then, to present as plainly as possible the facts about investing and leave the reader to reach his own conclusions.

One of the fundamentals of investing — in anything, cameras or diamonds or corporate paper — is that a profit is really no profit at all if it fails to beat the rate of inflation. This is a point the beginning or too-eager camera investor often overlooks. He thinks only in terms of increasing his capital, and is satisfied to do just that. If he can turn $1000 into $1500, he believes he has a profit of $500. In financial language this is called a "paper profit." It is a profit according to the arithmetic, but not necessarily a real profit.

If increasing one's capital automatically meant successful investment, there would be many ways of doing this, some of them carrying a much greater safety factor than buying and selling. A common savings account at the bank will increase your capital by $70 to $80 per year for each thousand dollars kept on deposit. This is a paper profit but a financial loss. Your capital is not growing as fast as the rate at which money loses its buying power. Withdrawing your capital (with interest) at the end of a year, and spending it, you can buy LESS than if the capital (without interest) had been spent a year ago.

In short you are getting poorer even though your capital is increasing.

For an investment to be successful, it must not only return a profit in cash but in purchasing power. This is why the quick profit, even if modest, has obvious advantages over the future gain — which may not be a gain at all! Selling quickly, you know precisely how much you must obtain to clear an actual profit. Selling on the long term, some paperwork may be necessary.

Investors are often advised to count on a prolonged holding period. This presupposes that values will continue rising as rapidly within (say) the next ten years as they did in the past ten. Is this really reasonable to expect? Probably not, if one examines all the various factors involved.

On the plus side of the ledger — tending to lead toward a conclusion that past performances will be duplicated — is overall growth in the hobby. Increased numbers of collectors entering the hobby will naturally benefit investors, as this means greater demand, more competition and higher

34 / INVESTING

prices. But to imagine that prices will continue rising at the pace of the late seventies and early eighties, simply because of continued growth in the hobby, may be erroneous.

The way in which one buys, not merely the selection of brands and models, also contributes to success (or failure) as an investor. In fact the approach to buying may really be the most vital element in investment. We all know that we can overpay for a camera. We all know that defects can be overlooked by a hurried buyer or one who fails to take a critical approach. Overpaying as a hobbyist may not be a sin, if that particular camera is an essential ingredient to your collection. When an investor overpays, he virtually eliminates any hope of turning a satisfactory profit.

Important factors to be considered when buying a camera chiefly for investment are:

Condition
Price in relation to the current market value
Future value-growth potential

Every investment purchase is a "tight" purchase insofar as there is little margin for error or miscalculation on any of these points.

Rather than buying what looks favorable at the moment, the serious investor ought to draw up a list of makes and models for his "portfolio," and not buy anything which is not included on this list. It is always tempting to take the advice of others, especially when their recommendations are backed by long experience in the hobby. But when someone offers a camera as a "good investment buy," one must keep in mind that this represents nothing more than a personal opinion — an opinion which may in fact be inspired by a desire to make a quick sale. The vast majority of antique cameras have climbed substantially in value within the past ten years, theoretically placing all of them in the category of "good investment buy" if past performance is the criterion. It is very commonplace today to use the investment angle as a device for selling all sorts of collector's items.

The investor should try to get his cameras in the best obtainable condition and, when possible, avoid paying the full market prices. In some instances this cannot be done, but with persistence the investor may find that fate and luck are on his side. Any advantage that can be obtained over paying the full market value is an immediate step in the direction of a successful investment, and may enable the investor to make a profitable sale without any waiting period.

Auction sale purchases of good investment grade cameras for WELL below 80% of book value are uncommon but once in a while they do happen. It is mostly a matter of being in the right place at the right time and keeping fully up to date with the market. Those who attend a sale of course have a marked advantage over absentee bidders. We would caution potential investors against bidding by mail or phone if they have not examined the cameras on which they're bidding. Auction sale regulations are so stringent that you will not likely have the chance to veto a purchase once it has been made. Even the hobbyist is unwise to gamble in this way, certainly unwise to make a practice of it. For the investor it is even more foolish.

Auction sales are not favorable for the investor in selling, simply because their outcome is unpredictable. The investor must sell in a manner which allows him to have full control over the price. Theoretically he has full control when selling to a dealer, as he can decline the offer. But he cannot actually set the price when selling to a dealer, and for this reason his best outlet is generally the private collector. The majority of investors sell their cameras to private collectors and this usually proves a good arrangement for both parties. The seller obtains a better price than he could hope to get from a dealer, and the collector saves a bit from the full retail market value. Generally the investor's selling price to a private collector is calculated at around 90% of the current market value, give or take some percentage points depending on any special circumstances that might be involved. Sometimes an investor will be able to obtain the full market value when selling to a private buyer.

The types of cameras most favorable for investment are not necessarily easy to select. One might be tempted to choose those which have shown the best performance records within past years, but cameras are not stock certificates. Some of the "blue chips" of camera investment might have reached values where they could no longer be expected to register profitable gains.

If the investor is already a collector, he has a distinct head start. If not, his first assignment will be to learn to think like a collector. When all is said and done, it is usually the collectors who set the trends and do the most toward influencing values. An investor must therefore examine the market in terms of the collector interest that is apt to be shown in various cameras within the coming years.

What will the collectors be buying?

What will they get tired of, and what will they discover afresh?

There are always new discoveries being made by collectors — little bandwagons that start rolling and gradually gather momentum, until a group of previously undervalued cameras is undervalued no longer.

FIRST MODELS. These would certainly have to be ranked high on any list of collector favorites, and for that reason should not be overlooked by the investor. Collectors in almost any field of manufactured objects have a special attraction to the prototypes or earliest available specimens. Perhaps the book collectors with their zest for "first editions" started it all. In any event, there are many camera collectors whose holdings consist of nothing but first models. This is strongly reflected in market values, as first models by the major manufacturers are generally much more valuable than their level of scarcity would seem to justify. It is not scarcity which brings about their lofty price realizations but the excessive demand.

It would be reasonable to assume that hobbyists will continue to pursue first model collecting, and quite likely this phase of the hobby will reach new heights in the future. The investor would be well advised, though, not to recklessly buy first models. The ones most worthy of his attention are first models by the larger or more historically important manufacturers.

NOVELTY TYPES. Investors often gravitate toward the older novelty cameras, such as pocket, palm, gun, and detective models, as well as cameras used to take miniature photos for application to pinback buttons.

On the whole the novelty types are no less favorable for investment, if one is careful to keep aware of the current market values. A certain type of novelty model put out by one maker may carry a very different market value than an almost identical type by another maker. The older one will not necessarily be the more valuable, nor will the better-looking one. There may in fact be no readily obvious reason for the difference in values, which might be learned only by probing into the background and history of each model.

The novelty types are a highly specialized group and one should approach them with reasonable caution, learning fully about them before doing any heavy investing. Their future collecting appeal is virtually assured, so there should be no need to entertain doubts along those lines.

EARLY STEREO CAMERAS. These certainly have their support from the collecting community and have been dabbled in by investors. They showed very satisfactory value increases in the period from 1977 to 1981 but their future outlook as investment material is open to question. They might be a little too "trendy" for the investor.

PRE-WAR GERMAN. These may well be the investment stars of the later 1980's and will certainly be if investors get to the point of taking a more objective, less romanticized, look at cameras available on the market. Many of the pre-war German cameras from the mid twenties up to about 1939 were marvels of their age from a technological viewpoint — ahead of anything that the rest of the world could produce. They began to seem less marvelous when the technology of other nations (notably Japan in the postwar years) caught up with them, and for this reason they went for some years not being fully appreciated by collectors and totally ignored by investors.

PRE-1900 AND EARLY 1900's PRESS CAMERAS. Some of these would appear to be underpriced on the current market, but there has never been any overwhelming interest in them as a group. If such an interest develops, they would be a very hot investment target.

EARLY COLOR CAMERAS (PRE-WORLD WAR I.) Though cameras like the Hicro certainly have their followers, the present level of collecting interest could be just a suggestion of things to come. Early color cameras have the definite potential to be more popular and more valuable monetarily. It is a worthy and interesting group which the investor will want to consider.

ORGANIZING A MUSEUM EXHIBIT

One way in which the hobbyist can increase his collecting enjoyment is to share his collection with the public. He can lend some of his cameras to the local museum for exhibition.

Antique cameras are ideal for loan shows, as they rank high in public interest but are seldom well represented (if at all) in a museum's permanent collection.

Almost any museum, whether its principle focus is art, science or history, will welcome the opportunity to stage a camera show. There is sure to be a museum of some kind in your area. Don't forget that museums depend for support on local residents, and support comes not only in the form of monetary contributions. You are doing your museum a valuable service by placing some of your cameras there on loan exhibition.

The first step is to contact the director or curator. In a small museum there will be one director for the whole facility. In a larger museum there are usually department heads and you should try to learn the name of the director of the appropriate department. Write this individual a letter outlining the fact that you have material available for a loan exhibition. Be specific. State the exact number of items that you can include in the exhibit and mention some of the rarer ones. Also state the length of time for which the material would be on loan. Museums have various policies as to the preferred length of loan exhibits. Since there is some labor involved in arranging a loan exhibit, most museums want to keep them running for six weeks to two months. A very large museum however, may wish to rotate its loan exhibits more frequently. If you can offer to consign your items for a minimum of two months, you are much more likely to receive a favorable response.

Tell the director that you are prepared to take part in mounting the exhibit and that full information will be furnished for each item. For an exhibit staged by a small local museum, it is preferred that the owner supply information cards for each object. These are usually placed on view in the exhibit cases just as the owner delivers them, without being retyped or checked for errors. Therefore it is worthwhile to take some time preparing them.

They need not be fancy. Use ordinary 3″ x 5″ index cards and type the description — one item to a card — on the unruled side. Type in capital letters only. This is important because sometimes the cards are at a distance from viewers, and not everyone has sharp eyesight. Work up a format for your exhibit cards. This would usually consist of the brand name, model name, date, and anything that would be of interest to the general public. Most people viewing the exhibit will not be collectors, so refrain from including any technical information unless it can be stated in simple language. Do not include the cash values of the cameras as this type of data is never proper for exhibition purposes. Also, do not make references to scarcity, and do not give any details about where and when you acquired the camera. Your name can (if you wish) be included at the bottom of each card, "LENT BY..."

Before making consignments to any museum or similar institution, check your insurance coverage to determine if your cameras will be fully protected at the museum and while in transit to and from it.

FIRST AID FOR OLD LEATHER BELLOWS

The antique leather-bellows camera which has been maintained in the best state of preservation by its former owners is the exception and not the rule. Quite often you will encounter a camera whose overall condition is acceptable, but on which the bellows has deteriorated to one degree or another.

This is unfortunate because in nearly every instance it is the fault of simple neglect (or perhaps ignorance of proper preservation methods) and could have easily been averted.

Some knowledge of the physical properties of leather bellows is essential in giving them correct maintenance.

The leather from which the bellows of antique cameras were made was obtained normally from the hides of cows, calves or sheep; occasionally from oxen, and, even less often, from pigskin. The hides were tanned and degreased before shipment to the factory, thereby reducing much of their natural moisture content. However some natural moisture did remain, as is always the case with freshly tanned leather. This residue of natural moisture served to keep the leather in respectable condition for the first several years of its life, regardless of the attention received from the owner.

Gradually the leather dried out. This would have first been noticeable by a loss of the original glossiness on the surface, which became duller and duller. Thereafter, the leather developed small cracks at the folds. These began as surface cracks to the uppermost layer of leather and eventually worked down deeper. Cracking was probably accompanied by flaking and peeling, too — some of the upper layer of leather chipped away here and there to reveal the undersurface.

You will find some antique cameras — not necessarily ancient ones either — in which the bellows are actually powdery and cannot be touched without some particles of leather chipping away. The best restorative and preservative for old leather is a regular treatment with oil dressing. With the bellows fully extended, gently rub the whole surface with leather dressing on a small cotton swab, working it in thoroughly.

You will note that it sinks into the leather almost immediately, and the surface looks dry again. This is because the leather is extremely thirsty, like a plant long overdue for watering. After the initial treatment you will need to repeat the process periodically. A bellows which has become really deteriorated through neglect cannot be brought back to the original appearance in this way, but further deterioration (which is otherwise inevitable) can be prevented.

If a great deal of flaking and chipping has occurred, and the exposed underlayer is lighter in color than the surface (which is usually the case,) you can darken these chipped spots by rubbing them with castor oil. Even the most puritanical collectors do not object to this, as castor oil imparts no color of its own. It cannot be considered a painted touch-up, as it merely darkens the existing color.

CAMERA CHRONOLOGY

NOTE: Some of the following dates are appropriate.

1614
Angelo Sala writes, "When silver nitrate is exposed to sunlight, it becomes the color of ink."

1725
Experiments toward development of sun images made in Germany by Johann Heinrich Schulze.

1765
Joseph Niepce born.

1787
Louis Daguerre born — full name Louis Jacques Mande Daguerre.

1799
Thomas Wedgwood, son of the renowned British pottery-maker, constructs a camera and attempts to make photographic images for use in pottery ornamentation. Wedgwood obtains positive images of twigs and leaves, but abandons the project upon discovering that the images soon fade and disappear.

1800
William Fox Talbot born.

1802
The *Journal of The Royal Institution* (London) publishes Thomas Wedgwood's account of his experiments with photography.

1824
Experiments in photography made in Paris by Joseph Niepce.

1826
Joseph Niepce of Paris designs his first camera, and has it built for him by a local optician.

1829
Oldest portrait photography still in existence today is taken, by Joseph Niepce. It portrays a French Cardinal.

1833
Joseph Niepce dies and his business associate, Daguerre, goes into partnership with Niepce's son.

1834
William H.F. Talbot Begins experiments with photography in England. Drawing upon the already published findings of Thomas Wedgwood, he seeks to discover a fixative that will prevent or reduce fading.

1835
The oldest preserved photo negative dates to this year (it may possibly be the first ever made). it was made by William H.F. Talbot of England and shows a window at his home. The negative is owned by the Science Museum of London, and is undoubtedly the most valuable piece of photographic memorabilia in existence.

1835
Daguerre uses mercury vapors for developing photo images and, by so doing, cuts the exposure time to a half hour or less.

1837
Daguerre uses sodium chloride as a fixative in developing.

1839
Louis Daguerre announces the successful results of his efforts to produce photo images.

1839
First commercially made cameras are offered to the public, the Daguerre and Giroux "Daguerreotype." On the side they carry a printed advertisement and guarantee of the manufacturers, and a red wax seal. Few specimens are still in existance.

1839
William H.F. Talbot, an Englishman, makes "Photogenic Drawings" on silver chloride paper.

1839
Translations begin to appear of Daguerre's handbook and soon are available in German, Spanish, English, Italian and several other languages.

1840
Alexander Wolcott becomes the first American to make significant contributions to photography, by use of the concave mirror.

1841
Willian H.F. Talbot introduces the calotype.

1841
Petzval develops the first lens made specifically for a camera (Daguerre and others had been using lenses from telescopes).

1841
Richard Beard opens the first photo studio in London.

40 / CAMERA CHRONOLOGY

1842
Edward Anthony founds the Anthony Co., first American maker of cameras and equipment. Official name at first is E. Anthony. The company later becomes Anthony and Scovill and then Ansco.

1849
David Brewster invents a stereoscope viewer.

1851
William Archer makes advances in bonding lightsensitive chemicals to glass plates.

1851
Stereoscope photos are shown at London's Great Exhibition and soon become the rage of Britain and Europe — and not long afterward America, too.

1852
Henry Anthony goes into partnership with his brother Edward, who ten years eariler had founded America's first camera and photographic equipment company.

1856
The *Dancer Stereo Camera* made by J.B. Dancer of Rochester, England.

1856
Introduction of tintype photographs.

1856
C.H. Kinnear designs a compact camera using paper negatives. It was not originally intended for production, but for Kinnear's personal use while touring Europe.

1860
Carte-de-visite photos becoming popular, their U.S. popularity soars following the Civil War.

1865
Alexander Gardner makes albumen print of the execution of Lincoln's conspirators (but John Wilkes Booth, who had been shot while resisting arrest, wasn't among them).

1866
Louis Bing develops an exposure meter.

1866
The "Rapid Rectillinear" lens is placed on the market in England.

1867
Scovill acquires American Optical Co. of New York, makers (at a later date) of the *Henry Clay* camera.

1878
Britannia Works Ltd. of Ilford, England, begins manufacturing silver bromide dry plates with gelatin base.

1879
Walter Woodbury introduces his exposure meter, an improvement on the model invented 13 years earlier by Louis Bing.

1880
Wooden plate camera called *Derogy Aplanat #2* made by Derogy of Paris; it has a brass barrel lens.

1880
The Blair Tourograph Co. is founded.

1881
Name of the Blair Tourograph Co. is changed to Blair Tourograph and Dry Plate Co.

1884
First true miniature camera is made, *Marion's Miniature Camera,* taking plates 1¼" by 1¼".

1885
J. Shew introduces the *Eclipse* camera.

1885
George Eastman begins selling the Eastman-Walker Roll Film Holder.

1885
Blair of Boston makes the *Lucidograph* folding plate camera with all wood body and brass-barrel single lens.

1885
Frank Brownell of Rochester, New York makes a stereo camera, one of the few cameras of his to be marketed under his name (most of his products were designed for Eastman Kodak).

1885
A collapsible-bellows view camera with non-folding bed is made by the Brooklyn Camera Co. of Brooklyn, New York.

1885
Anthony of Binghamton, New York makes its *Novelette* and *Patent Novelette* cameras in which back and bellows rotate as a unit.

1886
The Blair Tourograph and Dry Plate Co. becomes the Blair Camera Co.

1887
Rev. Hannibal Goodwin applies for a patent for rollfilm and is apparently its inventor. But the patent was not granted until 11 years later — in 1898 — by which time the credit for developing rollfilm had long since gone to Eastman.

1887
Duchess half plate field camera introduced in Britain.

1888
Original model of *Kodak* camera made by Frank Brownell for Eastman Dry Plate and Film Co. of Rochester, New York. It was factory loaded with 100 exposures in 2½" size. This was the first commercially marketed rollfilm camera.

1888
Compagnie Francaise de Photographie of France introduces its *Photosphere,* one of the first all metal cameras; it uses plates or rollfilm. Very valuable on the collector market.

1888
E. and H.T. Anthony of Binghamton, New York make the *Daylight Enlarging Camera*, a view camera and enlarger that accepts plates as large as 11½" by 11½".

1889
Kodak makes its *#1 Kodak* camera (acutally the second model as the first did not carry a numerical designation), produced for six years until 1895. It differs from the original type in that it has a sector instead of cylindrical shutter.

1890
Kodak introduces its *#3 Kodak,* placed on the market in January of that year and sold until 1897 — a string-set box camera factory loaded for 60 or 100 exposures.

1890
A *Junior* version of the *#3 Kodak* is introduced, factory loaded for 60 exposures. This particular model is scarce, but the production of Kodak Juniors increased enormously in following years.

1890
Beil and Freund ("Beil and Friend") of Berlin, Germany make a plate camera with Meniscus lens.

1890
V. Bischoff of Nunich, Germany (Bavaria) makes its *Detective Camera,* a box camera for 9 by 12 cm plates. It has a polished wood body.

1890
Rayment's Patent Camera is placed on sale by the English firm of Perken, Son and Rayment, at a retail price of seven pounds and five shillings for the half plate model. As the British pound was then exchanged at $5, this figured out to about $37.50.

1890
Blair acquires the Boston Camera Co.

1890
Kodak introduces service in which owners of its box cameras can ship their cameras, loaded with exposed film, to the company; Kodak would process the film, and return the camera loaded with a fresh roll.

1890
Detective camera made by the Dossert Detective Camera Co. of New York, a box plate model with reflex viewing, covered in leather and designed to be mistaken for a satchel.

1890
The *Vanneck* single lens reflex camera is marketed by Watson and Sons of Britain. The name, pronounced Van-Ek, was intended to suggest that you could produce pictures as fine as those painted by the Flemish artist Van Eyck (also pronounced Van-Ek).

1890
Anthony of Binghamton, New York makes the PDQ ("pretty darn quick") detective plate box camera. Retailed originally at $20 (not cheap for that time), it has multiplied in value about 25 times.

1890
Anthony of Binghamton, New York makes a 4" by 5" folding bed view camera with collapsible bellows.

1891
The Blair Camera Co. of Boston makes the *#6 Weno Hawkeye,* a Kodak-type box camera, one of many in its Hawkeye line.

1891
Blair of Boston introduces its *Kamaret,* the first American box camera to move the film spools to the front of the camera; it takes 100 exposures with automatic film counter.

1891
Anthony of Binghamton, New York makes the *Normandie* and refers to it in its advertising as "the lightest, most compact, and easily adjustable reversible back camera in the market."

1893
Birt Acres of Britain patents his "Chronophotograph," one of the earliest developments toward motion pictures.

1894
Burton's "Modern Photography" published.

1894
This is the final patent date for the *Folding Ansco* postcard-size rollfilm camera made by Anthony and Scovill, the company which later became Ansco.

1895
The *Henry Clay* camera (5" x 7" folding plate) is made by the American Optical Co. of New York. It is named after an unsuccessful Presidentaial candidate of the mid 1800's, who had no connection with photography.

1895
The first British motion picture is filmed (by Birt Acres, the "English Edison").

1895
Kodak introduces paper-backed rollfilm.

1895
The Boston Camera Co. makes its *Bullseye Box Camera,* a leather covered wooden camera for rollfilm; by this date the firm had been acquired by Blair but the name Boston Camera Co. was still being used.

1895
The Blair Camera Co. of Boston (soon to relocate at Rochester, New York) makes its *Hawkeye Junior* box camera for rollfilm or plates. This model remained in production about five years.

1895
Birt Acres of Britain patents his "Cinematograph," the most significant development toward motion pictures up to that time.

1895
The *Lightning Detective Camera* is made by Benetfink of London.

44 / CAMERA CHRONOLOGY

1895
    The American Camera Manufacturing Co., Inc. is founded in Northboro, Massachusetts. In 1899, it is sold to Eastman Kodak.

1895
    Adams of London makes *Minex*, single lens reflex camera for 3¼" x 4¼" exposures. At the same time, Adams is also manufacturing the *Yale #2 Detective Magazine Camera*, which makes twelve plates measuring 8 by 11 cm. The Yale has internal bellows focus.

1896
    The Borsum Camera Co. of Newark, New Jersey patents its 5 x 7 reflex camera; the patent was renewed the following year.

1896
    Close and Cone (with offices in several major cities) brings out its *Quad* box-plate camera with a quadruple plate holder.

1896
    Chicago Camera Co. of Chicago makes *Photake*, a seamless cylindrical camera taking five exposures on 2" square glass plates. The original selling price of this collector's item ($2.50) has now risen around 1,000% in the marketplace.

1896
    H. Bellieni et Fils ("Sons") of Nancy, France makes its *Stereo Jumelle* for 9 by 18 cm stereo plates, featuring a six speed shutter.

1897
    On the Kodak bandwagon, Adams and Westlake of Chicago are making *Adlake* cameras. Since distribution was still something of a problem in the trade, midwest makers felt they had a chance of capturing some share of Kodak's market. The Adlake is a manual plate changing box camera for twelve plates.

1897
    Thomas A. Edison of Orange, New Jersey, shoots his first motion pictrue, a western starring Bronco Billy Anderson. There's no plot, and for the final scene Anderson simply aims his 6-shooter at the audience and fires.

1897
    First "red window" rollfilm camera made.

1897
    The Blair Camera Co. of Boston (soon to relocate at Rochester, New York) makes its *Baby Hawkeye*, miniature version of its popular Kodak-style box cameras.

1897
    The Columbia Optical and Camera Co. of London makes its *Pecto #5*, a folding bed camera for 9 by 12 plates.

1897
    Bausch and Lomb introduces the Unicum shutter, the most successful in the company's history.

1897
 R. and J. Beck Ltd. of London makes the *Frena Detective Box Camera*, a magazine camera taking special sheetfilms. It is produced in three sizes. A deluxe version was introduced that same year, covered in brown calf leather.

1897
 The Aktien Gesellschaft fur Anilin-Fabrikation is established in Munich, Germany (Bavaria). Later it becomes known as Agfa (from the initial letters of words in its name) and eventually merge with Ansco and GAF.

1898
 Bullard Camera Co. of Springfield, Massachusetts makes a magazine camera for 18 plates in 4" by 5"

1898
 Le Stereocycle, a jumelle type stereo camera for twelve plates, is introduced by Bazin and LeRoy of Paris, France.

1898
 The *Tourist Hawkeye* is added to the line of Hawkeye camera made by the Blair Camera Co; it continues in production until 1904.

1898
 Using a name inspired by the Alsaka gold rush of the nineties, E. and H.T. Anthony of Binghamton, New York make the *Klondike* fixed-focus box-plate camera, featuring adjustable shutter speeds.

1899
 American Camera Manufacturing Co. of Northboro, Massachusetts (sold to Eastman Kodak in that same year) makes the *Buckeye #2*, rollfilm box camera for 4" by 5" exposures.

1899
 E. and H.T. Anthony (oldest camera company in the country, founded 1842) make the *Ascot* folding plate camera.

1899
 The Blair Camera Co. of Boston relocates in Rochester, New York and its eventually absorbed by Kodak.

1899
 The Chase Magazine Camera Co. of Newburyport, Massachusetts makes the *Chase Magazine Camera*, for twelve 4" by 5" plates. The plates were fed by turning a key at the side.

1899
 Rights to the *Cyclone* camera are acqured from Western Camera Co. by Rochester Optical Co. of Rochester, New York.

1900
 Kodak introduces its *#1 Brownie*, actually the second model Brownie as the first had been designated as number zero. A rarity in its original state as the back was redesigned only four months in production.

1900
 Use of aluminum baseboards for cameras begins.

46 / CAMERA CHRONOLOGY

1900
Perken, son and Rayment of England lowers the price on *Rayment's Patent Camera* to three pounds ten shillings — half the original cost of seven pounds and five shillings when it was introduced ten years earlier. This was one of the best selling British cameras of the nineties. Its price had to be cut because of competition from low-priced American makes.

1900
The Conley Camera Co. of Rochester, Minnesota makes a postcard-size folding plate camera.

1900
The Century Camera Co. is founded, bought out by Kodak three years later.

1900
Bullard Camera Co. of Springfield, Massachusetts makes a folding plate camera with wood interior and reversible back.

1901
British photographers make newsreel films of Queen Victoria's funeral procession.

1901
Kodak makes its *#2 Brownie,* a real "cheapo" with cardboard construction; but it sells like hotcakes.

1902
First year of production of Kodak's *#2A Brownie* box camera, made of cardboard.

1902
The Blair Camera Co. of Rochester, New York brings out its *#3 Folding Hawkeye* with horizontal format, wood interior and brown bellows.

1902
Anthony merges with Scovill and Adams. Five years later the company name becomes Ansco.

1903
Kodak buys the Century Camera Co.

1903
The Blair Camera Co. of Rochester, New York introduces model #4 of its *Folding Hawkeye* with horizontal design; it has nickel trim.

1904
The Blair Camera Co. of Rochester, New York makes its *#3 Combination Hawkeye,* which takes either rollfilm or plates.

1905
Ansco of Binghamton, New York (which did not actually begin using "Ansco" as the company name until 1907) makes the *Folding Pocket Ansco,* #5 in its series of box cameras.

1907
The company name Ansco is used for the first time, for the corporation which had been founded five years earlier by the merger of Anthony with Scovill/Adams. Their location is Binghamton, New York.

CAMERA CHRONOLOGY / 47

1907
Having bought the Century Camera Co. four years earlier, Kodak decides to continue operating it as a separate entity, calling it "Century Camera Division of the Eastman Kodak Co."

1907
Ansco of Binghamton, New York patents its *Ansco #10* folding rollfilm camera, featuring automatic shutter.

1907
Ansco of Binghamton, New York makes its *Folding Ansco Box Camera #6*, in Model C and Model D. Both have Wollensak lens and red leather bellows.

1908
The Bell Camera Co. of Grinnel, Iowa introduces *Bell's Straight-Working Panorama Camera;* "straight working" meant that everything on the camera was fixed or stationary, presumably to allow even the most inept operator to take decent pictures.

1910
The Chicago Ferrotype Co. of Chicago makes its *Wonder Automatic Cannon Photo-Button Machine,* a camera for taking pictures that can be made into buttons (pins). It produced prints 1" in diameter. Promoters had real success using this camera at amusement parks and similar locations.

1910
Ansco of Binghamton, New York makes the *Dollar* box camera. Good to its word, it really did sell for a dollar originally and sometimes even slightly less when retailed by supply houses.

1910
Stereo camera for 45 by 107 mm plates marketed by the Parisian firm of Demaria.

1910
Black gradually begins replacing red as the preferred color for camera bellows.

1910
Burke and James of Chicago makes its *Rexoette,* a box camera in its *Rexo* line which included *1A Folding Rexo, 1A Rexo Junior, 2C Rexo Junior* and others.

1912
W. Butcher and Sons of London makes its *Cameo 3½" by 5½"* plate camera with Ibso shutter.

1913
The Chicago Ferrotype Co. makes the *Mandel #2 Post Card Machine* — one of the few cameras that wasn't called a camera. The name "Post Card Machine" referred to the fact that it was designed to be used on the street.

1914
Autographic line introduced by Kodak.

1914
Importation of German cameras into Great Britain is halted due to World War I.

48 / CAMERA CHRONOLOGY

1916
Ansco of Binghamton, New York makes the *Speedex #1A* rollfilm camera for 116 film.

1919
Contessa merges with Nettel to become Contessa-Nettel in Stuttgart, West Germany.

1924
Contessa-Nettel of Stuttgart, Germany makes the *Miroflex* single lens reflex camera for 9" by 12" plates. When Zeiss took the company over, it kept this model in production.

1924
Contessa-Nettel of Stuttgart, Germany makes its *Citoskop Stereo* with Tessar lenses.

1924
Ansco makes the *Semi-Automatic Ansco* folding rollfilm camera, which takes six 2½" by 4¼" exposures.

1925
Ansco of Binghamton, New York makes its *Automatic,* a folding rollfilm camera which shoots six exposures in six seconds; it operates on a spring-wound film advance. When the Automatic hit the market it carried a pricetag of around $75, a whopping sum for a camera at that time.

1926
Certo Kamerawerk of Dresden, Germany (Saxony) makes the *Certonet,* a 6 by 9 cm folding camera for 120 film.

1926
Zeiss-Ikon Co. formed in Germany, as the result of a merger between the Carl Zeiss Optical Co. and other German manufacturers.

1927
Contessa-Nettel of Stuttgart, Germany makes the *Deckrullo Tropical* folding plate camera with teakwood body.

1927
Ansco makes the *Memo* for ½ frame exposures; it features lever film advance and automatic exposure counter.

1928
Ansco of Binghamton, New York merges with Agfa of Munich, Germany (Bavaria) to become Agfa-Ansco.

1929
The Chicago Ferrotype Co. makes its *Mandelette* direct positive street camera. The original selling price is $10, about a tenth of the sum now paid for it by collectors.

1929
Bakelite is used in making a camera body, *APM's #6 Rajar.*

1930
  Boy Scout camera introduced by Kodak, using 127 rollfilm. A vest pocket model with Boy Scout emblem. This one is now collected not only by camera enthusiasts but hobbyists interested in Scouting items.

1930
  Beau Brownie, two-tone colored version of the Brownie box camera, is marketed by Kodak.

1930
  Kodak makes its *Anniversary Box Camera* on the 50th anniversary of the Eastman Kodak Co. Nearly half a million of these were given away by the company to children, most of whom would have been hard pressed to afford a camera during the depths of the Depression.

1930
  Box cameras with brightly colored bodies begin going on the market, mostly made by Kodak by some by other firms as well.

1930
  Bentzin of Gorlitz, Germany, makes its *Planovista* twin-lens non-reflex folding camera, to be marketed by the London firm of Planovista Seeing Camera Co. Ltd.

1934
  Berning of Germany makes its *Robot I* 35 mm camera with spring motor automatic film advance, for 1″ by 1″ exposures. It features a rotating shutter.

1935
  Certo Kamerawerk of Dresden, Germany, (Saxony) makes the *Doppel* box camera which can take eight exposures at 6 by 9 cm or sixteen at 4½ by 6 cm.

1935
  Agfa of Munich makes the *Speedex,* inspired by the Jiffy Kodak. It becomes one of the company's best sellers.

1935
  Cornu of Paris introduces the *Ontobloc* 35 mm compact camera with body made of painted cast metal.

1936
  Argus of Ann Arbor, Michigan introduces its *Model A* 35 mm cartridge camera, which continues in production until the outbreak of World War II.

1936
  Adox Kamerwerk of Wiesbaden, Gemany, makes the 35 mm *Adox.*

1937
  Kodak makes its *Baby Brownie* with plastic body (brown or black).

1937
  Karl Arnold of Marienburg, Germany makes its *Karmaflex* with guillotine shutter, a variation of its basic *Karma* model. The name is not selected from the Indian work "karma" (or "mood") but by grouping various letters from the manuracturer's name and place of operation.

1937
Balda Werk of Dresden, Germany (Saxony) makes the *Rigona* folding camera; it makes 16 exposures on 127 film.

1937
Arugs makes its *Model AF,* similar to the *Model A* 35 mm cartridge camera which had been introduced earlier.

1937
Agfa of Munich makes the *Karat* remained in production about three years.

1938
Balda Werk of Dresden, Germany (Saxony) makes the *Jubilette* folding 35 mm camera; name derives from the jubilee for the 30th anniversary of the company's founding.

1938
Berning of Germany which had introduced its *Robot I* in 1934, brings out an improved version in *Robot II.*

1938
Pignone of Balaigues, Switzerland makes the *Bosley Reflex,* developed by Jacques Bosley before he emigrated to the U.S.

1938
Tri-Color Camera for making color separation negatives marketed by the Devin Colorgraph Co. of New York; made in at least two sizes.

1938
Candid Camera Corporation of America formed; no connection with the much later TV program of the same name.

1938
Argus makes its *Model C2* with coupled rangefinder. It remained in production four years.

1939
Argus makes its *Model A2* 35 mm cartridge camera, featuring extinction meter; it proves one of the most popular in the line and continues in production until about 1950.

1939
Argus makes its *Model K* with coupled extinction meter, an advance over its "A" series. It remained in production about two years.

1939
Agfa of Munic makes the *Memo,* in folding 24 by 36 mm format on 35 mm film with Afga Memar lens.

1939
Candid Camera Corporation of America makes its *Perfex Forty-four,* 35 mm CRF camera.

1940
Argus makes its *Model AA,* also known as *Argoflash,* a 35 mm catridge camera (a version of the *Model LA* introduced c. 1936).

1940
Detrola Corporation of Detroit makes its *Model GW,* a 127 film camera.

1940
Candid Camera Corporation of America introduces the *Perfex Thirty-Three.* It remains in production about two years.

1940
Agfa of Munich makes the *Plenax* folding rollfilm cameras, in models PD-16 and PB-20. Distribution of these potentially popular low-priced cameras to the U.S. is impeded by the war.

1941
Argus makes its *Colorcamera* with non-coupled selenium cell meter; it remained in production about two years.

1945
Name of the Candid Camera Corporation of America changed to Camera Corporation of America.

1946
Duca twelve exposure camera with zone focus made by Durst.

1946
Clarus Camera Manufacturing Co. of Minneapolis introduces the MS-35, a rangefinder 35 mm camera with Wollensak Velostigmatic lens. It remained in production six years.

1947
The Bosley Corporation of America (New York) makes the *Bosley B,* a compact 35 mm camera; it is followed by the B2 in 1949 with a double exposure prevention feature.

1948
Camera Corporation of America (formerly Candid Camera Corporation of America) makes the *Perfex One-O-One* with Alphax leaf shutter.

1948
Argus makes its *Argoflex* twin lens reflex camera, available in various body styles and models in the course of the following ten years.

1948
Bell and Howell makes its *Foton* 35 mm spring-motor driven cammera, shooting six frames per second.

1948
Automatic Radio Manufacturing Co. of Boston makes the *Tom Thumb Camera Radio,* which functions both as camera portable radio.

1949
Daiichi Kogaku of Japan makes the *Zenobia* folding camera modeled after the earlier Zeiss *Ikontas.*

1949
Ciro buys Camera Corporation of America.

52 / CAMERA CHRONOLOGY

1949
Ciro Cameras of Delaware, Ohio makes its *LCiro* 35, a 35 mm camera available in several models.

1949
Balda Werk of Dresden, Germany (Saxony) makes the *Beltica* folding 35 mm camera.

1950
Balda Werk of Dresden, Germany (Saxony) makes the *Baldalette* folding 35 mm camera with Pronto shutter.

1950
J.H. Dallmeyer of London makes the *Dan 35*, a compact camera for 15 exposures in 24 by 24 mm.

1950
Argus introduces its *Model FA* 35 mm cartridge camera, the last in its lengthy "A" series; it features two position focusing.

1950
Agfa-Ansco makes the *Rediflex*.

1950
The Bosley Corporation of America (New York) makes the *Bosley C*, which remains in production about six years.

1950
The American Safety Razor Corporation of New York gets into the camera business with the *ASR Foto-Disc*, a pocket camera taking eight exposures that measure a miniscule 22 by 24 mm — less than an inch square.

1951
Canon Camera Co. of Japan brings out the *Canon II*.

1951
Argus introduces its C4 with coupled rangefinder, made for about six years.

1952
Belca Werke of Dresden, Germany (Saxony) makes the *Belpasca*, a 35 mm stereo camera with Tessar lenses.

1953
Apparate and Kamerabau of Friedrichshafen, Germany, makes its *Akarex* 35 mm rangefinder camera, with rangefinder and lens interchangeable as a unit.

1953
Argus resurrects its "A" series of cameras by redesigning the body and bringing out the *Model A4*.

1954
Apparate and Kamerabau of Friedrichshafen, Germany, makes the *Akarelle*, a 24 by 36 mm camera with Prontor shutter.

1955
   The Bosley Corporation of America (New York) makes the *Jubilee*, a 35 mm camera with Gauthier leaf shutter.
1955
   Bencini of Italy makes its *Animatic 600* cassette camera.
1957
   Aires of Japan makes the *Aires 35V*, a 35 mm camera with rangefinder and meter.
1958
   Argus makes its *C4R*, an advnaced version of the C4 which had been introduced in 1951. The C4R has rapid film advance lever.
1958
   Astraflex of Germany makes the *Astraflex II*.
1960
   Argus makes its *Autronic*, sometimes known as Autronic 35 and sometimes as Autronic C3. It features automatic electric eye and rangefinder.
1960
   Corfield of England makes the *Periflex*, a 35 mm styled after the Leica.
1960
   Cannon Camera Co. of Japan introduces its *Canonet* camera.
1960
   Canon Camera Co. of Japan introduces its *Canonet* camera.
1961
   Canon Camera Co. of Japan makes the *Canon 7;* it remains in production until about 1964.
1964
   Canon Camera Co. of Japan redesigns its *Canon 7* and it becomes *Canon 7-S.*
1977
   Record prices set for an antique camera, $37,500 for a *Dancer Stereo Camera* made by J.B. Dancer of Rochester, England, c. 1856.

ABOUT THE PRICES IN THIS BOOK

Prices of cameras or virtually any collector's items are something on which universal agreement is not to be expected. Personal likes and dislikes enter into value; so do the circumstances under which a sale is made. The mere fact that a camera has been sold for X amount of dollars tells very little about its value. Was the seller a dealer or private individual? Was the seller fully aware of the camera's age, significance, and the demand for it? What condition was the camera in? Was it like new, or did it have missing parts or other major defects? Did the sale take place in a camera shop or in some kind of shop where collector cameras are seldom sold, and where the philosophy might have been "move it along at any price?" Was it a camera which comes up for sale regularly, and for which a fair value has been established through repeated sales? Or a scarce, odd, exotic or rare type, which is sold only occasionally? These and many other questions must be asked, before the validity of any single price in any single transaction can be judged. Isolated sales seldom provide any real basis for calculating the true value of a camera. A real sense of market value, even within the leeway of a *range* such as used in this book, can be obtained only when NUMEROUS sales have been analyzed.

Although we attempt in this book to provide value indications for the rarer cameras as well as the more standard, the reader should realize that values on rare, unusual and expensive models are not as firm or indicative. The more sales that occur on a given camera, the more data there is, with which to tabulate prices. If sales occur infrequently, which is generally the case with cameras in the $1,000 and higher price category, the available pricing information is scantier and less reliable. Say for example that in the course of a year, three recorded sales have occurred on a particularly rare camera. The three specimens might have differed considerably in condition and circumstances of sale. This makes it difficult to say what a fair price would be, for a specimen in any one grade of condition. Even assuming that all three were in identical condition, the prices might have varied drastically, one selling for $800, the next $1,200, and the third $1,500. Such variations in price are not at all uncommon where rare, seldom-offered models are concerned. These cameras do not carry really tight, standard prices because there is nothing "standard" about the market for them: they pass through the market unpredictably, sometimes doing exceptionally well, sometimes not as well.

What makes a price? Many prices are really arbitrary, in transactions occurring in the camera market. A dealer, or anyone with a camera for sale, will try to get the absolute maximum he can for it, which is nothing more than human nature. If someone could sell a $100 camera for $200, you can be quite sure he would ask $200 for it. And there are times when he can, if circumstances are right and Mr. Avid Collector comes along. This is precisely one of the ways in which established market prices change. Say a dealer had a Monroe folding plate Vest Pocket Camera in his stock last month. He put it out on sale with pricetag of $130 (in the neighborhood of the established market value). Ten minutes later, someone bought it — and didn't even haggle over the price. Of course the dealer was glad to make a quick sale, but at the same time he would not be human without wonder if he COULD have gotten more. This week, he gets another Monroe folding plate Vest Pocket Camera in the same grade of condition. Does he price it at $130? You can be quite certain he does not. Based on the success he had with that model last time, he will now charge a higher sum, perhaps $150 or $175. And what he does with his NEXT specimen will be determined chiefly by his success (or lack of it) in selling this one. If they keep selling fast at the prices he marks, he will con-

ABOUT THE PRICES IN THIS BOOK / 55

tinually raise the price — the sky is the limit so long as customers are paying the price. Of course, other dealers will hear of this along the market grapevine. They will say, "Well, if he can get more than the book price for HIS Monroe folding plate Vest Pocket Cameras, why can't I?" Gradually, a general increase in price for this model occurs throughout the entire trade. Though this is strictly a fictional example, it is typical of what actually does take place in the collector camera market. Prices on the whole for most collector cameras are CONSIDERABLY higher today than they were six or seven years ago. This could not have happened if everybody kept selling cameras for the price at which they sold the previous specimen.

Dealers cannot, however, manipulate the market to their advantage; nor can hobbyists or anyone else. There is no way to make prices artificially high and still keep selling the cameras. A dealer can ASK prices that are higher than book value — but he can't make his customers pay them if they choose not to. So the vital factor, in the movement of prices, is the level of interest on the part of the public, and its willingness to pay increased prices. Some cameras are unquestionably "underpriced," even in the current active market. The prices at which they sell do not reflect their scarcity or importance, but they continue to sell at these low prices because nothing has happened to boost them up. In some cases they are just overlooked, perhaps because of lack of publicity. Some obscure brands of cameras are scarcely known about by collectors. If collectors were more familiar with them, and had more opportunities to buy them, they would probably be more enthusiastic about them. In this hobby as in many others, "name and fame" go a long way.

Collectors are the regulators of the market. If they refuse to buy a camera priced above its book value, it does not move ahead in value. The seller must reduce its price to make a sale. If a camera consistently fails to sell for its established value, the established value drops; but this is rare, and tends to occur only when the overall economy is depressed.

Prices in this book should not be taken as hard and fast rules or dogma. They are simply guidelines to aid the buyer and seller. You can safely assume that sales have occurred both above and below these prices, and will do so again in the future. To better reflect the variations in price, a value RANGE has been used ($60-80, $100-130, $200-275 and so on), rather than a single price. You will note that is some cases the range is wider than in others. This is entirely a result of sales having occurred at sharply divergent prices. On the other hand, when most recorded sales have been in approximately the same range, the stated range will be much narrower.

Keep in mind that exceptional condition makes a vital difference in the value of a camera, as detailed in the comments on condition. There is greater competition among potential buyers for specimens in top grade condition, and a willingness to pay higher sums. Even among the dealers there is more willingness to pay premiums for specimens in the best condition. By the same token, an inferior specimen calls for a discount in the price, if the seller is serious about making a sale. An informed buyer will very rarely pay the full market price for a camera with damaged or missing components, unless it happens to be very rare.

CLUBS

Camera Clubs of America
2005 Walnut Street
Philadelphia, PA 19103

L.H.S.A. *(German made Leica Camera Collectors)*
P.O. Box 1626
Rome, GA 30161

Photographic Historical Society of New England
P.O. Box 403
Buzzards Bay, MA 02532

Photographic Historical Society of New York
P.O. Box 75
Radio City Station
New York, NY 10101

Western Photographic Collectors Association
P.O. Box 4294
Whittier, CA 90607

MUSEUMS

Center for Creative Photography
843 East University
Tucson, AZ 85719

International Center of Photography
New York, NY 10028

International Museum of Photography at George Eastman House
900 East Avenue
Rochester, NY 14607

Photographic Archives
University of Kentucky Libraries
Lexington, KY 40506

HOW TO USE THIS BOOK

The Official Price Guide To Antique and Classic Cameras has been designed for maximum convenience in use. All listings are grouped by manufacturer, and arranged alphabetically by the names of manufacturers. The Alphabetical format is also used in listing the products of each camera manufacturer. Thus, to find the latest market values for Kodak Brownies, just turn to K for Kodak, and Brownies will be at B. If more than one model is listed of any camera, the listings will be sequential by model number. For cameras having no model name, the listings will likewise be sequential by model number. After taking just a minute or two to familiarize yourself with the listings, you will be able to find any camera almost instantly.

Each Listing provides the basic information to positively identify the camera — that is, to avoid possible confusion with another model of the same manufacturer. When dates of manufacture are known, they have been given. In many cases, estimated dates are furnished, preceded by the symbol "c." ("circa"). Other pertinent information or observation are also included in many o the listings as an aid to collectors.

Beside each listing is a price range that represents generally the prices paid by collectors when buying from dealers. Prices paid by dealers are of course lower. A range is used rather than s single price to reflect the variations in price from one sale to another. Although the current market values have decreased somewhat from the prices listed, a gradual turn around is predicted in the upcoming months.

ADOX KAMERAWERK / 57

ACMA
(Australia)

☐ **Sportshot,** *620/120 film.*
................26.00   32.00

ACRO SCIENTIFIC PRODUCTS CO.

☐ **Acro,** *127.*
................45.00   55.00

ADAMS & CO.
(London)

☐ **Minex,** *single lens reflex c. 1895 for 3¼ x 4¼ exposures, similar to the Graflex.*
.... 165.00   185.00

☐ **Yale No. 2,** *c. 1895 detective magazine camera for 12 plates 8 x 11cm., lens f6.5, Adams Patent Shutter to 1/100, focus by internal bellows.*
.... 150.00   170.00

ADAMS & WESTLAKE CO.
(Chicago)

☐ **Adlake Cameras,** *manual plate changing box cameras for 12 plates in 3¼ x 4¼ and 4 x 5 inch sizes, c. 1897.*
................45.00   65.00

ADINA

☐ **6 x 9cm. camera,** *f6.3/105 Rodenstock Trinar lens in Adina shutter to 1/100 seconds.*
................15.00   18.00

ADORO
(See Contessa, Zeiss)

ADOX KAMERAWERK
(Wiesbaden)

☐ **Adox,** *35mm. camera c. 1936.*
................30.00   40.00

☐ **Adrette,** *35mm. camera with telescoping front, identical to Wirgin Edinex, Steinheil Cassar f3.5/50mm. or Schneider Radionar f2.9/50mm. in Prontor or Compur shutter.*
................35.00   50.00

☐ **Blitz,** *bakelite box camera for 6 x 6cm. exposures on 120 film, f6.3/75mm.*
................6.00   10.00

58 / AFIOM

- [ ] **Golf,** 6 x 6cm. folding camera, Adoxar f6.3 lens.
  ....16.00   20.00
- [ ] **Sport,** rollfilm camera for two formats, 4.5 x 6 or 6 x 9cm. on 120 film, folding bed type, Steinheil Cassar f6.3 or Radionar f4.5, Vario shutter, quite common.
  ....15.00   18.00

AFIOM
(Italy)

- [ ] **Wega IIa,** 24 x 36mm., Trixar f3.5/50mm., focal plane shutter to 1000, coupled RF, synchronized.
  .... 175.00   190.00

AGFA KAMERAWERKE
(Munich)

Originally "Aktien Gesellschaft für Anilin-Fabrikation" established in 1897. Agfa is an abbreviation from the original name. Eventually, it became part of the Agfa-Ansco and then GAF companies.

- [ ] **Ambi-Silette,** 35mm., 2.8/50 in Compur, f4/35mm. and f4/90mm. lenses also available, complete outfit.
  .... 125.00   150.00
- [ ] **Same as above,** with normal lens only.
  ....40.00   50.00
- [ ] **Antar,** box camera for 116 film.
  ....6.00   10.00
- [ ] **Billy,** Record, Clack, etc., folding rollfilm c. 1938 for 6 x 9cm. on 120 film, Apotar f4.5/105 or Solinar 4.5/105, or Agnar 6.3/105 or Igestar 6.3/105.
  ....10.00   14.00
- [ ] **Box cameras,** miscellaneous sizes, styles.
  ....5.00   7.00
- [ ] **Cadet,** all metal box camera.
  ....4.00   6.00
- [ ] **Captain,** box camera.
  ....5.00   7.00
- [ ] **Clack, Click,** box cameras.
  ....5.00   7.00
- [ ] **Clipper,** metal bodied collapsible camera with a rigid rectangular section which pulls out to the shooting position, for 16 exposures on 616 (PD-16) film, single-speed shutter and meniscus lens.
  ....4.00   6.00
- [ ] **Clipper Special,** like Clipper, but with f6.3 Anastigmat lens, and shutter 25-100, time and bulb, optical finder.
  ....8.00   12.00
- [ ] **Folding Rollfilm cameras,** common models for 116 and 120 films.
  ....12.00   15.00
- [ ] **Iso,** Isoflash, Isomat.
  ....8.00   12.00
- [ ] **Isolar,** 9 x 12cm. folding plate camera, Solinear f4.5/135 mm. dial Compur 200, DEB, metal body, GGB.
  ....35.00   45.00
- [ ] **Isolette,** folding rollfilm cameras similar in style to the Zeiss Ikonta and Nettar cameras, for 16 exposures 4.5 x 6cm. or for 12 exposures 6 x 6cm. on 120 film, models I-V, normally with f4.5/85 Apotar or Agnar lens in Pronto, Vario, or Compur.
  ....25.00   40.00
- [ ] **Isolette Super,** folding 6 x 6cm. on 120 film, f3.5/75 Solinar, CRF, Shutter to 500, MX synchronized, self-timer.
  ....85.00   100.00
- [ ] **Karat,** models 12 and 36 c. 1937-1940, folding 35mm. with self-erecting front, for 24 x 36mm. on Agfa Rapid Cassettes, many varied shutter/lens combinations from f6.3 to f2.
  ....35.00   50.00
- [ ] **Karomat,** f2.8 Schneider Xenar or f2 Xenon lens.
  ....45.00   55.00

AGFA KAMERAWERKE / 59

- ☐ **Major,** *folding bed camera for 6 x 9cm. exposures on 120 film.*
  ....10.00   15.00
- ☐ **Memo,** *c. 1939, folding 24 x 36mm. format on 35mm. film, 18 x 36mm. "half-frame" added as additional model in 1940, Agfa Rapid cassettes, rapid advance lever on back, f3.5, 4.5, or 5.6 Agfa Memar lens.*
  ....50.00   65.00
- ☐ **Nitor,** *6.5 x 9 plates or 6 x 9 rollfilm choice, Helostar f4.5/105, Compur to 250.*
  ....25.00   35.00
- ☐ **Optima,** *24 x 36mm., 35mm. Rangefinder, f2.8/45 color Apotar, Compur.*
  ....25.00   35.00

PD-16, PD-16 was Agfa's number for the same size film as Kodak 116 film. Several of the Agfa cameras use this number in their name, however we have listed them by their key word, Clipper, Plenax, etc.

- ☐ **Plate Cameras,** *6 x 9cm. with f4.5/105 and 9 x 12cm. size with f4.5/135 Double-Anastigmat or Solinar lenses, Compur dial-set shutter.*
  ....35.00   45.00
- ☐ **Plenax,** *c. 1940 folding rollfilm cameras, models PD-16 and PB-20, f6.3 Hypar.*
  ....8.00   12.00
- ☐ **Readyset,** *folding rollfilm, models 1, 1A, PB-20, Special, Royal, Eagle, Traveler, etc.*
  ....16.00   22.00
- ☐ **Schul-Prämie Box,** *originally given out as a school premium in Germany, which accounts for the inscribed title, a blue metal and plastic box for 6 x 9cm. rollfilm.*
  ....28.00   35.00
- ☐ **Selecta - M,** *c. 1965 fully automatic motor camera for 24 x 36mm., shutter speed regulated by BIM, Solinar f2.8/45, Compur 30-500 + B.*
  .... 115.00   135.00
- ☐ **Shurflash, Shurshot,** *box cameras.*
  ....6.00   10.00
- ☐ **Silette, Super Silette,** *c. 1950's 24 x 36mm. f3.5/45mm. Apotar.*
  ....28.00   38.00
- ☐ **Solinette, Super Solinette,** *with CRF, Solinette II pre-war folding 35mm. camera, f3.5/50 Apotar, Prontor.*
  ....25.00   35.00
- ☐ **Speedex,** *c. 1935 folding 4.5 x 6cm. styled like the Jiffy Kodak Cameras.*
  ....22.00   28.00
- ☐ **Same as above,** *c. 1940, styled like the Agfa Isolette for 6 x 6cm. f4.5 lens.*
  ....18.00   20.00

- ☐ **Standard,** *c. 1930's folding camera for 616 rollfilm, f6.3/130 mm. or 135mm. lens.*
  ....20.00   25.00
- ☐ **Same as above,** *for 6.5 x 9 sheet film, f4.5/105 mm.*
  ....30.00   40.00

60 / AIRES CAMERA CO.

- ☐ **Same as above,** *for 9 x 12 sheet film, f4.5 Anastigmatic.*
  ....40.00   50.00
- ☐ **Synchro,** *metal box for 6 x 9cm. on 120 rollfilm.*
  ....5.00   8.00
- ☐ **Ventura Deluxe,** *folding 120 film camera, f4.5 Apotar, Prontor.*
  ....15.00   20.00
- ☐ **View Cameras,** *3¼ x 4¼ and 4 x 5 inch sizes, wood construction, brass trim, no lens.*
  ....35.00   45.00
- ☐ **Viking,** *folding cameras for 120, 620, and 116 rollfilms, f6.3 or 7.7 lenses.*
  ....12.00   16.00

AIRES CAMERA CO.
(Japan)

- ☐ **Aires IIIc,** *Leica-styled 35mm. camera, f1.9/50mm. coral lens.*
  ....45.00   55.00
- ☐ **Aires 35 III L,** *coral f1.9/50mm, RF.*
  ....45.00   55.00
- ☐ **Aires 35V,** *c. 1957, 35mm. camera with rangefinder and meter, f1.5/45mm. coated lens.*
  ....80.00   110.00
- ☐ **Airesflex,** *6 x 6cm., TLR, f3.5/75 Coral.*
  ....35.00   50.00
- ☐ **Aires Penta 35,** *35mm. SLR, f2.8/50.*
  ....40.00   60.00
- ☐ **Aires Viscount,** *35mm. RF camera, Coral f1.9 or f2.8/45mm. lens.*
  ....35.00   45.00

AKA

An abbreviation for Apparate & Kamerabau. See listing under full name for Akarelle, Akarette, Akarex.

ALETHOSCOPE
(See Joux)

ALLIED

- ☐ **Carlton Reflex,** *cheap 6 x 6.*
  ....7.00   10.00

ALPA
(See Pignons)

ALPENFLEX

- ☐ **6 x 6cm.,** *TLR c. 1953.*
  ....30.00   40.00

ALPIN
(See Voigtlander)

ALTA
(See Reichenbach, Morey, & Will Co.)

ALTESSA
(See Boyer)

ALTIFLEX
(See Altissa, and Hofert)

ALTISCOP
(See Hofert)

ALTISSA KAMERAWERK
B. Altmann (Dresden)

Also associated with E. Hofert of Dresden. See also Hofert.

- ☐ **Altiflex,** *c. 1930's 6 x 6cm. TLR, Ludwig Victor f4.5/75 mm., Rodenstock Trinar f4.5/75mm., Trinar f3.5/75mm., Laack Pololyt f2.4/80mm.*
  ....35.00   45.00
- ☐ **Altissa,** *6 x 6cm. rollfilm box camera, Rodenstock Periscop f8 lens.*
  ....17.00   22.00
- ☐ **Altix,** *c. 1950's 35mm. camera, some models have focal plane shutter and interchangeable lenses such as Laack Tegonar f3.5/35mm. or Meyer Trioplan f2.9/50mm.*
  ....25.00   35.00

ALTURA
(See Contessa)

AL-VISTA
(See Multiscope & Film Co.)

AMBI-SILETTE, AMBION
(See Agfa)

AMEREX

☐ **Amerex,** Japanese, 16mm. subminiature styled like a 35mm. camera, made in post-war occupied Japan.
.... 25.00   30.00

AMERICAN ADVERTISING & RESEARCH CORPORATION
(Chicago)

☐ **Cub,** c. 1940's box camera for 3 x 4cm. exposures on 828 film, all plastic construction, simple lens and shutter, toothpaste premium.
.... 12.00   15.00

AMERICAN CAMERA MFG. CO., INC.
(Northboro, Mass. USA)

This company was founded by Mr. Blair, formerly of Blair Camera Co., in 1895 and subsequently sold to the Eastman Kodak Co. in 1899 and moved to Rochester, N.Y. It is not to be confused with the American Optical Company listed below. Having been in business such a short time, its well-made cameras are not as common as many other brands.

☐ **Buckeye No. 2,** c. 1899 rollfilm box camera for 4 x 5 exposures, similar to the Blair box cameras such as the Weno Hawkeye.
.... 60.00   70.00

☐ **Buckeye No. 3,** folding rollfilm camera c. 1895, maroon leather bellows, f8 lens.
.... 50.00   60.00

AMERICAN OPTICAL CO. / 61

☐ **Buckeye No. 1 Tourist,** c. 1895, folding rollfilm camera for 3¼ x 4¼, maroon bellows, wooden lens standard.
.... 95.00   115.00

☐ **4 x 5 folding plate camera,** No. 4 Sylvar f6.8/7" lens, Wollensak Auto shutter, red leather bellows.
.... 100.00   135.00

AMERICAN MINUTE PHOTO CO.
(Chicago)

☐ **American Sleeve Machine,** a street camera for tintypes, similar to cameras by the Chicago Ferrotype Co.
.... 165.00   185.00

AMERICAN OPTICAL CO.
(New York)

Acquired by Scovill c. 1867. *(See also Scovill.)*

☐ **Henry Clay Camera,** 5 x 7 inch folding plate camera c. 1895, a well made camera with many desirable features.
.... 330.00   350.00

☐ **Plate camera,** 5 x 8 size, horizontal format, complete with lens, back, etc.
.... 185.00   200.00

62 / AMERICAN SAFETY RAZOR CORP.

☐ **View camera,** *11 x 14 inch, with lens.*
.... 265.00   285.00

AMERICAN SAFETY RAZOR CORP.
(New York)

☐ **ASR Foto-Disc,** *c. 1950, a modern try to recreate the success of the Stirn Vest camera, takes 8 exposures 22 x 24mm. on a disc of film.*
.... 625.00   650.00

ANGO
(See Goerz)

ANIMATIC
(See Bencini)

ANSCHUTZ
(See Goerz)

ANSCO
(Binghamton, N.Y. USA)

Formed by the merger of Anthony and Scovill & Adams in 1902, the name was shortened to Ansco in 1907. Merger with Agfa in 1928 formed Agfa-Ansco. *(See also Agfa, Anthony, Scoville.)*

☐ **Anscoflex, Anscoflex II,** *cheap all-metal 6 x 6cm. TLR for rollfilm, c. 1950's, built-in close-up lens and yellow filter, with flash.*
.... 6.00   8.00

☐ **Anscoset,** *35mm. RF, BIM, f2.8/ 45mm., Rokkor lens.*
.... 30.00   40.00

☐ **Automatic,** *c. 1925 folding rollfilm camera for 6 exposure 2½ x 4¼ in six seconds, spring-wound automatic film advance, f6.3 Anastigmat lens, original price about $75.*
.... 225.00   250.00

☐ **Automatic Reflex,** *c. 1947-1949, 120 rollfilm TLR for 6 x 6cm. exposures, f3.5 Anastigmat 83mm. lens.*
.... 120.00   135.00

☐ **Buster Brown No. 2,** *box camera for 2¼ x 3¼ exposures on 4A film.*
.... 5.00   8.00

☐ **Buster Brown No. 2A,** *box for 2½ x 4¼ on 118 size film.*
.... 6.00   10.00

☐ **Buster Brown No. 2C,** *box for 2⅞ x 4⅞ exposures.*
.... 6.00   8.00

☐ **Buster Brown No. 3,** *box for 3¼ x 4¼.*
.... 6.00   10.00

☐ **Buster Brown No. 1 Folding,** *model B.*
.... 20.00   25.00

☐ **Buster Brown No. 2A Folding.**
.... 16.00   20.00

☐ **Buster Brown No. 3 Folding.**
.... 14.00   16.00

☐ **Buster Brown No. 3A Folding,** *the postcard size, Deltax or Actus shutter.*
.... 16.00   20.00

☐ **Buster Brown Junior,** *folding 116 roll.*
.... 16.00   20.00

☐ **Cadet,** *there are at least two common models, the Model B-2 box camera, and the more recent 127 film model with flash, in either case, they currently average just.*
.... 4.00   6.00

☐ **Clipper,** *Flash Clipper, Clipper Special.*
.... 5.00   8.00

☐ **Commander,** *folding, f6.3 Agnar.*
.... 16.00   20.00

☐ **Craftsman,** *a construction kit to build your own 2¼ x 3¼ box camera, c. 1940's, original unused kit with assembly instructions.*
.... 45.00   55.00

☐ **"Dollar" box camera,** *simple 4 x 3½ x 2½ box camera, c. 1910.*
.... 14.00   18.00

Goodwin Cameras.

Named in honor of the Rev. Hannibal Goodwin. Dr. Goodwin, it seems, invented rollfilm, or something similar, just a small step ahead of George Eastman. Goodwin's patent was applied for in 1887, but "owing to interference proceedings in the United States Patent Office," it was not issued until 1898.

- ☐ **Goodwin Jr. No. 1,** c. mid-1920's folding camera, front pulls straight out.
  ....18.00   22.00
- ☐ **Goodwin box cameras No. 2 & 3.**
  ....4.00   8.00
- ☐ **Karomat,** c. 1950's 35mm. camera.
  ....40.00   50.00
- ☐ **Lancer.**
  ....12.00   15.00

Memo, c. 1927. For ½-frame exposures, 18 x 23mm. 50 shots on 35 mm. film in special cassettes. f6.3/40mm. Wollensak Cine-Velostigmat or Ilex Cinemat lens. A rigid-bodied, upright box style with tubular optical finder on top. Lever film advance, automatic exposure counter. Some models focus, other are non-focusing types.

Note: This is not to be confused with the 1960's motor-driven ½-frame imported from Japan. It is, however, the forerunner of the Agfa Memo of c. 1937.

- ☐ **"Official Boy Scout Memo Camera,"** the wooden body is painted olive-drab color, and bears official insignia, much less common than the standard model.
  .... 145.00   165.00
- ☐ **Panda,** 120 and 620 rollfilm box cameras, a cute name for a camera, but still worth.
  ....6.00   10.00
- ☐ **Photo Vanity,** c. 1930's camera outfit designed as a lady's purse, grey colored.
  .... 1000.00   1200.00
- ☐ **Pioneer,** a cheap plastic box camera.
  ....3.00   6.00
- ☐ **Plenax,** PD-16 folding rollfilm cameras c. 1940, Agfa-Ansco.
  ....10.00   14.00
- ☐ **Readyflash,** another cheapie, complete with case, flash, and instructions, still just.
  ....5.00   7.00
- ☐ **Readyset,** No. 1, 1A, Viking Readyset, Readyset Royal, etc., folding models.
  ....20.00   24.00
- ☐ **Rediflex,** c. 1950.
  ....4.00   6.00
- ☐ **Regent,** 35mm. non-RF camera, f3.5/50mm. Apotar.
  ....25.00   35.00
- ☐ **Super Regent,** the same, but with RF, and Solinar f3.5/50mm.
  ....35.00   45.00
- ☐ **Semi-Automatic Ansco,** folding rollfilm camera c. 1924 for 6 exposures 2½ x 4¼, lever on left rear of drop bed actuates spring-wound advance system.
  .... 125.00   135.00

64 / ANSCO

Semi-Automatic Ansco

☐ **Shur-flash, Shur-shot,** *box cameras.*
.... 4.00   6.00

☐ **Speedex,** *No. 1A, c. 1916 rollfilm camera for 116 film, 2½ x 4¼, f6.3 Anastigmat, Ilex Universal shutter.*
.... 16.00   20.00

☐ **Speedex,** *No. 3A.*
.... 20.00   25.00

☐ **Speedex Special,** *c. 1940 horizontal style folding camera for 12 exposures 6 x 6cm. on 120 film, f4.5/85mm. Agfa Apotar, Vario or Prontor shutter.*
.... 18.00   25.00

☐ **Vest Pocket Ansco No. 0,** *c. WWI for 1⅝ x 2½ inch exposure, f6.3 Ansco Anastigmat or f7.5 Modico Anastigmat, front pulls straight out.*
.... 20.00   25.00

☐ **Vest Pocket Ansco No. 1,** *for 6 x 9cm., straight pull-out front, Actus shutter, patents to 1912, f8 lens or, rarely, f4.5/3.5 inch Goerz.*
.... 20.00   25.00

☐ **Vest Pocket Ansco No. 2,** *for 8 exposures 6 x 9cm. on 120 film, f6.3 Ansco Anastigmat or f7.5 Modico Anastigmat lens, Bionic or Gammax shutter, straight pull-out front and hinged lens cover.*
.... 28.00   35.00

☐ **Vest Pocket Model A,** *designed with folding bed, unlike the other vest pocket models, B&L Zeiss Tessar lens, Ansco shutter.*
.... 28.00   35.00

☐ **Vest Pocket Junior,** *8 exposures 6 x 9cm. on 120 rollfilm.*
.... 16.00   20.00

☐ **Viking,** *c. 1950's folding 6 x 9cm. 120 film camera manufactured by Agfa in Germany, f7.7 Major Anastigmar, or f4.5/105 Agnar or Somar.*
.... 10.00   14.00

☐ **Box cameras,** *miscellaneous models, black.*
.... 4.00   7.00

☐ **Same as above,** *miscellaneous colors other than black.*
.... 8.00   12.00

☐ **Folding cameras No. 1 Ansco Deluxe,** *RR lens, Ilex shutter.*
.... 22.00   28.00

☐ **Folding cameras No. 1 Special Folding Ansco,** *introduced c. 1924, the cheap version of the No. 1 Ansco Speedex, f7.5 Anastigmat, Ilex shutter.*
.................18.00   25.00

☐ **Folding cameras No. 1 Folding Ansco,** *f7.5 Anastigmat, Ilex shutter.*
.................16.00   20.00

☐ **Folding cameras No. 1A Ansco Jr.**
.................16.00   20.00

☐ **Folding cameras No. 1A Folding Ansco,** *for 116 film, f7.5 Ansco Anastigmat lens, Ilex Universal shutter.*
.................10.00   15.00

☐ **Folding cameras No. 2C Ansco Junior.**
.................12.00   18.00

☐ **Folding cameras No. 3 Folding Ansco,** *118 film.*
.................18.00   25.00

☐ **Folding cameras No. 3 Ansco Junior,** *118 film.*
.................20.00   25.00

☐ **Folding cameras No. 3A Folding Ansco,** *common post-card size, lenses: Wollensak, RR, Ansco Anastigmat, shutters: Ilex, Deltax, Bionic, Speedex.*
.................20.00   25.00

☐ **Folding cameras No. 4 Folding Ansco,** *c. 1905, models C and D, 3¼ x 4¼ on 118 film, horizontal format, mahogany drop bed, Wollensak lens, Cyko Automatic shutter, nickel trim.*
.................25.00   35.00

☐ **Folding cameras No. 5 Folding Pocket Ansco,** *c. 1905, Wollensak lens, Cyko Automatic shutter, black bellows.*
.................25.00   35.00

☐ **Folding cameras No. 6 Folding Ansco,** *c. 1907, models C and D, 3¼ x 4¼, Wollensak f4 lens, red leather bellows, for roll or cut film.*
.................30.00   35.00

☐ **Folding cameras No. 7 Folding Ansco,** *Anthony & Scovill Co., postcard-sized rollfilm camera, last patent date 1894, red bellows, brass-barrel Wollensak lens.*
.................25.00   30.00

☐ **Folding cameras No. 9 Ansco, Model B,** *horizontal style folding rollfilm for 3¼ x 5½, cherry wood body, leather covered, red bellows, Cyko shutter in brass housing, later models had black bellows and nickeled shutter.*
.................25.00   30.00

☐ **Folding cameras No. 10 Ansco,** *patented January 1907, folding rollfilm for 3½ x 5 on 122 film, model A has removeable ground glass back, Ansco Automatic shutter.*
.................35.00   40.00

☐ **View Camera,** *11 x 14 inch size, double extension bellows, sliding back, convertible lens, wide ranging prices.*
.... 300.00   500.00

ANTAR
(See Agfa)

ANTHONY

The oldest American manufacturer of cameras and photographic supplies. Begun by Edward Anthony in 1842 as E. Anthony. Edward's brother Henry joined him in 1852, and in 1862 the firm's name was

ANTHONY

changed to E. and H. T. Anthony and Company. In 1902, they merged with the Scovill Company, and five years later, the firm name was shortened to Ansco, a contracted form of the two names. At the same time, they moved from their original location on Broadway to Binghamton, N.Y. *(See also Agfa, Ansco, Scovill.)*

Ascot
Folding plate cameras c. 1899. *Note: The plate and hand camera division of E. & H. T. Anthony Camera Co. which made the Ascot Cameras merged with several other companies in 1899 to become the Rochester Optical and Camera Co.*

- **Ascot Cycle No. 1,** *4 x 5 size, original price in 1899, $8.00.*
  ....50.00   70.00
- **Ascot Folding No. 25,** *4 x 5 size.*
  ....70.00   90.00
- **Ascot Folding No. 29,** *4 x 5 size, original price in 1899, $15.00.*
  ....70.00   90.00

- **Ascot Folding No. 30,** *the big brother of the above cameras, this one takes 5 x 7 plates, like the others, it has a side door for loading and storage of plate holders.*
  ....75.00   90.00

Ascot cameras are quite uncommon, since they were made for such a short time.

- **Box Cameras,** *c. 1905 leather covered box for 3¼ x 4¼ on rollfilm.*
  ....28.00   35.00

- **Same as above,** *c. 1903, focusing model for 4 x 5 exposures on plates or with roll holder.*
  ....60.00   75.00
- **Buckeye,** *box cameras c. 1896 for 12 exposures on daylight-loading rollfilm, some models equipped for either plates or rollfilm, made in 3¼ x 4¼ and 4 x 5 sizes, these were Anthony competition for the Boston Bullseye and the Eastman Bullet cameras of the day.*
  ....50.00   65.00
- **Daylight Enlarging Camera,** *c. 1888, a view camera and enlarger for plates to 11½ x 11½ inches, rotating back and bellows, masking back for enlarging, without lens.*
  ....175.00   195.00
- **Klondike,** *fixed-focus box-plate camera c. 1898, adjustable shutter speeds and diaphragm, 3¼ x 4¼ size.*
  ....135.00   150.00

Lilliput
A detective camera in the shape of a miniature satchel. Also sold by Anthony. *(See also Lilliput Detective Camera.)*

- **Normandie,** *according to the Anthony 1891 Catalog, this was the "lightest, most compact, and easily adjustable, reversible back camera in the market," the spring-loaded ground glass back was a relatively new feature at that time, made in sizes from 4 x 5 to 14 x 17, current value of 5 x 7 to 8 x 10 with lens.*
  ....225.00   250.00
- **Novelette, Patent Novelette,** *view cameras c. 1885, back and bellows rotate as a unit, Anthony's patent, lightweight brass front standard assembly, originally made in all standard sizes from 4 x 5 to 11 x 14 inches in basic, single swing, and double swing models ranging from $15-$60. Presently, they range from.*
  ....150.00   350.00

ARGUS, INC. / 67

☐ **PDQ**, *detective plate box camera, c. 1890, 4 x 5 plates or film, original price $20. Now valued at about.*
.... 600.00   700.00

☐ **Stereo plate camera**, *5 x 8 inch, collapsible bellows style, some models had folding bed, others had rigid bed, with original lens.*
.... 375.00   425.00

☐ **View cameras**, *4 x 5 folding bed, collapsible bellows type c. 1890, 'E.A.' lens, case and holders.*
.... 85.00   115.00

☐ **Same as above**, *5 x 7.*
.... 100.00   120.00

☐ **Same as above**, *5 x 8, rigid "studio" or folding "field" types, c. 1888-1890, with lens and occasionally with accessory shutter.*
.... 150.00   175.00

☐ **Same as above**, *6½ x 8½, with RR lens in brass mount.*
.... 145.00   160.00

☐ **Same as above**, *8 x 10, with brass barrel lens.*
.... 235.00   250.00

☐ **Same as above**, *11 x 14, studio or field types, depending on type of lens.*
.... 250.00   350.00

ANTIQUE OAK DETECTIVE CAMERA
(See Scovill)

APOLLO

☐ **Apollo**, *120 film, Western Anastigmat f3.5/75, shutter 1-200, with case.*
.... 20.00   25.00

APPARATE & KAMERABAU
(Friedrichshafen, Germany)

☐ **Akarelle**, *c. 1954, 24 x 36mm. various lens types f2 to f3.5, Prontor shutter.*
.... 45.00   55.00

☐ **Akarette I & II**, *c. 1950, various lenses.*
.... 50.00   65.00

☐ **Akarex**, *c. 1953, 35mm. rangefinder camera, rangefinder and lens are interchangeable as a unit, normal lens: Isco Westar f3.5/45m., also available: Schneider Xenon f2/50mm., Tele-Xenar f3.5/90, and Xenagon f3.5/35mm.*
.... 125.00   140.00

APTUS
(See Moore)

ARETTE

☐ **Model W**, *German made non-rangefinder 35mm., f2.8/50 Wilow lens.*
.... 20.00   25.00

ARGUS
(See Nettel)

Monocular-shaped camera.

ARGUS, INC.
(Ann Arbor, Michigan and Chicago, Illinois.)

Originally International Research Corp., Ann Arbor, Michigan.

☐ **A**, *35mm. cartridge camera manufactured c. 1936-1941, f4.5/50mm. fixed focus anastigmat lens in collapsible barrel.*
.... 20.00   25.00

☐ **AF**, *1937-1938, similar but with focusing lens mount.*
.... 25.00   30.00

68 / ARGUS, INC.

- ☐ **AA,** 1940-1942, also known as Argoflash, similar to above, but with fixed focus lens, shutter for I & T, synched.
  .... 25.00   30.00

- ☐ **A2,** 1939-1950, similar to the "A", but with extinction meter, focus 6' to infinity.
  .... 20.00   25.00

- ☐ **A2B,** 1939-1950.
  .... 20.00   25.00

- ☐ **A2F,** 1939-1941, similar to all the other "A" series cameras, but with focus from 1¼ feet to infinity, extinction meter.
  .... 18.00   20.00

- ☐ **FA,** 1950-1951, the last of the "A" series with the original style, f4.5/50mm. Anastigmat, two position focus, 25-150, B, T. Sync.
  .... 20.00   25.00

- ☐ **A3,** 1940-1942, as all of the above, this camera is for 35mm. film, however, the style of this model, and the CC, is more sleek with rounded ends, extinction meter, f4/50 mm. Anastigmat, shutter 25-150.
  .... 18.00   22.00

- ☐ **A4,** 1953-1956, a newly styled body, later appearing as the C-20, f3.5/44mm. Cintar, full focus, Sync.
  .... 18.00   25.00

- ☐ **K,** 1939-1940, f4.5/50mm. Anastigmat, coupled extinction meter, it is probably this feature which makes it so desirable and thus high-priced, especially when compared to the other Argus cameras.
  .... 175.00   200.00

- ☐ **C,** 1938-1939, f3.5/50mm. Cintar, the original "brick" shaped camera with a noncoupled rangefinder.
  .... 22.00   28.00

- ☐ **CC,** 1941-1942, "Colorcamera," similar to the A3, but has non-coupled selenium cell meter instead of extinction type.
  .... 40.00   50.00

- ☐ **C2,** 1938-1942, like the "C", but rangefinder is coupled, introduced just after the model C in 1938, an early "brick."
  .... 25.00   30.00

- ☐ **C3,** 1939-1966, the most common "brick," like the C2, but with internal synch.
  .... 20.00   25.00

- ☐ **C3 Matchmatic,** basically a face-lifted C3 in two-tone finish, designed for use with a noncopuled clip-on selenium meter, price listed here is for camera and meter.
  .... 20.00   25.00

- ☐ **C4,** 1951-1971, f2.8/50mm. Cintar, coupled rangefinder.
  .... 30.00   35.00

☐ **C4R,** *1958, like the C4 above, this model is built on the style of the Model 21 which was introduced in 1947, the C4R features a rapid film advance lever, which gave it its "R" designation.*
..................45.00   55.00

☐ **C44,** *1956-1957, similar to C4, f2.8/ 50 Cintagon lens in interchangeable mount.*
..................50.00   60.00

☐ **C44R,** *1958-1962, similar to C44 but with rapid advance lever.*
..................55.00   65.00

☐ **C20,** *1956-1958, similar to model A4, but with brown simulated leather covering and coupled rangefinder, not too trustworthy, in general.*
..................25.00   30.00

☐ **C33,** *1959-1961, f3.5/50 Cintar, CRF and coupled meter, single stroke advance.*
..................40.00   50.00

☐ **21,** *Markfinder, 1947-1952, f3.5/ 50mm. Cintar, coated, interchangeable mount.*
..................20.00   25.00

☐ **Argoflex,** *twin lens reflex cameras in various body styles and model numbers from 1948 to 1958, models: E, EM, EF, 40, 75 black, 75 brown, Super 75, order of introduction.*
..................14.00   18.00

☐ **Autronic,** *Autronic 35 or Autronic C3, although the camera bore both designations during its short life, 1960-1962, it was really just one model, f3.5/50 mm. Cintar, sync. shutter 30-500, B, automatic electric eye, rangefinder.*
..................20.00   30.00

ARNOLD, KARL
(Marienburg)

The abbreviation KARMA comes from KArl ARnold, MArienburg.

☐ **Karma,** *6 x 6cm. rollfilm "box" camera for 120 film, Meyer Trioplan f3.5/75 coated lens, focal plane shutter 25-500, T, non-coupled rangefinder, Helix focus, trapezoid-shaped metal body with black leatherette.*
....   300.00   335.00

☐ **Karmaflex,** *4 x 4cm. format SLR for 127 film, c. 1937, Ludwig Vidar f4.5/ 60mm. or Laack Ragolyt f4.5/60, guillotine shutter 25-100, black leatherette covered metal body.*
....   300.00   350.00

ARROW

☐ **Arrow,** *14mm. subminiature novelty.*
..................8.00   12.00

Karmaflex

ASCOT
(See Anthony)

ASTRAFLEX

A successor to the Bentzin Primarflex. Apparently the Bentzin company became the Feinoptische Werke Görlitz and continued the Primarflex line of cameras under the Astraflex name.

☐ **Astraflex II,** *c. 1958, 6 x 6cm. SLR, interchangeable coated f3.5/105mm. Tessar, focal plane shutter to 1000, T, B.*
.... **150.00   175.00**

ATOM
(See Huttig, Ica)

AUTCORD
(See Minolta)

AUTOFLEX
(Kiyabashi Opt. Co. Tokyo)

☐ **6 x 6cm.,** *TLR styled like Rolleiflex, f3.5 Tri-Lausar lens.*
.................**28.00   38.00**

AUTOGRAPHIC

All Autographic cameras were made by the Eastman Kodak Co. See the various models of cameras under Eastman.

AUTOMATICA
(See Durst)

AUTOMATIC
(See Ansco)

AUTOMATIC RADIO MFG. CO.
(Boston)

☐ **Tom Thumb Camera Radio,** *c. 1948, identical in appearance to the "Cameradio" manufactured by Universal Radio Mfg. Co.*
.... **100.00   125.00**

AUTRONIC
(See Argus)

AVUS
(See Voigtlander)

BALDA-WERK
(Max Baldeweg, Dresden)

☐ **Baldalette,** *folding 35mm. c. 1950, f2.9/50 Schneider Radionar, Compur Rapid or Pronto shutter.*
.................**35.00   40.00**

☐ **Baldarette,** *folding camera for 5 x 8cm. on 127 film, Rodenstock Trinar f4.5/85, Vero shutter, T, B, 25-100, brown leathered body, brown bellows.*
.................**25.00   35.00**

☐ **Baldax,** *compact folding camera for 16 exposure 4.5 x 6cm. on 120, c. 1930's, available in a large variety of lens/shutter combinations, f2.6-f4.5.*
.................**30.00   40.00**

☐ **Baldaxette, Model I,** *for 16 exposure 4.5 x 6cm. on 120 film, f2.9/75 Hugo Meyer Trioplan or f2.8/80 Zeiss Tessar, Rimset Compur or Compur Rapid shutter with self-timer.*
.................**35.00   45.00**

☐ **Same as above,** *Model II for 12 exposure 6 x 6cm. on 120.*
.................35.00   45.00

☐ **Baldessa 1b,** *f2.8 Isco lens and meter.*
.................35.00   45.00

☐ **Baldi,** *c. 1930's for 16 exposure 3 x 4cm. on 127, f2.9 or 3.5/50mm. Trioplan.*
.................30.00   45.00

☐ **Baldina,** *c. 1930's folding 35, similar to the early folding Retina Cameras, common combinations include f3.5/50 Baldanar, f2/45mm. Xenon, f2.9/50 Xenar, Prontor-S or Compur Rapid shutter.*
.................25.00   35.00

☐ **Same as above,** *Super Baldina, similar, but with CRF, Zeiss Tessar f2.8, Compur Rapid, late 1930's.*
.................50.00   60.00

☐ **Baldinette,** *c. late 1930's Retina-style 35mm. various shutter/lens combinations.*
.................40.00   50.00

☐ **Same as above,** *Super Baldinette, with CRF, f2 lens.*
.................50.00   60.00

☐ **Beltica,** *c. 1949 folding camera for 35mm., Ludwig Meritar f2.9/50 or Zeiss Tessar f2.8/50 in Cludor or Ovus shutter to 1/200 second. See also Belca Beltica.*
.................25.00   35.00

☐ **Jubilette,** *c. 1938, the 30th anniversary of Balda-Werk, thus the name, a folding 35mm. similar to the Baldina, f2.9/50mm. Baltar or Trioplan, Compur shutter.*
.................28.00   38.00

☐ **Juwella,** *6 x 9cm. folding rollfilm camera, f4.5 Juwella Anastigmat, Prontor T, B, 25-125, self-timer.*
.................20.00   25.00

☐ **Piccochic,** *a vest-pocket camera for 16 exposure 3 x 4cm. on 127 film, normal lens Ludwig Vidar f4.5/50mm., also available: f3.5 Trioplan, f2.9 Vidar, f2.9 Schneider Xenar, Compur, Prontor, or Ibsor shutters, new prices ranged from $12.50 to $37.50.*
.................40.00   50.00

☐ **Poka,** *metal box camera for 6 x 9cm. exposures on 120 rollfilm, meniscus lens, single shutter.*
.................10.00   15.00

☐ **Rigona,** *c. 1937 folding camera for 16 exposure 3 x 4cm. on 127, similar to the Baldi, normal lenses f4.5 Vidanar, f2.9 Schneider Radionar, f2.9 Meyer Trioplan, Prontor shutter.*
.................30.00   50.00

☐ **Rollbox 120,** *all metal 6 x 9cm. box.*
.................8.00   12.00

☐ **Super Pontura,** *folding camera for 8 exposure 6 x 9cm. on 120 film, CRF, automatic parallax compensation, f3.8 or 4.5 Meyer Trioplan, Compur Rapid to 400, camera adaptable for 16 exposure 4 x 6cm.*
.................45.00   55.00

☐ **Wara,** *folding camera for 6 x 9cm. on rollfilm, f4.5/105 Xenar, Ring Compur to 250.*
.................20.00   25.00

BALDI
(See Balda-Werk)

BALDUR
(See Zeiss)

BANTAM
(See Eastman)

BAUER

☐ **Folding Camera,** *for 8 exposure 6 x 9cm. or 16 exposure 4 x 6cm. on 620, f4.5/105 Schneider Radionar, Vario synchronized shutter.*
.................20.00   25.00

BAUSCH & LOMB

- [ ] **Camera Obscura,** *made of oak with metal on front.*
  .... 300.00   350.00

BAZIN & LEROY
(Paris)

- [ ] **Le Stereocycle,** *c. 1898 jumelle-styled stereo camera for 12 plates 6 x 13cm., Ross Rapid Rectilinear lenses, guillotine shutter.*
  .... 275.00   350.00

BEACON
(See Whitehouse Products)

BEAU BROWNIE
(See Eastman)

BEAUTY, BEAUTYCORD, BEAUTYFLEX
(See Taiyodo Koki)

BECK
(R & J Beck, Ltd., London)

- [ ] **Frena,** *detective box cameras c. 1897, magazine cameras for special sheetfilms, made in three sizes: 2⅝ x 3½, 3¼ x 4¼, 4 x 5".*
  .... 170.00   190.00

- [ ] **Frena Deluxe,** *c. 1897, for 40 exposure 6.5 x 9cm. on special perforated sheet film, covered with brown calves leather, metal parts gold plated.*
  .... 450.00   550.00

BEBE
(See Ica, Zeiss)

BEICA

- [ ] **Beica,** *Japanese 14mm. novelty camera.*
  .... 8.00   10.00

BEIER
(Woldemar Beier, Freital, Germany)

- [ ] **Beira,** *35mm. camera c. early 1930's, f2.7/50mm. Dialytar, RF, Compur Rapid.*
  .... 150.00   160.00

- [ ] **Beirax,** *c. 1930's folding 6 x 9cm. rollfilm camera, E. Ludwig Victar f4.5/105, Prontor or Vario shutter.*
  .... 20.00   25.00

- [ ] **Beirette,** *compact folding 35mm. camera, horizontal style, Rodenstock Trinar lens: f2.9, 3.5, or 3.9 in Compur or Compur Rapid shutter.*
  .... 160.00   175.00

- [ ] **Beier folding sheet film cameras,** *3¼ x 4¼" or 9 x 12cm. sizes, Rodenstock Trinar Anastigmat f4.5 or Betar f4.5 in Compur shutter.*
  .... 30.00   40.00

- [ ] **Precisa,** *folding camera for 120 rollfilm, 75mm. lenses range from f2.9 to f4.5, AGC, Compur, or Compur Rapid shutter.*
  .... 30.00   40.00

- [ ] **Rifax,** *6 x 9cm. rollfilm, Rodenstock Trinar f3.8/105, Prontor II, 1-150, CRF.*
  .... 30.00   40.00

Beier Folding Sheet Film

BEIL & FREUND
(Berlin)

☐ **Plate Camera**, *9 x 12cm. c. 1890, f8 Anastoskop Meniscus lens.*
. . . . 100.00   120.00

BELCA-WERKE
(Dresden)

☐ **Belfoca,** *folding camera, post WWII, for 8 exposure 6 x 9cm. on 120, Prontor shutter, f4.5 Ludwig Meritar lens.*
. . . . 20.00   30.00

☐ **Belpasca,** *c. 1952 stereo 24 x 36mm. on 35mm. film, f3.5/37.5 Tessar lenses, synchronized shutter 1-200.*
. . . . 325.00   375.00

☐ **Beltica,** *post-war folding 35mm., Ludwig Meritar f2.9/50 or Zeiss Tessar f2.8/50, Ovus or Cludor shutter.*
. . . . 25.00   30.00

BELL AND HOWELL / 73
BELL CAMERA CO.
(Grinnell, Iowa)

☐ **Bell's Straight-Working Panorama Camera,** *c. 1908 panoramic camera in which neither the film nor lens swings, pivots, or moves, which justified the cumbersome name, this camera is basically an extra-wide folding camera for 5 exposure 3¼ x 11½ on rollfilm, also for 10 exposure 3¼ x 5½ if you prefer post-cards, knobs on top of camera allow user to change format in mid-roll.*
. . . . 475.00   550.00

BELL KAMRA

☐ **Model KTC-62,** *combination 16mm. cassette camera and shirt-pocket sized transistor radio.*
. . . . 115.00   140.00

BELL 14

☐ **Subminiature,** *novelty 16mm. camera styled like a 35mm.*
. . . . 10.00   15.00

BELL & HOWELL
(Chicago)

☐ **Colorist,** *TDC Stereo Colorist, stereo camera for 35mm. film, f3.5 Rodenstock Trinar lenses.*
. . . . 100.00   150.00

☐ **Dial 35,** *half-frame 35mm., auto wind, current value with case and flash.*
. . . . 40.00   75.00

☐ **Foton,** *c. 1948 35mm. spring-motor driven, 6 frames per second.*
. . . . 500.00   550.00

☐ **Vivid,** *TDC Stereo Vivid, f3.5 Trinar.*
. . . . 80.00   125.00

BELLIENI
(H. Bellieni & Fils, Nancy, France)

☐ **Jumelle,** *for 36 plates 9 x 12cm., Zeiss Protar f8/136mm., leather covered wood body.*
.... 220.00   260.00

☐ **Stereo Jumelle,** *c. 1896 for 9 x 18cm. stereo plates, f6.8/110mm. lenses in aluminum barrel with brass diaphragm ring, 6 speed shutter.*
.... 195.00   240.00

BELTAX

☐ **Beltax,** *35mm. camera, Leica styled, f4.5/40mm. Picner lens, Picny D shutter, 3 speeds.*
.................60.00   80.00

BELTICA
(See Belca)

BENCINI
(Italy)

☐ **Animatic 600,** *c. 1955 cassette camera for 126 film.*
...................3.00   6.00

BENETFINK
(London)

☐ **Lightning Detective Camera,** *c. 1895, ½ pl. Ilex string-cock shutter.*
.... 220.00   230.00

BENSON DRY PLATE & CAMERA CO.

☐ **Street Camera,** *with cloth sleeve, tank, and tripod.*
.... 160.00   180.00

BENTZIN
(Curt Bentzin, Görlitz, Germany)

(Succeeded by VEB Primar, Görlitz)

☐ **Planovista,** c. 1930, twin-lens folding camera, NOT a reflex, a "taking" camera topped by a second "viewing" or "finder" camera, separate lens and bellows for each half, for 8 exposure 4 x 6.5cm. on 127 film, Meyer Trioplan f3.5/75mm. in Pronto shutter 25-100, T, B, top lens tilts down for automatic parallax correction. The Planovista was made by Bentzin to be marketed by the Planovista Seeing Camera Co. Ltd. of London. The design is that of the Primarette, but with a new name.
.... 1000.00   1200.00

☐ **Primar,** *folding 120 rollfilm camera, Meyer Trioplan f3.8 or Zeiss Tessar f4.5, Deckel Compur shutter, 1-250.*
...................20.00   30.00

☐ **Primary,** *Plan Primar, 6.5 x 9cm. folding plate/sheetfilm camera, Meyer Trioplan f3.8 or Zeiss Tessar f4.5, Rimset Compur.*
...................70.00   85.00

☐ **Primar Reflex,** *6.5 x 9cm. or 9 x 12cm., Tessar f4.5 lens.*
.... 175.00   185.00

BIOFLEX / 75

- [ ] **Primar folding Reflex,** *klapp, 9 x 12cm., Meyer Trioplan or Tessar f3.5/ 210mm., focal plane shutter 1-300, T, B.*
  .... 165.00   175.00
- [ ] **Primarflex,** *Primar Reflex, c. 1930's 6 x 6cm. SLR, f3.5/105 Tessar, FP shutter.*
  .... 140.00   160.00
- [ ] **Stereo Reflex,** *6 x 13cm. stereo reflex, GGB, FP shutter 20-1000, f6 Roja Detective Aplanat.*
  .... 475.00   525.00

BERGHEIL
(See Voigtländer)

BERNING
(Otto Berning & Co., Westphalia, & Düsseldorf, Germany)

- [ ] **Robot I,** *c. 1934, for 1 x 1" exposure on 35mm. film, spring motor automatic film advance, Zeiss Tessar f2.8/32.5mm. lens, rotating shutter 2-500.*
  .... 100.00   125.00
- [ ] **Robot II,** *c. 1938, improved model of Robot I. Various lenses f1.9, f2, f2.8, f3.8, in 37.5 or 40mm. focal lengths.*
  .... 95.00   115.00
- [ ] **Robot Junior,** *postwar, Schneider Radionar f3.5/38mm.*
  .... 75.00   95.00
- [ ] **Robot,** *Luftwaffe model, most commonly found with 75mm. lens.*
  .... 180.00   190.00
- [ ] **Robot Royal 36,** *24 x 36mm. full-frame size, rather than the 24 x 24mm. format of the other models.*
  .... 300.00   350.00
- [ ] **Robot Star,** *f1.9 Xenon, MX sync.*
  .... 100.00   150.00
- [ ] **Robot Star II.**
  .... 225.00   275.00

BESSA, BESSAMATIC
(See Voigtländer)

BETTAX

- [ ] **Folding 6 x 9cm.,** *rollfilm camera, f4.5/100 Radionar, Compur shutter.*
  .... 30.00   40.00

BILLY
(See Agfa)

BILORA
(See Kürbi & Niggeloh)

BIOFLEX

- [ ] **6 x 6cm.,** *TLR, Hong Kong, plastic body, two speed shutter.*
  .... 10.00   15.00

BINOCULAR CAMERAS

Listed by manufacturer. See partial listing of manufacturers under the heading "Jumelle."

BISCHOFF
(V. Bischoff, Munich)

- **Detective camera,** c. 1890, box camera for 9 x 12cm. plates, polished wood body, Aplanat lens, iris diaphragm, 2-speed shutter.
  . . . . 675.00   750.00

BLAIR
(Blair Tourograph Co. - 1880.
Blair Tourograph & Dry Plate Co. 1881-1885.
Blair Camera Co. 1886-1899. Boston.
Blair Camera Co., Rochester N.Y. 1899-1906.
Blair Camera Division, E.K.C. after 1907.)

- **Combination Hawkeye,** somewhat similar to the No. 4 Screen Focus Kodak Camera, allowed use of No. 103 rollfilm or 4 x 5" plates, and allowed use of the groundglass with either, rollfilm holder pulls out from top like a drawer, double extension red bellows, wood interior, B&L RR lens, Blair/B&L pneumatic shutter.
  . . . . 525.00   575.00

- **No. 3 Combination Hawkeye,** c. 1904, similar to the above, but in 3¼ x 4¼ size.
  . . . . 465.00   485.00

- **Detective & Combination Hawkeye,** box camera for 4 x 5" plates in plate holders, c. 1890's, top back door hinges forward to change holders, leather covered wood construction, front door hinges down to reveal lens and shutter, internal bellows focus.
  . . . . 165.00   185.00

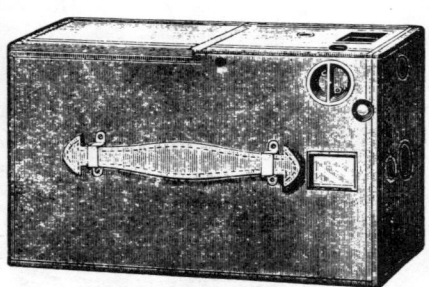

- **All wood detective Hawkeye,** no leather covering, an earlier style than the leather covered models, 4 x 5 size.
  . . . . 200.00   250.00

- **"Tool-box" style,** large detective camera, leather covered.
  . . . . 175.00   225.00

- **Hawkeye Junior,** 3.5 x 3.5" box for rollfilm or plates, c. 1895-1900.
  . . . . 85.00   125.00

- **Baby Hawkeye,** miniature box camera c. 1897, the smallest of the Hawk-eye cameras, comparable to Eastman's "Pocket Kodak" cameras, for 12 exposure 2 x 2½ on daylight loading "Blair's Sunlight Film."
  . . . . 150.00   200.00

Hawkeye Junior

- **Folding Hawkeye, 4 x 5,** c. 1895-1898, a 4 x 5 folding plate camera, basically a cube when closed, similar to the No. 4 Folding Kodak Camera of the same period, top back door for loading plate holders, could also use roll holder.
  . . . . 225.00   275.00
- **Folding Hawkeye 5 x 7,** c. 1890's, again, a cube-shaped camera when closed, top back door accepts plate holders or Eastman Roll Holder.
  . . . . 275.00   325.00

No. 3 Folding Hawkeye, Model 3, c. 1902 horizontal format folding rollfilm camera for 3 x 4" negatives, wood interior, maroon bellows, B&L RR lens.
. . . . 35.00   45.00

- **No. 4 Folding Hawkeye,** Models 3 & 4, c. 1903, horizontal format folding rollfilm camera for 4 x 5" exposure, red DEB, Rapid Symmetrical lens, Hawkeye pneumatic shutter, nickel trim, wood focus rails.
  . . . . 60.00   70.00
- **Stereo Hawkeye,** Stereo Weno, leather covered wood bodied stereo rollfilm camera for 3½ x 3½" exposure, maroon bellows, simple B&L stereo shutter in brass housing.
  . . . . 275.00   300.00
- **Tourist Hawkeye,** c. 1898-1904 folding rollfilm camera, 3½ x 3½ or 4 x 5" size, plain looking wooden standard conceals lens and shutter.
  . . . . 100.00   125.00
- **Same as above,** with optional accessory plate attachment.
  . . . . 135.00   165.00
- **No. 2 Weno Hawkeye,** 3½ x 3½, rollfilm box camera similar to the "Bulls-eye" series of the Boston Camera Co.
  . . . . 50.00   75.00

- **No. 3 Weno Hawkeye,** 3½ x 4½, box.
  . . . . 65.00   80.00

78 / BLITZ

- [ ] **No. 4 Weno Hawkeye,** *4 x 5, large box camera, single speed shutter, 2 finders.*
  . . . . .60.00   80.00
- [ ] **No. 6 Weno Hawkeye,** *c. 1891 box.*
  . . . . .50.00   75.00
- [ ] **No. 7 Weno Hawkeye,** *c. 1897 box camera for 3¼ x 5¼ rollfilm, most commonly found model of the Weno Hawkeyes.*
  . . . . .35.00   50.00

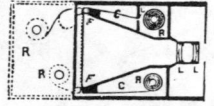

L Lens.
R R Film Rolls.
F F Focal Plane.

- [ ] **Kamaret,** *introduced in 1891, this large box camera, 5½ x 6½ x 8¾", was advertised as being "one-third smaller than any other camera of equal capacity" because it was the first American box camera to move the film spools to the front of the camera, made to take 100 exposures 4 x 5" on rollfilm, other features included double exposure prevention, automatic film counter,*

and an attachment for using plates or cut film, 4 x 5 size.
. . . . 475.00   525.00

- [ ] **Lucidograph,** *c. 1885-1886, a folding plate camera with all wood body, front door hinges to side, bed drops, and standard pulls out on geared track, tapered black bellows, brass-barrel single achromatic lens with rotating disc stops, made in several sizes: No. 1 for 3¼ x 4¼, No. 2 for 4¼ x 5½, No. 3 for 5 x 8", 5 x 8" model also has sliding front, these are not found often.*
  . . . . 700.00   800.00
- [ ] **View camera,** *5 x 7 or 5 x 8 field type, with lens.*
  . . . . 165.00   180.00
- [ ] **Same as above,** *6½ x 8½, with lens.*
  . . . . 200.00   225.00
- [ ] **Same as above,** *11 x 14.*
  . . . . 275.00   325.00

BLITZ
(See Adox)

BLOCK-NOTES
(See Gaumont)

BOB
(See Ernemann, Zeiss)

BOLSEY CORP. OF AMERICA
(New York)

See also Pignons for Alpa cameras which were designed by Jacques Bolsey.

- **Bolsey B,** c. 1947-1956 compact 35mm. camera with CRF, f3.2/44mm. anastigmat in helical mount, shutter to 200, T, B.
  ....20.00   25.00
- **Bolsey B2,** c. 1949-1956, similar to B, but with double exposure prevention and synchronized shutter.
  ....20.00   25.00
- **Bolsey B22,** Set-O-Matic, Wollensak f3.2 Anastigmat lens.
  ....18.00   25.00
- **Bolsey C,** c. 1950-1956 35mm. TLR, f3.2/44mm. Wollensak Anastigmat, Wollensak shutter, 10-200, B, T, synchronized.
  ....40.00   50.00
- **Same as above,** C22, similar but with Set-O-Matic.
  ....40.00   50.00
- **Explorer,** f2.8 lens, rapid wind.
  ....50.00   60.00
- **Bolseyflex,** 6 x 6cm. TLR, 120 film, f7.7/80mm. lens.
  ....15.00   20.00
- **Jubilee,** c. 1955-1956, 35mm., Steinheil f2.8/45mm., Gauthier leaf shutter 10-200, B, coupled rangefinder.
  ....35.00   40.00

- **Bolsey Reflex,** original model, c. 1938, manufactured by Pignons SA, Balaigues, Switzerland, this camera is identical to the Alpa I, both cameras being developed by Jacques Bolsey shortly before he moved to the United States, 35mm. SLR, 24 x 36mm. format, interchangeable Bolca Anastigmat lens f2.8/50mm., focal plane shutter 25-1000, focus with ground glass or split-image RF.
  ....325.00   375.00
- **Bolsey 8,** still or motion picture camera, stainless steel body, size of cigarette pack.
  ....100.00   140.00

BOLTA
(Nurnberg, Germany)

- **Photavit,** a compact 35mm. camera for 24 x 24mm. exposures on standard 35mm. film, but in special cartridges, film advances from one cartridge to the other, no rewinding needed, and the old supply cartridge becomes the new take-up cartridge, wide variety of shutter and lens combinations.
  ....75.00   100.00

BO-PEEP
(See Manhattan Optical Co.)

BORSUM CAMERA CO.
(Newark, NJ)
(See also Reflex Camera Co., post 1909)

- **5 x 7 Reflex,** patents 1896-1897, a very early American SLR, c. 1900, measures 15 x 11 x 8½ inches when closed, Goerz Dagor Serial III f7.7/16½ inch lens, focal plane shutter.
  ....300.00   350.00

80 / BOSTON

- [ ] **5 x 7 New Model Reflex,** *large box with internal bellows focus, small front door hinges down to uncover lens, identical to the 5 x 7 Reflex of the Reflex Camera Co.*
  .... 300.00   350.00

BOSTON CAMERA CO.
(Boston, Mass.)

The Boston Camera Co. was purchased by the Blair Camera Co. in 1890 and moved to Rochester in 1899. Boston was re-formed in the mid-1890's and made the Bullseye cameras.

- [ ] **Bullseye box cameras,** *introduced c. 1895, simple wooden box cameras, leather covered, for rollfilm, very similar to the later Blair and Kodak Bullseye cameras.*
  .... 45.00   60.00

- [ ] **Hawk-eye "Detective" box cameras,** *c. 1888-1892, large wooden box camera for 4 x 5" plates, rotating brass knob at rear of camera focuses by means of internal bellows, all wood box model.*
  .... 175.00   225.00
- [ ] **Same as above,** *leather covered model.*
  .... 175.00   195.00

BOWER-X
(See Schleissner)

BOX CAMERAS

The simplest, most common type of camera. Box cameras have been made by most camera manufacturers, and of most common materials from paper to plastic to metal. Many models are listed in this guide under the manufacturer, but to save you the trouble of looking, common boxes sell for Five Dollars or less, including sales tax, postage, and green stamps. They can make a fascinating collection, but without straining the average budget.

BOX TENGOR
(See Goerz, Zeiss)

BOY SCOUT CAMERA
(See Ansco, Eastman)

BOYER
(Paris)

- [ ] **Altessa,** *folding camera for 8 or 12 exposures on 120 film, tubular interchangeable Angenieux f3.5 lens, synchronized shutter.*
  .... 115.00   140.00
- [ ] **Boyer,** *plastic 120 cameras.*
  .... 10.00   15.00

BRACK & CO.
(Munich)

- [ ] **Field camera,** *18 x 24cm., square cloth bellows, black with red corners, extend backwards, a fine wood and brass camera with Rodenstock WA Bistigmat 24 x 30 lens with brass revolving stops.*
  .... 200.00   230.00

BRAUN
(Carl Braun, Nürnberg, Germany)

- [ ] **Colorette Super.**
  .... 35.00   45.00
- [ ] **Gloriette,** *non-RF 35mm. camera 24 x 36mm., f2.8/45m.. Steinheil Cassar, Prontor SVS shutter, BIM.*
  .... 20.00   30.00

- [ ] **Pax,** *models M2, M3, M4, f3.5 or 2.8/45mm. coated lens, shutter 10-300, B.*
  ....35.00   45.00
- [ ] **Paxette I,** *compact 35mm. RF camera c. late 1930's through 1950's, various models.*
  ....20.00   30.00
- [ ] **Paxette Automatic III,** *f2.8/50 Color Ennit lens.*
  ....30.00   40.00
- [ ] **Paxina,** *6 x 6cm. rollfilm camera, telescoping front, f3.5/75 Staebler Kataplast lens in Vario shutter.*
  ....15.00   20.00
- [ ] **Super Paxette,** *35mm. Xenar f2.8/50mm. or Enna Color Ennit, Prontor shutter.*
  ....25.00   35.00

BRILLIANT
(See Voigtländer)

BROOKLYN CAMERA CO.
(Brooklyn, NY)

- [ ] **Brooklyn Camera,** *c. 1885, ¼-plate, 3¼ x 4¼, collapsible-bellows view camera with non-folding bed.*
  .... 225.00   260.00

BROWNELL
(Frank Brownell, Rochester, NY)

- [ ] **Stereo Camera,** *c. 1885, a square bellows dry-plate camera for stereo exposures, historically significant, because Frank Brownell made very few cameras which sold under his own name, he made the first Kodak cameras for the Eastman Dry Plate & Film Co., and was later a Plant Manager for EKC.*
  .... 575.00   675.00

BROWNIE
(See Eastman Kodak Co.)

BUCCANEER
(See Universal Camera Corp.)

BUCKEYE
(See American Camera Mfg. Co., Anthony, and Eastman Kodak Co.)

BUESS
(Lausanne)

Multiprint, A special camera for 24 small exposures on a 13 x 18cm. plate which shifts from lower right to upper left by means of a crank on the back, Corygon lens. Rotating shutter 1-100. Reflex finder. Only 25 of these cameras were made. We know of only 1 example sold at auction in 1976 in Germany for $819.

BULLARD CAMERA CO.
(Springfield, MA)

- [ ] **Folding plate camera,** *4 x 5" c. 1900, wood interior, red bellows, reversible back, B&L or Rauber Wollensak lens, Victor shutter.*
  .... 165.00   195.00
- [ ] **Magazine camera,** *c. 1898 for 18 plates in 4 x 5" format, push-pull action of back advances plates, front bed hinges down and bellows extend, unusual, because the majority of the magazine cameras were box cameras, and did not employ folding bed or bellows.*
  .... 300.00   350.00

BULLET
(See Eastman)

BULLS-EYE
(See Boston, Eastman)

BURKE & JAMES
(Chicago)

- [ ] **Grover,** *4 x 5 view.*
  ....70.00   90.00
- [ ] **Ideal,** *6½ x 8½ view.*
  ....80.00   100.00
- [ ] **Ingento 1A Ingento Jr.,** *f6.3 lens.*
  ....16.00   20.00

82 / BUSCH CAMERA CO.

- ☐ **Ingento 3A Ingento Jr.,** *vertical format, Ilex lens, Ingento shutter.*
  ....20.00   30.00
- ☐ **Ingento 3A Folding Ingento,** *Model 3, horizontal format, Ilex lens, Ingento shutter.*
  ....28.00   38.00

Korelle
Marketed by Burke & James, but manufactured by Kochmann. *(See Kochmann.)*

- ☐ **Press 4 x 5,** *f4.7/127 Kodak Ektar.*
  ....85.00   105.00
- ☐ **Rexo Box camera,** *for 6 x 9cm. rollfilm.*
  ....6.00   8.00
- ☐ **Rexo 1A Folding Rexo,** *for 2½ x 4¼ on 116 film, Anastigmat lens.*
  ....15.00   20.00
- ☐ **Rexo 1A Rexo Jr.,** *folding camera for 2½ x 4¼ on 16 film, single achromatic or RR lens, Ilex shutter.*
  ....15.00   20.00
- ☐ **Rexo 2C Rexo Jr.,** *folding camera.*
  ....15.00   20.00
- ☐ **Rexo 3 Rexo,** *folding 3¼ x 4¼ rollfilm, RR or Anastigmat lens, Ilex shutter.*
  ....25.00   30.00
- ☐ **Rexo 3 Rexo Jr.,** *3¼ x 4¼, single achromatic lens, Ilex shutter.*
  ....15.00   20.00
- ☐ **Rexo Vest Pocket Rexo,** *Wolensak Anastigmat lens in Ultex shutter.*
  ....20.00   25.00
- ☐ **Rexo Rexoette,** *box camera 6 x 9cm. c. 1910.*
  ....15.00   20.00
- ☐ **Press/View cameras,** *without lens, 2¼ x 3¼ and 3¼ x 4¼.*
  ....50.00   55.00
- ☐ **Same as above,** *4 x 5.*
  ....75.00   100.00
- ☐ **Same as above,** *5 x 7.*
  .... 100.00   125.00
- ☐ **Same as above,** *8 x 10.*
  .... 150.00   165.00
- ☐ **Same as above,** *8 x 10, with lens.*
  .... 275.00   325.00
- ☐ **Watson-Holmes Fingerprint Camera,** *if the good folks at B&J named this specialty camera after the famous sleuth and his side-kick, it is aptly named, however, they made other Watson cameras, which adds to the mystery which we leave to our readers.*
  .... 150.00   160.00

BUSCH CAMERA CO.
(Chicago)

- ☐ **Pressman, 4 x 5,** *f4.7 Ektar, Optar, or Raptar lens, press camera style like Graphic.*
  .... 140.00   160.00
- ☐ **Pressman 2¼ x 3¼,** *miniature press camera.*
  ....80.00   100.00
- ☐ **Verascope F-40,** *c. 1950's stereo camera for 24 x 30mm. pairs or singles, f3.5/40mm. Berthiot lens, guillotine shutter to 250, RF.*
  .... 375.00   400.00

BUSTER BROWN
(See Ansco)

BUSY BEE
(See Seneca)

BUTCHER
(W. Butcher & Sons, London)

(See also Houghton-Butcher for any cameras not listed here.)

- ☐ **Cameo,** *3½ x 5½ plate camera c. 1912, Aldis f7.7 or f6.3 lens, Ibso shutter.*
  ....35.00   45.00
- ☐ **Carbine folding rollfilm,** *models c. 1920, quite a variety of models with various lens and shutter combinations, for a good clean example with a normal lens and shutter.*
  ....20.00

☐ **Same as above,** *a deluxe model with fast Tessar lens and Compur Rapid shutter.*
..................70.00

Note: Prices tend to be somewhat higher in Europe. The overabundance of cheap folding rollfilm cameras in the United States has kept enthusiasm low, even for some of the better models like these.

☐ **Carbine Postcard size folding camera,** f6.8/6½" Ross Homocentric lens, compound shutter.
..................35.00   40.00

☐ **Carbine No. 2,** *c. 1930's rollfilm box.*
..................10.00   12.00

☐ **Carbine Reflex,** *6 x 9cm. 120 film SLR c. 1920's, f7.7/4¼" Aldis Uno Anastigmat, two separate releases for T & I, body of wood covered with black leather.*
.... 160.00   175.00

☐ **Watch Pocket Carbine,** *compact folding rollfilm camera, horizontal style, for 6 x 6cm. exposure, normally with f7.7/3" Aldis Uno Anastigmat and Lukos II shutter.*
..................40.00   50.00

☐ **Klimax,** *4 x 5 folding plate camera c. 1912, DEB, Aldis f7.7 lens, with holders.*
..................50.00   60.00

☐ **Same as above,** *5 x 7, compound shutter, f7.7 lens.*
.... 100.00   125.00

☐ **Midg,** *box cameras c. 1950-1915, for film or plates, numbers 0, 00, 1a, 1, 2, 3, 4, 4a, 4b.*
..................50.00   75.00

CADET
(See Agfa, Ansco)

CADOT
(A. Cadot, Paris)

☐ **Scenographic Panoramique,** *Jumelle style 9 x 18cm. plate camera, one lens rotates to center position to change from stereo to panoramic mode.*
.... 350.00   400.00

CAMBINOX
(See Möller)

CAM-O-CORP.
(Kansas City, MO)

☐ **Ident,** *35mm. TLR, f9.5/114mm.*
..................70.00   85.00

CAMEL

☐ **Model II,** *Leica copy, f3.5 Camel lens.*
..................75.00   85.00

CAMEO
(See Butcher, Houghton-Butcher)

CAMEO STEREO
(See Ica)

CAMERA CORP. OF AMERICA
(See Candid Camera Corp.)

CAMERADIO
(See Universal Radio Mfg. Co.)

CAMERA-LITE

☐ **Cigarette-lighter spy camera,** *resembles Zippo lighter, made in USA in 1950's, similar to the Japanese Echo-8.*
.... 165.00   185.00

CAMERA-SCOPE

☐ **Kaleidoscope,** *novelty item disguised as a camera.*
..................20.00   30.00

CANDID CAMERA CORP. OF AMERICA

Original name 1938-1945 was shortened to "Camera Corp. of America" in 1945. It did no great good because in 1949, the company sold out to Ciro.

- **Perfex Speed Candid,** *1938-1939, 35mm. RF camera, interchangeable f3.5/50mm. or f2.8 Anastigmat, cloth focal plane shutter 25-500, B, non-coupled RF.*
  .... **70.00** **95.00**
- **Perfex Forty-Four,** *1939-1940, 35mm. CRF camera, interchangeable f3.5 or 2.8/50mm. Anastigmat, cloth focal plane shutter 1-1250, B, synchronized, extinction meter.*
  .... **30.00** **40.00**
- **Perfex Thirty-Three,** *1940-1941, f3.5/50mm. Anastigmat, focal plane shutter 25-500, B, synchronized, CRF, extinction meter.*
  .... **40.00** **50.00**
- **Perfex Fifty-Five,** *1940-1947, f3.5 or 2.8 lens, focal plane shutter 1-1250, B, synchronized, CRF, extinction meter, exposure calculator on early models only.*
  .... **30.00** **40.00**
- **Perfex One-O-One,** *1948-1950, f4.5/50mm. Wollensak Anastigmat, Alphax leaf shutter 25-150, T, B.*
  .... **30.00** **40.00**
- **Perfex One-O-Two,** *1948-1950, f3.5/50mm. Ektar lens, Compur Rapid 10-200, T, B.*
  .... **50.00** **60.00**

CANON CAMERA CO.
(Tokyo)

- **Demi,** *½ frame 35mm. with meter.*
  .... **35.00** **40.00**
- **L-1,** *RF, Hexanon f1.9, chrome.*
  .... **120.00** **150.00**
- **P,** *c. 1959-1963, f1.2 to 1.9/50mm., coupled rangefinder, and meter.*
  .... **175.00** **200.00**
- **VT,** *f1.8/50mm. c. 1956-1958.*
  .... **160.00** **170.00**
- **II,** *c. 1951, focal plane shutter to 500, no synchronization.*
  .... **120.00** **150.00**
- **II-B,** *similar to II, but with focus magnifier, with f1.9 Serenar.*
  .... **150.00** **175.00**
- **II-F,** *c. 1955, shutter to 500, f1.8 or 1.9.*
  .... **80.00** **95.00**
- **II-S,** *c. 1955, similar to II-F.*
  .... **120.00** **150.00**
- **III,** *f1.8 or 1.9 Serenar.*
  .... **90.00** **115.00**
- **IIIA,** *f1.8 or 1.9/50mm. Serenar.*
  .... **130.00** **150.00**
- **IV,** *1951, Serenar f1.9, shutter to 1000.*
  .... **140.00** **160.00**
- **IV-F,** *f1.8/50 Serenar, c. 1952.*
  .... **100.00** **115.00**
- **IV-S,** *similar to IV-F.*
  .... **100.00** **120.00**
- **IV-S2,** *c. 1952, f1.8 or 1.9 Serenar.*
  .... **135.00** **150.00**
- **7,** *c. 1961-1964, focal plane shutter to 1000, CRF, body only.*
  .... **175.00** **195.00**
- **Same as above,** *with f.95/50 Canon.*
  .... **350.00** **400.00**
- **Same as above,** *with f1.8/50mm. Canon.*
  .... **200.00** **250.00**
- **7-S,** *1964-1966, with f1.8/50mm. normal lens.*
  .... **335.00** **350.00**
- **Canonet,** *c. 1960, f1.9 or 2.8 lens.*
  .... **35.00** **45.00**
- **Dial 35,** *¼ frame, f2.8 lens.*
  .... **40.00** **50.00**

CAPTAIN
(See Agfa)

CARBINE
(See Butcher)

CARLTON
(See Allied)

CARMEN
(France)

☐ **Pygmee,** *c. 1930's camera for 24 x 24 exposures on 828 size rollfilm, Meniscus lens, simple shutter.*
.... **125.00**   **150.00**

CARPENTIER, JULES
(Paris)

☐ **Photo Jumelles,** *c. 1890's rigid-bodied, binocular styled camera, one lens is for viewing, the other for taking single exposures, this is not a stereo camera, as many jumelle-styled cameras are, magazine holds 12 plates, to change plates, a rod extending through the side of the camera is pulled out and pushed back in, various models in 6 x 9cm. and 4.5 x 6cm. sizes.*
.... **225.00**   **250.00**

CARTRIDGE KODAK
(See Eastman)

CASCA
(See Steinheil)

CENTURY / 85

CASPA
(See Demaria)

CENTURY 35
(See Graflex, Inc.)

CENTURY CAMERA CO.

Century began operations in 1900, which probably explains the company name well enough. In 1903, The Eastman Kodak Co. bought controlling interest in the company, and in 1907 it became "Century Camera Div., EKC." Following that, it was in the Folmer-Century Division of EKC which became Folmer Graflex Corp. in 1926.

☐ **Field cameras,** *classified by size, less lens, 4 x 5.*
.... **60.00**   **70.00**
☐ **Same as above,** *5 x 7.*
.... **95.00**   **115.00**
☐ **Same as above,** *6½ x 8½.*
.... **95.00**   **120.00**

86 / CERTO KAMARAWERK

☐ **Same as above,** *8 x 10.*
.... 130.00   140.00
☐ **Same as above,** *11 x 14.*
.... 175.00   195.00

CERTO KAMARAWERK
(Dresden, Germany)

☐ **Certosix,** *6 x 9cm. folding rollfilm camera for 120 film, Steinheil Certar f4.5/105mm., rim set Compur T, B, 1-250.*
.... 20.00   30.00

☐ **Certonet,** *c. 1926, 6 x 9cm. folding 120 film camera, f4.5/120mm. Schneider Radionar, Vario shutter, T, B, 25-100.*
.... 25.00   35.00

☐ **Certosport,** *folding plate cameras c. 1930's, 6.5 x 9 and 9 x 12cm. sizes, DEB, normally with f4.5 lens, Meyer or Schneider, in Compur or Ibsor shutter.*
.... 50.00   60.00

Dollina

☐ **Dollina II**
.... 70.00   80.00

☐ **Super Dollina,** *35mm. RF camera, f2.8/50 Tessar.*
.... 90.00   125.00

☐ **Certotrop,** *folding plate cameras, 6 x 9 and 9 x 12 sizes.*
.... 35.00   45.00

☐ **Dollina,** *folding 35mm. camera c. late 1930's, various shutter/lens combinations.*
.... 60.00   70.00

☐ **Dolly,** *compact folding camera for 16 exposures 3 x 4cm. on 127 film, f2.9, 3.5, or 4.5 lens, original price, about $20.*
.... 50.00   60.00

- **Supersport Dolly,** c. late 1930's folding camera for 12 exposures 6 x 6cm. or 16 exposures 4.5 x 6cm. on 120 film, later models have CRF, various lenses f2, 2.8, 2.9, rimset Compur.
  . . . . .50.00   60.00

- **Doppel Box,** c. 1935 box camera for 8 exposures 6 x 9cm. or 16 exposures 4.5 x 6cm. on 120 film, format changeable by turning dial, Certomat lens, single speed shutter.
  . . . . .45.00   55.00

- **Plate camera,** 9 x 12cm., DEB.
  . . . . .50.00   60.00

CHALLENGE
(See Lizars)

CHASE MAGAZINE CAMERA CO.
(Newburyport, Mass. USA)

- **Chase Magazine Camera,** c. 1899 for 12 plates 4 x 5", plates advanced, dropped, by turning large key at side, variable apertures, shutter speeds I & T.
  . . . . 125.00   135.00

CHAUTAUQUA
(See Seneca)

CHEVRON
(See Eastman Kodak Co.)

CHICAGO CAMERA CO.
(Chicago, Ill.)

- **Photake,** a seamless cylindrical camera c. 1896 made to take 5 exposures on 2 x 2" glass plates, f14/ 120mm. achromat lens, Guillotine shutter, a very unusual camera which originally sold for a mere $2.50.
  . . . . 2150.00   2250.00

CHICAGO FERROTYPE CO.
(Chicago, Ill.)

- **Mandel No. 2 Post Card Machine,** a direct positive street camera c. 1913-1930.
  . . . . 175.00   195.00

- **Mandelette,** direct positive street camera, 2½ x 3½ format, camera measures 4 x 4½ x 6", sleeve at rear, tank below, simple shutter and lens, a widely publicized camera which sold for about $10.00 in 1929.
  . . . . .75.00   100.00

- **PDQ Street Camera,** direct positive street camera.
  . . . . 120.00   135.00

- **Wonder Automatic Cannon Photo Button Machine,** an unusual all-metal street camera c. 1910 for taking and developing 1" diameter button photographs.
  . . . . 1000.00   1150.00

CHIYODO KOGAKU SEIKO CO. LTD.

- **Chiyoko,** 6 x 6cm. TLR, Seikosha MX shutter, f3.5 Rokkor lens.
  . . . . .50.00   60.00

- **Konan,** 16 Automat, c. 1952, 16mm. subminiature, the precursor of the Minolta 16.
  . . . . .65.00   75.00

Minolta
Although the Minolta cameras were made by Chiyoda, we have listed them separately under the more widely recognized name Minolta.

CIRKUT CAMERAS
(See Eastman)

CIRO CAMERAS, INC.
(Delaware, Ohio)

☐ **Ciro 35,** basically the same camera as the Cee-Ay 35 camera from the Camera Corporation of America, Ciro bought the design and dies and made only minor cosmetic changes, it still did not fare well, and soon was in the hands of Graflex, Graflex sold the Ciro 35, then modified it to make the Graphic 35, the Ciro 35 is a 35mm. RF camera c. 1949-1954, three models, R-f4.5, S-f3.5, and T-f2.8
................18.00   25.00

☐ **Ciroflex,** common 6 x 6cm. TLR c. 1940's, models A through F, all similar, with each new model offering a slight improvement.
................25.00   30.00

CITOSKOP
(See Contessa)

CLACK
(See Agfa, Reitzschel)

CLARISSA
(See Contessa)

CLAROVID
(See Rodenstock)

CLARUS CAMERA MFG. CO.
(Minnneapolis)

☐ **MS-35,** rangefinder 35mm. camera, made from 1946-1952, interchangeable f2.8/50mm. Wollensak Velostigmat lens, focal plane shutter to 1000, shutters tend to be erratic and slugish, which would decrease the value from the listed price.
................50.00   60.00

Note: The Clarus company never did well, because they could not escape their reputation, although they finally managed to make their camera work.

CLICK
(See Agfa)

CLIMAX
(See Anthony)

CLIPPER
(See Agfa, Ansco)

CLIX

☐ **Box camera,** cheap 120.
................4.00   6.00

CLOSE & CONE
(Chicago, Boston, and NY)

☐ **Quad,** box-plate camera c. 1896, the only camera using the new "quadruple plateholder", an unusual mechanism which turned the four plates into the focal plane, the camera which measured 4-5/8 x 4-5/8 x 6" for 3½ x 3½ plates was advertised in 1896 as "the largest picture and smallest camera combined ever made", and it cost $5.00 new.
................100.00   125.00

CMC

☐ **Novelty camera,** Japanese 14mm.
................10.00   12.00

COCARETTE
(See Contessa-Nettel, Zeiss)

COLLY

☐ **Novelty camera,** takes 14 x 14mm. exposures on 16mm. film, simple shutter, Meniscus lens.
................12.00   15.00

COLORETTE
(See Braun)

COLORFLEX
(See Agfa)

COLORIST STEREO CAMERA
(See Bell & Howell)

COLUMBIA OPTICAL & CAMERA CO.
(London)

☐ **Pecto No. 1A,** *4 x 5 plate camera, red bellows.*
.................60.00   75.00

☐ **Pecto No. 5,** *c. 1897 folding bed camera for 9 x 12cm. plates, B&L RR lens, Unicum shutter, DEB, rising front, leather covered wood body.*
.................60.00   70.00

COMBINATION CAMERA
(See Thompson)

COMMANDER
(See Ansco)

COMPAGNIE FRANCAISE DE PHOTOGRAPHIE

☐ **Photosphere,** *c. 1888, one of the first all-metal cameras, for 9 x 12cm. plates, or could take special roll back for Eastman film, shutter in form of a hemisphere.*
.... 1500.00   1650.00

Photosphere

COMPASS CAMERAS LTD.
(London)

☐ **Compass Camera,** *manufactured by Jaeger LeCultre & Cie., Sentier, Switzerland for Compass Camras Limited, the ultimate compact 35m. rangefinder camera system, a finely machined aluminum-bodied camera of unusual design and incorporating many built-in features which include f3.5/50mm. lens, RF, right-angle finder, panoramic and stereo heads, level, extinction meter, filters, ground glass focusing, etc., for 24 x 36mm. exposures on glass plates, or on*

film with optional roll back, camera only.
.... 800.00   900.00
☐ **Same as above,** complete outfit.
.... 1200.00   1400.00

COMPETITOR
(See Seneca)

CONCAVA
(See Tessina)

CONDOR
(See Galileo Optical Co.)

CONLEY CAMERA CO.
(Rochester, Minn.)

In addition to the cameras marketed under their own label, Conley also made many cameras for Sears, Roebuck & Company, which were sold under the Seroco label or with no identifying names on the camera.

☐ **Kewpie Box Camera No. 2,** *for 120 film, loads from side, rotating disc stops on front of camera.*
.... 15.00   20.00

☐ **Kewpie Box Camera No. 2A,** *for 2¼ x 4½ exposures.*
.... 15.00   20.00

☐ **Kewpie Box Camera No. 3,** *3¼ x 4¼.*
.... 15.00   20.00

☐ **Kewpie Box Camera No. 3A,** *3¼ x 5½ "postcard" size.*
.... 20.00   25.00

☐ **Folding Plate Camera 3¼ x 5½,** *postcard size, c. 1900-1910, vertical folding camera, fine polished wood interior, nickel trim, red bellows, f8/ 6½" lens in Wollensak Conley Safety Shutter, double extension.*
.... 50.00   60.00

☐ **Folding plate camera 4 x 5,** *c. 1900-1910, black leathered wood body, polished cherry interior, red bellows, usually with Conley Safety Shutter and one of the following lenses: Wollensak Rapid Symmetrical, Rapid Orthographic, Rapid Rectilinear, or occasionally with the Wollensak 6"-10"-14" Triple Convertible, worth more, normally found in case side by side with holders "cycle" style, the 4 x 5 is the*

most commonly found size of the Conley folding models.
.................65.00   75.00

☐ **Folding plate camera 5 x 7,** except for size, similar to the two previous listings.
.... 100.00   125.00

☐ **Folding rollfilm camera,** 3¼ x 5½ "postcard" size, on 122 film, Vitar Anastigmat f6.3 in B&L Compound shutter, similar to the Kodak folding rollfilm cameras which are much more common.
..................30.00   40.00

☐ **6½ x 8½ View Camera,** the least common size among Conley cameras.
.... 135.00   140.00

☐ **8 x 10 View Camera,** prices vary depending on accessories, particularly lens and shutter, since large format shutters and lenses still have some value as useful equipment.
.... 120.00   125.00

☐ **Conley Junior,** folding rollfilm cameras, similar in style to the better known Kodak folding rollfilm cameras.
..................20.00   25.00

☐ **Magazine Camera,** leather covered wooden box camera for 12 plates 4 x 5", plates advanced by crank on right side of camera.
..................70.00   75.00

☐ **Stereo box camera,** for 4¼ x 6½" plates, simple shutter, I & T, Meniscus lens.
.... 450.00   500.00

CONTAFLEX
(See Zeiss)

CONTAX
(See Zeiss)

CONTESSA, CONTESSA-NETTEL
(Stuttgart)

Contessa merged with Nettel in 1919. In 1926, a large merger joined Contessa-Nettel with Ernemann, Goerz, Ica, and the Carl Zeiss Optical Company to form Zeiss-Ikon. *(See also Nettel, Zeiss.)*

☐ **Adoro,** 9 x 12cm. folding plate camera, f4.5 Tessar, Compur, DEB.
..................35.00   45.00

92 / CONTESSA, CONTESSA—NETTEL

- **Altura,** 3¼ x 5½, Citonar 165mm. lens in dialset Compur shutter.
  ....50.00   65.00
- **Citoskop Stereo,** c. 1924, 45 x 107mm. f4.5/65mm. Tessar lenses, stereo Compur.
  ....300.00   350.00
- **Clarissa, Tropical model,** 4.5 x 6cm. plate camera, light colored wood body with red bellows, brass struts, standard, and lens barrel, focal plane shutter, 1/20 to 1000, Meyer Görlitz Trioplan f3/75mm.
  .... 1200.00   1400.00
- **Cocarette,** folding bed rollfilm cameras made in 2 sizes c. 1930's, 6 x 9cm. on 120 film and 2½ x 4¼" on 116 film, many combinations of shutters and lenses.
  ....20.00   35.00
- **Deckrullo-Nettel,** folding plate camera with focal plane shutter, 2 x 12cm. size with Zeiss Tessar f4.5/150mm., or 10 x 15cm. size with Tessar f4.5/180mm., black leather covered body, ground glass back.
  ....170.00   195.00
- **Deckrullo, Tropical model,** c. 1927 folding 9 x 12cm. plate camera, teakwood body partly covered with brown leather, light brown bellows, f4.5/120mm. Tessar, FP shutter to 1/2800 second.
  ....700.00   775.00
- **Deckrullo-Nettel Stereo,** 6 x 13cm. size, focal plane shutter, Tessar f4.5/90mm.
  ....375.00   425.00
- **Deckrullo Stereo, Tropical model,** folding teakwood bodied stereo camera for 9 x 12cm. plates, f2.7/65mm. Tessars, focal plane shutter to 2800, GG back, brown bellows, nickel trim.
  .... 1200.00   1400.00
- **Donata,** 6.5 x 9cm. and 9 x 12cm. sizes, folding plate or pack camera c. 1920's, f6.3 Tessar or f6.8 Dagor, Compur shutter, GGB.
  ....30.00   40.00
- **Duchessa,** 4.5 x 6cm. folding plate camera c. 1920's, f6.3/75mm. Citonar Anastigmat, Compur 1-100.
  ....140.00   160.00
- **Ergo,** monocular-shaped camera for 4.5 x 6cm. plates, earlier model was the Nettel Argus, later model was the Zeiss-Ikon Ergo, Tessar f4.5/55mm., Compur 25-100, B. right angle finder.
  ....950.00   1150.00
- **Miroflex,** single lens reflex c. 1924 for 9 x 12 plates, Tessar 4.5/150mm. lens, focal plane shutter to 2000, the later Zeiss-Ikon Miroflex is more often found than the Contessa models.
  ....220.00   250.00

☐ **Nic 63,** 9 x 12cm. folding plate camera, single extension bellows, GGB, Periskop Aplanat lens, simple TBI shutter.
.... 20.00   30.00

☐ **Onito,** 9 x 12cm. Nettar Anast, f4.5/135mm. Ibsor 1-100.
.... 20.00   30.00

☐ **Piccolette,** 1920's folding vest-pocket camera for 4 x 6.5cm. exposures on 127 film, f4.5/75mm. Tessar, f6.3 Triotar, or f11 Meniscus lenses, dial Compur or Achro shutter.
.... 85.00   95.00

☐ **Sonnar,** folding 9 x 12cm. plate camera, DEB, f4.5/135 Contessa-Nettel Sonnar, Compur 1-200.
.... 40.00   50.00

☐ **Sonnet,** folding plate camera c. 1920's, 4.5 x 6cm. and 6.5 x 9cm. sizes with teakwood bodies, f4.5 Zeiss lens, dial Compur 1-300, light brown bellows.
.... 725.00   825.00

☐ **Stereax,** stereo camera, 45 x 107mm. size, focal plane shutter.
.... 350.00   385.00

☐ **Steroco,** a cheaply made stereo camera for 45 x 107mm., f6.3 Tessars, Compur.
.... 120.00   135.00

☐ **Taxo,** 9 x 12cm. folding plate camera, f8/135 Extra Rapid Aplanat, Duval shutter to 100.
.... 20.00   30.00

☐ **Tessco,** 10 x 15cm. folding plate camera, DEB, GGB, Contessa-Nettel Sonnar f4.5/135mm., dial Compur 1-200.
.... 35.00   45.00

☐ **Tropical model plate cameras,** c. 1920's 6 x 9cm. size, Zeiss Tessar f4.5/120, Compur shutter 1-250, finely finished wood, reddish-brown bellows, brass trim or combination of brass and nickel trim, general guidelines, Bed-type with front shutter.
.... 400.00   550.00

☐ **Same as above,** strut-type with focal plane shutter.
.... 750.00 1250.00

☐ **Same as above,** single lens reflex.
.... 2000.00 3000.00

CONTINA
(See Zeiss)

CORFIELD
(England)

☐ **Periflex,** 35mm. Leica copy c. 1960 for 36 exposures 24 x 36mm., interchangeable f2.8/50mm. Lumax or f1.9 or f2.8/45mm., focal plane shutter to 1000, unusual through-the-lens periscope reflex rangefinder.
.... 250.00   300.00

CORNU CO.
(Paris)

☐ **Ontobloc,** c. 1935 35mm. compact camera, dark grey hammertone painted cast metal body, Som Berthiot Flor f3.5/50mm. lens in Prontor II, T, B, 1-200.
.... 35.00   40.00

☐ **Ontoflex,** TLR, Berthiot f3.5, Compur.
.... 850.00   950.00

CORONET

☐ **Reyna II,** *telescoping front 35mm. camera, Berthiot Flor f3.5/50, Compur Rapid to 500, front lens focus, black hammertone painted cast metal body.*
................20.00   30.00

☐ **Reyna Cross III,** *black painted cast aluminum bodied 35mm., f3.5 Berthiot or f2.9/45mm. Cross, two blade shutter, 25-200, B.*
................20.00   30.00

CORONET CAMERA CO.
(Birmingham, GB)

☐ **Midget,** *a small colored bakelite 16mm. novelty camera, Taylor Hobson Meniscus lens f10, single speed, 1/30, six exposures per special roll, original price $2.50.*
................45.00   55.00

☐ **"3-D" Stereo Camera,** *an inexpensive plastic stereo camera for 4 stereo pairs or 8 single exposures, 4.5 x 4.5cm. on 127 film, single speed shutter, twin Meniscus lenses.*
................35.00   40.00

☐ **Vogue,** *a brown bakelite-bodied folding camera which uses "Vogue 35" film, a spool film similar to Eastman Kodak 828, fixed focus lens, simple B & I shutter.*
................40.00   50.00

CORSAIR
(See Universal Camera Corp.)

COSMIC

☐ **Cosmic,** *Russian 35mm. of the mid-1960's, f4/40mm. lens, shutter 1/5-1/250.*
................20.00   25.00

COSMO-CLACK
(See Rietzschel)

CRAFTSMAN
(See Ansco)

CROSS
(See Cornu)

CRYSTAR

☐ **Crystar,** *novelty camera for 14 x 14mm. exposures on 16mm. film, paper backed rollfilm.*
................8.00   12.00

CUB
(See American Adv. & Research Corp.)

CUPID
(See Houghton)

CUPIDO
(See Ica)

CYCLONE

Cyclone cameras were originally manufactured by the Western Camera Co. until about 1899, when they were taken over by the Rochester Optical Co., which continued to produce Cyclone models. We have listed Cyclone models under each of these makers.

CYCLOPS

☐ **Cyclops,** *16mm. Japanese binocular camera c. 1950's, f4.5/35mm. lens, shutter 25-100, identical to the Teleca camera.*
.... 450.00   500.00

DACI

☐ **Daci,** German red metal box camera for 12 exposures 6 x 6cm. on 120 film.
.... 8.00   12.00

DAGUERREOTYPE CAMERAS

The earliest type of camera in existence, many of which were one-up or limited production cameras. Since so few of even the commercially made models have survived time, most Daguerrotype cameras are unique pieces, and price averaging is senseless. However, to keep the novice collector or casual antique dealer from making any big mistakes before consulting with a recognized authority, we will give one example: A half-plate American sliding box-in-box style is likely to be in the $7500.00 and up range.

DAIICHI KOGAKU
(Japan)

☐ **Zenobia,** c. 1949 folding camera for 16 exposures 4.5 x 6cm. on 120 film, styled like the early Zeiss Ikonta cameras, f3.5/75mm. Hesper Anastigmat, DOC Rapid shutter 1-500, B, similar to the Compur Rapid.
.... 20.00   30.00

DALLMEYER
(J. H. Dallmeyer, London)

☐ **Dallmeyer "Speed" Camera,** mid-1920's camera for 4.5 x 6cm. exposures, this press-type camera is equipped with the Dallmeyer "Pentec" f2.9 lens, the fastest anastigmat lens of its time, this lens, as well as the 1/8 to 1/000 second, focal plane shutter account for the camera's name.
.... 320.00   360.00

DAN 35

☐ **Dan 35,** c. 1950 compact camera for 15 exposures 24 x 24mm. on 828 film, Dan Anastigmat f4.5/40mm., shutter B, 25-100.
.... 30.00   45.00

DANCER
(J. B. Dancer, Rochester, England)

☐ **Stereo Camera,** c. 1856, for stereo pairs on 12 plates 3½ x 7", a nicely finished wooden stereo camera which set a new record for the highest price paid for an antique camera, $37,500.00 in 1977.

DANGELMEIER
(Reutlingen, Germany)

☐ **Decora I,** folding camera for 12 exposures, 6 x 6cm. on 120, Eunar f3.5/75, Prontor 1-100.
.... 8.00   14.00

DARLING 16

☐ **Darling 16,** subminiature.
.... 145.00   165.00

DAYDARK SPECIALTY CO.
(St. Louis, Mo.)

☐ **Photo Postcard Cameras,** "street" cameras for photo postcards or tintypes, complete with developing tank, dark sleeve, RR lens, and Blitzen Daydark shutter.
.... 175.00   225.00

☐ **Tintype Camera,** small amateur model, measures 4½ x 5 x 7¼.
.... 125.00   150.00

DAYLIGHT ENLARGING CAMERA
(See Anthony)

DAYLIGHT KODAK
(See Eastman)

DAYSPOOL
(See Lizars)

DAY-XIT
(See Shew)

DEBRIE
(Ets. Andre Debrie, Paris)

☐ **Sept,** c. 1920's spring motor drive camera for still, rapid sequence, or cine, 18 x 24mm. on 35mm. film, Roussel Stylor f3.5/50mm., one model has square motor, the other style has round motor.
.... 150.00   200.00

DECKRULLO
(See Contessa, Nettel)

DECORA
(See Dangelmeier)

DEHEL

☐ **Dehel,** French 120 rollfilm camera, f3.5/75mm. lens, AGC shutter.
.................16.00   20.00

DEJUR

☐ **Dejur,** TLR, f3.5 lens, 10-200 shutter.
..................30.00   40.00

DELMAR
(See Seroco)

DELTA
(See Krugener, also Delta)
DELTA STEREO

☐ **Delta Stereo,** American 35mm. stereo camera c. 1950's.
..................80.00   95.00

DEMARIA
(Demaria Freres, Denmaria-LaPierre, Paris)

☐ **Jumelle Caspa,** Denmaria Freres, 6 x 13mm. stereo camera.
.... 225.00   275.00

☐ **Stereo camera for 45 x 107mm. plates,** RR lenses, c. 1910.
.... 250.00   300.00

DERLUX
(France)

☐ **Derlux,** folding camera with polished aluminum body, Gallus Gallix f3.5/50mm., focal plane shutter B, 25-500.
..................50.00   60.00

DEROGY
(Paris)

☐ **Wooden plate camera,** c. 1880, 9 x 12cm. Derogy Aplanat Number 2 brass barrel lens, black tapered bellows, polished wood body, brass trim.
.... 200.00   300.00

DETECTIVE CAMERAS

The earliest "Detective" cameras were simply designed as a box or case. Before long, they were disguised in all shapes and sizes. Disguised and detective cameras seem to have a special appeal and therefore the prices have been staying well ahead of our inflationary economy. The original box, case, and satchel cameras are commonly referred to by the name "detective" cameras, while the later disguised/concealed varieties normally are not. In either case, they are listed by name of manufacturer.

DETROLA CORP.
(Detroit, Michigan)

- **Model B,** *127 film camera, Duomicroflex f7.9 lens.*
  .... **6.00**   10.00
- **Model D,** *same as above, f4.5 lens.*
  .... **6.00**   10.00
- **Model E,** *same as above, f3.5 lens.*
  .... **6.00**   10.00
- **Model GW,** *small 127 film camera c. 1940, basic f4.5 model.*
  .... **20.00**   25.00
- **Model HW,** *same as above, but with meter.*
  .... **20.00**   25.00
- **Model KW,** *with Anastigmat f3.5 lens.*
  .... **20.00**   25.00
- **Model 400,** *a Leica-inspired CRF 35mm. camera with interchangeable Wollensak Velostigmat f3.5 or f2.8 lens, focal plane shutter to 5000, synchronized, original cost about $70.*
  .... **300.00**   350.00

DEVIN COLORGRAPH CO.
(New York)

- **Tri-Color Camera,** *for making color separation negatives, original professional size for 5 x 7", Apo-Tessar f9/12" lens, dial Compur shutter.*
  .... **325.00**   400.00
- **Same as above,** *6.5 x 9cm. size, introduced c. 1938, Goerz Dogmar f4.5/5½" lens, compound shutter.*
  .... **325.00**   400.00

DEVRY
(QRS DeVry Corp., Chicago)

- **QRS Kamra,** *brown bakelite camera introduced in 1928, taking 35mm. film in special 40 exposure cartridges, Graf 7.7 Anastigmat lens, single speed shutter trips by counter-clockwise motion of winding crank, winding cranks often broken and missing, bakelite bodies tend to warp occasionally.*
  .... **45.00**   60.00

DIAL 35
(See Bell & Howell)

DIAX
(See Voss)

DICK TRACY

- **Dick Tracy,** *plastic camera for 127.*
  .... **18.00**   25.00

DIPLOMAT

- **Diplomat,** *14mm. novelty camera.*
  .... **8.00**   12.00

DIRECT POSITIVE CAMERA
(See Wabash)

DIVA
(See Phoba)

DOLLAR CAMERA
(See Ansco)

DOLLINA, DOLLY
(See Certo)

DONALD DUCK CAMERA
(See Herco)

DONATA
(See Contessa, Zeiss)

DOPPEL BOX
(See Certo)

DORIS

- **Doris,** *post-war folding 120 camera, f3.5/75mm. lens.*
  .... **10.00**   15.00

DOSSERT DETECTIVE CAMERA CO., NYC.

☐ **Detective Camera,** 4 x 5 box-plate detective camera with reflex viewing, c. 1890, leather covered to look like a satchel, sliding panels hide lens and ground glass openings, entire top hinges forward to reveal the plate holders for loading or storage.
.... 550.00   650.00

DOVER FILM CORP.

☐ **Dover 620A,** a plastic and chrome camera c. 1950 for 16 exposures 4.5 x 6cm. on 620 film, Somco f9 Meniscus lens, 5 rotary disc stops, single speed shutter, built-on flash.
.... 20.00   25.00

DUAFLEX, DUEX, DUO
(See Eastman)

DUBRONI
(Maison Dubroni, Paris)

The name Dubroni is an anagram formed with the letters of the name of the inventor, Jules Bourdin. Although anagrams and acronyms have always had a certain appeal to writers and inventors, the story in this case is quite interesting. It seems that young Jules, who was about twenty-two years old when he invented his camera, was strongly influenced by his father. The father, protective of the good reputation of his name, didn't want it mixed up with this new-fangled invention.

☐ **Le Photographe de Poche,** c. 1860's wooden box camera with porcelain interior for in-camera processing, five models were made, the smallest taking photos 5 x 5cm.
.... 3250.00   3500.00

DUCA
(See Durst)

DUCATI
(Milan, Italy)

☐ **Half-frame 35mm. RF camera,** for 15 exposures 18 x 24mm. on 35mm. film in special cassettes, c. 1938, interchangeable lenses, normally with f3.5 or 2.8 Vitor, or f3.5 Ducati Etar lens, 35mm. focal length, focal plane shutter to 500.
.... 225.00   250.00

DUCHESS

☐ **Duchess,** British ½-plate field camera c. 1887, mahogany body, brass trim, maroon bellows, RR brass barrel lens.
.... 200.00   225.00

DUCHESSA
(See Contessa)

DUPLEX
(See Ihagee, Iso (Duplex Stereo), Joux (Ortho Jumelle Duplex), Thornton-Picard (Duplex Ruby Reflex)

DURST S.A.

Most photographers know Durst for their enlargers. However, at one time they made some solid, well constructed, innovative cameras.

☐ **Automatica,** c. 1956 for 36 exposures 24 x 36mm. on standard 35mm. cartridge film, Schneider Durst Radionar f2.8/45mm., Prontor 1-300, B, and Auto, meter coupled to shutter by pneumatic cylinder.
.... 100.00   140.00

☐ **Duca,** c. 1946 for 12 exposures 24 x 36 on Agfa Karat Rapid cassettes, Ducan f11/50mm. T & I shutter, zone focus, rapid wind, aluminum body.
.... 70.00   85.00

☐ **Durst 66,** c. 1950 compact camera for 12 exposures 6 x 6cm. on 120 film, light grey hammertone painted aluminum body with partial red leather covering, Durst Color Duplor f2.2/80mm. lens, shutter ½-200, B, synchronized.
.... 50.00   75.00

EASTMAN DRY PLATE & FILM CO.
EASTMAN KODAK CO.

The first camera produced by the Eastman Dry Plate & Film Co. was called "The Kodak," and successive models were numbered in sequence. The first seven cameras listed here are the earliest Kodak cameras, and the remainder of the listings under Eastman Kodak Co. are in alphabetical order by series name and number. Some of the Eastman models listed are continuations of a line of cameras from another company which was taken over by Eastman. Earlier models of many of these cameras may be found under the name of the original manufacturer.

☐ **No. 1 Kodak Camera,** *1889-1895, similar to the original model, but with sector shutter rather than cylindrical, factory loaded for 100 exposures 2½" diameter, RR lens f9/57mm.*
.... 900.00   1200.00

☐ **The Kodak Camera,** *original model, c. June 1888 through 1889, made by Frank Brownell for the Eastman Dry Plate & Film Co., factory loaded with 100 exposures 2½" diameter, cylindrical shutter, string set, rapid Rectilinear lens f9/57mm., this was the first camera to use rollfilm and is a highly prized collectors' item.*
.... 3650.00   4000.00

☐ **No. 2 Kodak Camera,** *Oct. 1889-1897, also similar and still quite rare, but more common than the previous models, factory loaded for 60 exposures 3½" diameter.*
.... 450.00   550.00

☐ **No. 3 Kodak Camera,** *Jan. 1890-1897, a string-set box camera, factory loaded for either 60 or 100 exposures 3¼ x 4¼, Bausch & Lomb Universal lens, sector shutter.*
.... 400.00   500.00

100 / EASTMAN KODAK CO.

No. 3 Kodak

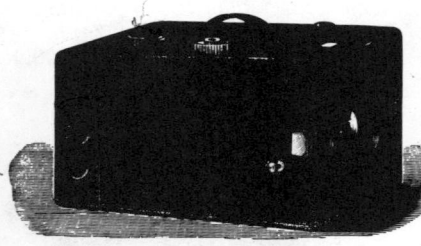

No. 3 Kodak Junior

No. 4 Kodak

5", but with capacity for 100 exposures for prolific photographers, B & L Universal lens, sector shutter.
.... **400.00   500.00**

No. 4 Kodak Junior

Anniversary Kodak Box

☐ **No. 3 Kodak Jr. Camera,** January 1890-1897, a relatively scarce member of the early Kodak family, factory loaded with 60 exposures 3¼ x 4¼ on rollfilm, could also be used with accessory plate back, B & L Universal lens, sector shutter, overall size: 4¼ x 5½ x 9".
.... **400.00   500.00**

☐ **No. 4 Kodak Camera,** January 1890-1897, string-set box camera, factory loaded for 48 exposures 4 x

☐ **No. 4 Kodak Jr. Camera,** January 1890-1897, similar to the Number 3 Kodak Junior Camera, but for 4 x 5", factory loaded for 48 exposures on rollfilm, B & L Universal lens, sector shutter, can also be fitted for glass plates.
.... **400.00   500.00**

☐ **Anniversay Kodak Box Camera,** a special edition of the Number 2 Brownie Kodak, issued to

commemorate the 50th anniversary of Eastman Kodak Company, approximately 400,000 were given away to children 12 years old in 1930, covered with a tan colored reptile-grained paper covering with a gold-colored foil seal on the upper rear corner of the right side, on a worn example, the gold coloring of the foil seal may have worn off and left it looking silver.
................15.00   20.00

☐ **Same as above,** *in mint condition.*
................30.00   40.00

AUTOGRAPHIC KODAK CAMERAS

The Autographic feature was introduced by Kodak in 1914, and was available on several lines of cameras. Listed here are those cameras without any key word in their name except Autographic, Kodak, or Special.

KODAK — AUTOGRAPHIC / 101

☐ **No. 1A,** for $2^{1}/_{4}$ x $4^{1}/_{4}$ exposures on No. A-116 film, RR lens f7.7/130mm., BB shutter 25-100, black leather and bellows.
................14.00   18.00

☐ **No. 3,** c. 1914-1926, $3^{1}/_{4}$ x $4^{1}/_{4}$ on 118 film, f7.7/130mm. lens, BB shutter.
................16.00   20.00

No. 3A

102 / KODAK — AUTOGRAPHIC JUNIOR

☐ **No. 3A,** c.1914-1924, 3¼ x 5½, post-card size, on 122 film, Kodak Anastigmat f7.7/170mm. Ilex or BB shutter, 25-100 seconds, this is the most common size of the Autographic Kodak Cameras.
.... 20.00   25.00

AUTOGRAPHIC KODAK JUNIOR CAMERAS

No. 1A

☐ **No. 1,** for 2¼ x 3¼ on 120 film, c. 1914-1924, Kodak Anastigmat f7.7 lens, BB shutter, 25-100, very common.
.... 10.00   15.00

☐ **No. 1A,** for 2½ x 4¼ exposures on 116 film.
.... 10.00   15.00

☐ **No. 2C,** c. 1925-1927 for 2⅞ x 4⅞, a very common size in this line.
.... 20.00   25.00

☐ **No. 3A,** 1918-1927, 3¼ x 5½" on 122.
.... 20.00   25.00

No. 2C

KODAK — AUTOGRAPHIC SPECIAL / 103

☐ **No. 2C**, *1923-1928.*
...................40.00   50.00

No. 3A

AUTOGRAPHIC KODAK SPECIAL CAMERA

No. 1A

☐ **No. 1**, *B & L lens.*
...................50.00   60.00
☐ **No. 1A**, *1914-1927, models with CRF, 1917-1928, 2½ x 4¼.*
...................60.00   75.00

☐ **No. 3**, *1914-1926, 3¼ x 4¼ on 118.*
...................20.00   30.00
☐ **No. 3A**, *1914-1927, models with CRF, 1916-1933, 3¼ x 5½ on 122.*
...................40.00   50.00
☐ **No. 3A, Model B.**
...................60.00   75.00

104 / KODAK — BANTAM

No. 3A

BANTAM CAMERA

June 1935-1941, for 28 x 40mm. exposures on 828 rollfilm.

F6.3

F5.6

- [ ] **f8,** *1938, Kodalinear f8/40mm., rectangular telescoping front rather than bellows.*
  .20.00   35.00
- [ ] **f6.3,** *1935, Kodak Anastigmat f6.3/ 53mm., collapsible bellows.*
  .20.00   25.00

F4.5

KODAK — BROWNIE / 105

- [ ] **f5.6,** *1938, Kodak Anastigmat f5.6/ 50mm., collapsible bellows.*
  ....20.00   25.00
- [ ] **f4.5,** *c. 1938, Kodak Anastigmat f4.5/ 47mm., Bantam shutter, 20-200, bellows.*
  ....20.00   25.00
- [ ] **f3.9 RF,** *c. 1953, non-interchangeable f3.9/50mm. Kodak Ektanon Anastigmat shutter 25-300, coupled rangefinder 3' to infinity.*
  ....25.00   35.00
- [ ] **Flash Bantam Camera,** *1947-1953, Kodak Anastigmat special f4.5/ 48mm., shutter 25-200, bellows, original price around $50.*
  ....25.00   30.00

Vest Pocket

BROWNIE CAMERAS

- [ ] **Bantam Special Camera,** *1936-1948, Compur rapid shutter, 1st model c. 1936-1940, is more common than the later model, c. 1941-1948, with Supermatic shutter, both models have coupled RF 3' to infinity, with Compur Rapid shutter.*
  .... 125.00   135.00
- [ ] **Same as above,** *with Supermatic shutter.*
  .... 195.00   220.00

BOY SCOUT KODAK CAMERA

- [ ] **Vest-pocket camera,** *c. 1930-1934, for 1⅝ x 2½" on 127 rollfilm, in olive drab color with official Boy Scout emblem engraved on bed.*
  ....50.00   75.00

- [ ] **No. 0,** *box, a small, 4 x 3¼ x 2½" box camera of the mid-teens for 127 film, slightly larger then the earlier "Pocket Kodak" of 1895.*
  ....15.00   20.00

106 / KODAK — BROWNIE

☐ **No. 1,** *box, introduced in February, 1900,* this box camera was made to take a new-size film, Number 117 for 2¼ x 2¼ exposures, the back of the camera fit like the cover of a shoe-box, constructed of cardboard, and measuring 3 x 3 x 5" overall, this camera lasted only four months in production before the back was re-designed, a rare box camera.
.... **500.00   600.00**

☐ **No. 1,** *box, improved, in May or June of 1900,* this improved model of the above was introduced, and became the first commercialy successful Brownie camera, although not rare, it is historically interesting.
...................**50.00   65.00**

☐ **No. 2,** *box, c. 1901,* cardboard construction, for 6 exposures 2¼ x 3¼ on 120 film, which was introduced for this camera, Meniscus lens, rotary shutter, later models even came in colors, black.
....................**4.00   6.00**

☐ **Same as above,** *colored.*
...................**10.00   14.00**

☐ **No. 2A,** *box, c. 1902,* cardboard box for 2½ x 4¼ on 116 film, some later models came in colors, black.
....................**4.00   6.00**

☐ **Same as above,** *colored.*
...................**10.00   14.00**

KODAK — BROWNIE / 107

☐ **No. 2C,** *box, c. 1916 for 2⅞ x 4⅞ on 130 film.*
.... 6.00   10.00

☐ **No. 3,** *c. 1902 for 3¼ x 4¼ on 124 film.*
.... 8.00   10.00

☐ **Beau Brownie Camera,** *c. 1930-1932, a simple Number 2 Brownie camera, box, for 120 film, but in classy two-tone color combinations.*
.... 40.00   50.00

☐ **Baby Brownie Camera,** *box c. 1937 made of brown or black plastic, for 4 x 6.5cm. exposures on 127 film.*
.... 10.00   15.00

☐ **Brownie Bullet Camera,** *c. 1957, a premium version of the Brownie Holiday Camera, 4.5 x 6cm., 1⅝ x 2½", on 127.*
.... 4.00   6.00

☐ **Brownie Bullseye Camera,** *c. 1954 for 6 x 9cm. on 620 film.*
.... 8.00   10.00

108 / KODAK — BROWNIE FOLDING

Brownie Bullseye

Brownie Flash

BROWNIE FOLDING CAMERAS

Identifiable by their square-cornered bodies and horizontal format.

- [ ] **Brownie Fiesta Camera,** c. 1962-1965.
  .... 4.00   6.00
- [ ] **Brownie Flash Camera,** 2¼ x 3¼ on 620.
  .... 4.00   6.00

Note: A special model of the No. 2 Brownie Camera was produced to celebrate the 50th Anniversary of Eastman Kodak Company. It is commonly called the Anniversary Kodak Box Camera, and is listed under "Anniv."

- [ ] **No. 2,** c. 1904, maroon bellows, wooden lens standard, for 2¼ x 3¼ on 120 film.
  .... 16.00   20.00
- [ ] **No. 3,** c. 1903, 3¼ x 4¼ on 124.
  .... 20.00   25.00
- [ ] **No. 3A,** c. 1909-1915, 3¼ x 5½ "postcard" size, maroon bellows.
  .... 20.00   25.00

KODAK — BROWNIE AUTOGRAPHIC FOLDING / 109

Folding Brownig, No. 3

Note: Of the Folding Brownie Cameras, the No. 3 and No. 3A are at least ten times more commonly found for sale than the No. 2, although prices are much the same. These cameras sell for about double the USA price in Europe.

BROWNIE AUTOGRAPHIC FOLDING CAMERAS

☐ **No. 1A.**
.................10.00   15.00

☐ **No. 2A,** c. 1921, 2½ x 4¼, the most common size of this line by far.
.................12.00   16.00

☐ **No. 2,** 2¼ x 3¼ on 120 film, c. 1916, very common.
.................12.00   16.00

☐ **No. 2C,** c. 1916, 2⅞ x 4⅞" exposures.
.................12.00   16.00

110 / KODAK — BROWNIE AUTOGRAPHIC FOLDING

No. 3A

No. 2

No. 2

No. 3A

No. 2

Brownie Hawkeye

KODAK — BROWNIE FOLDING POCKET / 111

Brownie Holiday

Brownie Reflex

Brownie Junior

☐ **No. 3A,** *c. 1916-1926, 3¼ x 5½.*
...................12.00   16.00

BROWNIE FOLDING POCKET CAMERAS

☐ **No. 2,** *introduced 1907, 2¼ x 3¼", 6 x 9cm.*
...................18.00   25.00

☐ **No. 2A,** *c. 1909, 2½ x 4¼ on 116 film, some with red bellows, some with black.*
...................20.00   25.00

☐ **No. 3,** *c. 1909, 3¼ x 4¼ on 124.*
...................20.00   30.00

Brownie Special

☐ **No. 3A,** *c. 1909, red bellows.*
...................20.00   30.00

☐ **Brownie Hawkeye Camera,** *molded plastic box camera for 6 x 6cm. exposure on 620 film.*
...................3.00   5.00

☐ **Brownie Holiday Camera,** *1953-1957, 4 x 6.5cm. exposures on 127 film.*
...................6.00   8.00

112 / KODAK — BROWNIE FOLDING POCKET

Brownie Six-16

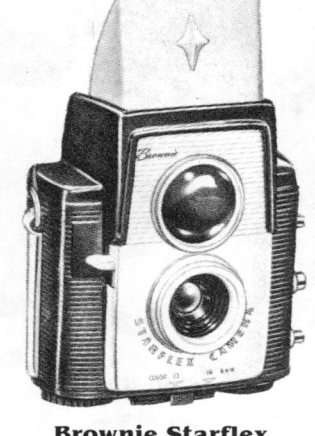

Brownie Starflex

Brownie Starlet

Brownie Six-20

- [ ] **Brownie Junior Camera,** *616 or 620 box.*
  . . . . 4.00   6.00
- [ ] **Brownie Reflex 20 Camera,** *c. 1959-1966, various models: Twin 20, Flash 20, Flashmite 20, Fiesta.*
  . . . . 4.00   6.00
- [ ] **Brownie Special Camera,** *c. 1940, trapezoid-shaped box, Six-16 or Six-20 models.*
  . . . . 4.00   6.00
- [ ] **Brownie Six-16 Camera,** *c. 1930, box.*
  . . . . 6.00   8.00
- [ ] **Brownie Six-20 Camera,** *cardboard box camera for 620 film.*
  . . . . 6.00   8.00
- [ ] **Brownie Starflex Camera,** *c. 1957-1963 for 4 x 4cm. on 127 film.*
  . . . . 6.00   8.00
- [ ] **Brownie Starlet Camera,** *c. 1956-1962 for 4 x 6.5cm. on 127, made in England.*
  . . . . 10.00   15.00
- [ ] **Brownie Starmatic Camera,** *1959-1961, 4 x 4cm. on 127 film.*
  . . . . 10.00   15.00

KODAK — BULLET / 113

Brownie Starmatic

Brownie Target

BUCKEYE CAMERA

☐ **Folding Bed Camera,** *c. 1899 when Eastman Kodak purchased the American Mfg. Co., who originated this model, the Eastman camera is nearly identical to the earlier version, all wooden construction, covered with leather, lens standard of polished wood conceals the shutter behind a plain front, an uncommon rollfilm model.*
.... 100.00   150.00

BULLET CAMERAS

☐ **Stereo Brownie Camera, No. 2,** *the successor to the Weno Stereo Camera, 1905-1910, for pairs of 3¼ x 2½" exposures on rollfilm, red bellows, Stereo Brownie Cameras are much less common than comparable Stereo Hawkeye Cameras.*
.... 225.00   240.00

☐ **Brownie Target Camera,** *616 or 620, metal and leatherette.*
.... 6.00   8.00

Bullet Camera

114 / KODAK — BULLET SPECIAL

☐ **Bullet Camera,** *plastic, cheap and simple torpedo-shaped camera with fixed focus lens mounted in a spiral-threaded telescoping mount, common, inexpensive, yet novel.*
.... 16.00   20.00

No. 2

No. 4

☐ **No. 2 Bullet Camera,** *1895-1896 and improved model, 1896-1900, box camera for 3½ x 3½ exposures on glass plates or on No. 101 rollfilm which was first introduced in 1895 for this camera, measures 4¾ x 4¾ x 6¼", some models named by year and marked on the camera.*
.... 40.00   50.00

☐ **No. 4 Bullet Camera,** *1897-1900, for 4 x 5" exposures on No. 103 rollfilm, or could be used with single plate holder which stores in the rear of the camera, a large leather box.*
.... 70.00   85.00

BULLET SPECIAL CAMERAS

Similar to the Bullet cameras No. 2 and 4, but with a higher quality RR lens in Eastman Triple Action Shutter.

☐ **No. 2.**
.... 75.00   85.00

☐ **No. 4.**
.... 100.00   125.00

BULLS-EYE KODAK CAMERAS

After Eastman took over the Boston Camera Co., they continued Boston's line of

KODAK — BULLS-EYES SPECIAL / 115

cameras under the Kodak name. *(See also Boston Bulls-Eye.)* Bulls-Eye cameras are often stamped with their year model as were other early Kodak cameras. Leather exterior conceals a beautifully polished wooden interior.

☐ **No. 4,** 1896-1904, nine models, side-loading 4 x 5" box for 103 rollfilm, internal bellows focus by means of outside lever.
................60.00   75.00

☐ **No. 2,** c. 1896-1913, leather covered wood box which loads from the top, 3½ x 3½ exposures on 103 rollfilm or double plateholders, rotary disc shutter, rotating disc stops.
................30.00   40.00

BULLS-EYE FOLDING CAMERA

☐ **No. 2,** c. 1899, for 3½ x 3½ exposures, scarce.
................130.00   150.00

BULLS-EYE SPECIAL CAMERAS

Similar to the Bulls-Eye (box) cameras, but with higher quality RR lens in Eastman Triple Action Shutter.

☐ **No. 3,** 1908-1913, this model loads from the side, 3¼ x 4¼ on No. 124 film, less common than the No. 2 and No. 4.
................40.00   50.00

116 / KODAK — CARTRIDGE

☐ **No. 2,** 3½ x 3½", c. 1898.
.... 65.00   75.00

☐ **No. 4,** 4 x 5" exposures on 103 rollfilm, c. 1896-1904.
.... 70.00   90.00

CARTRIDGE KODAK CAMERAS

Made to take "cartridge" film, as rollfilm was called in the early years.

☐ **No. 3,** c. 1900-1907, for 4¼ x 3¼ exposures on No. 119 rollfilm, which was introduced at the same time, this is the smallest of the series, Eastman Triple Action pneumatic shutter.
.... 70.00   85.00

☐ **No. 4,** c. 1897-1907, for 5 x 7" exposures on 104 rollfilm which was introduced for this camera, this is the first of the series, leather covered wood body, polished wood interior, red bellows, B&L RR lens, Kodak Automatic Shutter, original price about $25.
.... 50.00   70.00

☐ **No. 5,** c. 1898-1900, first model with wood lens board and bed, later model with metal lens board 1900-1907, for 7 x 5" exposures on No. 115 rollfilm, which was introduced in 1898 for this camera, or on plates, No. 115 rollfilm was 7" wide to provide the 7 x 5" vertical format, red bellows, Bausch & Lomb Rapid Rectilinear lens.
.... 95.00   125.00

CHEVRON

☐ **Chevron,** 1953-1956 for 2¼ x 2¼ on 620, Kodak Ektar f3.5/78mm. or Wollensak f2, synchronized Rapid 800 shutter.
.... 170.00   190.00

Chevron

CIRKUT CAMERAS, CIRKUT OUTFITS

Manufactured by the Century Camera Division of Eastman Kodak Co. beginning about 1905. Basically, a Cirkut OUTFIT is a revolving-back cycle view camera with an accessory Cirkut back, tripod, and gears. A Cirkut CAMERA is designed exclusively for Cirkut photos and cannot be used as a view camera. Both types take panoramic pictures by revolving the entire camera on a geared tripod head while the film moves past a narrow slit at the focal plane and is taken up on a drum which is connected via a pinion gear to the large stationary gear which is part of the tripod head. These cameras are commonly numbered according to film width, the common sizes being 5, 6½, 8, and 10".

Note: All prices listed here are for complete outfits with tripod and gears.

☐ **No. 5 Cirkut Camera,** with Turner Reich Triple Convertible lens.
.... 425.00   525.00

☐ **No. 6 Cirkut Camera,** Triple convertible.
.... 525.00   625.00

☐ **No. 6 Cirkut Outfit,** 5 x 7 RB Cycle Graphic, with Series II Centar lens.
.... 500.00   600.00

KODAK — DAYLIGHT / 117

☐ **Same as above,** with Graphic Rapid Rectilinear convertible 5 x 7 lens.
.... 600.00   700.00

☐ **No. 8 Cirkut Outfit,** also uses 6" film, 6½ x 8½ RB Cycle Graphic, with Triple Convertible lens.
.... 700.00   800.00

☐ **No. 10 Cirkut Camera,** also uses 6 or 8" film, with Triple Convertible lens.
.... 1250.00   1350.00

☐ **No. 16 Cirkut Camera,** also for 8, 10, or 12" film.
.... 2000.00   2500.00

DAYLIGHT KODAK CAMERAS

The Daylight Kodak Cameras are the first of the Kodak string-set cameras not requiring darkroom loading. All are rollfilm box cameras with Achromatic lens and sector shutter. Made from 1891 to 1895, each took 24 exposures on daylight-loading rollfilm.

☐ **"A",** 2¾ x 3¼", original cost $8.50.
.... 550.00   600.00

Daylight Kodak, "B"

118 / KODAK — DUAFLEX

☐ **"B",** *3½ x 4", original cost $15.00.*
.... 450.00   500.00

☐ **"C",** *4 x 5", original cost $25.00.*
.... 500.00   550.00

DUAFLEX

☐ **Duaflex,** *cheap TLR for 6 x 6cm. on 620, Models I-IV, 1949-1950, f8 Kodar lens.*
.... 6.00   8.00

DUEX

☐ **Duex,** *1940-1946 for 4.5 x 6cm. on 620 film, doublet lens.*
.... 10.00   15.00

Duex

DUO-620

☐ **Duo-620,** *1934-1937 folding camera for 16 exposures 4.5 x 6cm., 1⅝ x 2¼" on 620 film, made in Germany, f3.5/70mm. Kodak Anastigmat or Zeiss Tessar lens, Compur or Compur Rapid shutter.*
.... 50.00   60.00

KODAK — EUREKA / 119

to 1000, a precision camera which originally sold for $375 with the f1.9/50mm. lens.
.... 500.00   600.00

- [ ] **Same as above,** additional lenses: f3.5/90mm., f3.3/35mm., and f3.8/135mm.
.... 85.00   95.00

- [ ] **Same as above,** rare 153mm. lens.
.... 850.00   950.00

EUREKA

1898-1899 box camera for glass plates in standard holders which insert through side-opening door. Storage space for additional holders.

- [ ] **Duo-620 Series II,** *1937-1939, Rangefinder model 1939-1940, with Kodak Anastigmat f3.5/75mm. lens.*
.... 50.00   60.00

- [ ] **No. 2,** *3½ x 3½ exposures on plates or on Number 106 cartridge film in roll holder.*
.... 70.00   90.00

- [ ] **No. 2, Jr.,** *same size, but less expensive model when new, for plates only.*
.... 60.00   75.00

EASTMAN PLATE CAMERA

- [ ] **No. 4 Series D,** *c. 1903, 4 x 5" folding-bed cycle style plate camera with swing back more typical of some of Rochester Optical Company earlier models, double extending bellows, RR lens, Kodak shutter.*
.... 60.00   75.00

EKTRA

- [ ] **Ektra,** *35mm. RF camera c. 1940's, interchangeable lenses and magazine backs, focal plane shutter*

- [ ] **No. 4,** *made in 1899 only, for 4 x 5" exposures on Number 109 cartridge film in roll holder.*
.... 85.00   95.00

FALCON

☐ **No. 2,** *1897-1899 rollfilm box camera for 3½ x 3½" exposures on Number 101 rollfilm, knob on front of camera to cock shutter, leather covered wood.*
.................70.00   80.00

FIFTIETH ANNIVERSARY BOX CAMERA
(See Anniversary Kodak Box Camera)

FLAT FOLDING KODAK CAMERA

☐ **Flat Folding Kodak Camera,** *1895, Kodak's first folding camera with integral rollfilm back, rare, very few exist.*
.... 1200.00   1500.00

FLEXO

☐ **No. 2,** *1899-1913, box camera for 12 exposures 3½ x 3½" on Number 101 rollfilm, the most unusual feature is that the sides and back come completely off for loading, and are held together only by the leather covering, it is very similar in outward appearance to the Bulls-Eye series, but was slightly cheaper when new, the same camera was marketed in Europe under the name "Plico," achromatic lens, rotary shutter, original cost $5.00.*
...................50.00   60.00

No. 2

FLUSH BACK KODAK CAMERA

☐ **No. 3,** *c. 1902, an uncommon folding camera for 3¼ x 4¼ exposures on 118 film, or for glass plates, B & L RR lens in B & L, auto shutter.*
.... 100.00   125.00

FOLDING KODAK CAMERAS

There are two distinct styles of "Folding Kodak" cameras which share little more than a common name. The earlier models, numbered 4, 5, and 6 by size, resemble a carrying case when closed, and are easily identifiable by the hinged top door which hangs over the sides like a box cover. The later models can be distinguished from the early ones by their vertical format, rounded body ends, etc. in the more common style. We are listing the early models first, followed by the later ones.

☐ **No. 4 Folding Kodak,** *satchel-style, c. 1890-1892, improved model 1893-1897, for 48 exposures 4 x 5"*

KODAK — FOLDING POCKET / 121

on glass plates or rollfilm in rollfilm holder, non-tapered black bellows.
.... 500.00   600.00

☐ **No. 5,** similar specifications, but for 5 x 7" film or plates, B & L shutter.
.... 600.00   650.00

☐ **No. 6,** similar, but for 6½ x 8½, this size is even less common than the others.
.... 950.00   1050.00

FOLDING KODAK CAMERAS (LATER MODELS)

Actually, all but the No. 4A are Folding Pocket Kodak Cameras.

☐ **No. 1A,** c. 1902, f6.3/100mm. lens in Diomatic shutter.
.... 20.00   25.00

☐ **No. 2.**
.... 16.00   18.00

☐ **No. 3,** c. 1902, for 3¼ x 4¼ on 118 rollfilm, f5.6/130, Diomatic shutter.
.... 18.00   25.00

☐ **No. 3A,** 3¼ x 5½ on 122, f7.7/ lens in Diomatic shutter, red bellows.
.... 25.00   30.00

☐ **No. 4, Models A and B,** 1907-1914, for 4 x 5" exposures, red or black bellows, wood trim on bed, B & L RR lens, Kodak Automatic shutter.
.... 50.00   60.00

☐ **No. 4A,** April 1906-April 1915, for 6 exposures, 4¼ x 6½ on Number 126 rollfilm, 126 rollfilm was made from 1906-1949, and is not to be confused with the more recent 126 cassettes, B & L RR lens, B & L Auto shutter, red bellows.
.... 125.00   135.00

FOLDING POCKET KODAK CAMERAS

☐ **Original,** 1898-1904 for 2¼ x 3¼ exposures on Number 105 rollfilm, leather covered front pulls straight out, double finders concealed behind leather covered front, red bellows, the very earliest production models had brass struts.
.... 150.00   160.00

☐ **Same as above,** normally found with the nickeled struts indicative of later production models.
.... 60.00   70.00

☐ **No. 0,** similar in style to the original, made from 1902-1906 for 1⅝ x 2½" exposures on Number 121 film which was introduced also in 1902, it is the smallest of the series.
.... 110.00   125.00

☐ **No. 1,** 1898-1904, for 2¼ x 3¼ exposures, recognizable by the domed front door, red bellows, and the twin sprung struts for the lensboard, wooden lens standard, some models had a single finder.
.... 40.00   50.00

122 / KODAK — FOLDING POCKET

No. 1

☐ **Same as above,** *dual finders.*
.................**65.00** **75.00**

☐ **No. 1A,** *1899-1904, for 2½ x 4¼" exposures on 116 rollfilm, domed front door, twin sprung struts, red bellows, later models, lettered through D, with Pocket Automatic Shutter until 1915, original cost $12.*
.................**20.00** **40.00**

☐ **No. 2,** *1899-1903, a horizontal styled camera for square exposures 3½ x 3½ on Number 101 rolls, this model did not have a self-erecting front, as the two previous listings, bed folds down, and front standard pulls out on track, first model has leather covered lensboard with recessed lens and shutter, later models have wooden standard with exposed shutter and lens.*
.................**40.00** **60.00**

☐ **No. 3,** *early models, A and AB, c. 1900-1903, vertical style folding-bed type, leather covered lensboard conceals rotary shutter, for 3¼ x 4¼ exposures on 118 rollfilm.*
.................**30.00** **40.00**

KODAK — FOLDING POCKET SPECIAL / 123

No. 3

No. 3A

No. 4

- [ ] **No. 3,** *later models, c. 1904-1915, flat rectangular front door, B&L lens and shutter.*
  ....35.00   40.00

- [ ] **No. 3A,** *1903-1908, later models to 1915, 3¼ x 5½ on 122 film, flat, rectangular front door, red bellows, polished wood insets on bed, by far the most common model of the FPK series.*
  ....10.00   12.00

- [ ] **No. 4,** *4 x 5" size on Number 123 film, c. 1906-1915, red bellows, polished wood insets on bed, f8 RR lens, No. 2 B&L or Kodak BB shutter, original cost $20-25.*
  ....50.00   60.00

FOLDING POCKET KODAK SPECIAL CAMERAS

Similar to the Folding Pocket Kodak Cameras, but fitted with a better lens, shutter, or leather covering.

124 / KODAK — GIFT

☐ **No. 1A,** c. 1900-1912, 116 film, red leather bellows, RR lens and Kodak shutter.
..................50.00   60.00

☐ **Same as above,** with Cooke or Zeiss-Kodak Anastigmat lens in Compound shutter.
..................50.00   80.00

☐ **No. 3A,** with Zeiss-Kodak Anastigmat f6.3 in Compound shutter.
..................60.00   75.00

GIFT KODAK CAMERA

☐ **Gift Kodak Camera,** c. 1930-1931, a No. 1A Pocket Kodak Camera for 2½ x 4¼" exposures on Number 116 film, but in a special rendition, the camera is covered with brown genuine leather, and decorated with an enameled metal inlay on the front door, as well as a matching metal faceplate on the shutter, the case is a cedar box, the top plate of which repeats the art-deco design of the camera, original price in the 1930 Christmas season was just $15.00, camera only.
.... 125.00   135.00

☐ **Same as above,** with gift box.
.... 350.00   400.00

Gift Kodak

GIRL SCOUT KODAK CAMERA

☐ **Girl Scout Kodak Camera,** 1919-1934, for 1⅝ x 2½" on 127 film, bright green color with official GSA emblem engraved on bed.
................75.00   95.00

HAWKETTE

☐ **No. 2,** c. 1930's British made folding Kodak camera for 2¼ x 3¼ exposures on 120 rollfilm, folding style like the Houghton Ensignette with cross-swinging struts, body of bakelite plastic, black.
................10.00   12.00

☐ **Same as above,** colored.
................15.00   20.00

HAWKEYE CAMERAS

The Hawkeye line originated with the Blair Camera Co. and was continued by Kodak after they absorbed the Blair Co. *(See also Blair Hawkeye.)*

HAWKEYE, CARTRIDGE

☐ **Box camera No. 2,** 2¼ x 3¼ c. 1924-1930.
................10.00   12.00

☐ **Box camera No. 2A,** 2½ x 4¼, c. 1924-1930.
................10.00   12.00

HAWKEYE, FILM PACK

☐ **No. 2,** c. 1899-1916, box camera for 2¼ x 3¼ film packs, all metal construction.
................12.00   15.00

HAWKEYE, FOLDING CARTRIDGE

☐ **No. 2,** c. 1913-1930, 2¼ x 3¼ on 120 film, Kodex shutter.
................15.00   20.00

☐ **No. 2A,** 1913-1930, 2½ x 4¼ on 116 film, single Achromatic or RR lens.
................15.00   20.00

☐ **No. 3A,** 1913-1933, 3¼ x 5½ on 122 film, Kodex shutter, RR or Achromatic lens.
................25.00   30.00

HAWKEYE, FOLDING FILM PACK

☐ **No. 2,** c. 1923, Hawkeye shutter, Meniscus Achromatic lens, 2¼ x 3¼ exposures on film packs.
................16.00   20.00

HAWKEYE, FOLDING

☐ **No. 1,** 2¼ x 3¼.
................25.00   30.00

☐ **No. 1A,** 1913-1915, 2½ x 4¼, red bellows, various lens/shutter combinations, with Meniscus Achromat or RR lens in Kodak Ball Bearing shutter.
................15.00   20.00

☐ **Same as above,** with Zeiss-Kodak Anastigmat or Tessar IIB lens in Compound shutter.
................25.00   35.00

☐ **No. 2,** c. 1930-1940, 2¼ x 3¼ exposures on 120 film.
................15.00   20.00

☐ **No. 2A,** c. 1917, Kodex shutter.
................15.00   20.00

☐ **No. 3,** various models 1904-1915, 3¼ x 4¼ on 118 film, horizontal format.
................25.00   30.00

☐ **No. 3A,** various models 1908-1915, 3¼ x 5½ on 122 film, horizontal format.
................25.00   30.00

☐ **Folding Hawkeye Six-16 and Six-20,** c. 1933-1934, original price $9-16 depending on lens and shutter.
................20.00   30.00

☐ **Folding Hawkeye Special,** 1930, Kodex shutter, Kodak Anastigmat, f6.3 lens.
................20.00   25.00

RAINBOW HAWKEYE CAMERAS

In Green, Red, Brown, Black, or Blue. (Box cameras.)

- ☐ **No. 2,** *1931-1932, same as No. 2 Cartridge Hawkeye, but in colors.*
  .... 15.00   20.00
- ☐ **No. 2A,** *same, but in 2½ x 4¼ size.*
  .... 15.00   20.00

HAWKEYE, FOLDING RAINBOW

This series, made in 1931 and 1932 is similar to the regular Folding Hawk-eye series, but in colors.

- ☐ **No. 2,** *for 120 film, Kodex shutter, single or double lens.*
  .... 25.00   35.00
- ☐ **No. 2A,** *same, but for 2½ x 4¼", 6.5 x 11cm., on 116 film.*
  .... 30.00   40.00
- ☐ **No. 2 and 2A Special.**
  .... 30.00   35.00

HAWKEYE SPECIAL

- ☐ **No. 2 and 2A,** *1928-1930 rollfilm box cameras, f6.3 lens.*
  .... 15.00   20.00

HAWKEYE, STEREO

- ☐ **Stereo Hawkeye,** *a continuation of the Blair Stereo Hawkeye series, and labeled "Blair Division of Eastman Kodak Company," a folding stereo camera taking twin 3½ x 3½ exposures, various models 1904-1914 numbered in sequence, B & L RR lenses in Hawkeye shutter, mahogany interior, brass trim, red bellows.*
  .... 200.00   240.00
- ☐ **Target Hawkeye,** *No. 2, 2A, Six-16, Six-20 box cameras.*
  .... 5.00

- ☐ **Same as above,** *colored models.*
  .... 15.00   20.00
- ☐ **Vest Pocket Hawkeye,** *c. 1927-1931, with single or double lens.*
  .... 25.00   30.00
- ☐ **Weno Hawkeye,** *box cameras of various sizes: No. 2 for 3½ x 3½, No. 4 for 4 x 5", No. 5 for 3¼ x 4¼, No. 7 for 3¼ x 5½, etc.*
  .... 25.00   35.00

HOLIDAY, HOLIDAY FLASH
(See Eastman/Brownie Holiday)

JIFFY KODAK CAMERAS

Common rollfilm cameras with pop-out front with twin sprung struts. Twindar lens, zone focus.

- ☐ **Six-16,** *1933-1946, 2½ x 4¼ on 616.*
  .... 15.00   20.00
- ☐ **Six-20,** *1937-1939, 2¼ x 3¼ on 620.*
  .... 12.00   15.00
- ☐ **Vest Pocket,** *1935-1942, 1⅝ x 2½ on 127, black plastic construction.*
  .... 12.00   15.00

KODAK — KODET / 127

Note also: Two of Eastman's first cameras bore the name Junior along with their number. They are the No. 3 Kodak Jr., and the No. 4 Kodak Jr. Both are box cameras with string-set shutters, and are listed at the beginning of the Eastman Kodak section.

Six-20

Vest Pocket

KODAK JUNIOR CAMERAS

(See also "Autographic Kodak Jr." under the Eastman heading.)

☐ **No. 1,** c. 1914, 2¼ x 3¼ on 120 film, f7.7 Anastigmat lens.
................16.00   20.00
☐ **No. 1A,** c. 1914, 2½ x 4¼ on 116.
................12.00   15.00
No. 2C
(See Autographic Kodak Junior Cameras.)
No. 3A
(See Autographic Kodak Junior Cameras.)

KODET CAMERAS

☐ **No. 4 Kodet Camera,** 1894-1897, for 4 x 5" plates or rollfilm holder, leather covered wood box, front face hinges down to reveal brass-barrel lens and shutter, focusing lever at side of camera.
.... 135.00   150.00

128 / KODAK — MEDALIST

Kodak Junior, No. 1A

No. 4

☐ **No. 4 Folding Kodet Camera,** *folding-bed camera c. 1894 for 4 x 5 plates or special rollholder, basically cube-shaped when closed, very similar in appearance to the Blair Folding Hawkeye, variable speed shutter built into wooden lens standard, brass barrel lens with rotating disc stops.*
.... 150.00   185.00

MEDALIST CAMERAS

For 2¼ x 3¼ on 620 film, Ektar f3.5/100mm.

☐ **Medalist I,** *1941-1946, no flash sync, Supermatic shutter to 400, B. split image RF.*
.... 140.00   165.00

☐ **Medalist II,** *1946-1952, Flash Supermatic shutter.*
.... 180.00   200.00

MONITOR

☐ **Folding Rollfilm Camera Six-16,** *1939-1946, for 2½ x 4¼ on 616 film, f4.5/127 mm. in Supermatic shutter, 10-400, the less common of the two models.*
.................35.00   45.00

KODAK — NAGEL / 129

Medalist Camera II

Monitor, Folding Rollfilm, Six-20

Six-16

- [ ] **Folding Rollfilm Camera Six-20,** 1939-1946, 2½ x 3¼ on 620 film.
  ....**30.00** **40.00**

MOTORMATIC 35

- [ ] **Motormatic 35,** 1960-1969 35 mm. camera with spring-motor film advance, Ektanar f2.8/44mm., Auto Flash shutter 40-250, sync.
  ....**50.00** **60.00**

Motormatic 35

NAGEL CAMERAS

These cameras were made by Kodak A. G. (formerly the Dr. August Nagel Works) in Stuttgart.

- [ ] **Kodak Junior Six-20,** f7.7 Kodak lens in Compur shutter.
  ....**30.00** **35.00**

  Nagel Pupille, see Pupille.

ORDINARY KODAK CAMERAS

A series of cheap Kodak cameras made from 1891-1895. They were called "Ordinary" to distinguish them from the Daylight, Folding, Junior and Regular Kodaks, as they were called at that time. All are made for 24 exposures on rollfilm. All have Achromatic lens, sector shutter. They differ only in size and price.

- ☐ **"A"**, 2¾ x 3¼, original cost: $6.
  . . . . 1500.00   1600.00
- ☐ **"B"**, 3½ x 4", original cost: $10.
  . . . . 1000.00   1200.00
- ☐ **"C"**, 4 x 5", original cost: $15.
  . . . . 950.00   1150.00

PANORAM KODAK CAMERAS

A series of rollfilm panoramic cameras in which the lens pivots and projects the image to the curved focal plane. Although designed basically for wide views, it could also be used vertically.

- ☐ **No. 1 Panoram Kodak Camera,** April 1900-1914, for 2¼ x 7" exposures on No. 105 rollfilm for an angle of 112 degrees, original cost: $10, Model A.
  . . . . 240.00   260.00
- ☐ **Same as above,** Models B, C, and D.
  . . . . 200.00   225.00

- ☐ **No. 3A,** 1926-1928, takes 3¼ x 10⅜ exposures on 122 rollfilm, this is the least common of the series, having been made for only two years.
  . . . . 209.00

- ☐ **No. 4,** original model, 1899-1900, has no door to cover the swinging lens, for 3½ x 12" on No. 103 rollfilm, 142 degree angle, Rapid Rectilinear lens, original cost: $20.
  . . . . 375.00   450.00

POCKET KODAK CAMERAS

Except for the first camera listed here, the Pocket Kodak cameras are of the common folding rollfilm variety.

☐ Same as above, *later models of the No. 4 (B, C, and D) made through 1924, same as original model, but have door over lens.*
.... 200.00   225.00

PETITE

☐ **Petite,** *1929-1934, a Kodak Vest Pocket, Model B in colors, for 1⅝ x 2½" on 127, Meniscus lens, rotary shutter.*
.... 65.00   75.00

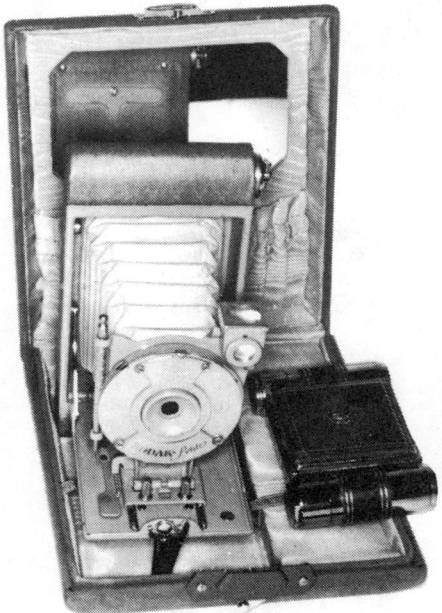

☐ **Same as above,** *also was available as the Kodak Ensemble, with matching lipstick, compact and mirror, current value for a complete Ensemble.*
.... 600.00   750.00

PLICO
(See EKC Flexo)

☐ **The Pocket Kodak,** *c. 1895-1900, a tiny box camera for 1½ x 2" exposures on No. 102 rollfilm, which was first introduced in 1895 for this camera, there are two models: one has the shutter mounted on the inside of the camera, and it is removed when loading film, the other model, which is less common, has*

132 / KODAK — POCKET

the shutter mounted on a separate board, both types could also be used with auxiliary plateholder, single lens, rotary shutter, pebble-grained leather.
.... 95.00   135.00

Pocket Kodak Cameras (folding types)
All of these incorporate the Autographic feature, but the word Autographic does not form part of the name.

No. 1, Series II

No. 1A

- ☐ **No. 1 Pocket Kodak Camera,** *May 1926-1931, 2¼ x 3¼ on 120, f7.9 Kodar lens in Kodex shutter.*
  .... 15.00   20.00
- ☐ **No. 1, Series II,** *1922-1924.*
  .... 15.00   20.00
- ☐ **No. 1A,** *c. 1926-1931, 2½ x 4¼ on 116 film, folding bed style.*
  .... 12.00   15.00
- ☐ **No. 1A, Series II,** *1923-1931.*
  .... 10.00   12.00
- ☐ **No. 1A,** *colored models, 1929-1931.*
  .... 20.00   25.00

KODAK — POCKET JUNIOR / 133

No. 1A, Series II

☐ **No. 3A,** *1927-1933, 3¼ x 5½ on 122.*
..................25.00   30.00

POCKET KODAK JUNIOR CAMERAS

☐ **No. 2C,** *1925-1932, 2⅞ x 4⅞ exposures on 130 film, Kodar f7.9, Kodex shutter.*
..................20.00   25.00

☐ **No. 3,** *1926-1934, 3¼ x 4¼ on 118.*
..................10.00   12.00

Pocket Kodak Junior, No. 1

134 / KODAK — POCKET SPECIAL

☐ **No. 1,** *1929-1931, 2¼ x 3¼ on 120 film, Meniscus Achromatic lens, Kodamatic shutter.*
.................18.00   20.00

☐ **No. 1,** *colored models.*
.................25.00   30.00

☐ **No. 1A,** *1929-1931, 2½ x 4¼ on 116 film, Achromatic lens, Kodamatic shutter, black.*
.................18.00   25.00

☐ **Same as above,** *colored models.*
.................30.00   35.00

POCKET KODAK SPECIAL CAMERAS

☐ **No. 1A,** *1926-1934, 2½ x 4¼ on 116.*
.................25.00   30.00

☐ **No. 3,** *1926-1934, 3¼ x 4¼ on 118 film, with f4.5, 5.6, or 6.3 Kodak Anastigmat lens.*
.................30.00   35.00

No. 1A

No. 3

KODAK — PREMO / 135

PONY CAMERAS

Pony Camera, II

Pony Camera, IV

Pony Camera, 135

☐ **II,** *1957-1962, for 24 x 36mm. exposures on 35mm. film, non-interchangeable Kodak Anastigmat f3.9/44mm., bakelite body.*
.................15.00   20.00

Pony Camera, 828

☐ **IV,** *1957-1961, 35mm. film, f3.5/44mm. Kodak Anastigmat "Kodak Flash 250" shutter.*
.................12.00   15.00

☐ **135,** *the first model for 35mm. film, 1950-1954, Models B and C through 1958, non-interchangeable Kodak Anastigmat f4.5/51mm. lens or f3.5/44mm. lens in focusing mount.*
.................12.00   15.00

☐ **828,** *1949-1959, the first in this series, it took No. 828 film, easily distinguished from the later 35mm. models by the lack of a rewind knob on the top right side of the camera next to the shutter release.*
.................12.00   15.00

PREMO CAMERAS

The Premo line was taken over by Kodak from the Rochester Optical Company, and was a very popular line of cameras. Cameras are listed here by size, since many models did not carry any model designation, and their identity is lost to all but an expert. *See also Rochester for earlier models.*

☐ **2¼ x 3¼,** *c. 1916-1922, such as Premo No. 12, folding cameras for packs or plates, various shutter/lens combinations.*
.................40.00   50.00

☐ **3¼ x 4¼ size.**
.................35.00   45.00

KODAK — PREMO CARTRIDGE

- ☐ 3¼ x 5½, "postcard" size cameras, such as No. 1, No. 8, or No. 9, B & L lens, BB shutter, red bellows, black leather covered.
  .... 45.00   55.00
- ☐ 4 x 5 size, including No. 8, and Sr. models, box or folding bed styles, RR lens, BB shutter.
  .... 40.00   50.00
- ☐ 5 x 7", including No. 9, and Sr. Special, Protar lens, Compur shutter, red bellows.
  .... 80.00   90.00

PREMO CARTRIDGE CAMERAS

- ☐ **No. 00**, c. 1916, simple box camera for exposures 1¼ x 1¾ on rollfilm, Meniscus lens.
  .... 40.00   50.00
- ☐ **No. 2**, c. 1918 rollfilm box for 2¼ x 3¼.
  .... 10.00   15.00
- ☐ **No. 2A**, similar but 2½ x 4¼" format.
  .... 20.00   25.00
- ☐ **Film Premo No. 1**, 1906-1916, wood-bodied folding bed camera for filmpacks, various sizes: 3¼ x 4¼ through 5 x 7, simple lens, BB shutter.
  .... 30.00   35.00
- ☐ **Film-Pack Premo**, box, 1903-1908, made in 3¼ x 4¼ and 4 x 5" sizes, Achromatic lens in Automatic shutter.
  .... 20.00   25.00
- ☐ **Film-Plate Premo**, c. 1910, folding camera for plates or packs, 3¼ x 4¼, 3¼ x 5½, or 4 x 5" sizes.
  .... 45.00   50.00
- ☐ **Film-Plate Premo Special**, 1912-1916, similar to above, but with Zeiss-Kodak Anastigmat or Tessar f6.3 lens in Compound or Optimo shutter, common sizes: 3¼ x 4¼ or 3¼ x 5½.
  .... 60.00   75.00

PREMO FOLDING CARTRIDGE CAMERAS

Folding-bed rollfilm cameras. Listed by size:

- ☐ **No. 2**, 2¼ x 3¼ on 120, RR lens, BB shutter.
  .... 10.00   12.00
- ☐ **No. 2A**, 2½ x 4¼ on 116, RR & BB.
  .... 10.00   12.00
- ☐ **No. 2C**, 2⅞ x 4⅞ on 130, RR & BB.
  .... 12.00   15.00
- ☐ **No. 3**, 3¼ x 4¼ on 124 film, RR & BB.
  .... 15.00   20.00
- ☐ **No. 3A**, 3¼ x 5½ on 122 film, RR & BB.
  .... 12.00   15.00

PREMO JUNIOR CAMERAS

Filmpack box cameras.

- ☐ **No. 0**, 1911-1916, 1¼ x 2⅜".
  .... 16.00   18.00
- ☐ **No. 1**, 1909-1916, 2¼ x 3¼".
  .... 12.00   15.00
- ☐ **No. 3**, 1909-1919, 3¼ x 4¼".
  .... 15.00   20.00
- ☐ **No. 4**, 1909-1914, 4 x 5".
  .... 20.00   25.00

PREMO, LONG-FOCUS
(See Rochester Optical)

POCKET PREMO CAMERAS

- ☐ **Pocket Premo**, 2¼ x 3¼, folding bed style camera with self-erecting front, made to take film packs only.
  .... 25.00   30.00
- ☐ **Pocket Premo C**, c. 1904-1916, for 3¼ x 5½" exposures on plates, B & L f8/6¼" lens in Kodak BB shutter, black bellows.
  .... 30.00   35.00

PONY PREMO CAMERAS

Folding plate cameras, Models A, C, D, E, 1, 2, 3, 4, 5, 6, and 7. Model numbers not related to size, so we have listed them here by size only, which determines value.

- [ ] **4 x 5"**, *B & L RR lens, Victor or Unicum shutter, all wood interior, red bellows.*
  ....**45.00**   **50.00**
- [ ] **5 x 7"**, *B & L Auto shutter, B & L or Goerz Dagor lens.*
  ....**70.00**   **85.00**
- [ ] **6½ x 8½**, *much less common.*
  ....**100.00**   **150.00**
- [ ] **Premo Senior** *6½ x 8½, red bellows.*
  ....**100.00**   **125.00**
- [ ] **Star Premo,** *c. 1903-1908, 4 x 5", various shutter/lens combinations.*
  ....**50.00**   **55.00**

PREMOETTE CAMERAS

The normal Premoette cameras, I, IA, and Special, are leather-covered wood-bodied "cycle" style cameras in vertical format.

- [ ] **No. 1,** *1906-1908, an inexpensive compact 2¼ x 3¼ film pack camera, Automatic shutter, Meniscus lens.*
  ....**35.00**   **40.00**
- [ ] **No. 1A,** *c. 1909-1912, 2½ x 4¼ filmpacks, otherwise like No. 1.*
  ....**25.00**   **35.00**

PREMOETTE JUNIOR CAMERAS

Leather covered aluminum bodied folding bed cameras. The bed folds down, but not a full 90 degrees. There is no track on the bed, but the front standard fits into one of several slots at the front of the bed for different focusing positions. Normal models have Achromatic lens.

- [ ] **Premoette Jr. (no number),** *c. 1911.*
  ....**20.00**   **25.00**
- [ ] **Premoette Jr. No. 1,** *c. 1912-1922, for 2¼ x 3¼ filmpacks, like the original model.*
  ....**25.00**   **30.00**
- [ ] **No. 1 Special,** *1913-1918, with Kodak Anastigmat f6.3 lens.*
  ....**30.00**   **35.00**
- [ ] **No. 1A,** *1912-1916, 2½ x 4¼.*
  ....**30.00**   **35.00**
- [ ] **No. 1A Special,** *Kodak Anastigmat f6.3.*
  ....**35.00**   **40.00**

Note: These cameras, although not terribly uncommon in the USA, are currently worth about double the US price in Europe.

PREMOETTE SENIOR CAMERAS

- [ ] **Premoette Senior Cameras,** *c. 1915-1922, similar in design to the Premoette Jr. models, various sizes including 3¼ x 5½, the 3¼ x 5½ size was not made in the other Premoette models.*
  ....**25.00**   **30.00**

PUPILLE

138 / KODAK — QUICK FOCUS

☐ **Pupille,** *1932-1934, made in Germany by the Nagel Works, Stuttgart, for 3 x 4cm. exposures on 127 film, Schneider Xenon f2/45mm. Compur shutter 1-300, rangefinder.*
.... **275.00   300.00**

QUICK FOCUS KODAK

☐ **Camera, No. 3B,** *1906-1911, box camera for 3¼ x 5½ exposures on No. 125 film, Achromatic lens, rotary shutter, original cost: $12.00, an unusual focusing box camera, focus knob on side of camera is set to proper focal distance, upon pressing a button, the camera opens, front pops straight out, to proper distance, focused and ready.*
.... **125.00   140.00**

RECOMAR CAMERAS

1932-1940. Kodak's entry into the crowd of popular compact folding long-extension precision view cameras. Made in Germany by the Nagel Works.

☐ **Model 18,** *2¼ x 3¼, Kodak Anastigmat f4.5/105mm. in Compur shutter.*
.... **60.00   75.00**

☐ **Model 33,** *3¼ x 4¼, similar, but 135mm. lens, more common than the smaller model.*
.... **60.00   75.00**

Model 18

Model 33

REFLEX KODAK CAMERAS

☐ **Kodak Reflex Cameras,** *f3.5 Anastigmat in Flash Kodamatic shutter, Models I, 1946-1948 and II, 1948-1954.*
.... **40.00   50.00**

KODAK — REGULAR / 139

Kodak Reflex

REGENT

☐ **Regent,** c. 1935, made by the Nagel Works in Stuttgart, Germany, 6 x 9cm., 2¼ x 3¼", on 620 film, Schneider Xenar f3.5/105mm. lens, Compur shutter, 1-250, coupled rangefinder.
.... 225.00   275.00

REGULAR KODAK

"Regular" is the term used in early Kodak advertising to distinguish the No. 2, 3, and 4 "string-set" Kodak cameras from the "Junior", "Folding", "Daylight", and "Ordinary" models. The "Regular Kodak" cameras are listed at the beginning of the Eastman section, where we have called them by their simple original names, No. 2, 3, and 4 Kodak cameras.

Kodak Reflex

Regent

140 / KODAK — RETINA

RETINA CAMERAS
Germany

A series of 35mm. cameras.

- **Retina,** *original model, 1934-1937, Xenar f3.5/50mm.*
  ....80.00   90.00

- **Model I,** *1936-1950, compact folding camera with Ektar f3.5 or Xenar f3.5 in Compur shutter, non-rangefinder type.*
  ....70.00   90.00

- **Model IA,** *similar, but shutter cocking mechanism coupled to film transport, Xenar f2.8 or 3.5, or Ektar f3.5, Compur Rapid or Synchro Compur shutter.*
  ....65.00   75.00

- **Model IB.**
  ....80.00   95.00

- **Model II,** *1937-1950, coupled rangefinder, Xenon, Ektar, or Rodenstock f2.*
  ....60.00   70.00

- **Model IIa,** *single window view/range finder, shutter cocking coupled to film advance, synch shutter, Xenon f2.*
  ....75.00   85.00

- **Model IIc,** *single stroke film advance, Xenon f2.8/50mm.*
  .... 100.00   120.00

- **Model IIIc,** *BIM, f2/50mm. lens.*
  .... 120.00   135.00

- **Model IIIC.**
  .... 135.00   160.00

KODAK — RETINETTE / 141

- **Model IIIs,** *1959-1961, non-folding type, Retina Xenon f1.9 or 2.8, Synchronized Compur.*
  ....80.00   95.00
- **Automatic I,** *c. 1960, f2.8/45mm.*
  ....65.00   80.00
- **Automatic III,** *c. 1960, Xenar f2.8/45mm., Compur 30-500.*
  ....70.00   85.00

RETINA REFLEX CAMERAS

- **Retina Reflex,** *c. 1958-1959 SLR, Xenon f2 or f2.8/50mm., Synchronized Compur 1-500.*
  ....80.00   90.00
- **Reflex-S,** *Xenon f1.9 or 2.8, Synchronized Compur.*
  ....80.00   95.00
- **Reflex III,** *f1.9 or 2.8 Synchronized Compur.*
  .... 100.00   120.00
- **Reflex IV,** *f1.9 or 2.8 Synchronized Compur.*
  .... 125.00   135.00

RETINETTE CAMERAS

- **Retinette, original model,** *folding 35mm. camera with self-erecting front, horizontal style, not like other folding Retina cameras, c. 1939, f6.3/50mm. Kodak Anastigmat.*
  ....55.00   70.00
- **Retinette II,** *vertical style folding 35mm. camera with self-erecting front, Schneider Anastigmat f4.5/50mm., c. 1940's.*
  ....65.00   75.00
- **Retinette IA,** *non-folding type, Schneider Reomar f2.8, 3.5, or 4.5 lens.*
  ....50.00   65.00

Model II

Model IIIC

SCREEN FOCUS KODAK CAMERAS

The first cameras to provide for the use of ground glass focus on a rollfilm camera. The rollfilm holder hinges up to allow focusing.

☐ **No. 4,** *1904-1909, for 4 x 5" exposures on No. 123 film, which was introduced at the same time, RR lens, Kodak Automatic shutter.*
.... 300.00   350.00

SIGNET CAMERAS

A series of cameras for 24 x 36mm. exposures on 35mm. film.

☐ **Signet 30,** *1957-1959, Ektanar f2.8/ 44mm. Anastigmat, CRF, Sync. shutter 4-250.*
.... 35.00   40.00

☐ **Signet 35,** *1951-1958, Ektar f3.5/ 44mm. in Kodak Synchro 300 shutter, CRF, double exposure prevention.*
.... 30.00   35.00

☐ **Signet, Signal Corps Model,** *special edition made for the U.S. Army Signal Corps, black satin finish, and no serial number on the body.*
.... 140.00   160.00

☐ **Signet 40,** *1956-1959, Ektanon Anastigmat f3.5/46mm. Kodak Synchro 400 shutter.*
.... 30.00   40.00

KODAK — SIX-16 / 143

☐ **Signet 50,** *1957-1960, BIM.*
................40.00   55.00

☐ **Signet 80,** *1958-1962, interchangeable f2.8/50mm. Ektanar in bayonet mount, Synchro 250 shutter, CRF, BIM, originally $130.*
................60.00   75.00

SIX-16 KODAK CAMERAS

A whole series of cameras of the 1930's for 2½ x 4¼" exposures on 616 rollfilm. Model names include:

☐ **Six-16.**
................20.00   25.00
☐ **Junior Six-16, Series I, II and III.**
................20.00   25.00
☐ **Senior Six-16.**
................20.00   25.00

Kodak Six-16

☐ **Six-16 Special,** *1937-1939, Kodak Anastigmat Special lens f4.5/127mm., Compur Rapid shutter, 1-400, T, B.*
................50.00   60.00

SIX-20 KODAK CAMERAS

Another whole series of cameras of the 1930's for 2¼ x 3¼ exposures on 620 film.

☐ Six-20.
.................15.00   18.00

☐ Junior Six-20, Series I, II, and III.
.................15.00   18.00
☐ Senior Six-20.
.................15.00   18.00

☐ Six-20 Special, *1937-1939, f4.5/ Kodak Anastigmat lens, Compur Rapid shutter.*
.................40.00   50.00

Super Six-20, *see Super.*

SPECIAL KODAK CAMERAS

☐ No. 1A Special Kodak Camera, *1912-1914, Zeiss-Kodak f6.3, compound shutter.*
.................80.00   95.00

☐ No. 3, *1911-1914, for 3¼ x 4¼ on 118 film, f6.3 Kodak Anastigmat in B & L Compound shutter.*
.................45.00   55.00

☐ No. 3A, *1910-1914, like the others of the series, this is a folding rollfilm camera, but this is for 3¼ x 5½ postcard-size photos, Kodak Anastigmat lens in B & L Compound shutter.*
.................75.00   90.00

KODAK — STEREO / 145

Kodak, No. 3 Special

No. 1A

Kodak, No. 3A Special

SPEED KODAK CAMERAS

- [ ] **No. 1A,** *April 1909-1913, for 2½ x 4¼ on 116 rollfilm, focal plane shutter to 1000, Zeiss, B & L, and Cooke lenses available.*
  . . . . **150.00   200.00**

- [ ] **No. 4A,** *1903-1913, for 4¼ x 6½" exposures on No. 126 film, No. 126 rollfilm, made from 1906-1949, focal plane shutter to 1000, Zeiss, Bausch & Lomb, Cooke, or Goerz lens.*
  . . . . **300.00   425.00**

STEREO KODAK CAMERAS

(See also Brownie Stereo and Hawkeye Stereo in the Eastman section.)

146 / KODAK — SUPER SIX-20

☐ **Stereo Kodak Camera, Model 1,** *original model 1917-1918, Ball Bearing Shutter model, 1919-1925, folding camera for 3⅛ x 3³⁄₁₆" pairs on No. 101 rollfilm, Kodak Anastigmat f7.7/130mm. lens.*
.... **200.00   350.00**

☐ **No. 2 Stereo Kodak,** *box camera, 1901-1905, for stereo exposures 3½ x 6" on No. 101 rolls, Periscopic f14/125mm. lens.*
.... **400.00   500.00**

☐ **Kodak Stereo Camera, 35mm.,** *1954-1959, for pairs of 24 x 24mm. exposures on standard 35mm. cartridge film, Kodak Anaston f3.5/ 35mm. lenses, shutter 25-200, common.*
.... **100.00   125.00**

SUPER KODAK SIX-20 CAMERA

☐ **Super Kodak Six-20 Camera,** *1938-1945, the first camera with coupled electric-eye for automatic exposure setting, takes 2¼ x 3¼ exposures on 620 film, Kodak Anastigmat Special lens, f4.5.*
.... **1250.00   1600.00**

KODAK 35 CAMERAS

☐ **Kodak 35 Camera,** *1938-1951 for 24 x 36mm. exposures on 35mm. cartridge film, five models with different shutter/lens combinations.*
.... **25.00   30.00**

☐ **Kodak 35 Camera with Rangefinder,** *1940-1951, various models.*
.... **25.00   30.00**

☐ **Kodak Automatic 35 Camera,** *c. late 1950's, Ektanar f2.8/44mm., Synchro 80 shutter.*
.... **40.00   50.00**

KODAK — TOURIST / 147

Kodak 35

Kodak 35

Tourist

Tourist II

TOURIST

☐ **Tourist,** *1948-1951, folding camera for 2¼ x 3¼ on 620 film, Kodak Anaston f8.8, 6.3, or 4.5 lenses.*
................20.00   25.00

☐ **Same as above,** *with Synchro-Rapid 800 shutter.*
................55.00   70.00

☐ **Tourist II,** *1951-1958, similar.*
................20.00   25.00

☐ **Same as above,** *with Synchro-Rapid 800 shutter.*
................50.00   60.00

148 / KODAK — VANITY
VANITY KODAK CAMERA

Vanity Kodak Ensemble

- ☐ **Vanity Kodak Camera,** *1928-1933, a Vest Pocket Kodak, Series III camera in color, for 1⅝ x 2½" exposures on 127 rollfilm, camera only.*
  ....75.00   85.00
- ☐ **Same as above,** *with deluxe case.*
  ....175.00   190.00
- ☐ **Vanity Kodak Ensemble,** *with lipstick, compact, mirror, and change pocket.*
  ....650.00   750.00

VEST POCKET KODAK CAMERAS

All cameras listed here are for 1⅝ x 2½" exposures on 127 film.

- ☐ **Vest Pocket Kodak Camera,** *1912-1914, painted metal or leather covered models, Autographic models 1915-1926, Model B and Model B Series III, including Autographic 1925-1934.*
  ....25.00   30.00

Vest Pocket Kodak

- ☐ **Vest Pocket Kodak Special Cameras,** *including Autographic Special, and Autographic Model B Special, 1912-1934.*
  ....30.00   40.00

KODAK — VIGILANT / 149

they are listed here as good second-hand cameras, the main value being their lenses. Prices given here are for cameras in Very Good condition, no lens.

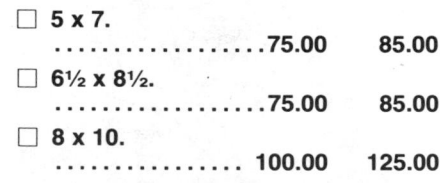

- [ ] 5 x 7.
  ....75.00   85.00
- [ ] 6½ x 8½.
  ....75.00   85.00
- [ ] 8 x 10.
  .... 100.00   125.00

VIGILANT CAMERAS

A series of cameras c. 1939-1948. Folding cameras for rollfilm in two sizes: 2½ x 4¼ on 116 film, and 2¼ x 3¼ on 620 film. Various models of each:

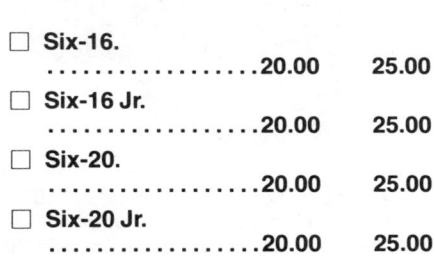

Vest Pocket Kodak

Vest Pocket Kodak Special

VIEW CAMERAS

Because of the many uses of view cameras, there are really no standard lens/shutter combinations, and because they are as much a part of the general used camera market as they are "collectible",

- [ ] Six-16.
  ....20.00   25.00
- [ ] Six-16 Jr.
  ....20.00   25.00
- [ ] Six-20.
  ....20.00   25.00
- [ ] Six-20 Jr.
  ....20.00   25.00

150 / KODAK — VOLLENDA

Six-16 Junior

VOLLENDA CAMERAS

1932-1937. Manufactured for Kodak by Nagel-Werk in Stuttgart.

☐ **127 size,** Schneider Radionar f3.5/ 50mm. Compur Rapid shutter.
................60.00   75.00

☐ **616 size,** f4.5/120mm. Radionar.
................50.00   60.00

☐ **620 size,** f4.5, 3.5, or 6.3 lens, Compur.
................30.00   45.00

WORLD'S FAIR FLASH CAMERA

☐ **World's Fair Flash Camera,** sold only at the 1964 New York World's Fair, the original box doubles the value of this camera, camera only.
................15.00   20.00

ZENITH KODAK CAMERA

☐ **No. 3,** a rare box camera for 3¼ x 4¼ plates, except for the name, it is identical to the Eureka cameras of the same period, 1898-1899, accepts standard plateholders through side-opening door, and allows room for storage of extra holders, not found often.
.... 150.00   200.00

EBNER, ALBERT & COMPANY
(Stuttgart)

- **Folding camera,** *for 8 exposures 6 x 9cm. on 120 film, bakelite body, Tessar f4.5/105mm. lens, rim-set Compur shutter 1-250, very similar to the Nagel Regent of the same vintage.*
  .... 275.00   325.00

EBONY 35
(See Hoei Industrial)

ECHO 8

- **Echo 8,** *Japanese cigarette-lighter camera, c. 1954, designed to look like a Zippo lighter, it also takes 5 x 8mm. photos with its Echor f3.5/15mm. lens on film in special cassettes.*
  .... 300.00   350.00

ECLIPSE
(See Horsman, Shew)

EDELWEISS
(See Zenith)

EDINEX
(See Wirgin)

EDIXA
(See Wirgin)

EHO
(See Hofert)

EKA
(See Krauss)

EKTRA
(See Eastman)

ELANER
(Stuttgart, Germany)

- **Elaner,** *folding camera for 120 film, Pronto shutter.*
  ....16.00   25.00

ELCA
(See Elop Camerawerk)

ELEGA
(Japan)

- **Elega,** *Leica-styled 35mm. camera, c. 1950's, f3.5 screw-mount lens, which does not interchange with Leica lenses.*
  .... 325.00   400.00

ELF
(See Spiegel)

ELJY
(See Lumiere)

ELOP KAMERAWERK
(Flensburg, Germany)

Also associated with the Uca Werkstatten of Flensburg. Makers of ELCA cameras. ELCA stands for ELop CAmera.

- **Elca,** *c. 1954, 35mm. camera with Eloca f4.5/35mm. lens, simple shutter, black painted and nickeled metal body.*
  ....40.00   50.00

EMMERLING & RICHTER
(Berlin)

- **Field Camera,** *for 13 x 18cm. plates, wooden body, nickel trim, without lens.*
  .... 100.00   125.00

EMPIRE STATE VIEW
(See View Cameras under the Eastman and Rochester headings)

EMSON

- **Emson,** *Japanese novelty camera, 14 x 14mm. exposures on 16mm. paper backed rollfilm.*
  ....10.00   15.00

ENCORE DELUXE CAMERA

- **Encore Deluxe Camera,** c. 1940's-1950's, an inexpensive cardboard novelty camera, factory loaded, user returns complete camera and film to factory with $1.00 for processing, vaguely reminiscent of the "You push the button..." idea which made Eastman rich and famous, but it didn't work.
  ....12.00   15.00

ENOLDE

- **Enolde,** 3¼ x 4¼ sheet film camera, f4.5/135 lens.
  ....50.00   60.00

ENSIGN, ENSIGNETTE
(See Houghton)

ERGO
(See Contessa-Nettel, Zeiss)

ERKO

- **Erko,** 2 x 12cm. folding plate camera, wood body covered with black leather, H. Bauer & Sons Splendar f4.5/135 lens, Ibso shutter, T, B, 1-150.
  ....50.00   60.00

ERMANOX
(See Ernemann)

ERNEMANN
(Heinrich Ernemann Werke Aktien Gesellschaft, Dresden, Germany)

Merged with Contessa-Nettel, Goerz, Ica, and Carl Zeiss Optical Company to form Zeiss-Ikon. This merger took place in 1926, and some Ernemann cameras continued under the Zeiss-Ikon name.

- **Bob 0,** folding camera for plates or rollfilm.
  ....40.00   50.00
- **Bob 1,** postcard size folding rollfilm or plate camera, f6.8 lens.
  ....40.00   50.00
- **Bob IV, Bob V.**
  ....50.00   60.00
- **Bobette I,** c. 1923 folding camera for 22 x 33mm. format on 35mm. film, this is a bedless folding type, front pops straight with bellows and struts.
  ....70.00   75.00
- **Same as above,** with Ernostar lens.
  .... 400.00   500.00
- **Box cameras,** c. 1926, some models bearing the Ernemann name, others Zeiss-Ikon, wood body, leather covered, for 8 exposures 6 x 9cm. on 120 film, two speed shutter, f12.5 Meniscus lens.
  ....30.00   40.00
- **Ermanox,** 4.5 x 6cm. rigid-bodied model, c. 1924, originally introduced as the "Ernox," metal body, covered with black leather, focal plane shutter, 20-1000, Ernostar f2/100mm. or f1.8/85mm. lens.
  .... 1250.00   1350.00
- **Ermanox,** collapsible bellows model, 6.5 x 9cm. size, f1.8 Ernostar lens.
  .... 1450.00   1650.00
- **Ernoflex,** c. 1925, strut-type folding reflex for 4.5 x 6cm. plates, Ernon F3.5/75 or Tessar f4.5/80, focal plane shutter to 1000, one of the smallest folding SLR cameras ever.
  .... 1200.00   1400.00
- **Ernoflex Simplex Stereo,** a stereo reflex camera for 45 x 107mm., ground glass focus on both sides, and reflex focus on one side only, Ernon f3.5/75mm., focal plane shutter 25-1000, unusual.
  .... 500.00   600.00

ERNEMANN / 153

☐ **Globus,** *c. 1900, 13 x 18cm. folding camera, double extended bellows, focal plane shutter, Goerz Double Anastigmat f4.6 brass-barreled lens, polished wood body with brass trim.*
.... 250.00   350.00

Heag
An acronym for Heinrich Ernemann Aktien Gesellschaft.

☐ **Heag 0,** *folding-bed camera for 6 x 9cm., single extension, black leathered wood body, detective Aplanat f6.8/135mm., Ernemann Automat shutter.*
.... 25.00   35.00

☐ **Heag I,** *folding plate cameras, 6 x 9 and 9 x 12cm. sizes, most commonly found with f6.8 lens and Ernemann Pneumatic or Automat shutter.*
.... 25.00   35.00

☐ **Heag II,** *series II, 9 x 12cm., Vilar f6.8/135mm. Double Anastigmat lens in Chronos shutter, double extension bellows.*
.... 35.00   45.00

☐ **Heag VII,** *6 x 9cm., Radionar Anastigmat f6.3/105, Pronto shutter.*
.... 30.00   40.00

☐ **Heag XIV,** *c. 1910, 4.5 x 6cm., Ernemann Doppel Anastigmat f6/80mm., shutter to 100.*
.... 40.00   50.00

☐ **Heag XV,** *vertical format folding plate camera, 4.5 x 6cm. "vest pocket" size, Ernemann Double Anastigmat f6.8/80 in Automat shutter 1-100.*
.... 45.00   55.00

Heag (tropical model)
(See Tropical Heag under this heading.)

☐ **4.5 x 6cm. "Miniature Klapp",** *c. 1925, body style like the bellow model Ermanox, but with front bed/door, Ernostar f2.7/75mm., focal plane shutter to 1000, possible the smallest focal plane camera ever?*
.... 525.00   625.00

4.5 x 6 cm., "Miniature Klapp"

☐ **Klapp,** *6.5 x 9cm., folding bellows camera with focal plane shutter, f3.5 Ernon lens.*
.... 195.00   245.00

☐ **Klapp,** *9 x 12cm., folding bellows camera, focal plane shutter to 1000, Tessar f4.5/150, c. 1925.*
.... 200.00   250.00

☐ **Liliput,** *4.5 x 6cm. folding bellows vest pocket camera c. 1913, this economy model sports a fixed-focus Achromatic lens and T, I shutter.*
.... 70.00   85.00

☐ **Liliput Stereo,** *c. 1915, folding stereo camera for 45 x 107mm., meniscus lens, guillotine shutter.*
.... 295.00   350.00

☐ **Reflex,** *4.5 x 6cm. format, a small box SLR with focal plane shutter and Ernoplast f4.5/75 lens.*
.... 325.00   450.00

☐ **Reporter,** *c. 1905, folding camera for 9 x 12 plates, Meyer Anastigmat f5.5/120mm., focal plane shutter to 250, wood body, black leathered.*
.... 165.00   195.00

☐ **Rolf,** *folding vest pocket camera for 127 film, f12/75mm. lens, 3 speed shutter.*
.... 70.00   95.00

154 / ERNEMANN

☐ **Tropical Heag,** *9 x 12cm., c. 1920, folding-bed style, not focal plane type, double extension bellows, mahogany body, brown bellows, brass fittings, Ernemann Vilar f6.8/135mm. lens in Ernemann shutter 1-300.*
.... **325.00   400.00**

Reflex

☐ **Simplex Stereo,** *c. 1920, non-collapsing "jumelle" style stereo camera for 45 x 107 mm. plates, Ernemann Doppel lens f11/60, guillotine shutter, T, B, I, not to be confused with the Ernoflex Simplex Stereo camera.*
.... **125.00   175.00**

☐ **Stereo box,** *c. 1912, for 9 x 18cm. stereo pairs, fixed focus meniscus lenses, B & I shutter.*
.... **400.00   475.00**

Tropical cameras
All tropical cameras, including Ernemann are relatively scarce. Prices have increased rapidly in the last few years. There is quite a difference in price between the FP shutter models and inter-lens shuttered types.

☐ **Tropical Klapp,** *9 x 12cm., horizontal format folding-bed focal-plane camera in teakwood with brass fittings, Ernostar f4.5/150mm. in Ernemann front shutter, focal plane shutter to 1000.*
.... **700.00   800.00**

☐ **Tropical Klapp,** *9 x 12cm., focal plane camera in vertical style, c. 1925, mahogany body, brown bellows, brass fittings, Ernon f3.5/150 lens, focal plane shutter to 1000.*
.... **1000.00   1200.00**

☐ **Tropical Klapp, Tropical Reporter,** *10 x 15cm. focal plane cameras c. 1915, strut-folding style, focal plane shutter to 1000, some models to 2500, Tessar f4.5/165mm. lens, wood body, brown leather bellows, and brass trim.*
.... 1000.00   1250.00

☐ **"Two-Shuttered Camera" (Zweiverschlusskamera),** *c. 1912 folding-bed camera for 9 x 12 plates, Goerz Dagor f6.8/120mm., Ernemann Pneumatic shutter 2-100, front, and Focal-plane shutter to 2500 at rear.*
.... 175.00   225.00

☐ **Unette,** *c. 1925 miniature box camera for 22 x 33mm. exposures on rollfilm, overall size: 3 x 3½ x 2¼, two speed T & I shutter, f12.5 meniscus lens, revolving stops.*
.... 100.00   140.00

ERNOFLEX
(See Ernemann)

ERRTEE
(See Talbot)

ESSEM

☐ **Essem,** *5 x 7 folding camera, RR lens in B & L shutter, mahogany interior, red bellows.*
.... 100.00   125.00

ETUI

Etui
A style of thin-folding plate camera c. 1930's. The most common model using the word Etui in its name is the KW Patent Etui made by Guthe & Thorsch.

EULITZ
(Dr. Eulitz, Harzburg)

☐ **Grisette,** *c. 1955 camera for 35mm. film, 45mm. Achromat lens, simple shutter.*
.................16.00   20.00

EXPO CAMERA / 155

EUMIG
(Austria)

☐ **Eumigetta,** *6 x 6cm. rollfilm camera, Eumar f5.6/80mm. lens.*
.................20.00   25.00

EUREKA
(See Eastman)

EXA, EXAKTA
(See Ihagee)

EXCELSIOR
(See Semmendinger)

EXCO

☐ **Exco,** *simple box-type stereo camera, also usable for single exposures, double anastigmat lenses.*
.... 100.00   150.00

EXPLORER
(See Bolsey)

EXPO CAMERA COMPANY
(New York)

☐ **Easy-Load,** *c. 1926, small box camera for 1⅝ x 2½ exposures on rollfilm in special cartridges, called Expo "Easy-Load" film, meniscus lens, rotary sector shutter.*
..................70.00   85.00

☐ **Police Camera,** *c. 1915, a tiny all-metal box camera for 12 exposures on special cassettes, fixed focus Achromatic lens,, 2 apertures, cloth focal plane shutter, T & I.*
.... 200.00   250.00

☐ **Watch Camera,** *introduced c. 1905 and produced for about 30 years, disguised as a railroad-type pocket watch, takes pictures through the "winding stem", while the "winding knob" serves as a lens cap, special cartridges, finder, original box, etc. add to this figure.*
.... 125.00   150.00

EXPRESS
(See Murer & Duroni)

EXTRA
(See Sida)

EYEMATIC
(See Revere)

FALCON
(See Eastman, very early box)
(See Utility, cheap 127 box)

FAVORIT
(See Ica, Zeiss-Ikon)

FAVORITE
(See Rochester)

FECA

- **Feca,** *German folding plate cameras, made in 6 x 9 and 9 x 12cm. sizes, f4.5 Tessar or Xenar lenses, DEB, GGB.*
  ....40.00   65.00

FED

- **Fed,** *Russian Leica copies, various models, No. 1, 2, 3, and 4, dating from the 1930's on, most models with Fed f3.5 lens, some with f2.8 Fed lens.*
  .... 100.00   125.00

FED-FLASH

- **Fed-Flash,** *cheap camera for 127 film.*
  ....10.00   15.00

FEINAK-WERKE
(Munich)

- **Folding plate camera, 10 x 15cm.,** *horizontal format, double extension bellows, Schneider Xenar f4.5/165mm., Dial Compur to 150, leather covered metal body.*
  .... 125.00   150.00

- **Special Wiphot,** *9 x 12cm. folding bed plate camera, DEB, Reitzschel Linear f5.5/120mm. lens in Compound shutter.*
  ....50.00   75.00

FEINOPTISCHE WERKE
(Görlitz, Germany)

Successors to the Curt Bentzin Company.

- **Astraflex II,** *c. 1958, 6 x 6cm. SLR modeled after the Bentzin Primarflex, Tessar f3.5/105 coated lens, focal plane shutter, T, B, to 1000.*
  .... 150.00   165.00

FEINWERK TECHNIK GmbH
(Lahr)

- **Mec 16,** *c. late 1950's gold-colored subminiature for 10 x 14mm. exposures on 16mm. film in cassettes, f2.8 lens, shutter to 1000.*
  ....50.00   60.00

- **Mec 16 SB,** *similar but with built-in coupled Gossen meter and f2 Rodenstock Heligon lens.*
  ....90.00   115.00

FELICA

- **Felica,** *German 6 x 6cm. metal box camera for 120 film,, meniscus lens, zone focus, simple shutter, 25, 50, B, light grey colored.*
  ....20.00   25.00

FERRANIA
(Milan, Italy)

Associated with the Galileo Optical Company of Milan.

Condor
(See Galileo.)

Wooden View Camera, *8" x 10", Graflex focal plane shutter attached to rear* **$200.00-$250.00**

Top Left to Right: **Makina III** by Plaubel & Co., c. 1950, rapid Compur, roll film back, **$200.00-$250.00; Canon Model SII** by Canon Camera Co., Auto-Up accessory range finder, **$160.00-$200.00;** Bottom Left to Right: **Polyscop** by Ica, c. 1910, stereo camera, Busch Anastigmat lens, **$150.00-$200.00; Stereo Realist** by David White Co., c. 1950, 35mm., f3.5 lens, **$125.00--$155.00.**

Left to Right: **Century Graphic,** *by Graflex Inc., Kodak Ektar lens,* **$150.00-$175.00; Miniature Speed Graphic,** *by Graflex Inc., c. 1945, Kodak Ektar lens,* **$70.00-$120.00.**

Series B *by Folmer Graflex Corp., c. 1925, Kodak Anastigmat lens,* **$75.00-$125.00**

Rembrandt by Burke and James, Inc., portrait camera model I, comes with wooden film canister, not pictured, **$100.00-$150.00**

Top Left to Right; **Super Ikonta IV,** *by Zeiss Ikon, Synchro-Compur lens, 120 film,* **$50.00-$75.00; Primar** *by Curt Bentzin, c. 1959, 120 film, Compur shutter,* **$30.00-$40.00;** Bottom Left to Right: **Avus** *by Voigtlander,* **$40.00-$60.00; Vest Pocket Autographic Kodak Camera** *by Eastman Kodak Co., c. 1919,* **$15.00-$25.00; Vest Pocket Kodak Camera Model B,** *by Eastman Kodak Co.,* **$15.00-$25.00**

Top Left to Right: **Twin Lens Reflexes** *by Franke & Heidecke —* **Rolleiflex Model 2.8E,** *c. 1957, f2.8/75mm., 120 film, no meter,* **225.00-$250.00; Rolleimagic II,** *c. 1965, 3.5/75 mm., 120 film,* **$145.00-$160.00; Rolliflex Automat,** *c. 1939, f3.5/75mm., 120 film,* **$55.00-$65.00;** Bottom Left to Right: **Primo Jr.** *by Tokyo Kogaku, f3.5 lens, 127 film,* **$100.00-$125.00; Yashica 44** *by Yashica, c. 1956, f3.5 lens, 127 film,* **$65.00-$70.00**

Fotochrome by Fotochrome, Inc., c. 1965, direct positive film load, **$30.00-$40.00**

☐ **Rondine,** *miniature all metal box camera for 4 x 6.5cm. exposures on 127 film, measures 3½ x 3 x 2½, meniscus f7.5 linear focusing lens, simple shutter with flash synchronized.*
.................30.00   35.00

FERROTYPE
(See Chicago, Keystone, Moore)

FIESTA
(See Eastman Brownie Fiesta)

FILMET
(See Seneca)

FINETTA WERK
(P. Saraber, Goslar)

☐ **Finetta 99,** *spring motor camera c. 1940's, for 36 exposures 24 x 36mm. on 35mm. film, interchangeable Finetar f2.8/45mm. lens, focal-plane shutter 25-1000, light grey.*
...............140.00   175.00

☐ **Finette,** *f5.6/43mm. Achromat Finar, simple shutter, T, B, I, aluminum body.*
.................18.00   25.00

FINGERPRINT CAMERA
(See Graflex, Burke & James)

FIRSTFLEX

☐ **Firstflex,** *c. 1951 Japanese 6 x 6cm. TLR for 120 film, f3.5 lens, cheaply made.*
.................15.00   20.00

FLEKTAR

☐ **Flektar,** *6 x 6cm. TLR made in USSR occupied East Germany, Row Pololyt f3.5/75.*
.................30.00   35.00

FLEXARET
(See Meopta)

FLEXO
(See Eastman)

FLUSH-BACK
(See Eastman)

FOITZIK TRIER

☐ **Foinix,** *c. 1955 6 x 6cm. folding camera, Steiner f3.5/75mm. coated lens, Pronto 25-200.*
.................20.00   25.00

☐ **Unca,** *6 x 6cm., f3.5 Prontor-S shutter.*
.................40.00   50.00

FOLDEX
(See Photak Corp.)

FOLMER & SCHWING
**Folmer & Schwing (NYC) - 1881
Folmer & Schwing Mfg. Co. (NYC) - 1890
Folmer & Schwing Co. (Rochester)(EKC) - 1905
Folmer & Schwing Dept., Eastman Kodak - 1908
Folmer Graflex Corp. - 1926
Graflex, Inc. - 1943**

Because of the many organizational changes in this illustrious company which are outlined above, and in order to keep the continuous lines of cameras together, we have chosen to list their cameras as follows, regardless of age of camera or official company name at time of manufacture:
Cirkut Cameras - See Eastman Kodak Co. Graflex, Graphic Cameras - See Graflex.

FOTH
(C. E. Foth & Co., Berlin)

158 / FOTOCHROME, INC.

- [ ] **Foth Derby,** *Models I & II, c. 1930's compact cameras for 16 exposures 3 x 4 cm., 1¼ x 1⅝", on 127 film, focal plane shutter 25-200 + B, Foth Anastigmat f3.5 or f2.5/50mm., model II has CRF.*
  ....50.00   65.00

- [ ] **Fothflex,** *c. 1934 TLR for 6 x 6cm. on 120, f3.5/75mm., Foth Anastigmat, cloth focal plane shutter 25-500 + B.*
  ....90.00   110.00

- [ ] **Folding rollfilm camera,** *for 116 film, Foth Anastigmat f4.9/120mm., waist level and eye level finders.*
  ....30.00   35.00

FOTOCHROME, INC.
(U.S.A.)

- [ ] **Fotochrome Camera,** *c. 1965, "unusual" is a kind description for this machine, designed by the film company to use a special direct-positive film loaded in special cartridges, the camel-humped body houses a mirror which reflects the image down to the bottom where the "color picture roll" passed by on its way from one cartridge to another.*
  ....30.00   40.00

FOTOFLEX

- [ ] **Fotoflex,** *cheap plastic TLR.*
  ....6.00   8.00

FOTON
(See Bell & Howell)

FOTRON
(See Triad Corp.)

FRANCIA
(See Mackenstein)

FRANKA-WERK
(Beyreuth, Germany)

- [ ] **Rolfix,** *c. WWII, pre- and post, a folding camera for 8 exposures 6 x 9cm. or 16 exposures 4.5 x 6cm. on 120 film, post-war models made in U.S. occupied zone from pre- and post-war parts.*
  ....35.00   45.00

- [ ] **Solida,** *folding camera for 12 exposures 6 x 6cm. on 120, f6.3/75mm., pre- and post-war.*
  ....25.00   35.00

FRANKE & HEIDECKE
(Braunschweig)

Heidoscop
c. 1920's and 1930's three-lens stereo camera for stereo pairs on plates or cut film, in two sizes: 45 x 107mm. and 6 x 13cm., it was named for the designer, Reinhold Heidecke.

- [ ] **Heidoscop 45 x 107mm. size,** *Zeiss Tessar f4.5/55mm., Stereo Compound shutter.*
  .... 250.00   300.00

- [ ] **Heidoscop 6 x 13cm. size,** *Zeiss Tessar f4.5/75mm. lenses in Stereo Compound shutter.*
  .... 300.00   400.00

- [ ] **Rollei-16,** *submini for 12 x 17mm. exposures on 16mm. film, Tessar f2.8/25mm.*
  ....60.00   85.00

FRANKE AND HEIDECKE / 159

☐ **Rollei-35,** *Tessar f3.5/50mm.*
.... 75.00   100.00

Rolleicord
6 x 6cm. TLR, introduced in 1933, main identifying features listed with each model.

☐ **I, first model,** *Zeiss Triotar f4.5/75mm., Compur T, B, 1-300, nickel plated body.*
.... 100.00   125.00

☐ **1a,** *black leathered body, f4.5 Triotar, Compur to 300, not synched.*
.... 75.00   100.00

☐ **II,** *f3.5 Triotar, Compur 1-300, no synch.*
.... 45.00   55.00

☐ **III,** *f3.5 Triotar or f3.5 Schneider Xenar Compour Rapid 1-500 Synchronized, eye level, waist level, and sports finders.*
.... 75.00   100.00

☐ **IV,** *MX Synchronized, double exposure preventer.*
.... 80.00   125.00

☐ **V,** *self-timer.*
.... 90.00   120.00

☐ **Rolleidoscop,** *c. 1926, the rollfilm version of the Heidoscop stereo camera, actually, some of the very earliest production models of the Rolleidoscop still bore the name Heidoscop, perhaps the name which is now so famous was once an afterthought? like the Heidoscop, this is three-lens reflex, the center lens, for reflex viewing, is a triplet f4.2/75mm., taking lenses are Carl Zeiss Tessar f4.5/75mm., Stereo Compound shutter 1-300, for 6 x 13cm. on 120 rollfilm.*
.... 750.00   850.00

☐ **Rolleidoscop 45 x 107,** *a smaller size for 127 film, Tessar f4.5/55mm. lenses, much less common than the normal 6 x 13cm. size.*
.... 1500.00   1600.00

☐ **Rolleiflex, Twin Lens Reflex camera, original model,** *1929, the "little sister" of the already well-known Heidoscop and Rolleidoscop, readily identified by the rim-set Compur shutter and the film advance system, which on this early model was not automatic, and so there is no exposure counter, with f4.5, or more often with f3.8/75mm. Tessar, this first model was made to take 6 exposures on No. 117 film, later models were switched to 120, the first version of this model had no distance scale on the focus knob, and the back is not hinged, but fits into a groove, the second version of the Rolleiflex I had focus scale and hinge.*
.... 160.00   195.00

☐ **Rolleiflex, Twin Lens Reflex camera, standard model,** *c. 1932*
.... 100.00   125.00

☐ **Rolleiflex, Twin Lens Reflex camera, 4 x 4 or "Baby" model,** *for 4 x 4cm. on 127 film, f3.5/60 Xenar or f2.8/60 Tessar, black, 1931.*
.... 250.00   300.00

- [ ] **Same as above,** *grey, 1957 type.*
  .... 150.00   200.00
- [ ] **Rolleiflex Sport,** *c. 1932, Tessar f3.5/75mm., Compur 1-300.*
  .... 100.00   150.00
- [ ] **Rolleimagic 6 x 6cm. TLR camera I,** *Xenar f3.5/75, Prontormat shutter.*
  ....80.00   95.00
- [ ] **Rolleimagic 6 x 6cm. TLR camera II,** *c. 1959, auto exposure control with built-in Gossen meter.*
  .... 145.00   165.00

FRENA
(See also Beck)

- [ ] **FT-2,** *c. 1955 Russian panoramic camera for 12 exposures 24 x 110mm. on 35mm. film, Industar f5/50mm., shutter 100-400.*
  .... 300.00   350.00

FUJI PHOTO FILM COMPANY, FUJICA
(Japan)

- [ ] **Lyra, Semi-Lyra,** *compact folding camera for 16 exposures 4.5 x 6cm. on 120 rollfilm, made before and after World War II, f3.5/75 Anastigmat, Fujico shutter to 200.*
  ....35.00   50.00

- [ ] **Mini,** *very small half-frame camera for 35mm. film in special cartridges, f2.8/25mm.*
  .... 100.00   125.00

FUTURA WERK
(Fritz Kuhnert, Freiburg)

- [ ] **Futura-S,** *a very well constructed 35mm. RF camera from pre-war Germany, continued through the 1950's, Kuhnert Frilon f1.5/50mm. lens, Compur Rapid 1-400, B, CRF.*
  ....80.00   95.00

GALILEO OPTICAL
(Milan, Italy)

Associated with Ferrania, also of Milan.

- [ ] **Condor I,** *Leica copy.*
  .... 100.00   125.00
- [ ] **Gami 16,** *c. mid-1950's subminiature for exposures approximately 11 x 17mm. on 16mm. film in cassettes, f1.9/25mm. lens, shutter 2-1000, coupled meter, parallax correction, spring-motor wind for up to 3 rapid-fire shots, complete outfit with all accessories: f4/4x telephoto, flash, filter, 45 degree viewer, wrist strap, etc. sells for 2 to 3 times the cost of the camera and case only.*
  .... 700.00   800.00

GALLUS
(Usines Gallus, Courbevoie, France)

- [ ] **Stereo camera,** *rigid "Jumelle" style all metal camera c. 1920's for stereo exposures in the two popular formats: 6 x 13cm. or the smaller 4.5 x 10.7cm., simple lenses, I & B shutter.*
  .... 200.00   250.00

GALTER PRODUCTS
(U.S.A.)

☐ **Hopalong Cassidy Camera,** *c. 1950 plastic box camera for 8 exposures 6 x 9cm. on 120 rollfilm, simple shutter and meniscus lens, the front plate depicts the famous cowboy and his horse.*
................30.00   35.00

GAMI
(See Galileo Optical because GAMI is an abbreviation for GAlileo, MIlano)

GAMMA

☐ **Gamma,** *Italian Leica copy.*
...............450.00   500.00

GARLAND
(London, England)

☐ **Wet Plate camera,** *8 x 10", c. 1865, Ross lens.*
...............1650.00   1800.00

GAUMONT
(L. Gaumont & Cie., Paris)

☐ **Block-Notes 4.5 x 6cm.,** *compact folding plate camera c. 1904, f6.8 Tessar, Hermagis Anastigmat, or Darlot lens.*
...............200.00   250.00

☐ **Block-Notes 6 x 9cm.,** *similar but larger, with f6.3 Tessar lens, less common than the smaller model.*
...............200.00   245.00

☐ **Block-Notes Stereo,** *compact folding cameras like the other Block-Notes models, but for the 6 x 13cm. and 45 x 107mm. stereo formats, f6.3 lenses, variable speed guillotine shutter, for single plateholders or magazines.*
...............425.00   525.00

☐ **Spido Stereo,** *black leather covered jumelle style stereo camera for 9 x 18cm. stereo plates, Krauss Zeiss Protar f12.5/189mm., six speed Decaux Stereo Pneumatic shutter.*
...............225.00   325.00

☐ **Stereo cameras,** *miscellaneous or unnamed models, 6 x 13cm., f6.3/85mm. lenses and guillotine shutter.*
...............135.00   175.00

GELTO
(See Takahashi Kogaku)

GEM
(See Rochester, Gem Poco, Wing, New Gem)

GEMFLEX

☐ **Gemflex,** *c. 1954 TLR novelty camera for 14 x 14mm. exposures, quite unusual, it stands out in a collection of novelty cameras.*
...............185.00   210.00

GENIE CAMERA CO.
(Philadelphia, Pa.)

☐ **Genie,** *c. 1892 focusing magazine-box camera for 3¼ x 4" plates, push-pull action changes plates and actuates exposure counter on brass magazine, string-set shutter.*
...............525.00   625.00

GENNERT
(G. Gennert, NYC)

☐ **Montauk,** *detective type plate camera c. 1890 for plate holders which load from the side, shutter-tensioning knob on the front next to the lens opening, internal bellows focusing via radial focus lever on top of camera.*
...............125.00   150.00

162 / GENOS K.G.

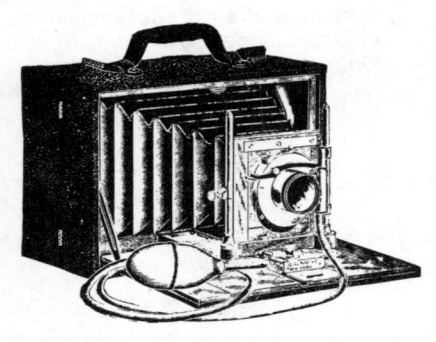

- **Folding Montauk,** *folding plate cameras, leather covered wood bodies, "cycle" style, Wollensak Rapid Symmetrical, Ross Patent, or Rapid Rectilinear lens, 4 x 5 or 5 x 7".*
  .... 75.00   85.00
- **Montauk rollfilm camera,** *c. 1914.*
  .... 30.00   40.00

- **"Penny Picture" camera,** *c. 1890, a 5 x 7 studio camera with sliding back and masks to produce multiple small images on a single plate.*
  .... 300.00   350.00

GENOS K. G.
(Nurnberg, Germany)

- **Genos Rapid,** *c. 1950 plastic camera for 12 exposures 6 x 6cm. on 120 film.*
  .... 15.00   20.00

GEORGE, HERBERT
(See Herco)

GEVAERT
(Germany)

- **Gevabox,** *c. 1950 box cameras for 120 film, two sizes: 6 x 6 and 6 x 9cm.*
  .... 7.00   9.00

GEWIRETTE
(See Wirgin)

GIFT KODAK
(See Eastman)

GILLES-FALLER
(Paris)

- **Studio camera,** *c. 1900, 18 x 24cm., Hermagis Delor f4.5/270mm. lens with iris diaphragm, finely finished light colored wood.*
  .... 300.00   350.00

GIRL SCOUT CAMERAS
(See Eastman, Herco)

GLOBAL

- **Global,** *Japanese 14mm. novelty camera.*
  .... 10.00   12.00

GLOBUS
(See Ernemann)

GLORIETTE
(See Braun)

GLUNZ
(S. Glunz Kamerawerk, Hannover)

☐ **Folding plate camera,** c. 1920's, 9 x 12cm. size, Dial Compur shutter, Goerz Tenastigmat f6.8, or Zeiss Tessar f4.5 lens, double extension bellows, wood body, leather covered.
.................50.00   60.00

☐ **Folding rollfilm model,** f6.3 Tessar, Compur shutter.
.................35.00   40.00

GLYPHOSCOPE
(See Richard)

GOEKER
(Copenhagen, Denmark)

☐ **Field camera,** 18 x 24cm., Carl Zeiss Series II f8/140mm. lens.
................125.00   135.00

GOERZ
(C. P. Goerz, Berlin, Germany)

Also associated with American Optical Company.
Note: Goerz merged with Contessa-Nettel, Ica, Ernemann, and Carl Zeiss Optical Company in 1926 to form Zeiss-Ikon. Some Goerz models were continued under the Zeiss name.

☐ **Ango,** *strut-type folding camera with focal plane shutter, introduced c. 1899 and produced for at least 30 years, Goerz Dagor f6.8, Dogmar f3.5, Syntor f6.8, Double Anastigmat f4.6, or Celor f4.8 are among the lenses you could expect to find.*
...............200.00   250.00

☐ **Ango Stereo,** c. 1906, similar to the Ango but for stereo format.
...............250.00   300.00

☐ **Anschutz,** *another bedless "strut" type folding focal plane camera, introduced c. 1890 and quite common with the press during the early part of the century, most often found in the 6 x 9cm., 9 x 12cm., and 4 x 5" sizes.*
...............135.00   145.00

☐ **Anschutz Stereo,** c. 1890-1900, *a focal plane strut-folding bedless stereo camera for paired exposures on 8 x 17cm. plates, panoramic views are also possible by sliding one lens board to the center position, with Goerz Dagor Double Anastigmat or Goerz Wide-Angle Aplanat lenses, a relatively uncommon camera.*
...............275.00   350.00

Folding Reflex

164 / GOERZ

☐ **Folding Reflex,** a compact folding single lens reflex camera for 4 x 5" plates, c. 1912, this camera competed for attention with the Bentzin, Goltz & Breutmann Mentor, and Ihagee Patent Klappreflex, all of which were designed to operate as an efficient full-size SLR, but be as portable as an ordinary press camera when folded.
. . . . 225.00   350.00

☐ **Folding rollfilm cameras,** for 120 or 116 rollfilms, various models with Goerz lens and Goerz or Compur shutter.
. . . . 20.00   30.00

☐ **Minicord,** C. P. Goerz, Vienna, c. 1951 subminiature TLR for 10 x 10mm. exposures in 16mm. film in special cartridges, f2/25mm. Goerz Helgor lens, metal focal plane shutter, 10-400, synchronized.
. . . . 175.00   235.00

☐ **Minicord III and IV.**
. . . . 200.00   250.00

☐ **Stereo Photo Bincole,** c. 1899, an unusual disguised detective binocular camera in the form of the common field glasses of the era, in addition to its use as a single-shot camera on 45 x 50mm. plates, it could use plates in pairs for stereo shots, or could be used without plates as a field glass, f6.8/75mm. Dagor lenses.
. . . . 3250.00   3500.00

☐ **Tenax folding camera, 4.5 x 6cm. Vest Pocket Tenax,** c. 1909 strut-type folding camera for plates, Goerz Double Anastigmat Celor f4.5/75mm. or f6.8 Dagor or Syntor lens, compound shutter 1-250 + B.
. . . . 150.00   165.00

☐ **4 x 6.5cm. Vest Pocket Rollfilm Tenax,** for 127 film, similar to the folding vest pocket cameras of Kodak and Ansco, f6.3/75 Dogmar in Compur shutter to 300.
. . . . 50.00   60.00

6 x 9 cm.

☐ **6.5 x 9cm. Coat Pocket Tenax,** *for plates or film packs, Goerz Dagor f6.8/90 or Dogmar f4.5/100, compound shutter T, B, 1-250.*
................90.00   110.00

☐ **6 x 9cm.**, *bed-type folding rollfilm model, style similar to the American cameras of the same period, Tenastigmat f6.3/100mm. in Compur shutter 1-250.*
................20.00   30.00

☐ **8 x 10.5cm.**, *3¼ x 4¼, bedless strut-folding camera, for plates, c. 1915-1920.*
................85.00   100.00

☐ **8 x 10.5cm.**, *bed-folding type, for rollfilm.*
................30.00   35.00

☐ **8 x 14cm.**, *3¼ x 5½, postcard size, folding bed type rollfilm camera, bed focus.*
................30.00   40.00

☐ **9 x 12cm. Tenax, Manufok Tenax,** *plate cameras c. 1920, folding bed type on common square-cornered plate camera style, Goerz Dogmar f4.5/150mm., Dial Compur 1-150, double extension bellows, ground glass back.*
................50.00   60.00

☐ **10 x 15cm. Tenax,** *folding-bed plate camera, c. 1912, Goerz Dagor f6.8/168mm., or f6.3 Tenastigmat, Compound or Compur shutter.*
................60.00   70.00

GOLDMANN / 165

☐ **Stereo Tenax,** *strut-type folding stereo camera for 45 x 107mm. plates or packs, Goerz Syntor f6.3/60 or f4.5/60 Dogmar or Celor, stereo Compur or Compound shutter.*
.... 185.00   210.00

☐ **Tengor,** *box, c. mid-1920's for 6 x 9cm. exposures on 120 film, Goerz Frontar f11 lens.*
................25.00   30.00

☐ **Tengor,** *folding rollfilm, Vest Pocket size for 4 x 6.5cm. on 127 film, Goerz Frontar f9/45 lens, shutter, T, B, 25-100.*
................40.00   50.00

GOLDECK 16

☐ **Goldeck 16,** *subminiature for 10 x 14mm. exposures on 16mm. film, interchangeble f2.8/20 Enna-Color Ennit lens, behind the lens shutter, B, 1-200, rapid wind lever, bright frame finder.*
.... 125.00   135.00

GOLDI

☐ **Goldi,** *c. 1930 folding-bed camera for 16 exposures 3 x 4cm. on 127 film, f2.9 or 4.5 Zecanar lens, Vario, Prontor, or Compur shutter.*
................50.00   60.00

GOLDMANN
(R. A. Goldmann, Vienna)

☐ **Press camera,** *c. 1900 bedless strut-folding 9 x 12cm. plate camera, Zeiss Tessar f6.3/135, focal plane shutter, T, B, ½-90, black wood body, leather bellows, nickel trim and struts.*
.... 175.00   185.00

☐ **Field camera,** *13 x 18cm., c. 1900, reversible back, Aplanat lens, mahogany body with brass trim.*
.... 150.00   160.00

GOLDEN STEKY
(See Riken)

GOLF
(See Adox)

GOLTZ & BREUTMANN
(Dresden, Germany and Görlitz, Germany)

All Mentor cameras are listed here, including any manufactured by the "Mentor Kamerawerk, Dresden" or Rudolph Grosser, Pillnitz.

- **Mentor Compur Reflex,** *c. 1928 SLR box for 6 x 5 x 9cm. plates, Zeiss Tessar f4.5/105 or f2.7/120mm. lens, Compur shutter 1-250, reflex viewing, ground glass at rear, and adjustable wire frame finder, black metal body, partly leather covered.*
  .... 165.00   175.00

- **Mentor Folding Reflex, Klappreflex,** *compact folding SLR c. 1915-1930, 6 x 9cm., 9 x 12cm., and 4 x 5" sizes, Zeiss Tessar lenses, usually f2.7 or 4.5, focal plane shutter to 1000.*
  .... 180.00   190.00

- **Mentor Stereo Reflex,** *bellows focusing focal plane box reflex for stereo pairs in the two common European stereo sizes: 45 x 107mm., with Tessar f4.5/75mm. lens, and 6 x 13cm. size with Tessar f4.5/90mm. lens, both sizes have focal plane shutter 15-1000.*
  .... 600.00   650.00

- **Mentor Reflex,** *like Graflex, basically a cube when closed, fold-up viewing hood, bellows focus, focal plane shutter, three common sizes: 6.5 x 9cm., 9 x 12cm., and 10 x 15cm. for plates or packs, most common lenses are f4.5 Tessar, Heliar, and Xenar.*
  .... 130.00   140.00

- **Mentor II,** *c. 1907, a strut-folding 9 x 12cm. plate camera, not a reflex, Paul Wächter Triplan f6/125mm., focal plane shutter, wood body covered with black leather, GGB.*
  .... 175.00   200.00

- **Mentor Dreivier,** *c. 1930, an eye-level camera for 16 exposures 3 x 4cm. on 127 film, styled much like a 35mm. camera, Tessar f3.5/50mm. lens in Compur shutter, 1-300.*
  .... 140.00   150.00

Mentorett, c. 1935 TLR for 12 exposures 6 x 6cm. on 120 film, Mentor f3.5/75mm., variable speed focal plane shutter, looks somewhat like a Rolleiflex, but with focal plane shutter.
.... **145.00   165.00**

☐ **Klein-Mentor,** a relatively simple SLR for 6 x 9 and 6.5 x 9cm. formats, fold-up viewing hood, measures 3½ x 4 x 4¾ when closed.
.................**90.00   110.00**

GOODWIN FILM & CAMERA CO.

Named for the Reverend Hannibal Goodwin, the inventor of flexible film, but taken over by Ansco. (See Ansco for listing of "Goodwin" camera.)

GRAFLEX, INC.

Also including Folmer-Schwing and Folmer-Graflex products from 1881-1943 except Cirkut cameras which are listed under Eastman.

☐ **Century 35,** c. 1961 Japanese-made 35mm. camera, f3.5 or 2.8 lens.
.................**30.00   40.00**

☐ **Century Universal 8 x 10 View,** less lens.
.... **150.00   175.00**

☐ **Ciro 35,** c. 1950 35mm. RF camera, f4.5, 3.5, or 2.8 lens, Alphax or Rapax shutter.
.................**30.00   40.00**

☐ **Graflex Ia,** for 2¼ x 4¼, B & L Tessar f4.5.
.... **100.00   125.00**

☐ **Graflex 22,** TLR for 6 x 6cm. on 120 film, Graftar f3.5/85, Century Synchromatic shutter.
.................**50.00   60.00**

☐ **Graflex 3A,** "postcard" size, 3¼ x 5½ on 122 film, focal plane shutter, with one of the many available lenses.
.................**90.00   120.00**

168 / GRAFLEX, INC.

- **Auto Graflex camera,** 2¼ x 3¼ "Junior", c. 1915-1924, with focal plane shutter, and price listed is for camera with normal lens.
  . . . . 120.00   150.00
- **Same as above,** 3¼ x 4¼, c. 1907-1923.
  . . . . 100.00   115.00
- **Same as above,** 4 x 5.
  . . . . 100.00   115.00
- **Same as above,** 5 x 7.
  . . . . 140.00   150.00

- **RB Auto Graflex camera** 3¼ x 4¼, c. 1909-1942.
  . . . . 120.00   150.00
- **RB Auto Graflex camera** 4 x 5.
  . . . . 100.00   135.00
- **Compact Graflex,** 3¼ x 5½" postcard size, although our price average is based only on complete and working examples, there have been numerous incomplete and/or not working examples on the market in recent years for considerably less.
  . . . . 125.00   175.00
- **Series B Graflex,** c. 1925-1942, complete, working, with lens, G-VG condition, 3¼ x 4¼.
  . . . . 60.00   85.00
- **Same as above,** 4 x 5, many inoperable examples available for lower prices.
  . . . . 80.00   90.00

Series B Graflex

- **Same as above,** 5 x 7, less common.
  . . . . 160.00   195.00

GRAFLEX, INC. / 169

RB Graflex Series C

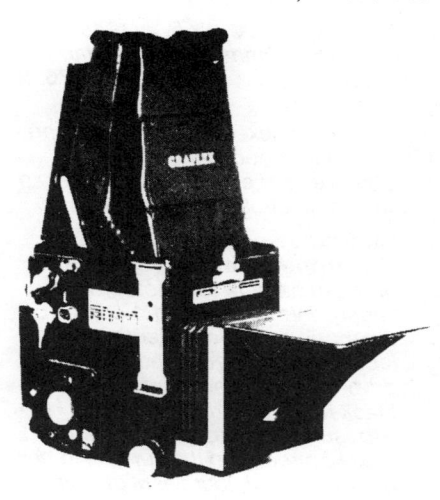

RB Graflex Super D

RB Graflex Series D

Graflex "Inspectograph" Fingerprint

- **RB Graflex Series B,** *complete, working, with lens, G-VG condition,* 2¼ x 3¼, c. 1925-1951.
  . . . . .80.00   90.00
- **Same as above,** 3¼ x 4¼, c. 1925-1942.
  . . . . .75.00   85.00
- **Same as above,** 4 x 5, c. 1923-1942.
  . . . . .90.00   110.00

- **RB Graflex Series C,** c. 1926-1935, 3¼ x 4¼.
  . . . . .75.00   95.00
- **RB Graflex Series D,** 3¼ x 4¼.
  . . . . .75.00   125.00
- **Same as above,** 4 x 5, c. 1929-1945.
  . . . . 100.00   135.00
- **RB Graflex Super D,** 3¼ x 4¼, c. 1941-1963.
  . . . . 150.00   225.00

170 / GRAFLEX, INC.

- ☐ **Same as above,** 4 x 5, c. 1948-1957, with f5.6/190mm. Ektar or Optar.
  . . . . 275.00   375.00

Note: This price is considerably higher than other Graflexes, and we are listing the lens mainly because it is a very useable piece of equipment, and not so much a "collectible" to gather dust.

- ☐ **Graflex "Inspectograph" Fingerprint Camera,** a special-purpose camera for photographing fingerprints or making 1:1 copies of other photos or documents, pre-focused lens is recessed to the proper focal distance inside a flat-black rigid shroud, to make exposure, camera front opening is placed directly on the surface to be photographed, four flashlight-type bulbs provide illumination.
  . . . . 125.00   150.00

- ☐ **Home Portrait Graflex,** c. 1912-1942, a 5 x 7 focal plane SLR with an unusual feature, the focal plane shutter could be set to pass one, two, or more of the aperture slits for a single exposure, thus allowing a very broad range of "slow" speeds.
  . . . . 145.00   175.00

- ☐ **National Graflex,** Series I, 1933-1935, and Series II, 1934-1941, SLR for 10 exposures 2¼ x 3¼ on 120 film, focal plane shutter, B & L Tessar f3.5/75mm.
  . . . . 135.00   150.00

- ☐ **Naturalist's Graflex Camera,** 1907-1921, probably the rarest of the Graflex cameras, it has a long body and bellows to accommodate lenses up to 26" focal length, viewing hood can be used from top or back position.
  . . . . 2650.00   2750.00

- ☐ **Press Graflex,** 5 x 7, c. 1907-1923.
  . . . . 175.00   225.00

- ☐ **Stereo Auto Graflex,** 5 x 7, c. 1907-1922, for stereo exposures on a 5 x 7" plate, the viewing hood featured a pair of stereo prisms so that the photographer could see one stereo image on the ground glass, that has to be the ultimate composing aid for stereo photographers, B & L Kodak Anastigmat f6.3 or B & L Tessar f4.5/135mm. lenses, focal plane shutter.
  . . . . 1600.00   1800.00

GRAPHIC / 171

Press Graflex

Tele-Graflex

Stereo Auto Graflex

- **Tele-Graflex,** *designed with a long bellows to allow the use of lenses of various focal lengths, c. 1914-1924, 3¼ x 4¼.*
  ....80.00   120.00
- **Same as above,** *4 x 5.*
  .... 150.00   170.00

GRAPHIC CAMERAS

The folding-bed type press cameras most common during the second quarter of the century. Rather than our normal alphabetical listing, we are listing these cameras chronologically by four major periods: Early, Pre-Anniversary, Anniversary, and Pacemaker. Other models of Graphic cameras follow the major period lists.

- **Early Graphic No. 0,** *c. 1909-1920's, focal plane Graphic camera for 127 filmm, f6.3 Zeiss Kodak Anastigmat lens.*
  .... 300.00   350.00
- **Early Graphic RB Cycle,** *wood body, leather covered, folding-bed type with polished wood interior, double or triple extension red bellows, 5 x 7 or 6½ x 8½ sizes with B & L RR lens, higher with convertible lenses.*
  .... 160.00   180.00

172 / GRAPHIC

☐ **Early Graphic Stereo,** c. 1900, focal plane shutter added c. 1908, this was a professional camera used for making the commercial stereo views which were popular around the turn of the century, not to be confused with the Stereo Graphic 35mm. camera c. 1950's which appears near the end of the Graphic listings.
.... 1150.00   1275.00

☐ **Pre-Anniversary Speed Graphic Cameras,** prior to 1940, identifiable by the wooden bed with single focus knob, pre-1938 models have Newton-finder, negative diopter lens with rear post sight, sportsfinder is of the hinged rather than telescoping type, all pre-anniversary models are Speed Graphics with focal plane shutters, made in 2½ x 3½, 3¼ x 4¼, 3¼ x 5½, and 4 x 5" sizes.
.... 110.00   135.00

Note: Often found in poor condition or missing lens or back, or with stiff curtain, etc. for much less.

☐ **Anniversary Speed Graphic Cameras,** c. 1940-1947, distinguished from the earlier models by the metal bed with two focus knobs, telescoping sportsfinder, distinguished from later models by lack of body release for front shutter, 2¼ x 3¼.
.... 100.00   125.00

☐ Same as above, 3¼ x 4¼.
.... 75.00   115.00
☐ Same as above, 4 x 5.
.... 95.00   120.00
☐ Same as above, 4 x 5 "Combat Graphic", the World War II olive-drab model for the armed forces.
.... 225.00   275.00

Pacemaker Graphic Cameras c. 1947. Distinguishable from earlier models by the built-in body release with cable running along bellows, metal lensboard, adjustable infinity stops on bed are hinged type.

☐ **Pacemaker Crown Graphic,** as described above but does not have focal plane shutter, prices vary tremendously on these, 2¼ x 3¼ and 3¼ x 4¼ sizes.
.... 120.00   135.00
☐ Same as above, more commonly used 4 x 5 models run a more stable average, all prices for complete working camera and lens.
.... 165.00   195.00
☐ **Pacemaker Speed Graphic,** as above but with focal plane shutter, prices on all three sizes.
.... 125.00   225.00
☐ Same as above, usually available.
.... 160.00   195.00
☐ **Century Graphic,** an economy model press camera with a plastic body instead of metal, c. 1950, 2¼ x 3¼ size.
.... 125.00   175.00
☐ **Stereo Graphic,** c. mid-1950's for stereo pairs on 35mm. film, Graflar f4/35mm. lenses in simple 1/50 second shutter.
.... 90.00   125.00
☐ **Super Graphic,** 4 x 5 press camera, Optar f4.7/135mm. lens in synchronized shutter 1-400.
.... 240.00   285.00
☐ **Graphic View,** c. 1941-1950's, 4 x 5" monorail view camera, no lens, l.
.... 115.00   135.00

☐ **Same as above,** *II.*
.... 145.00   175.00
☐ **Graphic 35,** *c. 1955-1958 35mm. RF camera, Graflar f3.5 or 2.8/ 50mm. in helical mount with unique push-button focus, coupled split-image rangefinder, Prontor 1-300.*
.... 40.00   60.00

GRAFTEX PRODUCTS

☐ **Hollywood Reflex,** *a cheap 6 x 6cm. TLR.*
.... 10.00   15.00

GRAY
(Robert D. Gray, NYC)

☐ **View camera,** *8 x 10" c. 1880, Periscope Number 4 lens with rotary disc stops.*
.... 175.00   195.00

GRIFFITHS
(Walter M. Griffiths & Co., Birmingham, England)

☐ **Magazine camera,** *c. 1890, for 3¼ x 4¼ plates.*
.... 75.00   95.00

GRISETTE
(See Eulitz)

GROSSER
(Rudolph Grosser, Pillnitz)

Manufacturer of Mentor cameras during the 1950's, however, all Mentor Cameras are listed in this edition under Goltz & Breutmann.

GROVER
(See Burke & James)

GUNDLACH OPTICAL COMPANY, GUNDLACH-MANHATTAN OPTICAL COMPANY
(Rochester, N.Y.)

☐ **Korona cameras,** *3¼ x 4¼ and 3¼ x 5½, folding plate cameras, including "Petit" models, cherry wood body, leather covered, red bellows.*
.... 60.00   65.00
☐ **Same as above,** *4 x 5" size, folding bed view camera.*
.... 60.00   65.00
☐ **Same as above,** *5 x 7" size.*
.... 90.00   100.00
☐ **5 x 7 Stereo,** *folding plate camera for stereo exposures on standard 5 x 7 plates, leather covered wood body with polished wood interior, simple stereo shutter.*
.... 375.00   425.00
☐ **Same as above,** *6½ x 8½ view, less lens.*
.... 100.00   125.00
☐ **Same as above,** *8 x 10 view, less lens.*
.... 100.00   150.00
☐ **Same as above,** *7 x 17, 8 x 20, and 12 x 20 "Banquet" view, without lens, but with holder.*
.... 325.00   375.00

GUTHE & THORSCH KAMERA WERKSTATTEN
(Dresden, Germany)

KW Patent Etui
c. 1930, as the name Etui denotes, this is an extremely flat folding plate camera, folding bed style with double extension bellows, the whole works folds to a thickness of about an inch.

☐ **6 x 9cm. size,** *Tessar f4.5/100-120mm. with focus knob on bed, Ibsor or Compur shutter, black leather and bellows.*
.... 45.00   65.00
☐ **6 x 9cm. Deluxe Model,** *tastefully finished in brown leather with light brown bellows.*
.... 225.00   250.00

- **9 x 12cm. size,** the most common size, f4.5 or f6.3 Rodenstock Eurynar, Schneider Radionar, Erkos Fotar, Zeiss Tessar, or Schneider Isconar, shutter: Ibsor, Vario, or Compur.
  ....50.00   60.00
- **KW folding plate camera,** 6 x 9cm., f4.5/105 lens, Compur shutter.
  ....40.00   50.00
- **Same as above,** 9 x 12cm., f4.5/135mm., Compur.
  ....45.00   55.00
- **KW Reflex Box,** c. 1930, SLR for 8 exposures, 6 x 9cm. on 120 rollfilm in horizontal format, KW Anastigmat f6.3/105mm., or f4.5/105mm. KW or Steinheil, three speed segment shutter 25-100, B, folding top viewing hood.
  ....85.00   115.00

KAWEE

- **Kawee,** compact "Etui" type folding bed plate camera in 6 x 9 and 9 x 12cm. sizes, Schneider Radionar or Xenar, or Rodenstock Trinar, Compur or Gauthier shutter.
  ....45.00   55.00
- **Pilot 6,** c. 1930's SLR for 12 exposures 6 x 6cm. on 120 film, Laack Pololyt f3.5/75 or 80mm. or KW Anastigmat f6.3/75mm., metal guillotine shutter B, 20-200.
  ....60.00   75.00
- **Pilot Reflex,** c. 1930's, TLR for 16 exposures, 3 x 4cm. on 127 film, Tessar f2.8/50mm.
  ....85.00   95.00
- **Pilot Super,** SLR for 12 exposures 6 x 6cm. on 120 film, could also be used for 16 exposures 4.5 x 6cm. with mask, built on the same chassis as the Pilot 6, but easily distinguished by the addition of a small extinction meter attached to the viewing hood, Ennastar f4.5, Pilotar f4.5, or Laack f2.9 or 3.5.
  ....70.00   80.00

- **Prakti,** c. 1960, 35mm. with automatic electric drive, Domitron or Meyer lens.
  ....30.00   40.00
- **Praktica,** 35mm. SLR, f2.8 lens.
  ....35.00   45.00
- **Praktica FX,** 35mm. SLR, Westanar or Tessar f2.8 or 3.5 lens, focal plane shutter 2-500.
  ....35.00   45.00
- **Praktica Nova,** with f2.8 lens.
  ....45.00   55.00
- **Praktiflex,** 35mm. SLR c. 1938, Victor f2.9/50mm. or Tessar f3.5, focal plane shutter 20-500.
  ....40.00   50.00
- **Praktiflex FX,** Tessar f2.8 or Primoplan f1.9 lens.
  ....50.00   60.00
- **Praktiflex II,** Victor f2.9/50mm.
  ....50.00   65.00
- **Praktina IIa,** 35mm. SLR, Jena T 2.8/50mm., focal plane shutter to 1000, spring motor drive.
  .... 120.00   135.00
- **Praktisix,** 6 x 6cm. SLR, interchangeable bayonet mount Meyer Primotar f3.5/80mm., focal plane shutter, 1-1000, changeable prism.
  .... 175.00   195.00

HAKING
(W. Haking, Hong Kong)

- **Halina,** 35mm., f2.8 or 3.5, shutter 25-200.
  ....16.00   20.00

HALL CAMERA COMPANY
(Brooklyn, N.Y.)

- **Mirror Reflex Camera,** c. 1910 Graflex-style SLR, 4 x 5" size with f4.5/180 lens.
  .... 100.00   125.00

HALLOH
(See Ica)

HAMCO

☐ **Hamco,** *Japanese 14mm. novelty camera.*
.... 8.00   10.00

HANDY
(See Rochester Optical Company)

HANEEL TRI-VISION COMPANY
(Alhambra, Ca.)

☐ **Tri-Vision Stereo,** *plastic and aluminum stereo camera for 28 x 30mm. pairs on 828 rollfilm, f8 Meniscus lenses with three stops, usually found in excellent condition with original box, stereo viewer, etc.*
.... 30.00   40.00

HAPO
(See Photo Porst because Hapo is just an abbreviation for HAns POrst)

HAPPI-TIME

☐ **Happi-Time,** *plastic camera for 127.*
.... 6.00   8.00

HAPPY

☐ **Happy,** *Japanese novelty camera.*
.... 8.00   10.00

HARBOE, A. O.
(Altona, Germany)

☐ **Wood box camera,** *c. 1870, for glass plates, typical of the type of camera made in Germany during the 1870-1890 period, although it pre-dated the "Kodak", it was made for the ordinary person to use, brass barrel lens, simple shutter, ground glass back.*
.... 650.00   750.00

Wood Box

HARE
(George Hare, London)

☐ **Tourist camera,** $1/2$-*plate, c. 1865, with Fallowfield Rapid Doublet lens with iris diaphragm, changing box.*
.... 750.00   850.00

☐ **Stereo camera,** *c. 1865, full plate size, for stereo views in two separate exposures using the same lens on a sliding panel, mahogany body, dark red bellows, Dallmeyer lens.*
.... 900.00   975.00

HARMONY

☐ **Harmony,** *Japanese.*
.... 8.00   10.00

HARVARD
(See Mason, Perry & Co.)

HAWKEYE
(See Blair, Boston, Eastman)

HEAG
(See Ernemann)

HEIDECKE, HEIDOSCOP
(See Franke & Heidecke)

HELIOS
(See Hüttig)

HEMAX

- **Hemax,** 9 x 12cm. folding plate camera, H. Roussel Anastigmat f6.8/135mm.
  ....25.00   35.00

HENRY CLAY CAMERA
(See American Optical Co.)

HERCO
(Herbert George Co.)

- **Donald Duck Camera,** c. 1940's plastic 127 film camera for 1⅝ x 1⅝" exposures, figures of the Disney ducks, Donald, Huey, Louie, and Dewey, in relief on the back, meniscus lens, simple shutter.
  ....30.00   40.00
- **Same as above,** with original cardboard carton.
  ....18.00   25.00
- **Imperial,** pre-war folding 127 camera, Ludwig f4.5/50mm. lens.
  ....8.00   12.00
- **Imperial Reflex,** c. mid-1950's plastic 6 x 6cm. TLR for 620 film, simple lens and shutter.
  ....6.00   8.00
- **Imperial Satellite Flash.**
  ....5.00   8.00
- **Roy Rogers and Trigger,** plastic marvel for 620 film.
  ....20.00   30.00

Note: The Trigger in this case is not a shutter release, but a horse. Pardon the pun.

- **Official "Scout" cameras,** Boy Scout, Brownie Scout, Cub Scout, Girl Scout, in black or in official scout colors.
  ....10.00   15.00

HERLANGO AG
(Vienna)

- **Folding camera,** for 7 x 8.5cm. plates or rollfilm back, Tessar f4.5/105mm., Compur shutter 1-250.
  ....20.00   40.00

HERMAGIS
(J. Fleury Hermagis, Paris)

- **Velocigraphe,** c. 1892 detective style drop-plate magazine camera for 12 plates 9 x 13cm. in metal sheaths, polished wooden body built into a heavy leather covering which appears to be a case, front and back flaps expose working parts.
  .... 2750.00   3000.00

HESS-IVES CORPORATION
(Philadelphia, Pa.)

- **Hicro Color Camera,** c. 1915 box-shaped camera for color photos 3¼ x 4¼" by the separation process via multiple exposures with filters, Meniscus lens, Wollensak Ultro shutter, made for Hess-Ives under contract by the Hawkeye Division of E.K.C.
  .... 185.00   195.00

HETHERINGTON & HIBBEN
(Indianapolis)

☐ **Hetherington Magazine Camera,** *c. 1892 magazine camera for 4 x 5 plates, dark brown leather covered, plate advancing, aperture setting, and shutter tensioning are all controlled by a key, this camera was once marketed by Montgomery Ward & Company.*
.... 550.00   650.00

HEXACON
(Dresden)

☐ **Hexacon,** *35mm. SLR, Contax copy, f2/50mm. Cooke Amotal or Zeiss Tessar.*
.................70.00   85.00

HICRO
(See Hess-Ives)

HIT

☐ **Hit,** *Japanese novelty camera for 14 x 14mm. exposures on 16mm. paper backed rollfilm.*
.................10.00   15.00

HIT, STEREO

☐ **Stereo Hit,** *Japanese plastic stereo camera for 127 film, f4.5 lens, synchronized shutter.*
.................80.00   95.00

HOEI INDUSTRIAL COMPANY
(Japan)

☐ **Ebony 35,** *c. 1950 bakelite camera for 25 x 37mm. exposures on 828 rollfilm, f11 meniscus lens, simple B & I shutter.*
.................10.00   12.00

HOFERT
(Emil Hofert, EHO Kamera Fabrik, Dresden, Germany)

Emil Hofert, often abbreviated to "Eho" in camera names, worked closely with B. Altmann, founder of Altissa Kamerawerk, Dresden, and many cameras bear both names. *(See also Altissa.)*

☐ **Eho Altiflex,** *c. 1930's 6 x 6cm. TLR for 120 films, f4.5/75mm. Ludwig Victar, f4.5 or 3.5 Rodenstock Trinar, or f2.8 Laack Pololyt lenses, Prontor or Compur shutter.*
..................50.00   60.00

☐ **Eho-Altmann Juwel Altissa,** *c. 1938, pseudo-TLR box camera for 12 exposures on 120 film, the finder on this model is like many of the cheap TLR cameras, just an oversized brilliant finder, not coupled to focusing mechanism, Rodenstock Periscop f6 lens, simple shutter, black hammertone finish.*
..................20.00   25.00

☐ **Eho box camera,** *c. 1932, for 3 x 4cm. on 127 film, f11/50mm. Duplar lens, simple shutter, B & I, metal body.*
..................50.00   60.00

☐ **Eho Stereo Box camera,** *c. 1930's for 5 stereo pairs 6 x 13cm. or 10 single 6 x 6cm. exposures on 120, B & I shutter, f11/80 Duplar lens.*
..................90.00   110.00

HOLIDAY
(See Eastman, Brownie Holiday)

HOLLYWOOD

☐ **Hollywood,** *novelty mail-in camera.*
..................15.00   20.00

HOLLYWOOD REFLEX
(See Graftex)

HOLOGON
(See Zeiss-Ikon)

HOMEOS
(See Richard)

HOMER 16

- **Homer 16,** *Japanese novelty camera for 13 x 13mm. exposures on 16mm. film, meniscus lens, single shutter.*
  ....12.00   15.00

HOPALONG CASSIDY CAMERA
(See Galter)

HORIZONT

- **Horizont,** *Russian 35mm. panoramic camera with f2.8 pivoting lens for 120 degrees.*
  .... 375.00   425.00

HORSMAN
(E. I. Horsman Co. N.Y.C.)

- **No. 3 Eclipse,** *c. 1896, folding bed, collapsible bellows, polished cherywood view camera for 4½ x 6½ plates, styled like the more common Scovill Waterbury camera, brass barreled meniscus lens, rubberband powered shutter.*
  .... 185.00   210.00

HOUGHTON
(George Houghton & Son Ltd., Houghton's Ltd., pre 1925, Houghton-Butcher, after 1925, London, England)

- **All Distance Ensign Camera,** *an euphemistic term for "fixed focus", ths name was applied to box and folding model cameras for 2¼ x 3¼", 6 x 9cm., on rollfilm, box models.*
  ....10.00   12.00
- **Same as above,** *rollfilm models, including Ensign Pocket Models I and II.*
  ....15.00   20.00
- **Autorange 220 Ensign,** *c. 1941, folding camera offering a choice of 12 or 16 exposures on 120 film, f4.5 Tessar in Compur 1-250, focus by radial lever on bed.*
  ....50.00   60.00
- **Box cameras, Ensign.**
  ....12.00   15.00

  Cameo, Carbine, see Butcher.

- **Cupid,** *c. 1920, simple camera for 4 x 6cm. exposures on 120 film, meniscus achromatic lens, f11.*
  ....60.00   80.00
- **Ensignette,** *c. 1910-1930, all-aluminum bodied folding rollfilm camera of the bedless strut type, similar to the Vest-Pocket Kodak camera but has extensions on both ends of the front panel which serve as table stands, made in two sizes: No. 1 for 1½ x 2¼ and No. 2 for 2 x 3", originally available over a large price range, featuring different lens/shutter combinations.*
  ....45.00   60.00
- **Ensign folding rollfilm camera,** *postcard size for 3¼ x 5½" exposures on 122 film.*
  ....25.00   30.00
- **Klito,** *c. 1905 magazine box camera for 3¼ x 4¼ plates.*
  ....60.00   70.00
- **Folding Klito,** *for 3¼ x 4¼ sheet films, double extension bellows, f6.8 Aldis Plano.*
  ....50.00   75.00
- **May Fair,** *metal box camera, T & I shutter.*
  ....20.00   25.00
- **Midget Ensign,** *c. 1912 compact folding camera for 3.5 x 4.5cm. exposures on 127 film, meniscus lens, shutter 25-100.*
  ....50.00   65.00

HURLBUT MANUFACTURING / 179

☐ **Ensign Reflex and Popular Reflex,** c. 1915-1930 Graflex-style SLR for 3¼ x 4¼ plates, focal plane shutter to 1000, Cooke Luxor lens.
.... 105.00   120.00

☐ **Ensign Rollfilm Reflex,** c. 1920's for 6 x 9cm. exposures on 120 film, two models, non-focusing model, vertical format.
.................75.00   110.00

☐ **Same as above,** focusing model, horizontal format.
.................75.00   85.00

Sanderson cameras
Even though manufactured by Houghton, all Sanderson cameras are listed under Sanderson.

☐ **Selfix 16-20,** c. 1950's, for 16 exposures, 4.5 x 6cm. on 120 film, this style of camera was often called a "semi" at the time, because it took half-size frames on 120, f4.5/75 Ensar of f3.8 Ross Xpress.
.................40.00   60.00

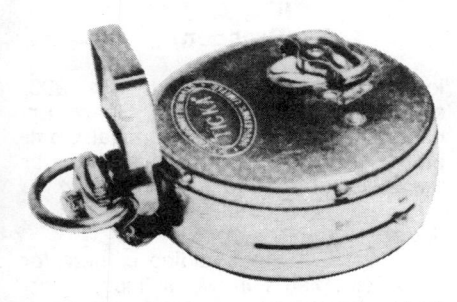

☐ **Ticka,** c. 1905, pocket-watch styled camera manufactured under license from the Expo Camera Company of New York, and identical to the Expo Watch Camera, for 25 exposures 22 x 16mm. on special cassette film, fixed focus f16/30mm. lens, meniscus, I & T shutter.
.... 185.00   200.00

☐ **Ticka,** focal plane model, with focusing lens, rare, exposed works make it easy to identify.
.... 2750.00   3000.00

☐ **Ticka Enlarger,** to enlarge the 166 x 22mm. Ticka negative to 6 x 9cm., meniscus lens.
.................60.00   70.00

HUCKLEBERRY HOUND

☐ **Huckleberry Hound,** modern novelty camera for 127 films featuring the cartoon character on the side.
.................4.00   6.00

HUNTER
(R. F. Hunter, Ltd. London)

☐ **Purma Special,** c. late 1930's bakelite and metal camera for 16 exposures 32 x 32mm., 1¼" square, on 127 film, three speed metal focal plane shutter, speeds controlled by gravity, fixed focus f6.3/2¼" Beck Anastigmat plastic lens, one of the first cameras to use a plastic lens.
.................50.00   70.00

HURLBUT MANUFACTURING COMPANY
(Belvidere, Ill.)

180 / HÜTTIG

☐ **Velox Magazine Camera,** c. 1890, an unusual magazine-plate detective camera, plates are dropped into the plane of focus and returned to storage by turning the camera cover.
.... 850.00   950.00

HÜTTIG
(R. Hüttig A.G., Dresden, R. Hüttig & Son, Dresden)

Claimed in 1910 advertisements to be the oldest and largest camera works in Europe. Soon became Ica, then merged to form Zeiss-Ikon in 1926.

☐ **Atom,** c. 1908 plate camera for 4.5 x 6cm., f8/90mm. lens, Compound shutter 1-250.
.... 150.00   175.00

☐ **Folding plate camera,** c. 1906, for 9 x 12cm. plates, black leathered wood body, aluminum bed, red bellows, Pneumatic shutter 25-100.
.... 40.00   50.00

☐ **Helios,** strut-type folding plate camera, 9 x 12cm., 185mm., Anastigmat lens, focal plane shutter 6-1000.
.... 120.00   150.00

☐ **Ideal,** c. 1908 9 x 12cm. folding-bed plate camera, Huttig Extra Rapid Aplanat Helios f8, Automat shutter B, T, 25-100, aluminum standard and bed, red bellows.
.... 45.00   55.00

☐ **Ideal Stereo,** c. 1908, 6 x 13cm. plates,, Extra Rapid Aplanat Helios f8/105mm., Huttig Stereo Automat shutter T, B, 1-100.
.... 135.00   180.00

☐ **Lloyd,** folding camera for 3¼ x 4¼ rollfilm or 9 x 12 plates, Goerz Dagor f6.8/135, Compound shutter 1-250, double extension red bellows.
.... 50.00   70.00

☐ **Magazine cameras,** c. 1900, including varied Monopol models, 9 x 12cm. drop-plate type box cameras, leather covered, focusing aplanat lens and simple shutter.
.... 140.00   160.00

☐ **Record Stereo Camera,** for 9 x 18cm. plates, Hugo Meyer Aristostigmat f6.8/120mm. lenses, focal plane shutter.
.... 170.00   190.00

☐ **Stereolette,** c. 1909 small folding stereo camera for 45 x 107mm. plates, f8/65mm. Helios lens, I, B, T shutter.
.... 200.00   250.00

☐ **Tropical plate camera,** 6 x 9cm. folding-bed type, double extension bellows, brown, Steinheil Triplan f4.5/135 lens in Compound shutter f-150, fine wood body with brass trim and bed.
.... 600.00   650.00

ICA A.G.
(Dresden)

Ica became a part of Zeiss-Ikon in 1926, along with Contessa-Nettel, Goerz, Ernemann, and Carl Zeiss Optical Company. Some modes were continued under the Zeiss name. *(See also Zeiss-Ikon.)*

Atom

c. 1910-1920. Small folding camera for 4.5 x 6cm. plates. In two distinctly different models, both in appearance and current value.

☐ **Horizontal-format Atom,** *a folding bed type with self-erecting front, generally with f4.5/65mm. Tessar or f6.8 Hekla, Compound shutter, 1-300, unusual location of reflex brilliant finder, viewing lens on front center of bed, but mirror and objective lens extend below the bed.*
.... 325.00   350.00

ICA A.G. / 181

☐ **Vertical format Atom,** *in the more traditional folding bed style, Reflex finder is still on the front of the bed, but remains above the bed.*
.... 180.00   195.00

Bebe
Folding plate cameras in the common sizes, but again two quite different styles, most easily distinguished by format orientation.

☐ **Horizontal format Bebe,** *40/2 for 4.5 x 6cm. plates, bedless strut-type folding style, Tessar f4.5/75mm. in dial-set Compur shutter which is built into the flat front of the camera.*
.... 195.00   225.00

☐ **Vertical format Bebe,** *in the normal drop-bed folding style, such as the Bebe A, Tessar f3.5 or 4.5 lens, dial-set Compur shutter.*
.... 40.00   50.00

☐ **Cameo Stereo,** *c. 1912 folding bed stereo camera for 9 x 18cm. plates, Extra Rapid Aplanat Helios lenses, Automat Stereo shutter, ½-1000, T, B, twin tapered bellows, black covered wood body.*
.... 200.00   225.00

☐ **Cupido,** *folding bed camera for 6 x 9cm. plates or rollfilm back, Tessar f4.5/12cm. lens, Compur dial-set shutter.*
.... 40.00   50.00

☐ **Favorit 425,** *c. 1925 folding-bed camera for 13 x 18cm., 5 x 7", plates, square black DE leather bellows, f6.3/210mm. Tessar, Compur dial-set 1-150, an uncommon size.*
.... 125.00   150.00

☐ **Folding plate cameras,** *miscellaneous models, in 6 x 9 and 9 x 12cm. sizes.*
.... 30.00   40.00

Cupido

☐ **Halloh,** *Models 505, 510, 511, folding rollfilm cameras, also for plate backs, in the 8 x 10.5 cm., 3¼ x 4¼", size, f4.5/12cm. Tessar, or f6.8/135 Litonar, Dial Compur shutter 1-250, B, T.*
.... 40.00   50.00

☐ **Icar,** *c. 1920 folding bed plate camera for 9 x 12cm., Ica Dominar f4.5/135, Compur dial-set shutter, T, B, 1-200.*
.... 40.00   50.00

☐ **Icarette,** *folding bed rollfilm cameras for 120 film, two basic styles, the horizontally styled body for 6 x 6cm. exposures, such as the Icarette A, and the vertical body style for 6 x 9 cm., such as the Icarette C, D, and L, prices average the same for either style.*
.... 50.00   60.00

182 / ICA A.G.

- **Ideal,** 6 x 9cm., c. 1920's folding-bed vertical style plate cameras, double extension bellows, see also Zeiss for the continuation of this line of cameras, f6.8/90 Hekla, f6.3/90 Tessar, or f4.5/105 Litonar, Compur 1-150.
  ....40.00   50.00
- **Same as above,** 9 x 12cm., f4.5/150mm. Tessar, Compur.
  ....40.00   50.00
- **Same as above,** 13 x 18cm., 5 x 7", f4.5/210mm. Tessar in dial Compur shutter, this larger size is much less common than the others.
  ....75.00   100.00
- **Juwel, Universal Juwel,** c. 1925, also continued as a Zeiss model after 1926, a drop-bed folding plate camera of standard style, except that it has square format bellows and rotating back, it also incorporates triple extension bellows, wide angle position, and all normal movements.
  ....75.00   100.00
- **Lloyd, Stereo model,** c. 1910, folding stereo, or panoramic, camera for plates or rollfilm, Stereo Compound shutter 1-100, f6.8/90mm. Double Anastigmat Maximar lenses.
  .... 200.00   275.00
- **Maximar,** folding bed double extension precision plate camera, although the Zeiss-Ikon Maximar is much more common, it originated as an Ica model, 9 x 12cm. size with f4.5/135 Novar, f6.8/135 Hekla, f4.5/135 Litonar, in Compound, Compur, or Rulex shutter.
  ....40.00   50.00
- **Minimal,** folding bed double extension sheet-film camera, 9 x 12cm. with f6.8/135 Hekla, or f6.8/120 Goerz Dagor, Ica Automat or Compound shutter, leather covered wood body.
  ....40.00   50.00

- **Minimum Palmos,** c. 1935 compact vertical format folding bed camera for 4.5 x 6cm. plates, most unusual feature is the focal plane shutter, T, B, 50-1000, this is Ica's smallest focal plane camera, Zeiss Tessar f2.7/80.
  .... 225.00   295.00
- **Nelson 225,** c. 1915 folding bed double-extension plate camera for 9 x 12cm., Tessar f4.5/150, Dial Compur T, B, 1-150.
  ....40.00   60.00

- **Nero,** c. 1905 magazine box camera for 9 x 12cm. plates, guillotine shutter, T & I.
  ....65.00   80.00
- **Niklas,** c. 1920's folding bed plate cameras, 6 x 9 and 9 x 12cm. sizes, f4.5 Litonar or Tessar lens in Compur shutter.
  ....40.00   50.00
- **Nixe,** c. 1920's folding bed camera for 9 x 12 plates of 122 rollfilm.
  ....40.00   50.00

ICA A.G. / 183

☐ **Periscop,** 9 x 12cm. plate camera, Alpha lens.
.................40.00   50.00

☐ **Plascop,** c. 1925 rigid-bodied stereo camera for 6 x 13cm. plates or packfilm, Ica Novar Anastigmat f6.8/75mm lens in guillotine shutter, T & I, black leather covered wood body with black painted metal parts, reflex and wire frame finders.
.... 165.00   185.00

☐ **Polyscop,** c. 1910-1925, rigid bodied stereo camera in two common formats: 45 x 107mm., and 6 x 13cm., some models had plate backs, some had magazine backs, could also be used as panoramic cameras by using one lens in the center position and removing the septum, f4.5 or 6.3 Tessar lenses.
.... 200.00   225.00

☐ **Cheaper models,** with simple lenses and without magazine backs.
.... 195.00   225.00

☐ **Reflex 756, 756/1,** c. 1910-1925 Graflex style SLR for 8.5 x 11cm., 3¼ x 4¼", plates, examples: "Artists" reflex, Tudor, etc., f4.5/150mm. Tessar lens, focal plane shutter to 1000.
.... 140.00   160.00

☐ **Folding Reflex,** a very compact SLR which folds to about one-third the size of the box model, f4.5 Tessar or Dominar.
.... 200.00   250.00

☐ **Sirene,** folding plate cameras, 6 x 9 or 9 x 12cm. sizes, economy models with f11 Periskop or f6.8 Eurynar lens, Ibso shutter.
.................22.00   26.00

☐ **Stereo camera,** for 122 rollfilm, f6.3 Zeiss lens.
.... 225.00   250.00

☐ **Stereo Ideal,** folding stereo camera for 9 x 18cm. plates, like type 660, twin f6.3 Tessar lenses, Compound shutter to 150, twin black bellows.
.... 200.00   250.00

☐ **Stereo Ideal, type 651,** c. 1910 folding bed stereo camera for 6 x 13cm. plates, 90mm. lenses, f4.5 or 6.3 Tessar or f6.8 Double Anastigmat, in Stereo Compound shutter, magazine back.
.... 200.00   250.00

☐ **Stereolette,** c. 1912-1926 compact folding-bed type stereo camera for 45 x 107mm. plates, variety of available lens/shutter combinations.
.... 200.00   250.00

☐ **Stereolette Cupido, type 620.**
.... 175.00   195.00

☐ **Teddy,** 9 x 12cm. folding plate camera, f8/130mm. Extra Rapid Aplanat Helios or f6.8/135 Double Anastigmat Heklar, Automat shutter.
..................20.00   30.00

184 / ICARETTE

- □ **Toska,** 9 x 12cm. folding plate camera, Zeiss Double Amatar f6.8/135, or f8/130 Rapid Aplanat Helios, Ica Automat or Compound shutter.
  .... 20.00   30.00

- □ **Trilby 18,** c. 1912 magazine box camera for 6 plates 9 x 12cm., or 12 exposures on sheet film, Ica Achromat lens, guillotine shutter, T & I, automatic exposure counter.
  .... 125.00   135.00

- □ **Trix,** c. 1915 cut film cameras in 4.5 x 6cm size.
  .... 115.00   135.00

- □ **Same as above,** 9 x 12cm. size.
  .... 40.00   60.00

- □ **Trona,** 6 x 9 or 9 x 12cm. double extension plate cameras, f4.5 Tessar, Compur shutter.
  .... 40.00   60.00

- □ **Tropica 285,** tropical model folding-bed 9 x 12cm. plate camera, square back style, double extension bellows, finely finished wood body with brass trim.
  .... 750.00   850.00

- □ **Victrix,** c. 1912-1925 folding bed camera for 4.5 x 6cm. plates, Ica Dominar f4.5/75 or Hekla f6.8/75mm., Automat or Compur shutter, focus by radial lever on bed.
  .... 125.00   140.00

ICARETTE
(See Ica, Zeiss)

IDEAL
(See Ica, Huttig, Zeiss, Burke & James)

IDEAL TOY CORPORATION
(Hollis, N.Y.)

- □ **Kookie Kamera,** c. 1968, certainly in the running for the most unusual camera design of all time, from the plumbing pipes to the soup can, it looks like a modern junk sculpture, but takes 1¾ x 1¾" photos on direct positive paper for in-camera processing.
  .... 50.00   70.00

IDENT
(See Cam-co)

IHAGEE
(Kamerawerk, Steenbergen & Co., Dresden, Germany)

Duplex cameras
Ihagee used the name "Duplex" for two distinctly different cameras.

- □ **Duplex two-shuttered,** folding bed plate camera c. 1920's, square body, focal plane shutter, in addition to the front inter-lens shutter, this was the camera which inspired the name, made in 6 x 9 and 9 x 12cm. sizes.
  .... 175.00   195.00

- □ **Duplex, vertical format,** c. 1940's folding bed plate camera, f3.5 or 4.5 Steinheil lens, Compur shutter, double extension.
  .... 40.00   50.00

IHAGEE / 185

☐ **Exa,** 35mm. focal plane SLR, models I, Ia, II, IIa, IIb, with normal lens, f2.8 Meritar or f2.9 Domiplan.
................50.00   60.00

☐ **Exakta, original model, A,** introduced in 1933, it was the first small focal plane SLR, for 8 exposures 4 x 6.5cm. on 127 rollfilm, f3.5 Exaktar or Tessar, focal plane shutter 25-100, black finish, some models with slow speeds to 12 seconds, some models not synched.
...............200.00   225.00

☐ **Exakta B,** similar to model A, main body still black leather covered, but some models have chrome finish on metal parts, focal plane shutter 25-1000, + slow speeds to 12 seconds and self timer, with normal lens, f2.8 or f3.5 Tessar or Xenar.
...............175.00   195.00

☐ **Exakta Junior,** similar to model B, but speeds only 25-500, no self timer.
...............120.00   130.00

☐ **Night Exakta,** similar to model B, but wider lens flange size for special fast lenses, not a common model, probably because of non-standard lens mount, it was available in all-black or in black and nickel, with Biotar or Xenon lens.
...............300.00   350.00

Note: Some people think that the half-moon on the top of the viewing hood identifies this camera. Not true. The half-moon and rising sun is a trademark of the Ihagee company, and it appears on many Exakta models, as well as other Ihagee cameras. The easiest way to make a quick identification is that the serial number is on the viewing hood and not on the lens flange.

☐ **Exakta C.**
...............175.00   185.00

☐ **Exakta II, Kine Exakta,** c. 1935, for 35mm. film, interchangeable bayonet-mount lenses, f2.8 or 3.5/50 Tessar, f2.8/50 Westar, f2/50 Schneider Xenon.
...............60.00   75.00

☐ **Exakta V,** c. 1950, 35mm. film, with normal lens as listed above.
...............70.00   80.00

☐ **Exakta VX,** c. 1950's, 35mm. with lens similar to Exakta II.
...............60.00   80.00

☐ **Exakta VX IIA.**
...............70.00   85.00

Exakta 66
Single lens reflex for 12 exposures. 6 x 6cm. on 120 rollfilm. f2.8 Tessar or Xenar. Two distinct body styles.

186 / IKKO SHA

- **Exakta 66 Pre-war model,** c. 1938, horizontal body style and film transport, like most 35mm. cameras, or like the 6 x 6cm. Korelle reflex, focal plane shutter, 12 seconds to 1/1000.
  . . . . 350.00   400.00
- **Exakta 66 Post-war style,** vertical style, much like the twin-lens reflex shape, but with only one lens, scattered prices.
  . . . . 350.00   500.00

- **Ihagee folding plate cameras,** 6 x 9 size, with f4.5/105 Tessar, Compur shutter.
  . . . . 40.00   60.00
- **Same as above,** larger 9 x 12cm. size with similar lens/shutter.
  . . . . 45.00   65.00
- **Ihagee folding rollfilm camera,** for 8 exposures 6 x 9cm. on 120 film, f4.5 anastigmat lens in Compur or Prontor shutter.
  . . . . 25.00   35.00
- **Paff,** c. 1920's SLR box camera for 120 film, simple meniscus lens, single speed shutter.
  . . . . 80.00   100.00

- **Parvola,** c. 1930's camera for 127 rollfilm, telescoping front, three models: 3 x 4cm., 4 x 6.5cm., and the "twin" or "two-format" model for either size, could also use plates or packs.
  . . . . 75.00   100.00
- **Patent Klapp Reflex,** c. 1920's compact folding SLR for 6.5 x 9 or 9 x 12cm., focal plane shutter to 1000, f4.5 Dogmar, Tessar, or Xenar.
  . . . . 350.00   400.00
- **Stereo camera,** folding bed style for 6 x 13cm. plates, Meyer Trioplan f6.3/80mm., Stereo Prontor shutter.
  . . . . 200.00   250.00
- **Ultrix, Auto,** c. 1930 folding bed camera for rollfilm, small size for 4 x 6.5cm. on 127 film, larger size for 6 x 9cm. on 120.
  . . . . 40.00   60.00
- **Ultrix, Cameo, Weeny,** models with telescoping screw-out lens mount like the Parvola.
  . . . . 80.00   100.00

IKKO SHA
(Japan)

- **Start 35,** a simple plastic eye-level camera for 828 film, despite the name, this is one of few cameras for 828 film ever made outside of the United States.
  . . . . 20.00   25.00

IKOFLEX, IKOMAT, IKONETTE, IKONTA
(See Zeiss-Ikon)

ILOCA
(See Witt)

ILOCA TOWER
(See Tower)

IMPERIAL
(See Herco)

INGENTO
(See Burke & James)

INSPECTOGRAPH
(fingerprint camera)
(See Graflex)

INSTANTOGRAPH
(See Lancaster)

INTERNATIONAL RESEARCH CORPORATION
(See Argus)

IRIS
(See Universal Camera Corp.)

IRWIN
(U.S.A.)

☐ **Irwin,** *cheap cameras such as Irwin Reflex, Irwin Kandor, etc.*
................10.00   12.00

ISO
(Italy)

☐ **Duplex,** *c. 1950 stereo camera for 24 pairs of 24 x 24mm. exposures on 120 film, the 24 x 24 format was the common format for 35mm. stereo, but putting the images side-by-side on 120 film advanced vertically was a novel idea.*
.... 125.00   150.00

ISO, ISOFLASH, ISOLAR, ISOLETTE, ISO RAPID
(See Agfa)

JAPY & CIE
(France)

☐ **le Pascal,** *c. 1898 box camera with spring-motor transport for 12 exposures 40 x 55mm. on rollfilm, meniscus lens with 3 stops, shutter has 2 speeds + B, leather covered wood and metal body with brass trim, the first motorized rollfilm camera.*
.... 750.00   850.00

JEANNERET & CIE
(Paris)

☐ **Monobloc,** *c. 1915-1926 stereo camera for 6 x 13cm. plates, f4.5 Boyer Sapphir or f6.3 Roussel Stylor 85mm. lenses, built-in magazine, pneumatic shutter, metal body, partly leather covered.*
.... 200.00   250.00

JEM
(J. E. Mergett Co., Newark, N.J.)

☐ **Jem Jr. 120,** *all metal box camera c. 1940's, simple lens and shutter.*
...................6.00   8.00

JIFFY
(See Eastman)

JOS-PE
(Joseph Peter, Hamburg and Munich)

☐ **Tri-Color Camera,** *c. 1925 all-metal camera for single-shot 3-color separation negatives, made in 4.5 x 6cm. and 8.5 x 11cm. sizes.*
.... 1500.00   1800.00

JOUX
(L. Joux & Cie, Paris, France)

☐ **Alethoscope,** *c. 1912 stereo camera for 45 x 107mm. plates, 5-speed guillotine shutter.*
.... 175.00   200.00

☐ **Ortho Jumelle Duplex,** *c. 1895 rigid-bodied "jumelle" style camera for 6 x 9cm. plates, f8/110mm. Zeiss Krauss Anastigmat, five speed guillotine shutter, plate magazine, an uncommon camera.*
.... 200.00   225.00

JUBILAR
(See Voigtlander)

JUBILEE
(See Bolsey)

JUBILETTE
(See Balda)

Jumelle
(See French manufacturers such as: Bellieni, Carpentier, Gaumont, Joux, Richard, etc.) Jumelle is the French word for "twins," also meaning binoculars. Commonly used to describe stereo cameras of the European rigid-body style, as well as other "binocular-styled" cameras where one of the two lenses is a viewing lens and the other takes single exposures.

JUWEL
(See Hofert, Ica, Zeiss)

JUWELLA
(See Balda)

KALART COMPANY
(New York City)

☐ **Press camera,** 3¼ x 4¼ size, f4.5/127mm. Wollensak Raptar in Rapax shutter.
.... 200.00   250.00

KALIMAR
(Japan)

☐ **Kalimar A,** c. 1950's 35mm. non-RF camera, f3.5/45mm. Terionar lens.
.................20.00   25.00

KALLOFLEX
(See Kowa)

KAMRA
(See Bell, Devry)

KAMARET
(See Blair)

KAMERET

☐ **Kameret Jr. No. 2,** c. 1930's Japanese box camera for 1¼ x 2" cut film.
.................25.00   35.00

KAMREX
(See Lancaster)

KARAT
(See Agfa)

KARDON
(See Premier Instrument Company)

KARMA
(See Arnold)

KAROMAT
(See Ansco, Agfa)

KAWEE
(See Guthe & Thorsch)

KEMPER
(Alfred C. Kemper, Chicago)

☐ **Kombi,** c. 1890's, the mini-marvel of the decade, a 4 ounce seamless metal miniature box camera with oxidized silver finish, made to take 25 exposures 1⅛" square on rollfilm, then double as a transparency viewer, from whence the name "Kombi," sold for $3.00 new, and Kemper's ads proclaimed "50,000 sold in one year," although not rare, they are a prized collector's item.
.... 200.00   250.00

KENFLEX

☐ **Kenflex,** Japanese 6 x 6cm. TLR, f3.5 First lens.
..................35.00   40.00

KENGOTT
(W. Kengott, Stuttgart)

☐ **6 x 9cm. plate camera,** c. 1920's, folding-bed style, double extension, f4.8/105mm. Leitmeyr Sytar lens in Ibsor 1-125 shutter.
..................30.00   40.00

- [ ] **10 x 15cm. plate camera,** *with revolving back, triple extension bellows, Kengott, Paris, Double Anastigmat f6.8/180mm. lens in Koilos shutter 1-300, leathered wood body.*
  ....50.00   75.00

- [ ] **Tropical model 10 x 15cm. plate camera,** *Steinheil Unofocal f4.5/150 lens in Kengott Koilos 1-100, T, B shutter, candlewood body, gold plated brass trim, light brown leather bellows.*
  .... 700.00   800.00

KENT

- [ ] **Kent,** *Japanese 14mm. novelty camera.*
  ....10.00   15.00

KEWPIE
(See Conley)

KEYS STEREO PRODUCTS (U.S.A.)

- [ ] **Trivision Camera,** *c. 1950's for 6 stereo pairs or 12 single shots on 828 film, fixed focus f8 lenses, single speed shutter.*
  ....30.00   40.00

KEYSTONE FERROTYPE CAMERA COMPANY
(Philadelphia, Pennsylvania)

- [ ] **Street camera,** *suitcase style direct-positive street camera with ceramic tank inside, various masks allow taking different sized pictures.*
  .... 150.00   200.00

KIEV
(Moscow, USSR)

- [ ] **Kiev,** *c. 1945-1960's 35mm. RF camera, Contax copy, f2/50mm. Jupiter lens.*
  .... 100.00   125.00

KILFITT
(Hans Kilfitt, Munich, Germany, Heinz Kilfitt Kamerabau, Vaduz, Liechtenstein, Metz Aparatebau, Nürnberg, Germany)

- [ ] **Mecaflex,** *a well-made 35mm. SLR in an odd format, 24 x 24mm., for 50 exposures on regular 35mm. cartridge film, interchangeable bayonet mount lenses, f3.5 or 2.8/40mm. Kilar, Prontor-Reflex behind-lens shutter, entire top cover of camera hinges forward to reveal the waist-level reflex finder, rapid-wind lever, exposure counter, etc., when closed, the matte-chromed cast metal body with its grey leatherette covering looks somewhat like a sleek, knobless Exakta, not too many were made, and it was never officially imported into the United States.*
  .... 475.00   575.00

KINAX
(See Kinn)

KINDER

- [ ] **Kindar Stereo camera,** *35mm. film in standard cartridges, f3.5 Steinheil Cassar lenses.*
  .... 100.00   125.00

KING
(See Metropolitan Supply Company)

KING
(Germany)

- [ ] **Regula,** *35mm. cameras various models: 1, IIID, B, KG, PD, etc., f2.8 Cassar, Gotar, or Ennit lens.*
  ....30.00   50.00

KING CAMERA
(Japan)

190 / KING POCO

☐ **King Camera,** *cardboard miniature box camera for single plate holder, single speed shutter, ground glass back.*
.... 25.00   30.00

KING POCO
(See Rochester)

KINN
(France)

☐ **Kinax,** *folding camera for 8 exposures on 120 film, f4.5/105 Berthiot lens.*
.... 25.00   30.00

KIRK

☐ **Stereo Camera, Model 33,** *brown bakelite body.*
.... 35.00   40.00

KIYABASHI KOGAKU
(Japan)

☐ **Autoflex,** *6 x 6cm. TLR for 120 film, f3.5 Tri-Lausar lens.*
.... 35.00   40.00

KLACK
(See Reitzschel)

KLAPP

Klapp is included in the name of many German cameras, it simply means "folding." Look for another key reference word in the name of the camera.

KLEFFEL
(L. G. Kleffel & Sohn, Berlin)

☐ **Field camera,** *c. 1890, 13 x 18cm., 5 x 7", horizontal format, brown square-cornered bellows, wood body with brass trim, brass barrel lens.*
.... 200.00   225.00

KLIMAX
(See Butcher)

KLITO
(See Houghton)

KLONDIKE
(See Anthony)

KNACK DETECTIVE CAMERA
(See Scovill)

KOCHMANN
(Franz Kochmann, Dresden)

Korelle cameras
There are several basic types of Korelle cameras which appear regularly on today's market, the most common of these by far is the reflex. All types, even if not identified by model name or number on the camera, are easily distinguished by size and style. For this reason, we have listed the Korelle cameras here in order of increasing size.

☐ **Korelle camera, 18 x 24mm. Korelle K,** *compact 35mm. half-frame camera in vertical format, body of thermoplastic is neither folding nor collapsing type, shutter/lens assembly is a fixed part of the body, front lens focusing, Tessar f2.8/35mm. in Compur 1-300.*
.... 150.00   200.00

- [ ] **Korelle camera, 3 x 4cm.**, *style similar to the model K, or like a Wirgin Klein-Edinex, for 16 exposures on 127 film, this model has telescoping front like the Edinex, Schneider Radionar f2.9/50, Compur 1-300, T, B.*
  ....60.00   80.00
- [ ] **Korelle camera, 4 x 6.5cm.**, *strut-folding rollfilm type, for 8 exposures on 127 film, Schneider Radionar f3.5/75mm. or Xenar f2.8/75mm., Compur or Compur Rapid shutter, c. 1930, basically the same as the Korelle "P", but with rounded ends added to the length of the body to house the film rolls.*
  ....70.00   100.00
- [ ] **Korelle camera, 4 x 6cm.**, *Korelle "P", for plates, strut-folding type, similar to the rollfilm model, but shorter and with square ends, a fine quality vest-pocket plate camera, Tessar f2.8/75mm., or f2.9 Xenar, Compur shutter 1-250, leather covered metal body.*
  .... 100.00   150.00
- [ ] **Korelle camera, Reflex Korelle**, *also called Meister Korelle, and Master Reflex, introduced c. 1934, single lens reflex for 12 exposures 6 x 6 cm. on 120 film, probably the earliest 6 x 6cm. SLR, the first model is identifiable by the focal plane shutter 1/25 to 1/500 only, + B, later models extended the range to 1/10-1/1000.*
  .... 100.00   125.00

KODAK
(See Eastman)

KOGAKU

Kogaku is Japanese for "Optical." This term is found in the name of many Japanese firms, usually preceded by the key name of the manufacturer. (However, if you are reading the name from a lens, it may only be the maker of the lens and not the camera.)

KONISHIROKU KOGAKU / 191

KOLA
(Czechoslovakia)

- [ ] **Kola**, *c. 1936, an unusual camera for various formats on either of two types of film, takes 4 x 4cm. or 3 x 4cm. exposures on 127 film or 24 x 36mm. exposures on 35mm. film with different masks, Zeiss f2.8/60mm. Tessar or f2.9/50mm. Xenar, Compur shutter, quite uncommon.*
  .... 200.00   250.00

KOLIBRI
(See Zeiss)

KOMAFLEX

- [ ] **Komaflex**, *c. 1960's SLR for 4 x 4cm. on 127 film, one of very few 4 x 4SLR's ever made.*
  .... 100.00   150.00

KOMBI
(See Kemper)

KONAN
(See Chiyoda Kogaku)

KONICA
(See Konishiroku)

KONISHIROKU KOGAKU
(Japan)

- [ ] **Konica**, *c. 1951 35mm. RF, f2.8 or 3.5 Hexanon lens.*
  ....50.00   60.00
- [ ] **Konica II.**
  ....50.00   60.00
- [ ] **Konica III.**
  ....60.00   70.00
- [ ] **Pearl, Baby**, *folding camera for 16 exposures on 127 film, f4.5/50 Optor lens.*
  ....45.00   55.00
- [ ] **Pearl II**, *folding 6 x 9cm. rollfilm, c. 1920's for 120 film, typical folding-bed rollfilm camera style.*
  ....40.00   50.00

192 / KOOKY

Pearl, Baby

☐ **Pearl II,** folding 4.5 x 6cm. rollfilm, c. 1950 for 120 film "semi" or half-size frames, f4.5/75mm. Hexar, rangefinder coupled on some models.
.................50.00   60.00

☐ **Pearlette,** c. 1920's and 1930's folding, via trellis-type struts, camera for 4 x 6.5cm. exposures on 127 film, Rokuohsha Optar f6.3/75mm. in Echo shutter 25-100.
.................50.00   60.00

☐ **Semi-Pearl,** c. 1930's-1950's folding bed camera for 16 exposures, 4.5 x 6cm. on 120 film, some post-war models with rangefinder, Hexar f4.5/75mm. lens.
.................50.00   60.00

KOOKY (NOVELTY CAMERA)
(See Ideal Toy)

KORELLE
(See Kochmann)

KORNER & MAYER
(See Nettel)

KORONA
(See Gundlach)

KOSMO KLACK
(See Reitzschel)

KOWA OPTICAL

☐ **Kalloflex,** c. 1955, TLR, 6 x 6cm. on 120.
.... 165.00   185.00

KRAUSS
(G. A. Krauss, Stuttgart, E. Krauss, Paris)

☐ **Eka,** Paris, c. 1924, for 100 exposures, 35 x 45mm. on 35mm. unperforated film, Krauss Zeiss Tessar f3.5/50, Compur 1-300.
.... **2150.00   2250.00**

☐ **Peggy I,** Stuttgart, c. 1935, 35mm. strut-folding camera, Tessar f3.5/50mm., Compur shutter 1-300.
.... **800.00   900.00**

- **Peggy II,** Stuttgart, c. 1935, basically the same as Peggy I, but with coupled RF, often with f2 or 2.8 Tessar.
  . . . . 800.00   900.00
- **Photo Revolver,** c. 1920's for 18 x 35mm. exposures on 48 plates in magazine or rollfilm in special back.
  . . . . 2400.00   2600.00
- **Polyscop,** c. 1910 stereo camera for 45 x 107mm. plates in magazine back.
  . . . . 200.00   225.00
- **Rollette,** c. 1920's folding rollfilm cameras with Krauss Rollar f6.3/90mm. lens in Pronto 25-100 shutter, focus by radial lever on bed.
  . . . . 50.00   75.00
- **Takyr,** Paris, c. 1906, strut-folding camera for 9 x 12cm. plates, Krauss Zeiss Tessar f6.3/136mm. focal plane shutter.
  . . . . 225.00   250.00

KRUGENER
(Dr. Ronald Krugener, Bockheim/Frankfurt, Germany)

KRUGENER / 193

- **Delta folding plate camera,** 9 x 12cm., black leather covered wood body, aluminum standard, nickel trim, f6.8/120mm. Dagor or Euryscop Anastigmat lens, Delta shutter 25-100.
  . . . . 50.00   60.00
- **Delta Magazine Camera,** c. 1892, for 12 exposures, 9 x 12cm. on plates which are changed by pulling out rod at front of camera, Achromat lens, simple spring shutter.
  . . . . 600.00   700.00
- **Delta Periscop,** c. 1900 folding bed camera for 9 x 12cm. plates, Krugener Rapid Delta Periscop f12 lens in Delta shutter 25-100, wood body covered with leather, red bellows.
  . . . . 90.00   110.00
- **Jumelle-style magazine camera,** for 18 plates, 6 x 10.7cm., brass-barrel Periscop lens, leather covered wood body, built-in changing magazine.
  . . . . 200.00   250.00
- **Simplex Magazine Camera,** c. 1889 TLR with changing mechanism for 24 plates, 6 x 8cm. Steinheil or Periscop f10/100mm. lens, Sector shutter, polished mahogany.
  . . . . 1250.00   1400.00

KULLENBERG, O.
(Essen, Germany)

- **Field camera,** *13 x 18cm., 5 x 7", vertical format field camera with red tapered bellows, brass-barreled Universal Aplanat f8 lens with iris diaphragm, Rouleau shutter.*
.... 200.00   250.00

KUNICK, WALTER KG
(Frankfurt)

- **Petie,** *c. 1958 subminiature for 16 exposures, 14 x 14mm. on 16mm. film, meniscus f9/25mm. in simple shutter.*
.................60.00   70.00

- **Tuxi,** *for 14 x 14mm. on 16mm film, Achromat Röschlein f7.7/25mm. lens in two-speed synchronized shutter.*
..................50.00   60.00

- **Tuximat,** *14 x 14mm. on 16mm. film, meniscus lens, f7.7/25mm., two-speed synchronized shutter, simple built-in meter.*
..................70.00   80.00

KURBI & NIGGELOH
(Germany)

- **Bilora Bella 44,** *127 film.*
..................15.00   20.00

- **Bilora Blitz Boy,** *red-brown bakelite box for 6 x 6cm. on 120, f6.3/75mm.*
..................10.00   12.00

- **Bilora Boy,** *c. 1950 bakelite box for 4 x 6.5cm. exposures on 127, simple lens/shutter.*
..................10.00   12.00

- **Bilora Radix,** *postwar, 24 x 24mm. on 35mm. Rapid cassettes, Biloxar Anastigmat f5.6/38mm. behind-the-lens rotary shutter.*
..................30.00   40.00

K.W. (KAMERA WERKSTATTEN A.G.)
(See Guthe)

LAACK
(Julius Laack & Sons, Rathenow)

- **Padie,** *9 x 12cm. folding plate camera, Laack Pololyt f6.8/135mm., Rulex 1-300 shutter.*
...................40.00   50.00

LADIES CAMERA
(See Lancaster)

LAMPERTI & GARBAGNATI
(Milan)

- **Detective camera,** *9 x 12cm. c. 1890, polished wood body, leather changing sack, without lens.*
.................300.00   350.00

LANCASTER, J.
(Birmingham, England)

- **Instantograph ½ plate view,** *c. 1894, wood body, brass-barrel Lancaster lens.*
................250.00   325.00

- **Instantograph ¼ plate view,** *c. 1891, brass barrel Lancaster f8 or f10 lens in Lancaster rotary shutter, iris diaphragm, tapered red bellows, wood body.*
.................300.00   350.00

- **Kamrex,** *c. 1900 ¼-plate camera, red leather bellows, mahogany with brass trim.*
.................140.00   160.00

- **Ladies Camera,** *c. 1890's, ½-plate reversible-back camera, Achromatic lens, iris diaphragm, single speed pneumatic shutter.*
.................600.00   700.00

- **Le Merveilleux,** *c. 1890's ¼-plate camera, aplanat lens.*
.................225.00   250.00

LANCER
(See Ansco)

LeCOULTRE
(See Compass)

LE PASCAL
(See Japy & Cie)

LEHMANN
(A. Lehmann, Berlin)

Cane Handle Camera c. 1903. Obviously, a rare camera like this cannot be shackled with an "average" price, two known sales were for $5,000, and $8,000.

LEICA
(See Leitz)

LEIDOLF
(Wetzlar)

☐ **Leidox II,** c. 1951, for 4 x 4cm. Triplet f3.8/50mm. lens in Prontor-S shutter to 300.
.................60.00   70.00

☐ **Lordomat, Lordomatic** 35mm. camera with interchangeable f2.8/50mm. Lordonar, Prontor-SVS shutter, CRF & BIM, two-stroke film advance.
.................50.00   60.00

☐ **Lordox,** compact 35mm., f2.8/50 or f3.8/50, Pronto shutter, body release.
.................30.00   45.00

LEITZ
(Ernst Leitz GmbH, Wetzlar)

Leica cameras
All models listed are for full-frame (24 x 36mm.) exposures, and all are listed in chronological order by date of introduction. Although we have included a few basic identification features for each camera, these are meant only for quick reference. For more complete descriptions, serial number lists, or history of each model, we would suggest that you refer to a specialty book on Leica cameras. There are a number of good references, among which are: *Leica, The First Fifty Years* by C. Rogliatti, published by Hove Camera Foto Books in England;

LEITZ / 195

Leica Illustrated Guide by James L. Lager, published by Morgan & Morgan in New York. The collecting of Leica cameras is a distinct specialty within the camera collecting field for several reasons. The Leica line has always been one of extremely good quality, and the many varieties of camera bodies, lenses, and accessories have been well documented. The fact that the Leica was the first commercially successful 35mm. still camera adds historical significance to the Leica. The ready availability of accurate information on any Leica product gives collectors a good sense of organization and direction for their collection. It is not a good specialty for those on a tight budget, however.

☐ **Ur-Leica,** display model of the original 1913 prototype, reproduced by Leitz for museums, etc.
.... 500.00   625.00

☐ **Leica "A", I,** 1925-1930, the first commercially produced model, non-interchangeable lenses, Anastigmat f3.5/50mm., 1925, very few made, perhaps 100-150.
.... 8000.00   9000.00

☐ **Same as above,** Elmax f3.5/50mm., 1925-1926.
.... 5500.00   6500.00

☐ **Same as above,** Elmar f3.5/50, 1926-1930, priced by Serial Number, 4-digit.
.... 600.00   675.00

☐ **Same as above,** 5-digit.
.... 600.00   700.00

☐ **Leica "B", I,** 1926-1930, the "Compur" Leica, approximately 1500 were made in two variations, both with Elmar f3.5/50, dial-set Compur, 1926-29.
.... 5000.00   6000.00

☐ **Same as above,** rim-set Compur, 1929-1930.
.... 4500.00   5000.00

196 / LEITZ

☐ **Leica "C", I,** *1930-1931, the first Leica with interchangeable lenses, non-standardized lens mount, lenses were custom fitted to each camera because the distance from the lens flange to the film plane was not standard, the lens flange is not engraved, but each lens is numbered with the last three digits of the body serial number, with matching engraved lens.*
.... 1000.00   1100.00

☐ **Same as above,** *standardized, the lens mount on the body has a small "o" engraved at the top of the body flange, lenses now standardized and interchangeble from one body to another with f3.5/50mm.*
.... 275.00   350.00

☐ **Leica "D", II,** *1932-1948, the first one with built-in coupled rangefinder, body only, black or chrome.*
.... 195.00   235.00

☐ **Same as above,** *with f3.5/50 Elmar, mint.*
.... 225.00   275.00

☐ **Leica "E", Standard,** *1932-1948, similar to the standardized "C," but with smaller, 12mm. diameter, rewind knob, which pulls out to make rewinding easier, body only.*
.... 250.00   350.00
☐ **Same as above,** *with f3.5/50 Elmar.*
.... 300.00   400.00
☐ **Same as above,** *with f2/50 Summar.*
.... 300.00   400.00

☐ **Leica "F", III,** *1933-1939, the first model with slow-speed dial, carrying strap eyelets, and diopter adjustment on rangefinder eyepiece, shutter to 500, body only, black or chrome.*
.... 125.00   150.00
☐ **Same as above,** *with f3.5/50 Elmar.*
.... 200.00   250.00
☐ **Same as above,** *with f2/50 Summar.*
.... 200.00   250.00

☐ **Leica "FF", 250, Reporter,** *1934-1943, like Model F, but body ends extended and enlarged to hold 10 meters of 35mm. film for 250 exposures, only about 950 were made, later models, called GG, are built on a model G body and have shutter speed to 1000.*
.... 3500.00   4000.00

☐ **Leica "G", IIIa,** *1935-1950, basically like the "F", but with the addition of 1/1000 second shutter speed, chrome only, body only.*
.... 125.00   150.00
☐ **Same as above,** *with f3.5/50 Elmar.*
.... 150.00   175.00
☐ **Same as above,** *with f2/50 Summar.*
.... 150.00   175.00
☐ **Same as above,** *with f2/50 Summitar.*
.... 160.00   185.00

☐ **Leica, IIIa, "Monte en Sarre,"** assembled after World War II, between 1950 and 1955, in the French occupied German state of Saarland, from pre- and post-war parts, very few were made, the top of the body is engraved "Monte en Sarre" below the normal "Ernst Leitz, Wetzlar" engraving.
.... **3000.00   3500.00**

☐ **Leica "G", IIIb,** 1938-1946, similar to the IIIa, but rangefinder and viewfinder eyepieces are next to each other, diopter adjustment lever below rewind knob, body only.
.... **125.00   150.00**

☐ **Leica IIIc,** 1940-1946, die-cast body is 1/8 inch longer than earlier models, one-piece top cover with small step for advance-rewind lever, body only.
.... **100.00   125.00**

☐ **Same as above,** with f3.5/50 Elmar.
.... **125.00   150.00**

☐ **Same as above,** with f2/50 Summar.
.... **115.00   145.00**

☐ **Same as above,** with f2/50 Summitar.
.... **115.00   145.00**

☐ **Leica IIIc, "K-Model,"** the letter K at the end of the serial number and on the front of the shutter curtain stands for "kugellager" (ball-bearing), the ball-bearing shutter was produced during the war years, primarily for the military, usually blue-grey painted.
.... **550.00   580.00**

☐ **Leica IIIc, Luftwaffe and Wehrmacht models,** engraved "Luftwaffe Eigentum."
.... **650.00   750.00**

☐ **Same as above,** engraved "W.H."
.... **1150.00   1250.00**

☐ **Leica IIc,** 1948-1951, like the IIIc, but no slow speeds, top shutter speed 500, body only.
.... **125.00   150.00**

☐ **Leica Ic,** 1949-1951, no slow speeds, no built-in finders, two accessory shoes for mounting separate view and range finders.
.... **200.00   250.00**

☐ **Leica IIIf,** 1950-1956, has MX synchronized, "black-dial," shutter speed dial is lettered in black, with speeds 30, 40, 60.
.... **100.00   150.00**

☐ **Same as above,** "Red-dial," shutter speed dial is lettered in red, with speeds 25, 50, 75.
.... **100.00   150.00**

☐ **Same as above,** "Red-dial" with self-timer.
.... **145.00   165.00**

☐ **Leica IIf,** 1951-1956, like the IIIf, but no slow speeds, black dial body.
.... **150.00   160.00**

☐ **Same as above,** red dial body.
.... **150.00   160.00**

☐ **Leica If,** 1952-1956, no slow speed dial nor finders, separate finders fit accessory shoes, flash contact in slow speed dial location, body only.
.... **250.00   300.00**

☐ **Same as above,** with 3.5 Elmar.
.... **300.00   350.00**

☐ **Leica IIIg,** 1956-1960, the last of the screw-mount Leicas, bright-line finder and small window next to viewfinder window which provides light for finder illumination, with 50mm. f2.8 Elmar.
.... **500.00   600.00**

☐ **Leica IIIg, Swedish Crown Model,** 1960, a batch of 125 black-finished cameras for the Swedish Armed Forces were among the very last IIIg cameras produced, on the back side of the cameras and on the lens are engraved three crowns, the Swedish coat-of-arms, camera and lens.
.... **4500.00   5000.00**

198 / LENINGRAD

- ☐ **Leica Ig,** *1957-1960, like IIIg, but no finders or self-timer, two accessory shoes accept separate range and view finders, top plate surrounds the rewind knob, covering the lower part when not extended, only 6,300 were made, body only.*
  .... 600.00   700.00
- ☐ **Leica Single-Shot,** *c. 1936, ground glass focus, single metal film holder, Ibsor shutter.*
  .... 1450.00   1650.00
- ☐ **Leica M3,** *1954-1966, two variations, single-stroke film advance, body only.*
  .... 300.00   400.00
- ☐ **Same as above,** *double-stroke advance, body only.*
  .... 250.00   300.00
- ☐ **Leica M2,** *1957-1967, like the single-stroke M3, but with external exposure counter, finder has frame lines for 35, 50, and 90mm. lenses, all early models and some later ones were made without self-timer, body only.*
  .... 350.00   400.00
- ☐ **Luxus,** *gold-plated A-Elmar camera with lizard skin covering.*
  .... 14,000.00 16,000.00
- ☐ **Luxus Replica.**
  .... 1750.00   1850.00

LENINGRAD

- ☐ **Leningrad,** *Russiam 35mm. RF Leica copy, f3.5/50mm. lens in Leica mount, motor drive.*
  .... 250.00   300.00

LENZ

- ☐ **Lenz,** *novelty camera for 16mm. film.*
  .... 8.00   10.00

LEONAR KAMERAWERK
(Hamburg)

- ☐ **Leonar,** *9 x 12cm. folding plate camera, Leonar Aplanat f8/140mm. or Periscop Aplanat f11/140mm., shutter 25-100.*
  .... 20.00   30.00

LEOTAX
(See Showa Optical Company)

LEROY
(Lucien LeRoy, Paris)

- ☐ **Minimus,** *rigid body stereo.*
  .... 200.00   300.00
- ☐ **Stereo Panoramique,** *c. 1906, black, all-metal camera for 6 x 13cm. plates in stereo, or by rotating one lens to center position, panoramic views, Krauss Protar f9/82 or Goerz Doppel Anastigmat f8.5/80mm., five speed shutter.*
  .... 225.00   325.00

LEULLIER
(Louis Leullier, Paris)

- ☐ **Summum Special,** *c. 1925 for 6 x 13cm. stereo plates, Roussel Stylor f4.5/75 fixed focus lens, stereo shutter 25-100, changing magazine for 6 plates.*
  .... 175.00   200.00

LEVY-ROTH
(Berlin)

- ☐ **Minigraph,** *c. 1915 camera for 18 x 24mm. exposures on 35mm. film in special cassettes, the first European still camera to use cine film, f3.5/54mm. Minigraph Anastigmat lens, flap shutter.*
  .... 1850.00   2250.00

LEWIS
(W. & W.H. Lewis, New York)

- ☐ **Wet plate camera,** *c. 1862, large size, for plates up to 12 x 12", folding leather bellows, plates and ground glass load from side, a rare camera.*
  .... 3000.00   4000.00

LIEBE
(V. Liebe, Paris)
(See also Jeanneret Monobloc)

- **Monobloc,** *c. 1920, for 6 x 13cm. stereo plates, Boyer Saphir f4.5/85mm. lenses in pneumatic spring shutter, metal body is partly covered with leather.*
  .... 200.00   250.00

LIFE-O-RAMA III

- **Life-O-Rama III,** *German 6 x 6cm. on 120, f5.6/75 or f3.5 Ennar, Vario shutter, synchronized.*
  ....10.00   12.00

LIGHTNING DETECTIVE CAMERA
(See Benetfink)

LILIPUT
(See Ernemann)

LILIPUT DETECTIVE CAMERA

- **Liliput Detective Camera,** *sold by Anthony, a detective camera in the shape of a miniature satchel, takes 2½ x 2½" exposures on plates in double holders.*
  .... 1650.00   1850.00

LINEX
(See Lionel)

LINHOF PRAZISIONS KAMERAWERK
(V. Linhof, Munich)

- **Silar,** *for 10 x 15cm. plates, triple extension bellows, Meyer Aristostigmat f5.5/180mm. lens in Compound shutter 1-150.*
  .... 100.00   150.00

- **Stereo Panorama,** *c. 1920, for 6 x 13cm. exposures, stereo or panoramic, two Reitzschel Sextar f6.8/120mm. lenses and one Reitzschel Linar f5.5/150mm., compound shutter, metal body, leather covered.*
  .... 275.00   325.00

- **Technika I,** *c. 1930, various sizes: 6 x 9, 9 x 12, or 13 x 18cm., with f4.5 Tessar in compound or Compur shutter.*
  .... 250.00   300.00

LIONEL MFG. CO.
(The train people)

- **Linex Stereo,** *c. late 1940's cast metal subminiature, for pairs of 16 x 20mm. exposures on rollfilm, f8/30 lenses, guillotine shutter, synched.*
  ....75.00   100.00

LIPCA
(Lippische Camerafabrik, Barntrup)

- **Rollop,** *c. 1957 TLR for 6 x 6cm. on 120, Ennit f2.8/80mm., or Enna f3.5/75mm., Prontor-SVS shutter 1-300.*
  .... 125.00   150.00

LITTLE WONDER

- **Little Wonder,** *miniature box-plate camera for 2 x 2", made of 2 cardboard boxes sliding into one another.*
  .... 175.00   200.00

LIZARS
(J. Lizars, Glasgow)

- **Challenge, Challenge Dayspool,** *c. 1905 for 3¼ x 4¼ exposures on rollfilm or plates, leather covered mahogany construction, f6 or f8 Aldis or Beck lens, or f6.8 Goerz.*
  .... 110.00   115.00

200 / LLOYD

☐ **Challenge Dayspool, tropical model,** *with polished Spanish mahogany body, rather than leather covered, red leather bellows.*
.... 525.00   600.00

☐ **Challenge Dayspool,** 4½ x 6½", *c. 1900, for rollfilm, leather covered, red bellows, Beck Symmetrical lens.*
.... 100.00   150.00

☐ **Challenge Stereo Camera, Model B,** *c. 1905, for 3¼ x 6¾" plates, teak with brass trim, B & L RR, or Aldis Anastigmat lenses in B & L Stereo shutter.*
.... 850.00   950.00

☐ **Challenge Stereo Camera, Model 1-B,** *c. 1910, a beautiful and finely finished stereo camera in Spanish mahogany with brass trim, focal plane shutter, Aldis Anastigmat lenses.*
.... 950.00   1050.00

LLOYD
(See Huttig, Ica)

LLOYD, ANDREW J. & COMPANY
(Boston)

☐ **Box camera,** *for 4 x 5" glass plates.*
.... 40.00   50.00

LOEBER BROTHERS
(New York)

The Loeber Brothers manufactured and imported cameras c. 1880's and 1890's.

☐ **Folding plate camera,** *full-plate, British, fine polished wood, black bellows, brass trim, brass-barreled lens with waterhouse stops.*
.... 200.00   250.00

LOISIR

☐ **Loisir,** *French plastic rollfilm camera for 8 or 16 exposures on 120 film, Radior lens, simple shutter, T & I.*
.... 20.00   30.00

LONDON STEREOSCOPIC & PHOTO COMPANY

This company imported and sold under their own name many cameras which were manufactured by leading companies at home and abroad. We are listing two cameras here which we can't positively link to another manufacturer.

☐ **Tailboard stereo camera,** *c. 1885, Swift & Son 4" lenses, side board panel, 3½ x 6¼" plate, Thornton rollerblind shutter, dark maroon bellows.*
.... 500.00   575.00

☐ **Wet plate camera,** *c. 1855, 4 x 5" sliding box style, light colored wood body, 7 x 7½ x 6¼" overall, which extends to 10", London Stereoscopic Petzval-type lens in brass barrel.*
.... 3250.00   3500.00

LORDOMAT, LORDOX
(See Leidolf)

LUBITEL

☐ **Lubitel,** *c. 1949, Russian 6 x 6cm. TLR for 12 exposures on 120 film, T-22 lens, f4.5/75, variable speed shutter 10-200.*
.... 20.00   30.00

LUCIDOGRAPH
(See Blair)

LUMIERE & CIE
(Lyon, France)

☐ **Eljy,** c. 1937 for 24 x 36mm. exposures on unperforated 35mm. film in special cassettes, Lypar f3.5/ 50mm. lens in Eljy shutter.
.................80.00   100.00

☐ **Luminor,** 9 x 12cm. folding-bed plate camera.
.................25.00   35.00

☐ **Lumix F,** simple folding 6 x 9 rollfilm.
.................20.00   25.00

☐ **Sinox,** 6 x 9cm. folding rollfilm, Nacor Anastigmat f6.3/105mm., central shutter 25-100.
.................20.00   25.00

☐ **Sterelux,** c. 1920, folding stereo camera for 116 rollfilm, 6 x 13cm. format, Spector Anastigmat f4.5/ 80mm.
.... 200.00   225.00

☐ **No. 49 box camera,** for 122 film.
.................20.00   25.00

LUNDELIUS MFG. CO.
(Port Jarvis, N.Y.)

☐ **Magazine Camera,** c. 1895 for 12 plates in vertical format, leather covered wood body, measures 10 x 8 x 4½" overall.
.... 125.00   150.00

LURE

☐ **Lure,** plastic miniature.
.................6.00   8.00

LÜTTKE
(Dr. Lüttke & Arndt, Wandsbek, Hamburg, and Berlin, Germany)

☐ **Folding rollfilm camera,** 8 x 10cm., Lüttke Periplanat lens, black leathered body with red cloth bellows, nickel trim.
.................50.00   60.00

☐ **Folding bed plate camera,** 9 x 12cm., horizontal format, Lüttke Periscop lens with rotary stops, brass shutter, red-brown bellows, black leathered wood body.
.................75.00   100.00

LYNX
(See Pontiac)

LYRA
(See Fuji Photo Film Company)

MACKENSTEIN
(H. Mackenstein, Paris)

☐ **Francia,** strut-folding stereo camera for 45 x 107mm. plates, c. 1906, Max Balbreck or Sumo Aplanat lenses, guillotine shutter with variable speeds, red leather bellows.
.... 200.00   225.00

☐ **Stereo Jumelle,** c. 1893, for 18 plates 9 x 18cm. in magazine, Goerz Double Anastigmat 110mm. lens, variable speed guillotine shutter.
.... 200.00   225.00

MACRIS-BOUCHER
(Paris)

☐ **Nil Melior Stereo,** 6 x 13cm., c. 1920, Boyer Sapphir or E. Krauss Tessar f4.5 lens in seven-speed spring shutter, large newton finder, 12-plate magazine.
.... 175.00   200.00

MADISON

☐ **Madison, I,** folding camera for 6 x 6cm. on 620 film, f4.5 lens, shutter to 200.
.................16.00   18.00

MAGIC INTRODUCTION
COMPANY
(N.Y.)

- [ ] **Photoret Watch Camera,** c. 1894 for 6 exposures ½ x ½", 12 x 12mm., on round sheet film, meniscus lens, rotating shutter.
.... 600.00   700.00

MAJOR
(See Agfa)

MAKINA, MAKINETTE
(See Plaubel)

MAMIYA CAMERA COMPANY
(Tokyo)

- [ ] **Mamiya 6,** c. 1950's, basically, a folding-bed camera for 12 square exposures 6 x 6cm. on 120, some models featured the option of 16 vertical exposures 4.5 x 6cm. as well, camera body is in horizontal style, f3.5/75 Zuiko lens in Copal or Seikosha shutter, coupled rangefinder, unusual feature: knurled focusing wheel just above the back door of the camera moves the film plane to focus while the lens remains stationary.
.... 50.00   75.00

- [ ] **Mamiya 16,** c. 1950's subminiature for 20 exposures 10 x 14mm. on 16mm. film, various models including: Original model, Deluxe, with plain, smooth body, Super, like original, but with sliding filter, Automatic, built-in meter, no significant price difference among these models.
.... 30.00   40.00

- [ ] **Mamiyaflex,** c. 1940's-1950's, 6 x 6cm. TLR cameras, Rolleiflex-style, early models with f3.5/75mm. lens.
.... 75.00   100.00

MANDEL, MANDELETTE
(See Chicago Ferrotype Company)

MANHATTAN OPTICAL COMPANY
(New York)
(See also Gundlach-Manhattan)

- [ ] **Bo-Peep, Model B,** c. late 1890's, 4 x 5 folding plate camera, red bellows, brass shutter, similar to other brands of same period.
.... 60.00   75.00

- [ ] **Bo-Peep, 5 x 7",** larger size, double extension bellows, brass lens with rotating stops. 100.00   125.00

- [ ] **Night-Hawk Detective,** c. 1895 for 4 x 5" plates, leather covered wood, string-set shutter, T & I, ground glass or scale focus, rapid Achromatic lens.
.... 375.00   400.00

- [ ] **Wizard folding plate camera,** 4 x 5 size, including Baby, Cycle, Wide Angle, Senior, Junior, A, and B models.
.... 63.00   73.00

- [ ] **Same as above,** 5 x 7 size, including Cycle, B, and Senior models.
.... 100.00   120.00

- [ ] **Long-Focus Wizard,** 5 x 7", including Cycle and Senior models, triple extension bellows, RR lens, Unicum shutter.
.... 100.00   150.00

MARION & COMPANY, LTD.
(London)

- [ ] **Perfection,** 10 x 12" folding field camera c. 1890, fine polished wood, Dallmeyer f8 RR lens in brass barrel with iris diaphragm.
.... 200.00   300.00

- [ ] **Soho Reflex,** Graflex-type SLR for 2¼ x 3¼, f4.5/120mm. Tessar, focal plane shutter.
.... 250.00   350.00

- [ ] **Same as above,** ¼-plate size, 3¼ x 4¼", with Ross Xpres f3.5/5½" lens.
.... 175.00   225.00

☐ **Soho Tropical Reflex,** 3¼ x 4¼", Dallmeyer f3.5/150mm. Dalmac, or Ross Xpres f3.5/6½" lens, revolving back, fine polished wood, red bellows and viewing hood, brass trim, a beautiful tropical camera.
.... 2000.00 2500.00

MARS
(See Wunsche)

MARVEL
(See Putnam)

MARVELFLEX

☐ **Marvelflex,** *twin-lens-reflex, f4.5.*
.... 20.00 25.00

MASCOT DETECTIVE CAMERA
(See Scovill)

MASHPRIBORINTORG
(See Kiev)

MASON
(Perry Mason & Company, Boston)

☐ **Harvard camera,** c. 1890 for 2½ x 3½ plates, meniscus lens, all metal, black with gold pinstriping.
.... 175.00 200.00

MASTER REFLEX

Master Reflex
(See Kochmann.) The anglo version of the pre-war Meister-Korelle.

MATCH-MATIC
(See Argus)

MAXIMAR
(See Ica, Zeiss)

MAY FAIR
(See Houghton)

MAZO
(E. Mazo, Paris)

☐ **Field & Studio camera,** c. 1900, for 13 x 18cm., 5 x 7" on plates, fine wood body, GG back, double extension bellows, horizontal format, Mazo & Magenta Orthoscope Rapid f8 lens in Thornton-Picard shutter.
.... 200.00 250.00

McBEAN
(Edinburgh)

☐ **Stereo Tourist,** 9 x 18cm., Steinheil Antiplanat lens, Thornton-Picard shutter 1-225.
.... 365.00 425.00

MEC
(See Feinwerk Technik)

MECAFLEX
(See Kilfitt)

MEDALIST
(See Eastman)

MEISTER KORELLE
(See Kochmann Korelle)

MEISUPPII

☐ **Meisuppii,** *half-frame 35mm.*
.... 50.00 60.00

MELIOR
(See Macris-Boucher)

MEMO
(See Agfa, Ansco)

MENDEL
(Georges Mendel, Paris)

☐ **Detective camera,** for 12 plates 3¼ x 4¼, RR lens, rotating shutter, iris diaphragm.
.... 175.00 200.00

MENTOR, MENTORETT
(See Goltz & Breutmann)

MEOPTA
(Prague, Czechoslovakia)

- [ ] **Flexaret,** 6 x 6cm. TLR, Belar f3.5/80mm. in Prontor II shutter, crank wind, lever focus.
  ....40.00   60.00
- [ ] **Mikroma,** c. 1949, 16mm. subminiature, Mirar f3.5/20mm. lens, spring shutter 25-200, rapid-wind slide.
  ....95.00   115.00
- [ ] **Mikroma II,** c. 1964, similar.
  .... 100.00   125.00
- [ ] **Stereo Mikroma,** for stereo exposures on 16mm. film, Mirar f3.5/25mm. lenses, shutter 1/5-1000.
  .... 200.00   250.00

MERCURY
(See Universal)

MERGETT
(See Jem)

MERIDIAN

- [ ] **Meridian,** 4 x 5 press view, f4.5/135.
  .... 175.00   200.00

MERIT

- [ ] **Merit,** c. 1935 German brown bakelite box for 4 x 6.5cm. on 127 film, f11/75mm. Rodenstock lens, T & I shutter.
  ....20.00   30.00

MERVEILLEUX
(See Lancaster)

METEOR
(See Universal)

METROPOLITAN SUPPLY CO.
(Chicago)

- [ ] **King Camera,** small 2 x 2 x 3½" cardboard camera for glass plates, back fits on like shoe-box cover, similar to Yale & Zar, not to be confused with the Japanese King Camera of the post-World War II era.
  ....80.00   100.00

- [ ] **MF Stereo Camera,** 45 x 107mm. plates, f6.8 Luminor lenses.
  .... 100.00   150.00

MICK-A-MATIC

- [ ] **Mick-A-Matic,** a 126 cartridge camera in the shape of Mickey Mouse's head, meniscus lens in nose.
  ....30.00   40.00

MICRO

- [ ] **Micro,** Japanese novelty camera
  ....10.00   15.00

MICRO-16
(See Whittaker)

MIDAS

- [ ] **Midas,** British 9.5mm. hand-crank camera/projector, f2.5 lens.
  ....80.00   100.00

MIDG
(See Butcher)

MIDGET
(See Coronet, Houghton)

MIGHTY
(See Tokyo Shashin)

MIKADO

- [ ] **Mikado,** 6 x 6cm., f3.5/75 Wester.
  ....30.00   45.00

MIKROMA
(See Meopta)

MIKUT COLOR CAMERA

- [ ] **Mikut Color Camera,** c. 1937, for 3 color-separation negatives 4 x 4cm. on a single plate 4.5 x 13cm., Mikutar f3.5/130mm., Compur shutter 1-200.
  .... 1250.00   1450.00

MIMOSA

☐ **Mimosa I,** *c. 1947 compact 35mm., Meyer Triplan f2.9/50, Compur Rapid shutter, unusual boxy style for 35mm. camera.*
.... **175.00**   200.00

☐ **Mimosa II,** *f2.9 Trioplan, Velax shutter, 10-200.*
.... **125.00**   150.00

MINETTA

☐ **Minetta,** *Japanese 16mm. rollfilm novelty camera.*
.... **10.00**   15.00

MINEX
(See Adams & Company)

MINICORD
(See Goerz)

MINIMAL
(See Ica)

MINIMUM
(See Ica, Zeiss)

MINIMUS
(See Leroy)

MINOLTA
(Chiyoda Kogaku Seiko Company, Ltd., Osaka, Japan)

☐ **"A" type 35mm. cameras,** *A, A2, A5, etc., f3.5 or 2.8 Rokkor.*
.... **30.00**   40.00

☐ **Autocord, Minoltacord Autoflex,** *6 x 6cm. TLR, Rolleiflex-style, early models without meters.*
.... **70.00**   95.00

☐ **Semi-Minolta, Auto Semi-Minolta,** *folding cameras for 16 exposures 4.5 x 6cm. on 120 rollfilm, f4.5/75mm. Coronar or Promar Anastigmat lens, Crown or Crown Rapid shutter.*
.... **50.00**   65.00

☐ **Minolta Six,** *c. late 1930's folding camera for 6 x 6cm. exposures on 120 film, horizontal body style, no bed, no struts, standard pulls out with telescoping snap-lock frames around bellows, an unusual design in a camera format popular at the time, f4.5 or 5.6/80 Coronar lens in Crown shutter.*
.... **50.00**   75.00

☐ **Minolta 16,** *subminiature c. 1950's for 10 x 14mm. exposures on 16mm. film in special cassettes, f3.5 or 2.8 Rokkor lens, 3-speed shutter, 25, 50, and 200.*
.... **20.00**   25.00

☐ **Minolta 16-II,** *f2.8 Rokkor, 6 speeds.*
.... **20.00**   25.00

☐ **Minolta 16-EE,** *f2.8/25mm. Rokkor, electric eye.*
.... **35.00**   40.00

☐ **Minolta 16-EE-II,** *with case.*
.... **25.00**   30.00

☐ **Minolta 16-MG,** *with case and chain.*
.... **30.00**   40.00

☐ **Minolta 16-P,** *with case and original instructions.*
.... **20.00**   30.00

☐ **Minolta 16-PS,** *with case and strap.*
.... **20.00**   30.00

☐ **Minolta 16-QT,** *with case, electric flash, etc.*
.... **35.00**   50.00

☐ **Minolta 35,** *c. 1948-1950's, rangefinder cameras, Leica copies, for 24 x 32mm., and later 24 x 36mm. on standard 35mm. cartridges, most commonly found with f2.8/44mm. Rokkor, models I, F, II, IIB.*
.... **100.00**   125.00

MINOX

Subminiature cameras for 8 x 11mm. exposures on 9.5mm. film in special cassettes. The original model, designed by Walter Zapp, was made in 1937 in Riga, Latvia.

206 / MINUTE 16

- ☐ **Original model,** *stainless steel body, made in Riga, Latvia by Valsts Electro-Techniska Fabrika, guillotine shutter ½-1000, Minostigmat lens, f3.5/15mm.*
  .... 500.00   600.00
- ☐ **Minox "Made in USSR,"** *stainless steel model made during the short time the Russians held Latvia before the German occupation, approximately Spring to Fall, 1940.*
  .... 700.00   800.00
- ☐ **Minox II,** *made in Wetzlar, Germany, aluminum body.*
  ....60.00   80.00
- ☐ **Minox III.**
  ....60.00   80.00
- ☐ **Minox III, Gold plated.**
  .... 575.00   650.00
- ☐ **Minox III-S.**
  ....65.00   80.00
- ☐ **Minox A,** *Wetzlar, Complan f3.5.*
  ....75.00   90.00
- ☐ **Minox B,** *built-in meter.*
  ....80.00   95.00

MINUTE 16
(See Universal)

MIRANDA G

- ☐ **Miranda G,** *35mm. SLR.*
  ....90.00   115.00

MIROFLEX
(See Contessa, Zeiss)

MIRROR REFLEX CAMERA
(See Hall)

MITSUKOSHI
(Japan)

- ☐ **Picny,** *c. 1935 compact camera for 3 x 4cm., ½-frame, exposures on 127 film, very similar in size and shape to the Gelto-D by Takahashi, but rounded ends and better finish almost make it look like a stubby Leica, even the collapsible lens mount is a direct copy of the Leica styling.*
  .... 100.00   135.00

MÖLLER
(J.D. Möller, Hamburg, Germany)

- ☐ **Cambinox,** *c. 1956, a combination of high quality 7 x 35 binoculars and a precision camera for 10 x 14mm. exposures on 16mm. film, interchangeable f3.5/90mm. lenses, rotary focal plane shutter 30-800.*
  .... 900.00   1150.00

MOMENT, MOMEHM

- ☐ **Moment, Momehm,** *Russian copy of Polaroid 95, f6.8/135mm. "BTL" shutter, 10-200+ B, black bellows.*
  .... 100.00   150.00

MONITOR
(See Eastman)

MONOBLOC
(See Jeanneret, Liebe)

MONROE CAMERA COMPANY
(Rochester, N.Y.)

Merged in 1899 with several companies to form Rochester Optical & Camera Company.

- ☐ **Folding plate camera,** *c. 1898, folds to a very compact size, only about 1½" thick including brass double plateholder, 2 x 2½", Vest Pocket size.*
  .... 150.00   175.00
- ☐ **Same as above,** *3½ x 3½, Pocket Size.*
  .... 125.00   175.00

☐ **Same as above,** 3¼ x 4¼, Pocket Poco A, the last of the series by Monroe before the merger.
.... 175.00   225.00

☐ **Monroe Model 7,** 5 x 7", a "cycle" style plate camera, double extension maroon bellows, RR lens, Gundlach shutter, this camera looks like the Rochester it is about to become.
.... 90.00   125.00

MONTANUS
(Solingen, Germany)

☐ **Montiflex,** 6 x 6cm. TLR, Steinheil Cassar f2.8/80mm. Prontor-SVS shutter.
.... 80.00   125.00

MONTAUK
(See Gennert)

MONTE
(See Monti)

MONTGOMERY WARD & COMPANY

☐ **Model B,** 4 x 5", rapid convex lens, Wollensak shutter.
.... 50.00   60.00

Note: Most of the cameras sold through Montgomery Ward were not marked with the company name. Sears was one step ahead of Wards in that respect.

MONTI
(Charles Monti, France)

☐ **Monte 35.**
.... 20.00   25.00

☐ **Monte Carlo,** pre-war folding camera for 6 x 9cm. on 120 film, f3.5 or 4.5/90mm.
.... 20.00   25.00

MOORE & COMPANY
(Liverpool, England)

☐ **Aptus Ferrotype Camera,** c. 1895 for 4.5 x 6.3cm. plates, meniscus lens, black leather covered wood body, suction bulb takes unexposed plate and swings it into position for exposure.
.... 350.00   400.00

MOSCOW, MOSKWA

Russian copies of the Zeiss Super Ikontas.

☐ **Moscow 4,** copy of 6 x 9cm. Super Ikonta, f4.5/110mm. Industar.
.... 75.00   100.00

☐ **Moscow 5,** copy of Super Ikonta C, f3.5/105 lens, synchronized shutter.
.... 80.00   110.00

MOTORMATIC
(See Eastman)

MULTI-EXPOSURE
(See Simplex, Wing)

MULTIPRINT
(See Buess)

MULTISCOPE & FILM COMPANY
(Burlington, Wis.)

Al-Vista Panoramic Cameras
Patents 1891-1901. Takes panoramic pictures (model number gives film width in inches) in lengths of 4, 6, 8, 10, or 12 inches on rollfilm.

MURER AND DURONI

- **Al-Vista Panoramic Camera,** *Model 4B.*
  .... 175.00   200.00
- **Al-Vista Panoramic Camera,** *Model 5B.*
  .... 200.00   235.00
- **Al-Vista Panoramic Camera,** *Model 5D.*
  .... 240.00   275.00
- **Al-Vista Panoramic Camera,** *Model 5F, the convertible model, this camera has two fronts which use the same back, one front is the swinging lens panoramic, and the other is a folding-bed front which looks like the typical folding plate cameras of the day, an unusual and rare set.*
  .... 450.00   500.00

MURER & DURONI
(Milan, Italy)

Folding Plate

- **Express,** *magazine box camera c. 1900, for various sized plates: 4.5 x 6cm., 6 x 9cm., 7 x 8cm., 8.5 x 11cm. (3¼ x 4¼") and 9 x 12cm., Murer Anastigmat f4.5 or 6.3, focal length depending on size of camera, focal plane shutter.*
  .... 100.00   145.00
- **Folding plate cameras,** *focal plane models, strut folding style, in various sizes.*
  .... 175.00   225.00
- **Reflex,** *for 6 x 9cm. plates, Murer Anastigmat f4.5/120mm, focal plane shutter 15-1000.*
  .... 100.00   125.00
- **Stereo,** *folding camera for 45 x 107mm., focal plane shutter, 150-1000, Murer Anastigmat f4.5/60mm.*
  .... 290.00   310.00

MURO SUTER
(See Suter)

MUTSCHLER, ROBERTSON, & CO.

Manufacturer of the "Ray" cameras, which were later sold and labeled under the "Ray Camera Co." name. *(See Ray.)*

MYCRO
(See Sugaya Optical Co.)

MYRACLE
(See Sugaya Optical Co.)

NAGEL
(Dr. August Nagel Camerawerk, Stuttgart, Germany)

- **Nagel 18,** *folding-bed plate camera, 6 x 9cm., c. 1928, like the Kodak Recomar, which was made by Nagel, with Nagel Anastigmat f6.3 or other normal lens.*
  ....60.00   80.00
- **Same as above,** *with Leitz Elmar f4.5 lens.*
  .... 200.00   225.00

☐ **Nagel 30, 33,** *similar, but 9 x 12cm. size, Nagel Anastigmat f6.3/135, or Laudar, Compur shutter 1-250.*
.................50.00   75.00

☐ **Pupille,** *c. 1930 for 16 exposures 3 x 4cm. on 127, with Schneider Xenar f2, 2.9, or 3.5/50mm. in Compur or Ibsor shutter.*
.................200.00   250.00
☐ **Same as above,** *with Leitz Elmar f3.5/50mm. lens.*
.................400.00   450.00
☐ **Ranca,** *c. 1931, 3 x 4cm. on 127 film, similar to Pupille, but cheaper, has front-lens focusing, Nagel Anastigmat f4.5/50mm. in Ibsor shutter 1-150.*
.................175.00   200.00
☐ **Recomar 33,** *for 9 x 12cm. plates, double extension bellows, Compur 1-250, T, B, with normal f4.5/135 lens.*
.................40.00   60.00
☐ **Same as above,** *with Leitz Elmar f4.5/135mm. lens.*
.................300.00   350.00
☐ **Regent,** *6 x 9cm., Schneider Xenar f3.5/105 in Compur shutter 1-250.*
.................200.00   250.00
☐ **Vollenda,** *4 x 6.5 on 127 or 6 x 9 on 120, with normal lens.*
.................40.00   50.00
☐ **Same as above,** *with Leitz Elmar.*
.................225.00   275.00

NETTEL KAMERAWERK / 209

NATIONAL CAMERA
(England)

☐ **Folding field camera,** *½ plate, fine wood finish, reversible back, tapered black bellows, Ross f6.3/7" Homocentric lens, Thornton-Picard roller-blind shutter.*
.................125.00   150.00

NATIONAL PHOTOCOLOR CORP.
(N.Y.)

☐ **One-Shot Tri-color camera,** *5 x 7", less lens.*
.................325.00   425.00

NELSON
(See Ica)

NERO
(See Ica)

NESCON

☐ **Nescon 35,** *f3.5/40mm.*
.................20.00   25.00

NETTAR, NETTAX
(See Zeiss-Ikon)

NETTEL KAMERAWERK
(Sontheim-Heilbronn, Germany)

Formerly Süddeutsches Camerawerk - Körner & Mayer. Later became Contessa-Nettel in 1919 and Zeiss-Ikon in 1926.

☐ **Argus,** *monocular-styled camera, the precursor to the Contessa-Nettel Ergo, right angle finder in monocular eyepiece, an unusual disguised camera, less common than the later Contessa and Zeiss models.*
.................1000.00   1250.00
☐ **Deckrullo,** *9 x 12cm. plate camera, Zeiss Tessar f6.3/135mm., focal plane shutter 2-300.*
.................110.00   135.00

210 / NEW GEM

- **Folding plate camera,** 9 x 12cm., double extension bellows, Tessar f6.3/135, dial Compur 1-250.
  . . . . .40.00   60.00
- **Sonnet, tropical model,** 4.5 x 6cm., Tessar f4.5/75mm., compound shutter 1-300, teakwood with light brown bellows.
  . . . . 750.00   850.00

NEW GEM
(See Wing)

NEW IDEAS MFG. CO.
(N.Y.)

- **Magazine camera,** polished wood box detective camera, string-set shutter.
  . . . . 350.00   400.00

NEW IDEAL SIBYL
(See Newman & Guardia)

NEW YORK FERROTYPE CO.

- **Tintype camera,** c. 1906 professional model with three-section plateholder for postcards, 1½ x 2½" tintypes, and "button" tintypes, two-speed Wollensak shutter, with tank and black sleeve.
  . . . . 150.00   200.00

NEWMAN & GUARDIA
(London)

- **Folding Reflex,** a single-lens-reflex which takes 6 x 9cm. plates, Ross Xpress f2.9 lens, folds to compact size.
  . . . . 175.00   200.00
- **Magazine camera,** c. 1895, wood box for 12 plates 9 x 12cm., leather changing bag, meniscus lens.
  . . . . 200.00   250.00
- **Sibyl,** 6 x 9cm. plates, c. 1907, folding-bed cameras c. 1907-1920's, rollfilm models and plate models, Tessar f6.3/120mm., N&G special shutter.
  . . . . 110.00   175.00
- **Same as above,** Sybil Deluxe, 9 x 12cm., DEB, Zeiss Protar f6.3/122mm., N&G shutter 2-100.
  . . . . 100.00   165.00
- **Baby Sibyl,** 4 x 6cm., c. 1913, Tessar or Ross Xpress f4.5/75. N&G shutter 2-200.
  . . . . 150.00   175.00
- **New Ideal Sibyl,** 3¼ x 4¼ plate, c. 1913, f4.5/135mm. Tessar, N & G shutter.
  . . . . .95.00   115.00

- **New Special Sibyl,** for 6 x 9cm. exposures on 120 rollfilm, Ross Xpress f4.5/112mm., N & G Special shutter.
  . . . . .75.00   100.00

- [ ] **Special Box magazine camera,** *for 3¼ x 4¼ plates, internal bellows allow front of box to slide out for copy work or close-ups.*
  .... 175.00   225.00

NIC
(See Contessa-Nettel)

NICCA CAMERA WORKS
(Japan)

- [ ] **Nicca III,** *Leica copy, f2 Nikkor or f3.5 Simlar.*
  .... 125.00   150.00
- [ ] **Nicca IIIS,** *copy of Leica IIIa, c. 1955, f2/50mm. Nikkor-H, focal plane shutter 1-500.*
  .... 125.00   150.00

NIKON
(Nippon Kogaku, Tokyo)

- [ ] **Nikkorex,** *c. 1959 35mm. SLR, f1.4/50mm. Nikkor, copal metal focal plane shutter 1-1000.*
  .... 125.00   150.00
- [ ] **Nikon F,** *f1.4/50 Auto Nikkor.*
  .... 125.00   150.00
- [ ] **Nikon S.**
  .... 125.00   150.00
- [ ] **Nikon S2.**
  .... 120.00   150.00
- [ ] **Nikon S3.**
  .... 425.00   500.00
- [ ] **Nikon SP.**
  .... 500.00   600.00

Note: All of above with f1.4/50mm. lens.

NIL MELIOR
(See Macris Boucher)

NIPPON KOGAKU
(See Nikon)

NISHIDA KOGAKU
(Japan)

- [ ] **Westar,** *for 120 film, f3.5/75mm.*
  .... 25.00   35.00

NITOR
(See Agfa)

NIXE
(See Ica, Zeiss)

NODARK
(See Popular Photograph Company)

NOMAR

- [ ] **Nomar No. 1,** *metal box for 127 film.*
  .... 12.00   15.00

NORMANDIE
(See Anthony)

NORRIS

- [ ] **Norris,** *120 folding camera, f2.9/75 Cassar lens in Compur shutter.*
  .... 28.00   35.00

NORTON
(See Universal)

NOVELETTE
(See Anthony)

NOVIFLEX

- [ ] **Noviflex,** *German SLR c. 1935 for 6 x 6cm. on 120 film, Schneider Radionar f2.9/75.*
  .... 100.00   125.00

OKAM
(Czechoslovakia)

- [ ] **Okam,** *c. 1935, box camera for 4.5 x 6cm. plates, Meyer f6/105mm. lens in Patent 2 disc shutter 5-1000.*
  .... 475.00   550.00

Okam

OLYMPUS KOGAKU
(Japan)

- **Pen, original model,** c. 1959, for 18 x 24mm. "half" frame exposures on 35mm., f3.5 lens.
  ....35.00   45.00
- **Pen D,** f1.9.
  ....40.00   50.00
- **Pen F,** f1.8/38mm.
  .... 125.00   140.00
- **Pen FT,** f1.8/38mm. Zuiko.
  .... 150.00   160.00
- **Olympus 35,** f2.8/48mm. Zuiko, shutter 1-500, rangefinder.
  ....35.00   45.00

OMEGA
(See Simmon)

OMPEX

- **Ompex 16,** German subminiature similar to the Tuxi by Walter Kunick.
  ....40.00   55.00

ONITO
(See Contessa-Nettel, Zeiss-Ikon)

ONTOBLOC
(See Cornu)

ONTOFLEX
(See Cornu)

OPEMA

- **Opema,** Czechoslovakian Leica copy, Opemar f2.
  .... 100.00   135.00

OPTIMA
(See Agfa)

ORDINARY KODAK
(See Eastman)

ORION WERK
(Hannover)

- **Orion box camera,** 6 x 9cm., f17 meniscus lens simple shutter, for glass plates.
  ....50.00   75.00
- **Folding plate cameras,** 6 x 9 and 9 x 12cm. sizes, leather covered wood body with metal bed, f4.5 or 6.3 Meyer Trioplan, Helioplan, or Orion Special Aplanat, Vario or Compur shutter.
  ....30.00   40.00
- **Orion Rio Tropical,** c. 1920 folding-bed 9 x 12cm. plate camera, teak and brass, brown double extension bellows, Xenar f4.5/150 in Compur shutter 1-150.
  .... 600.00   650.00

ORIX
(See Zeiss)

ORTHO JUMELLE
(See Joux)

OWLA
(Japan)

- **Owla Stereo,** c. 1958, Owla f3.5/36mm. lenses, for stereo pairs on 35mm. film.
  .... 100.00   150.00

P.D.Q.
(See Anthony, Chicago Ferrotype Company)

PD-16
(See Agfa)

PADIE
(See Laack)

PAFF
(See Ihagee)

PALMER & LONGKING

☐ Bellows style Daguerreotype camera, ½ plate.
.... 7500.00 12,500.00
Note: Seek advice if unsure.

PALMOS
(See Ica, Zeiss)

PANDA
(See Ansco)

PANORAM
(See Eastman)

PAPIGNY
(Paris)

☐ Jumelle Stereo, c. 1890, for 8 x 8cm. plates, magazine back, Chevalier lenses.
.... 200.00   225.00

PARVOLA
(See Ihagee)

PASCAL
(See Japy & Cie)

PATENT DETECTIVE
(See Schmid)

PATENT KLAPP REFLEX
(See Ihagee)

PATENT

☐ Patent, 3¼ x 4¼ magazine box camera with shifting front.
.... 75.00   100.00

PAX, PAXETTE, PAXINA
(See Braun)

PEARL, PEARLETTE
(See Konishiroku)

PECTO
(See Columbia Optical & Camera Company)

PEERFLEKTA
(East Germany)

☐ Peerflekta, c. 1956 6 x 6cm. TLR for 120, f3.5/75mm. Pololyt in Prontor shutter 1-300.
.... 30.00   40.00

PEGGY
(See Krauss)

PEN
(See Olympus)

PENTACON
(Dresden, Germany)

☐ Contax FB, Zeiss Biotar f2/58mm., focal plane shutter 1-1000.
.... 100.00   125.00
☐ Pentacon, 35mm. SLR, f2.8/50mm. focal plane shutter, ½-1000.
.... 75.00   100.00
☐ Pentacon F, Meyer Primotar f3.5/50.
.... 40.00   60.00
☐ Pentacon FB, Steinheil f1.9/55.
.... 70.00   85.00
☐ Pentacon FBM, c. 1950, f2 or 2.8.
.... 60.00   80.00
☐ Penti, 18 x 24mm. on 35mm. film, Meyer Trioplan f3.5/30, gold colored with blue-green enamel.
.... 35.00   45.00

214 / PERFECT

- **Werra,** 35mm. Jena T f2.8/50mm. lens, 1-500 shutter, olive green leather.
  ....40.00   60.00

PERFECT
(See Photo Hall)

PERFECTA
(See Welta)

PERFECTION
(See Marion & Company)

PERFEX
(See Candid Camera Corporation)

PERIFLEX
(See Corfield)

PERISKOP
(See Ica, Krugener)

PERKA PRAZISIONS KAMERAWERK
(Munich, Germany)

- **Perka,** c. 1922 folding-bed plate camera, double extension bellows, Tessar f4.5/150 Compur 1-200, construction allows tilting of back and lensboard, standard, for architectural photos.
  .... 150.00   200.00

PERKEN, SON, & RAYMENT
(London)

- **Studio camera,** c. 1890's, full-plate 6½ x 8½ size.
  .... 200.00   250.00

PERKEO
(See Voigtlander)

PERLE
(See Welta)

PETAL
(See Sakura)

PETER, JOSEPH
(See Jos-Pe)

PETIE
(See Kunick)

PETITAX

- **Petitax,** German novelty camera for 14 x 14mm. exposures on rollfilm, f11/25mm. lens, simple shutter.
  ....20.00   25.00

PETITE
(See Eastman)

PETRI CAMERA CO.
(Japan)

- **Petri 6 x 6,** folding camera for 6 x 6cm. exposures on 120, Ikonta copy, c. 1948, f3.5/75mm., shutter 1-200, synchronized, RF.
  ....25.00   35.00

PHOBA A.G.
(Basel, Switzerland)

- **Diva,** 6 x 9cm. folding-bed plate camera, Titar f4.5/105mm., Compur.
  ....25.00   35.00

PHOTAK CORP.
(Chicago)

- **Foldex,** folding camera for 620, all metal, Octvar or Steinheil lens.
  ....8.00   10.00

PHOTAKE
(See Chicago Camera Co.)

PHOTAVIT-WERK
(Nürnberg, Germany)

- **Photavit,** a compact 35mm. camera for 24 x 24 mm. exposures on standard 35mm. film in special cartridges.
  .... 100.00   120.00
(See Bolta for description)

PHOTINA

☐ **Photina,** German 6 x 6cm. TLR, post WWII, Cassar f3.5/75 in Prontor SVS shutter.
.................25.00   35.00

PHOTOLET

☐ **Photolet,** c. 1932, French.
.................75.00   85.00

PHOTO MASTER

☐ **Photo Master,** c. 1948, for 16 exposures 3 x 4cm. on 127 film, Rollax 50mm. lens, single speed rotary shutter, plastic body.
..................4.00   6.00

PHOTO-PORST
(Hans Porst, Nürnberg)

Makers of Hapo cameras. Hapo = HAns POrst.

☐ **Hapo 35,** c. 1955, folding 35mm., Enna Haponar f2.9/50mm., Prontor SVS 1-300, CRF.
.................35.00   45.00

☐ **Hapo 36,** 35mm., non-coupled RF, f2.8 Steinheil in Pronto shutter.
.................35.00   45.00

☐ **Hapo 66,** 6 x 6cm., Enna Haponar f3.3/75mm., Pronto synchronized shutter ½-200.
.................50.00   60.00

PHOTORET
(See Magic Introduction Co)

PHOTO REVOLVER
(See Krauss)

PHOTOSCOPE
(See Ross)

PHOTOSCOPIC
(Brussels, Belgium)

☐ **Photoscopic,** c. 1930, unusual designed early 35mm. camera for 50 exposures 24 x 24mm. on 35mm. film in special cassettes, O.I.P. Gand Labor f3.5/45mm. lens, Pronto or Ibsor shutter.
.... 475.00   525.00

PHOTO-SEE

☐ **Photo-See,** an art-deco box camera and developing tank for photos in 5 minutes, an interesting simple camera, they would have beat Polaroid to the marketplace, but as rumor goes, the first batch of cameras were all made when it was discovered that the viewfinders were all on backwards, that was just enough discouragement, so they never printed the instructions or sold the cameras.
.................20.00   30.00

PHOTOSPHERE
(See Compagnie Francaise de Photographie)

PHOTO VANITY
(See Ansco)

PHOTRIX QUICK B

☐ **Photrix Quick B.**
.................15.00   20.00

PICCOCHIC
(See Balda)

PICCOLETTE
(See Contessa, Zeiss)

PICNY
(See Mitsukoshi)

PIGNONS AG
(Ballaigues, Switzerland)

☐ **Alpa Alnea,** model 7, c. 1952, 35mm. SLR, f1.8/50, focal plane shutter 1-1000, synchronized, CRF.
.... 125.00   150.00

216 / PILOT

☐ **Alpa,** *model 6, c. 1958, 35mm. SLR, f3.5/50mm. Alorar, or f1.9/50 Alpa Xenon.*
.... 150.00   200.00

☐ **Alpa,** *model 9d, 35mm. SLR c. 1964, Tele Xenar 50mm. lens, focal plane shutter 1-1000, the first European camera with through-the-lens metering.*
.... 200.00   250.00

☐ **Alpa Reflex,** *original model, c. 1940, 35 mm. SLR, focal plane shutter 1-1000, identical to the Bolsey model, both of these cameras were designed by Jacques Bolsey before he moved to the United States and started the Bolsey Camera Co.*
.... 325.00   375.00

☐ **Bolsey,** *c. 1938 35mm. SLR, Bolca Anastigmat f2.8/50, focal plane shutter, this is the camera which was originally called the Bolca, and grew into the Alpa line of cameras.*
.... 500.00   550.00

PILOT
(See Guthe & Thorsch)

PINETTA

☐ **Pinetta,** *35mm. camera, f2.8.*
.................20.00   25.00

PIONEER
(See Ansco)

PIPON
(Paris)

☐ **Magazine camera,** *c. 1900 leather covered wood box for 9 x 12cm. plates, Aplanoscope f9 lens.*
.... 100.00   125.00

☐ **Self-Worker,** *c. 1895, Jumelle camera for 9 x 12cm. plates, Goerz Double Anastigmat 120mm. lens, 6-speed guillotine shutter.*
.... 190.00   210.00

PITTSBURGH CAMERA CORP
(Penn.)

☐ **Ulca TSL,** *c. 1935 for 20 x 20mm. on rollfilm, meniscus lens, simple shutter, cast steel body.*
...................40.00   50.00

PIXIE
(See Whittaker)

PLANOVISTA SEEING CAMERA LTD.
(London)

Imported a camera with their name on it. Actually a Bentzin camera. *(See Bentzin)*

PLASCOP
(See Ica)

PLASMAT GmbH - ROLAND
(See Roland)

PLATOS

☐ **"Pocket Platos",** *French 6.5 x 9cm. folding plate camera, Splendor f6.2/90mm. lens in Vario shutter.*
.... 110.00   145.00

PLAUBEL & CO.
(Frankfurt, Germany)

☐ **Folding-bed plate cameras,** *6 x 9 and 9 x 12cm. sizes, double extension bed and bellows, Anticomar or Heli-Orthar lens, Ibso or Compur shutter.*
...................30.00   40.00

☐ **Makina,** *c. 1920 compact strut-folding sheet film camera, f2.9/Anticomar lens, Compur shutter, 4.5 x 6cm. or 6.5 x 9cm.*
.... 225.00   250.00

☐ **Makina II,** *Anticomar f2.9, Compur to 200, coupled rangefinder.*
.... 190.00   215.00

Makina

☐ **Makina III,** *c. 1930, 6 x 9cm. strut-folding camera, Anticomar f2.9/100mm., rim-set Compur 1-200, CRF.*
.... 200.00   250.00

☐ **Roll-Op,** *folding bed camera, 16 exposures 4.5 x 6cm. on 120 rollfilm, c. 1935, Anticomar f2.8/75mm., Compur Rapid 1-250, coupled rangefinder.*
.... 110.00   150.00

☐ **Stereo Makina,** *c. 1930, strut-folding stereo camera for 6 x 13cm. plates, Anticomar f2.9/90mm. lenses in stereo shutter 1-100, black bellows, black metal body, partly leather covered.*
.... 700.00   800.00

PLENAX
(See Agfa, Ansco)

PLICO
(See Eastman Flexo)

POCKET Z
(See Zion)

POCO
(See Rochester, Monroe)

POKA
(See Balda)

POLAROID

Polaroid cameras, using the patented process of Dr. Land, were the first commercially successful instant picture cameras which were easy to use, and were not in need of bottles of chemicals, etc. The idea of in-camera development is not new. Jules Bourdin invented a simple system which was marketed as early as 1860. Many other attempts met with mediocre success. Polaroid caught on and became a household word. We are listing these cameras strictly by number, without descriptions. They are quite common, and not very old. There is more supply than demand in the present market.

☐ J-33 ....12.00   15.00
☐ J-66 ....10.00   12.00
☐ SX-70 ....75.00   85.00
☐ 80 ....10.00   12.00
☐ 80A 10.00   12.00
☐ 80B 10.00   12.00
☐ 95 ....20.00   25.00
☐ 95A 18.00   20.00
☐ 95B 18.00   20.00
☐ 100 ....25.00   30.00
☐ 110 ....50.00   60.00
☐ 110A 60.00   70.00
☐ 110B 70.00   80.00
☐ 150 ....25.00   30.00
☐ 180 .... 225.00   235.00
☐ 210 ....20.00   25.00

☐ 800 ....20.00   25.00
☐ 900 ....20.00   25.00

POLICE CAMERA
(See Expo)

POLYSCOP
(See Ica, Krauss)

PONTIAC
(Paris)

☐ **6 x 9cm.,** *folding rollfilm camera, Berthiot Special f4.5/105mm. lens, shutter 25-150, for 8 exposures on 120 film.*
............20.00   25.00

☐ **Lynx,** *for 16 exposures, 3 x 4cm. on 127 film, Berthiot f2.8/50mm. coated lens in Leica-style collapsible mount, focal plane shutter.*
............65.00   75.00

PONTURA
(See Balda)

PONY
(See Eastman)

POPULAR PHOTOGRPH COMPANY
(New York)

☐ **Nodark Tintype Camera,** *c. 1899, all-wood box camera for 2½ x 3½ ferrotype plates, the camera has a capacity of 36 plates.*
............1000.00   1200.00

POPULAR PRESSMAN
(Busch, London)

☐ **3¼ x 4¼ SLR,** *Aldis Anastigmat f3.4 or Tessar f2.7/165mm.*
............125.00   175.00

POUVA
(Karl Pouva, Freital, Germany)

☐ **Start,** *c. 1954 telescoping camera for 6 x 6cm. exposures on 120 rollfilm, Duplar f8 lens.*
............15.00   20.00

PRAKTI
(Praktica, Praktiflex, Praktina, Praktisix)
(See Guthe & Thorsch)

PRECISA
(See Beier)

PREMIER
(See Rochester)

PREMIER INSTRUMENT COMPANY
(New York)

☐ **Kardon,** *c. 1945, 35mm. Leica IIIa copy, made for the Signal Corps, and also for civilians, Ektar f2/47mm., cloth focal plane shutter for 1 to 1000, coupled rangefinder.*
............200.00   250.00

"PREMIUM"

☐ **"Premium" box-plate camera,** *c. 1895, an unusual box-plate camera for single exposures, 4 x 5", black papered wood body, primitive meniscus lens, wooden lens cap.*
............200.00   250.00

PREMO, PREMOETTE
(See Eastman, Roch)

PRESSMAN
(See Busch)

PRIMAR
(See Bentzin)

PRIMO
(See Sawyer, Tokyo Kogaku)

PROMINENT
(See Voigtlander)

PUCK
(See Thornton-Picard)

PUPILLE
(See Eastman, Nagel)

PURMA
(See Hunter)

PUTNAM
(E. Putnam, N.Y.)

☐ **Marvel,** *5 x 8" horizontal folding view camera c. 1890, Scovill Waterbury lens with rotating disc stops.*
.... **125.00   175.00**

PYGMEE
(See Carmen)

Q.P.

☐ **Q.P.,** *pronounced "Kewpie," Japanese novelty camera for 16mm. paper backed rolls.*
.................**10.00   12.00**

Q.R.S.
(See DeVry)

QUAD
(See Close & Cone)

QUICK
(See Photrix)

QUICK FOCUS KODAK
(See Eastman)

RAACO

☐ **Raaco,** *box camera for 4.5 x 6cm., cardboard construction, meniscus lens, segment shutter.*
.... **100.00   125.00**

RADIX
(See Kurbi & Niggeloh)

RAY / 219

Raaco, Raaco

RAJAR

☐ **Rajar No. 6,** *English folding camera for 120 film, c. 1920's, T & I shutter.*
.................**20.00   25.00**

RANCA
(See Nagel)

RAY CAMERA COMPANY
(Successors to Mutschler Robertson & Company, Rochester, N.Y.)

☐ **Ray No. 1,** *c. 1899, 4 x 5 wooden plate camera, red bellows, brown leather covered.*
.................**45.00   60.00**

☐ **Ray No. 2,** *5 x 7 folding plate camera, similar construction, dark mahogany interior, red bellows, double pneumatic shutter.*
.................**50.00   65.00**

☐ **Ray Jr.,** *c. 1897 for 2½ x 2½ plates.*
.................**65.00   75.00**

220 / READYFLASH

Ray No. 1

Ray No. 2

Ray Jr.

☐ **Box camera,** *for glass plates, 3½ x 3½", rear section of top hinges up to insert holders.*
.... 60.00   70.00

READYFLASH
(See Ansco)

READYSET
(See Agfa)

REALIST
(See White)

RECOMAR
(See Eastman, Nagel)

RECORD
(See Huttig)

RECTAFLEX
(Italy)

☐ **Rectaflex Standard,** *c. 1950 SLR, Schneider Xenon f2.8/50mm. or Angenieux f1.8/50, focal plane shutter 25-1300, synchronized.*
.... 150.00   200.00

REDIFLEX
(See Ansco)

REFLECTA
(See Welta)

REFLEX CAMERA COMPANY
(Newark, N.J.)

Took over the Borsum Camera Company in 1909.

☐ **Focal plane postcard camera,** *a vertical styled folding plate camera in the post-card size, but with a focal plane shutter, c. 1912, Cooke Anastigmat or Ilex RR lens in plain mount.*
.... 150.00   175.00

REGENT
(See Ansco, Eastman)

REGENT

☐ **Regent,** *14mm. novelty camera, Japan.*
.... 10.00   15.00

REGULA
(See King)

REGULAR KODAK
(See Eastman)

REICHENBACH, MOREY & WILL CO.
(Rochester, N.Y.)

☐ **Alta D,** *5 x 7 folding plate camera.*
.... 100.00   125.00

REICKA
(See Wunsche)

REID & SIGRIST
(Leicester, England)

☐ **Reid,** *c. 1953, copy of Leica IIIb, collapsible Taylor Hobson f2/50mm., focal plane shutter 1-1000, synchronized.*
.... 250.00   300.00

RIETZSCHEL
(A. Heinrich Rietzschel GmbH Optische Fabrik, Munich, Germany)

☐ **Clack,** *9 x 12cm. or 10 x 15cm. c. 1910, red bellows, black leathered wood body, aluminum standard, nickel trim, f6.3 or f8.*
.... 60.00   75.00

☐ **Heli-Clack,** *9 x 12 or 10 x 15cm., horizontal format folding plate cameras, double extension bellows, double Anastigmat f6.8 in Compound shutter.*
.... 70.00   95.00

☐ **Junior Reflex,** *box camera c. 1903 for 3¼ x 4¼ plates, simple lens, 4-speed sector shutter coupled to mirror, a simple SLR box.*
.... 140.00   160.00

☐ **Patent Reflex Hand Camera,** *an early model leather covered 4 x 5" SLR box camera, internal bellows focus, focal plane shutter, red focusing hood, fine finished wood interior, without lens.*
.... 350.00   425.00

☐ **Reflex camera,** *4 x 5", leather covered wood box with tall viewing hood, internal bellows focus, without lens.*
.... 200.00   275.00

☐ **5 x 7 Reflex,** *c. 1898, f16/210mm. Anastigmat.*
.... 310.00   340.00

REGAL MINIATURE

☐ **Regal Miniature,** *for 127 film.*
.... 5.00   8.00

Clack

☐ **Cosmo Clack Stereo,** c. 1914, 45 x 107mm. format, double Anastigmat f6.3, Rietzschel f4.5/60mm. in Compur 1-250, panoramic photos also possible.
.... 250.00   350.00

☐ **6 x 9 folding plate camera,** Dialyt f6.8/105 in dial-set Compur 1-250, DEB.
................30.00   50.00

☐ **Special Wiphot,** 9 x 12cm. folding plate camera, Rietzschel Lesican Anastigmat f5.5/120mm. in Compound shutter 1-200.
................50.00   75.00

REPORTER CAMERA
(See Ernemann)

RETINA, RETINETTE
(See Eastman)

LE REVE

☐ **Le Reve,** c. 1908 French folding camera for 3¼ x 4¼ plates or rollfilm with special rollfilm back, Beckers f6.3 or Roussel f6.8/135mm. Anastigmat lens, Unicum shutter, red bellows.
.... 200.00   250.00

REVERE

☐ **Eyematic EE,** c. 1958, 127 film, Wollensak f2.8/58mm.
................30.00   40.00

☐ **Stereo 33,** Amaton or Wollensak f3.5/35mm., shutter 2-200, MFX synchronized, rangefinder.
.... 100.00   125.00

REVIEW
(See Zorki Model III)

REX KAYSON

☐ **Rex Kayson,** Japanese 35mm. RF camera, f3.5/45mm. lens, Compur 1-300, looks like a small Leica M.
................40.00   50.00

REX MAGAZINE CAMERA COMPANY
(Chicago)

☐ **Rex Magazine Camera,** c. 1899, 4 x 5 format, simple lens and shutter, unusual plate changing mechanism.
.... 150.00   175.00

☐ **Rex Magazine Camera,** 2 x 2" format, the baby brother of the above model.
.... 125.00   150.00

REXO, REXOETTE
(See Burke & James)

REYGONAUD
(Paris)

☐ **Stand Camera,** c. 1870, Jamin Darlot lens, brass trim, for 8 x 11cm. plates.
.... 500.00   600.00

REYNA
(See Cornu)

REYNOLDS & BRANSON

☐ **Field camera,** full plate, 6½ x 8½ size, without lens.
................75.00   115.00

RICHARD
(Jules Richard, Paris, France)

- **Glyphoscope,** c. 1905 45 x 107mm. stereo camera of simple construction, meniscus lens, guillotine shutter, all metal.
  ....90.00   135.00
- **Homeos,** c. 1914, the first stereo for 35mm. film, 25 exposures on standard 35mm. cine film, Zeiss Krauss Anastigmat f4.5/28, guillotine shutter.
  .... 2600.00   2850.00
- **Verascope, simple models,** c. 1898, fixed-focus lenses single speed shutter, all metal body.
  .... 100.00   125.00
- **Verascope, better models,** with higher quality lenses and shutters, more common than the simple models.
  .... 125.00   150.00

RICOH
(Japan)

- **Golden Ricoh 16,** c. 1955, subminiature for 25 exposures 9 x 13mm. on 16mm. film, f3.5/25mm., synchronized shutter 50-200.
  .... 100.00   125.00
- **Ricoh 35,** c. 1955 Leica-style 35mm., f3.5, 2.8, or f2 lens.
  ....25.00   35.00
- **Ricohflex,** c. 1953, 6 x 6cm. TLR, Ricoh Anastigmat f3.5.
  ....20.00   25.00

RIFAX
(See Beier)

RIGONA
(See Balda)

RIKEN OPTICAL
(Japan)

- **Golden Steky,** subminiature for 10 x 14mm. on 16mm. film, fixed focus f3.5/25mm. lens, shutter 50-200.
  .... 125.00   150.00
- **Same as above,** with auxiliary f5.6/40mm. telephoto.
  .... 155.00   180.00
- **Steky,** c. 1949, subminiature for 10 x 14mm. on 16mm. film, Stekinar f3.5/25mm. Anastigmat shutter 25, 50, 100.
  ....40.00   50.00
- **Steky II, III, IIIa, IIIb.**
  ....40.00   55.00

RILEX
(See Riley Research)

RILEY RESEARCH
(Santa Monica, Calif.)

- **Rilex Press,** 2¼ x 3¼ press camera, Tessar f4.5, chrome and stainless.
  .... 125.00   150.00

RIVAL REFLEX

- **Rival Reflex,** 35mm. SLR made in USSR occupied Germany, Wetzlar Vastar f2.8/50mm., focal plane shutter, synchronized.
  ....30.00   40.00

ROBOT
(See Berning)

ROBRA

- **Robra,** German folding camera.
  ....25.00   35.00

ROCHESTER

Various official company names during the history of the company and its mergers: Rochester Camera & Supply Co., Rochester Optical Co., Rochester Optical & Camera Co., etc. Sold out to Eastman Kodak Co. in 1907 and became Rochester Optical Division, then Rochester Optical Department. Other companies which merged into the Rochester family included: Monroe Camera Co., Mutschler & Robertson (Ray Cameras), and Western Camera Mfg. Co. (Cyclone Cameras). *(See also Eastman Kodak Co. listings for later examples of many of the Rochester cameras, particularly the "Premo" line.)*

Cyclone Cameras
Formerly Western, prior to 1901.

☐ **Cyclone Magazine,** *No. 2, 4, or 5, c. 1898, for 3¼ x 4¼ or 4 x 5" plates, black leathered wood box, meniscus lens, sector shutter.*
................**50.00   60.00**

☐ **Cyclone Junior,** *plate box camera for 3½ x 3½" glass plates in standard holders, top door hinges forward to load plateholders, a cheaper alternative to the more expensive magazine cameras.*
................**25.00   35.00**

☐ **Cyclone Senior,** *plate box camera, 4 x 5" for standard plateholders.*
................**25.00   30.00**

☐ **Favorite,** *8 x 10" c. 1890, Emile No. 5 lens with waterhouse stops.*
.... **200.00   250.00**

☐ **Handy,** *c. 1892 detective box-plate camera, 4 x 5", internal bellows focus, a simple, less expensive version of the Premier.*
.... **100.00   150.00**

☐ **Ideal,** *folding view cameras, cherry wood, brass trim, sizes 4 x 5 to 8 x 10, ranging in price, depending on size.*
.................**75.00   150.00**

Poco Cameras
First introduced in 1893, listed here by size.

☐ **3¼ x 4¼ Pocket Poco,** *red bellows, single pneumatic shutter.*
.................**50.00   75.00**

☐ **4 x 5 Cycle Poco,** *folding-bed plate cameras, leather covered wood body and bed, nicely finished wood interior, often with B & L RR lens and Unicum shutter, models 1-7, B, C.*
.................**60.00   75.00**

☐ **5 x 7 Cycle Poco,** *c. 1902, black leather covered wood body, polished interior, red bellows, RR lens, Unicum shutter, models 1-5.*
.... **100.00   150.00**

☐ **8 x 10 Poco,** *similar, but larger, double extension bellows, B & L Symmetrical lens.*
.... **125.00   175.00**

ROCHESTER / 225

☐ **Gem Poco,** *4 x 5" box for plates, focuses by sliding lever at left front, shutter tensioned by brass knob on face.*
................**50.00**   **75.00**

☐ **Gem Poco, folding,** *c. 1895, for 4 x 5" plates in standard holders, red bellows.*
................**60.00**   **75.00**

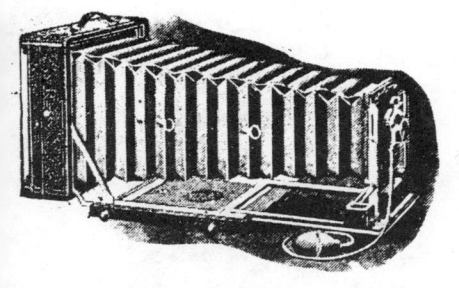

☐ **King Poco,** *5 x 7" folding view.*
................**75.00**   **100.00**

☐ **Telephoto Poco Camera, 4 x 5,** *c. 1891, folding plate camera, triple extension red leather bellows, B & L lens in Auto shutter, storage in back of camera for extra plateholders.*
................**65.00**   **80.00**

☐ **Telephoto Poco Camera, 5 x 7,** *c. 1902, folding plate camera, red leather bellows, double or triple extension, B & L RR lens, Auto shutter.*
................**115.00**   **135.00**

☐ **Telephoto Poco Camera, 6½ x 8½ and 8 x 10 sizes.**
................**150.00**   **185.00**

☐ **Premier Detective box camera,** *c. 1891, internal bellows focus with external control knob, side panel opens to insert plate holders, made in 4 x 5 and 5 x 7" sizes.*
................**135.00**   **150.00**

☐ **Premier folding camera,** *c. 1892, 4 x 5 or 5 x 7 size, for plates, B & L pneumatic shutter.*
................**175.00**   **195.00**

Premo Cameras
(See also Eastman for their continuation of the Premo line.) Prices here are for cameras with normal shutter/lens combinations, often B & L lenses, Victor shutters.

☐ **Premo Camera 4 x 5",** *c. 1900 folding plate cameras, including: Pony Premo, Star Premo, Premo A-E, 3B, 4, and 7, red bellows.*
................**60.00**   **75.00**

☐ **Premo Camera, 5 x 7",** *c. 1900 folding plate cameras, including: Pony Premo, Pony Premo Senior, Premo No. 6, Premo B, red bellows.*
................**75.00**   **90.00**

226 / RODENSTOCK

☐ **Long Focus Premo,** *triple extension red bellows, sizes 4 x 5, 5 x 7, 6½ x 8½ inch.*
.................90.00   125.00

☐ **Reversible Back Premo,** *5 x 7", looks like a Long Focus Premo, but back shifts from horizontal to vertical.*
...............100.00   150.00

☐ **Rochester Stereo Camera,** *5 x 7 or 6½ x 8½" size, B & L shutter, red bellows.*
...............425.00   475.00

☐ **Rochester View Cameras,** *miscellaneous models, with folding bed, normal lens, maroon bellows, 4 x 5 size.*
.................85.00   115.00

☐ **Same as above,** *other sizes to 8 x 10, all averaged.*
...............125.00   140.00

RODENSTOCK
(Optische Werke G. Rodenstock, Munich)

☐ **Clarovid,** *c. 1932 folding-bed rollfilm camera for 6 x 9cm. exposures, Trinar Anastigmat f4.5/105 or f3.8/105, rim-set Compur 1-250, CRF.*
.................45.00   60.00

☐ **Folding rollfilm cameras,** *4.5 x 6 and 6 x 6cm. models for 120 film, Rodenstock Trinar f2.9 lens, rim-set Compur 1-250.*
.................20.00   30.00

☐ **Folding plate/sheetfilm camera,** *9 x 12cm., f2.9, f3.8, or f4.5 Trinar.*
.................25.00   35.00

ROKUOH-SHA
(Pearl cameras)
(See Konishiroku)

ROLAND

This camera was designed by Dr. Winkler in association with Dr. Paul Rudolph, who designed the various Plasmat lenses. The camera was built by Plasmat GmbH. It was highly regarded for its six-element lens and sold new in 1934-1937 for $93-143.

☐ **Folding camera,** *for 4.5 x 6cm. exposures on 120 rollfilm, c. 1931, telescoping front, Plasmat f2.7/70mm. lens in rim-set Compur 1-250 shutter, coupled rangefinder.*
...............1450.00   1650.00

ROLF
(See Ernemann)

ROLFIX
(See Franka)

ROLLEI
(See Franke & Heidecke)

ROLLETTE
(See Krauss)

ROLLOP
(See Lippische Camerawerk, Lipca, also Plaubel & Company)

ROM
(Italy)

☐ **Scat,** *c. 1950 subminiature for 8 x 11mm. exposures on 9.5mm. film in Minox cassettes, f3.5 lens, revolving shutter, leather covered metal body, uncommon.*
.... 175.00   215.00

RONDINE
(See Ferrania)

ROROX

☐ **Rorox,** *3 x 4cm., ½-frame, on 127 film.*
.................35.00   45.00

ROSS
(Thomas Ross & Company)

Very few Ross cameras appear on the U.S.A. market, so it is impossible for us to figure any averages. However, those we have on record compare with other British cameras of the same type and age.

Sutton Panoramic Camera
c. 1861. This camera, made for Thomas Sutton by Ross, takes curved glass plates in special curved holders. And wet-plates at that! Only about 30 were made. Lens is water-filled and gives an angle of 120 degrees. We can only tell you that two of these cameras sold at auction in 1974 for approximately $25,000 and $28,000.

ROUSSEL
(H. Roussel, Paris)

☐ **Stella Jumelle,** *c. 1900, 9 x 12cm. plates, Roussel Anti-Spectroscopique f7.7/130mm. in 7-speed guillotine shutter, leather covered wood body.*
.... 250.00   300.00

ROY ROGERS CAMERA
(See Herco)

ROYER
(France)

☐ **Savoyflex,** *35mm. SLR, Som Berthiot f2.8/50mm. lens, Prontor Reflex inter-lens shutter, 1-500.*
.................65.00   75.00

RUBIX 16

☐ **Rubix 16,** *c. 1950's Japanese subminiature for 50 exposures, 10 x 14mm. on 16mm. cassette film, Hope f3.5/25mm., shutter 25-100.*
.................80.00   95.00

RUBY REFLEX
(See Thornton Picard)

RUTHINE

☐ **Ruthine,** *35mm. CRF camera, Friedrich Corygon f2.8/45mm., shutter 1-500, B.*
.................20.00   35.00

SABRE 620

☐ **Sabre 620.**
.................10.00   12.00

ST. LOUIS

☐ **St. Louis,** *reversible back camera No. 116, c. 1890, for 8 x 10" plates, with lens.*
.... 135.00   150.00

SAKURA
(Japan)

228 / SAMOCA

☐ **Petal,** *subminiature camera about the size of a half-dollar, approximately 30mm. diameter, takes 6 exposures on circular film, original price about $10, round model.*
.... 100.00   125.00
☐ **Same as above,** *octagonal model.*
.... 200.00   250.00

SAMOCA
(Sanei Sangyo, Japan)

☐ **Samoca Super,** *c. 1956, 35mm. camera for 36 exposures, 24 x 36mm. on standard cartridges, Ezumar f3.5/50mm., shutter 10-200, CRF, built-in selenium meter.*
.................40.00   50.00
☐ **Same as above,** *other models, 35, 35II, 35III, c. 1950's, simpler models.*
.................30.00   35.00

SANDERSON CAMERA WORKS
(England)

All Sanderson cameras incorporate the patented lens panel support system designed by Frederick H. Sanderson. The majority of the cameras were actually built by Houghton's.

☐ **Sanderson "Regular" and "Deluxe" models,** *3 x 4", 3¼ x 4¼", and 3½ x 5½" sizes, folding plate cameras with finely polished wood interior, heavy leather exterior.*
.... 175.00   325.00

SAVOYFLEX
(See Royer)

SAWYERS, INC.
(Portland, Oregon)

☐ **Mark IV,** *same as Primo Jr., TLR for 4 x 4cm. on 127 film, Topcor f2.8 lens, Seikosha MX shutter to 500, auto wind.*
.... 100.00   115.00

☐ **View-Master Mark II Stereo,** *for stereo pairs on 35mm film, Trinar f2.8/20mm.*
.... 125.00   150.00
☐ **View-Master Personal Stereo,** *c. 1960, for making your own viewmaster slides, Anastigmat f3.5/25mm. lenses, brown and beige or black models.*
.... 100.00   150.00
☐ **Sawyers Europe View-Master Stereo Color,** *the European model, made in Germany, for stereo exposures 12 x 13mm. on 35mm. film, Rodenstock f2.8/20mm. lenses and single-speed shutter.*
.... 100.00   150.00

SCAT
(See Rom)

SCENEX

☐ **Scenex,** *American black plastic novelty camera for 3 x 4cm. exposures on 828 film, meniscus lens, single speed shutter.*
.................15.00   20.00

SCENOGRAPHE
(See Cadot)

SCHIANSKY

☐ **Universal Studio Camera,** *all metal, for 7 x 9¼" sheet film, with reducing back for 13 x 18cm, 5 x 7", Zeiss Apo-Tessar f9/450mm., black bellows extend to 1 meter, only 12 were made, one sale in 1976.*
.... 500.00   600.00

SCHLEISSNER

☐ **Bower,** *35mm., Meritar f4.5 lens in Prontor shutter to 200.*
.................30.00   35.00
☐ **Bower Jr., Bower X,** *620 folder, Steinheil f6.3/105mm., Vario shutter 25-200.*
.................15.00   20.00

SCHLEUSSNER
(Dr. C. Schleussner Fotowerke GmbH., Wiesbaden, Germany)
(See Adox)

SCHMITZ & THIENEMANN
(Dresden)

- **Uniflex "Reflex Meteor,"** *c. 1931* SLR box for 6.5 x 9cm., Meyer Trioplan f4.5/105mm. in self-cocking Pronto shutter 25-100.
  .... 200.00   275.00

SCHUL-PRÄMIE
(See Agfa)

SCOUT
(See Ansco, Herco, Eastman for "Girl Scout" and "Boy Scout" models. See Wittnauer, Seneca for cameras named "Scout" which are not related to the scout clubs.)

SCOVILL MANUFACTURING COMPANY
(N.Y.)

Brief summary of name changes and dates: Scovill & Adams - 1889; Anthony & Scovill - 1902; Ansco - 1907. Scovill produced some excellent cameras, all of which are relatively uncommon today. *(See also Anthony and Ansco.)*

- **Antique Oak Detective,** *c. 1890*, 4 x 5" box-plate camera finished in beautiful golden oak, string-set shutter, variable speeds.
  .... 650.00   750.00

- **Knack Detective,** *c. 1891*, the Antique Oak Detective camera with a new name.
  .... 550.00   650.00

- **Mascot,** *c. 1890-1892*, 4 x 5" format leather covered wood box camera, similar to the Waterbury detective camera, but with an Eastman Roll Holder, string-set shutter.
  .... 500.00   600.00

- **Scovill Detective,** *c. 1886*, leather covered box detective camera for 4 x 5" plates in standard plateholders, entire top of camera hinges open to one side to reveal the red leather bellows and to change plates, the bottom of the camera is recessed, and the controls are located there, out of sight, a very uncommon detective camera.
  .... 1000.00   1150.00

- **Triad Detective,** *c. 1892*, leather covered 4 x 5" box detective camera for plates, rollfilm, or sheet film, various speed string-set shutter.
  .... 350.00   450.00

- **Waterbury Detective Camera, original model,** *c. 1888*, black painted all wood box, but at least one leather-covered model has surfaced, side door for loading plates, focused by means of sliding bar extending through the base of the camera, recessed bottom stores an extra plateholder, 4 x 5".
  .... 500.00   550.00

- **Same as above, 5 x 7".**
  .... 525.00   625.00

- **Waterbury Detective, improved model,** *c. 1892*, same as the original model, except focus knob is at top front.
  .... 450.00   500.00

Field / View 5" 8" or 6½" x 8½"

230 / SCREEN FOCUS

☐ **Field/View cameras, 4 x 5",** *square black box with folding beds on front and rear, bellows extend both directions, top and side doors permit loading the plateholders either way into the revolving back when only the front bellows are being used, nickel plated Waterbury lens.*
.... 175.00   200.00

☐ **Field/View camera, 5 x 8" or 6½ x 8½",** *c. 1888, horizontal format, light wood finish, brass barrel Waterbury lens.*
.... 150.00   200.00

☐ **Field/View camera, 8 x 10",** *c. early 1880's, light colored wood body.*
.... 200.00   250.00

☐ **Stereo 5 x 8",** *c. 1885, all wood body, Scovill Waterbury lenses.*
.... 350.00   400.00

☐ **Stereo Solograph,** *c. 1899, a compact folding stereo camera for 4 x 6½", stereo RR lenses in Automatic Stereo shutter.*
.... 350.00   400.00

☐ **Waterbury 4 x 5" view,** *c. 1888, folding-bed collapsible bellows view camera, Eurygraph 4 x 5 RR lens, Prosch Duplex shutter.*
.... 150.00   200.00

SCREEN FOCUS KODAK
(See Eastman)

SEAGULL

☐ **No. 203,** *Chinese 6 x 6cm. TLR for 120 film, copy of Zeiss Ikonta IV, 12 or 16 exposures on 120 film, f3.5/75mm.*
.... 50.00   75.00

SEARS
(See Seroco, Tower)

SECAM
(Paris)

Stylophot cameras
c. 1950's "Pen" style cameras, according to the name, but even if compared to the large deluxe European fountain pens, it ends up looking a bit hefty. The pocket clip is the closest resemblance to a pen, for 18 exposures use 10 x 10mm. on 16mm. film in special cartridges. Shutter cocking and film advance via pull-push sliding mechanism which pushes film from cartridge to cartridge, automatic exposure counter, weight: 3 ounces (85 grams).

☐ **Stylophot "Standard" or "Color" model,** *the cheaper of the two models, with fixed focus two-element f6.3 coated lens, single speed shutter, 1/50 seconds, original price $15.00.*
.... 100.00   125.00

☐ **Stylophot "Luxe" or "Deluxe" model,** *with f3.5/27mm. Roussel Anastigmat lens, iris diaphragm, focus to 2½ feet, (0.8m.), single speed shutter, 1/75, synched for flash, original price, $33.00, this model very uncommon.*
.... 175.00   200.00

☐ **Stereophot,** *an unique stereo camera consisting of two Stylophot cameras mounted side-by-side on a special mounting plate, awkward, maybe, but rare.*
.... 750.00   850.00

SELECTA
(See Agfa)

SELFIX
(See Houghton)

SELF WORKER
(See Pipon)

SEMI-AUTOMATIC
(See Ansco)

SENECA CAMERA COMPANY
(Rochester, N.Y.)

- **No. 9 Folding Plate Camera,** *4 x 5", maroon bellows, Velostigmat lens, Compur shutter.*
  ....45.00   55.00

- **Box-plate camera,** *4 x 5", fixed focus, all black.*
  ....40.00   50.00

- **Busy Bee,** *c. 1903, 4 x 5" box-plate camera, fold-down front reveals a beautiful interior.*
  ....90.00   120.00

- **Chautauqua,** *4 x 5" folding plate camera, Wollensak lens, Seneca Uno shutter, a very plain all-black camera.*
  ....50.00   60.00

Chautauqua

- **Chief 1A,** *rollfilm camera.*
  ....15.00   20.00

- **Competitor View, 5 x 7 or 8 x 10",** *a folding field camera, light colored wood or medium colored cherry wood.*
  .... 125.00   150.00

- **Filmet,** *c. 1916 folding film-pack camera for 3¼ x 4¼" packs, single speed shutter, rotating disc stops.*
  ....25.00   35.00

- **Folding plate camera,** *3¼ x 4¼, Wollensak f16 lens, Uno shutter.*
  ....45.00   55.00

Folding Plate, 4" x 5"

232 / SENECA CAMERA COMPANY

- **Folding plate camera, 3¼ x 5½,** black double-extension bellows and triple convertible lens.
  . . . . 50.00   60.00
- **Folding plate camera, 4 x 5",** black leathered body with nickel trim, double extension bellows, Seneca Uno or Auto shutter.
  . . . . 55.00   65.00
- **Folding plate camera, 5 x 7",** similar, black interior, black leathered wood body, 7" Rogers or Seneca Anastigmat in Auto shutter.
  . . . . 65.00   75.00

- **Pocket Camera Jr. No. 1,** 2¼ x 3¼ exposures folding rollfilm camera, Ilex shutter.
  . . . . 30.00   50.00
- **Pocket Camera No. 3A,** *double extension bellows, rapid convertible lens, Auto shutter 1-100.*
  . . . . 40.00   60.00
- **Pocket Camera No. 29,** c. 1905 folding plate camera for 4 x 5 plates, Seneca Uno shutter, lens f8.
  . . . . 40.00   60.00

- **No. 2A Folding Scout,** c. 1916, Wollensak lens, Ultro shutter.
  . . . . 20.00   25.00
- **No. 3 Folding Scout,** c. 1916, Ultro shutter.
  . . . . 15.00   20.00
- **No. 3A Folding Scout,** c. 1916, Seneca Trio shutter, 122 film.
  . . . . 20.00   25.00
- **Box Scout No. 2, 2A, 3, 3A.**
  . . . . 10.00   12.00
- **Stereo View,** c. 1910, 5 x 7 format folding-bed collapsible bellows view camera with wide front lensboard, style similar to the Competitor view, Wollensak lenses.
  . . . . 275.00   350.00
- **Trio No. 1A,** *folding camera for 120.*
  . . . . 20.00   25.00

- **Uno,** c. 1910, 3¼ x 4¼ folding filmpack camera, leather covered wood body, Wollensak brass barrel lens, black bellows.
  . . . . 25.00   30.00
- **Vest Pocket,** *compact folding camera for 127 film, f7.7 Seneca Anastigmat lens, shutter 25-100.*
  . . . . 35.00   45.00

SEROCO / 233

☐ **View Camera, 8 x 10", including improved model,** *with Wollensak Velostigmat Ser. 2, f4.5/12" lens, or double anastigmat lens in Optimo or Wollensak Regular shutter.*
.... 160.00   175.00

SEPT
(See Debrie)

SEROCO

An abbreviation for Sears, Roebuck & Company, whose cameras were made by other companies for sale under the Seroco name. The Conley company made many cameras for Sears around the turn of the century. *(See also Tower for other Sears models.)*

☐ **Delmar,** *box camera for plates, top rear door hinges up to insert plateholders, storage space for extra plateholders, for 3¼ x 4¼ plates or 4 x 5" plates.*
.................40.00   50.00

Vest Pocket

☐ **View Camera, 5 x 7",** *Seneca Rapid convertible or Goerz Syntor f6.8 lens, Ilex shutter 1-100, black double extension bellows, polished wood body.*
.... 115.00   135.00

☐ **View Camera, improved 5 x 7",** *Wollensak Planatic Series III lens, Auto shutter, black leather bellows, fine wood body.*
.... 100.00   130.00

☐ **Seroco 4 x 5" folding plate camera,** *c. 1901, black leathered wood body with polished interior, red bellows, Seroco 4 x 5 Symmetrical lens and Wollensak shutter are common.*
..................65.00   75.00

☐ **Seroco 5 x 7" folding plate camera,** *similar to the above except for size.*
..................75.00   85.00

234 / SHALCO

- [ ] **Seroco 6½ x 8½" folding plate camera,** *red double extension bellows.*
  .... 100.00   125.00

- [ ] **Seroco Stereo,** *for 5 x 7" plates, brown leather covered mahogany body with polished interior, red leather bellows, Wollensak Stereo shutter and lenses.*
  .... 305.00   325.00

SHALCO
(Japan)

- [ ] **Shalco,** *novelty camera.*
  .... 15.00   20.00

SHEW
(J. F. Shew & Company, London)

- [ ] **Eclipse,** *c. 1890, 3¼ x 4¼" plates, Wray f8/5" lens in brass barrel, Thornton-Picard shutter, mahogany with dark brown bellows.*
  .... 300.00   350.00

- [ ] **Xit,** *c. 1900, almost identical to the Eclipse with aluminum and mahogany construction.*
  .... 250.00   300.00

- [ ] **Xit Day,** *c. 1910 variation of the Xit, meniscus lens, synchronized shutter, black leathered wood body.*
  .... 150.00   175.00

SHOWA OPTICAL WORKS, LTD.
(Japan)

- [ ] **Leotax,** *35mm. Leica copy, f1.5 or 3.5 Simlar or f1.8 or 3.5 Topcor lens.*
  .... 150.00   175.00

- [ ] **Semi-Leotax,** *folding camera for 4.5 x 6cm. exposures on 120 film, f3.5 lens.*
  .... 40.00   60.00

SHUR-FLASH
(See Agfa, Ansco)

SHUR-SHOT
(See Agfa, Ansco)

SHUR-SHOT

- [ ] **Shur-Shot,** *tiny all-wood box plate camera for single exposures 2½ x 2½" on glass plates, simple rotary shutter.*
  .... 200.00   250.00

Note: This is not to be confused with the later model box cameras by Agfa and Ansco for rollfilms.

SIBYL
(See Newman & Guardia)

SICO
(See Simons)

SIDA
(Berlin)

☐ **Extra,** *c. 1936 camera for 10 exposures 24 x 24mm. on unperforated special rollfilm, black cast metal body, side Optik f8/35mm. lens, single speed guillotine shutter.*
.................60.00   75.00

SIGNAL
(See Zeiss-Ikon)

SIGNET
(See Eastman)

SILAR
(See Linhof)

SILETTE
(See Agfa)

SIMDA
(LePerreux, France)

☐ **Simda Stereo,** *c. 1950 stereo camera for 16mm. film, fixed focus Angenieux f3.5/25mm. lenses, stereo shutter 1-250 synchronized, grey covered metal body.*
.... 500.00   550.00

SIMMON BROTHERS, INC.
(N.Y.)

☐ **Omega 120,** *c. 1954, a professional rollfilm press camera for 9 exposures 2¼ x 2¾ on 120, Omicron f3.5/90mm. lens, synchronized shutter 1-400, coupled rangefinder.*
.... 200.00   250.00

SIMONS
(Wolfgang Simons & Company, Bern, Switzerland)

☐ **Sico,** *c. 1923, for 25 exposures 30 x 40mm. on unperforated 35mm. paper-backed rollfilm, Rudersdorf Anastigmat f3.5/60mm. lens in focusing mount, iris diaphragm to f22, dial Compur shutter 1-300, dark brown wooden body with brass trim.*
.... 2550.00   2750.00

SIMPLEX, SIMPLEX STEREO, SIMPLEX ERNOFLEX
(See Ernemann)

SIMPLEX MAGAZINE
(See Krugener)

SIMPLEX POCKETTE

☐ **Simplex Pockette,** *16mm., f3.5.*
.................30.00   40.00

SINCLAIR
(James A. Sinclair & Company, Ltd., London)

☐ **Una,** *c. 1895 ½-plate camera, heavy wood construction, folding type, Goerz f6.8/7" Double Anastigmat lens, revolving back.*
.... 200.00   260.00

SINGLO

☐ **Singlo,** *French folding 9 x 12cm. plate camera.*
.................35.00   50.00

SINGLO-TEX

☐ **Singlo-Tex,** *German subminiature, collapsing lens.*
.... 165.00   200.00

SINOX
(See Lumiere)

SIRENE
(See Ica, Zeiss)

SIX-16, SIX-20
(See Eastman)

SMYTH
(John M. Smyth, Chicago)

☐ **5 x 7 view camera,** Wollensak RR lens, Regno shutter 1-100, reversible back, black leather covered, black interior.
.................75.00   125.00

SOENNECKEN & COMPANY
(Munich)

☐ **Folding camera, 6 x 9cm.,** *double extension, Steinheil Unofocal f5.4/105mm. lens.*
.................20.00   30.00

SOHO
(See Marion)

SOLIDA
(See Franka)

SOLIGOR I & II

☐ **Soligor I & II,** 6 x 6cm. TLR for 120 film, f3.5/80 Soligor in Rektor rimset shutter.
.................25.00   35.00

SOLINETTE
(See Agfa)

SOLOGRAPH
(See Scovill & Adams)

S.O.M.

☐ **S.O.M.,** 9 x 12cm. folding plate camera, Berthiot f4.5/135 lens in dial Compur.
.................25.00   30.00

SONNAR
(See Contessa-Nettel)

SONNET
(See Contessa-Nettel, Nettel)

SPARTUS CORPORATION
(U.S.A.)

☐ **Spartus cameras,** *including Spartus 120, Spartus 35, 35F, Spartus folding, and Spartaflex.*
.................10.00   12.00

SPEED CAMERA
(See Dallmeyer)

SPEED CANDID
(See Candid)

SPEED KODAK
(See Eastman)

SPEEDEX
(See Agfa, Ansco)

SPEED-O-MATIC CORPORATION
(Boston, Mass.)

☐ **Speed-O-Matic,** an early instant-picture camera with meniscus lens, single speed shutter.
.................20.00   25.00
☐ **Same as above,** clear plastic salesman's "demo" model.
.................30.00   35.00

SPIDO
(See Gaumont)

SPIEGEL ELF

☐ **Box.**
.................15.00   20.00

SPORT
(See Adox)

SPUTNIK
(U.S.S.R.)

☐ **Sputnik Stereo,** c. 1960 for 6 x 13cm. stereo pairs on 120 film, f4.5/75mm. lenses, shutter 15-125, ground glass focus.
.... 175.00   225.00

STANDARD
(See Agfa)

STAR
(See Robot)

STARFLEX
(See Eastman, Brownie Starflex)

STARLET
(See Eastman, Brownie Starlet)

STAR LITE

☐ **Novelty,** *Japanese.*
.... 10.00   15.00

STARMATIC
(See Eastman, Brownie Starmatic)

START
(See Pouva, Ikko Sha)

STEGEMANN
(A. Stegemann, Berlin)

☐ **Field camera,** *13 x 18cm., 5 x 7", mahogany body, single extension square cloth bellows, normally with Meyer or Goerz lens.*
.... 175.00   225.00

STEINECK KAMERAWERK
(Tutzing)

☐ **Steineck ABC Wristwatch camera,** c. 1949, for 8 exposures on circular film in special magazine, Steinheil f2.5/12.5mm. fixed focus lens, single speed shutter.
.... 475.00   525.00

STEINHEIL
(G. A. Steinheil Sons, Munich)

STERE-ALL / 237

☐ **Casca I,** c. 1948 Leica copy, Culminar f2.8/50mm. lens, focal plane shutter, 25-1000.
.... 125.00   150.00

☐ **Detective camera,** c. 1895, for 12 exposures on 9 x 12cm. plates, wood body with nickel trim, Steinheil or Periskop lens, rotary or guillotine shutter.
.... 550.00   600.00

☐ **Tropical camera,** 9 x 12cm. plates, double extension brown tapered bellows, fine wood with nickel trim.
.... 525.00   600.00

STEKY
(See Riken)

STELLA JUMELLE
(See Roussel)

STERE-ALL
(See Universal Camera Corporation)

STEREAX
(See Contessa-Nettel)

STERELUX
(See Lumiere)

STEREOCRAFTERS
(Milwaukee, Wisc.)

- **Videon,** *c. 1950's stereo camera for standard 35mm. cassettes, metal and plastic construction, Ilex Stereon Anastigmat f3.5/35mm. lenses, synchronized shutter.*
  ....75.00   100.00

STEREOCYCLE
(See Bazin & Leroy)

STEREFLEKTOSKOP
(See Voigtlander)

STEREOLETTE
(See Huttig, Ica)

STEROCO
(See Contessa-Nettel)

STIRN
(C. P. Stirn, Stirn & Lyon, N.Y., Rudolph Stirn, Berlin)

- **Concealed Vest Camera, Size No. 1,** *c. 1886 for 6 photos 1¾" diameter on 5" diameter glass plates, original price, $10.00, and early ads proclaimed, "Over 15,000 sold in first 3 years," needless to say, many are lost.*
  .... 850.00   975.00

STÖCKIG
(Hugo Stöckig, Dresden)

- **Union camera,** *early folding plate cameras with leather covered wood body and finely polished interior, made in 9 x 12 and 13 x 18cm. sizes, with Meyer Anastigmat f7.2 or Union Aplanat f6.8 lens in Union shutter, double extension bellows.*
  ....75.00   100.00

STYLOPHOT
(See Secam)

SÜDDEUTSCHES CAMERAWERK
(See Nettel)

SUGAYA OPTICAL COMPANY, LTD.
(Japan)

- **Mycro Myracle, Model II,** *Hope Anastigmat f4.5, shutter 25-100, red leather.*
  ....25.00   30.00

SUMMUM
(See Leullier)

SUMNER
(J. Chase Sumner, Foxcroft, Me.)

- **Stereo rollfilm box camera,** *similar to the No. 2 Stereo Kodak box camera.*
  .... 400.00   500.00

SUNART PHOTO COMPANY
(Rochester, N.Y.)

- **Sunart folding view,** *c. 1898, 4 x 5 or 5 x 7" sizes, black leather covered wood body with polished cherry interior, double extension bellows, B & L RR lens, Unicum shutter, 4 x 5 size.*
  ....50.00   75.00
- **Same as above,** 5 x 7 size.
  ....75.00   100.00
- **Sunart Jr.,** *3½ x 3½ and 4 x 5" plate box cameras similar in style to the Cyclone Senior.*
  ....30.00   40.00

SUPERB
(See Voigtländer)

SUPERFLEKTA
(See Welta)

SUPER IKONTA
(See Zeiss)

SUPER KODAK 620
(See Eastman)

SUPER NETTEL
(See Zeiss-Ikon)

SUTER
(E. Suter, Basel, Switzerland)

- **Detective magazine camera,** c. 1890, early model for 12 plates, 9 x 12cm., Periskop lens, guillotine shutter, polished wood with nickel trim.
  .... 500.00   600.00
- **Detective magazine camera,** c. 1893, later model for 20 exposures on 9 x 12cm. plates, Suter f8 lens with iris diaphragm, rotating shutter, leather covered mahogany box with brass trim.
  .... 400.00   500.00
- **Stereo Muro,** c. late 1890's for 9 x 18cm. plates, f5/85mm. Suter lenses.
  .... 325.00   375.00

SUTTON PANORAMIC CAMERA
(See Ross)

SYNCHRO
(Box cameras)
(See Agfa)

TAISEI KOKI
(Japan)

- **Welmy Six,** folding camera for 6 x 6cm. on 120 film, Terionar f4.5/75mm. or f3.5/75mm., shutter 1-300.
  ....25.00   35.00
- **Welmy 35,** a non-RF folding 35mm. camera, f2.8/50mm. lens.
  ....25.00   35.00
- **Welmy Wide,** c. 1958, 35mm. camera with Taikor f3.5/35mm. lens.
  ....25.00   35.00

TALBOT / 239

TAIYODO KOKI
(Japan)

- **Beauty Super L,** f1.9.
  ....25.00   30.00
- **Beautycord,** 6 x 6cm. TLR for 120.
  ....25.00   35.00
- **Beautyflex,** 6 x 6cm. TLR, c. 1954, f3.5/80mm. Doimer Anastigmat lens, simple shutter.
  ....25.00   35.00

TAKAHASHI KOGAKU
(Japan)

- **Gelto D III,** c. 1930's ½-frame 127 film camera, 3 x 4cm., Grimmel f3.5/50mm. collapsible lens, gold and chrome finished.
  ....40.00   50.00

TAKIV
(See Walker)

TAKYR
(See Krauss)

TALBOT
(Romain Talbot, Berlin)

Makers of the Errtee cameras. In German the letters R.T. (for R. Talbot) are pronounced "Err-Tee."

- **Errtee button tintype camera,** a cylindrical "cannon" for 100 button tintypes 25mm. diameter, processing tank hangs below camera, and exposed plates drop through chute, Laack f4.5/60mm. lens, single speed shutter.
  .... 950.00   1050.00
- **Errtee folding plate camera,** 9 x 12cm., double extension bellows, Laack Pololyt f4.5/135mm. lens, Compur shutter 1-200.
  ....30.00   40.00

240 / TANAKA OPTICAL

☐ **Errtee folding rollfilm camera,** *for 6 x 9cm. on rollfilm, Anastigmat Talbotar f4.5/105mm. in Vario shutter 25-100, brown bellows and brown leather covering.*
.................30.00   40.00

TANAKA OPTICAL COMPANY, LTD.
(Japan)

☐ **Tanack, Type IV-S,** *copy of Leica IIIb, Tanar f2/50mm. lens, shutter 1-500.*
.... 115.00   145.00

TARGET
(See Eastman, Brownie, Hawkeye)

TAUBER

☐ **Folding plate,** *German, c. 1920's, Rapid Aplanat f8/135.*
.................25.00   35.00

TAXO
(See Contessa-Nettel, Zeiss)

TAXONA
(See Zeiss)

TDC
(See Bell & Howell)

TECHNIKA
(See Linhof)

TEDDY
(See Ica)

TELECA

☐ **Binocular,** *16mm.*
.... 275.00   350.00

TELEPHOT VEGA
(See Vega)

TENAX
(See Goerz, Zeiss)

TENGOR
(See Goerz, Zeiss)

TENNAR

☐ **Folding,** *for 620 film.*
.................15.00   20.00

TESSCO
(See Contessa-Nettel)

TESSINA
(Manufactured by Concava, S.A., Lugano, Switzerland)

☐ **Side-by-Side Twin Lens Reflex,** *c. 1960, for 14 x 21mm. exposures on 35mm. film in special cartridges, the camera is about the size of a package of cigarettes, one lens reflects upward to the ground glass for viewing, the other lens, a Tessinon f2.8/25mm., reflects the image to the film below, the film travels across the bottom of the camera, shutter speeds 2-500, spring-motor advance for 5-8 exposures per winding.*
.... 185.00   235.00

THOMPSON
(W. J. Thompson Company)

☐ **Direct positive street camera.**
.... 125.00   175.00

THORNTON-PICARD MANUFACTURING COMPANY
(Altringham, England)

☐ **Folding Ruby,** 3¼ x 4¼, *revolving back, fine wood interior, various correctional movements, Cooke Anastigmat f6.5 lens.*
.... 100.00   135.00

☐ **Folding plate camera,** 5 x 7", *c. 1890, Zeiss Unar f5/210mm., focal plane shutter 15-80.*
.... 160.00   180.00

☐ **Puck Special,** 4 x 5" *plate box camera, focus and shutter adjustable.*
.... 65.00   85.00

☐ **Reflex model,** 2¼ x 3¼ SLR, *c. 1925, Dallmeyer or Cooke lens.*
.... 100.00   150.00

☐ **Reflex model,** 4 x 5" SLR, *Wray Lustrar f4.5/6" lens, focal plane shutter.*
.... 100.00   150.00

☐ **Ruby Deluxe,** *c. 1912,* ¼-*plate SLR, Goerz Dogmar or Ross Xpres f4.5 lens, focal plane shutter 10-1000.*
.... 75.00   100.00

☐ **Ruby Duplex Reflex,** ¼-*plate SLR, "tropical" model, teak and brass, double extension orange bellows, focal plane shutter to 1000, Cooke Anastigmat f6.3 lens.*
.... 1650.00   1850.00

☐ **Special Ruby Reflex,** 2¼ x 3¼, *Cooke Anastigmat f4.5/5" lens, focal plane shutter.*
.... 100.00   150.00

☐ **Stereo Puck,** *c. 1920's cheap rollfilm box for 6 x 8.5cm. on 120 film, meniscus lenses, simple shutter, black covered wood body.*
.... 100.00   125.00

THORNWARD DANDY

☐ **Box-plate camera,** *detective-type, for 4 x 5 plates.*
.... 50.00   75.00

THOWE CAMERAWERK
(Freital & Berlin)

☐ **Folding plate camera,** 9 x 12cm., *c. 1910, leather covered wood body, Doxanar f6/135mm., shutter 25-100.*
.... 30.00   50.00

☐ **Horizontal-format field camera,** 9 x 12cm., *rear bellows extension, blue square bellows with black covers, Meyer Primotar f3.5/115mm.*
.... 100.00   135.00

TICKA
(See Houghton)

TINTYPE CAMERAS
(See American Minute, Chicago Ferrotype, Popular Photograph, New York Ferrotype, etc.)

TISDELL & WHITTELSEY
(pre-1893)
TISDELL CAMERA & MANUFACTURING COMPANY
(post 1893)
(New York)

- **T & W Detective Camera,** *c. 1888, detective box camera for 3¼ x 4¼ plates, all wood box, truncated pyramid rather than bellows for focusing, achromatic meniscus lens.*
.... 1400.00   1600.00

- **Tisdell Hand Camera,** *c. 1893, in 1893, the name of the T & W Detective Camera was changed to "Tisdell Hand Camera," leather covered, internal bellows focus.*
.... 700.00   800.00

TIVOLI

- **½-plate camera,** *c. 1895, English, mahogany body, Rectilinear lens.*
.... 200.00   250.00

TOGODA OPTICAL COMPANY
(Japan)

- **Toyoca 35,** *c. 1955, 35mm. camera, f2.8 Lausar or f3.5 Owla 45mm. lens.*
.... 20.00   25.00

TOKYO KOGAKU
(Japan)

- **Primo Jr.,** *4 x 4cm. TLR for 127 film, sold in the U.S.A. by Sawyers.*
.... 100.00   125.00

TOKYO SHASHIN
(Japan)

- **Mighty,** *made in Occupied Japan, subminiature for 13 x 13mm. exposures on 16mm. rollfilm, meniscus lens, single speed shutter.*
.... 35.00   45.00

TOM THUMB
(See Automatic Radio Manufacturing Company)

TONE

- **Subminiature,** *16mm., f3.5/25mm. lens in 3 speed shutter.*
.... 40.00   55.00

TOP

- **Japanese subminiature,** *14 x 14mm. exposures on special 16mm. rollfilm, meniscus lens, single speed shutter, aluminum body.*
.... 25.00   35.00

TOSCA
(See Ica)

TOURIST
(See American Camera Manufacturing Company, Blair, Eastman, Hare, McBean, Sandringham, Vive)

TOWER

- **Type 3,** *made in Occupied Japan, and sold by Sears, copy of Leica III, Nikkor f2/50mm. is most common lens.*
.... 100.00   125.00

- **Stereo,** *made in Germany by Iloca for Sears, Isco-Westar f3.5/35mm. lenses, Prontor-S shutter 1-300.*
.... 100.00   125.00

TRAMBOUZE
(Paris)

- **Plate camera,** *13 x 18cm., 5 x 7", with brass barreled f8 lens.*
.... 175.00   225.00

TRAVELER

- Novelty camera, *Japanese.*
  ....10.00   15.00
- Reflex, *simple plastic TLR, shutter 25, 50.*
  ....15.00   20.00

TRIAD CORPORATION
(Encino, Calif.)

- Fotron & Fotron III, *grey and black plastic cameras of the 1960's, originally sold by door-to-door salesmen for prices ranging from $150 to $300 and up, the cameras were made to take exposures 1 x 1" on special cartridge film, 35mm. wide, they featured many high-class advancements such as built-in electronic flash with rechargeable batteries, electric film advance, etc., at the time these cameras were made, these were expensive features, still, the Fotron camera campaign is considered by many to be the greatest photographic "rip-off" of the century.*
  ....35.00   50.00

TRIAD DETECTIVE CAMERA
(See Scovill)

TRI-COLOR CAMERAS
(See manufacturers such as Devin, Jos-Pe, Mikut, National)

TRILBY
(See Ica)

TRIO
(See Seneca, Welta)

TRIPLE VICTO
(See Victo)

TRI-VISION
(See Keys Stereo Products)

TRIX
(See Ica, Zeiss)

TRONA
(See Ica, Zeiss)

TROPICA
(See Ica)

TRUMPREFLEX

- Trumpreflex, *German-made 6 x 6cm. TLR sold in the U.S. by Sears, parallax correction accomplished by the taking lens tilting up at close focusing distances, Meyer f3.5/75mm. or Triolar f4.5/75mm. lens, shutter 1-300.*
  ....30.00   40.00

TURRET CAMERA COMPANY
(Brooklyn, N.Y.)

- Panoramic camera, *c. 1905, for 4 x 10" panoramic views.*
  .... 625.00   725.00

TUXI, TUXIMAT
(See Kunick)

TWINFLEX
(See Universal Camera Corp.)

TWO-SHUTTERED CAMERA
(See Ernemann)

TYNAR CORPORATION
(Los Angeles, Calif.)

- Tynar, *c. 1950, for 10 x 14mm. exposures on specially loaded 16mm. cassettes, f6.3/45mm. lens, single speed guillotine shutter.*
  ....45.00   55.00

UCA
(Uca Werkstatten für Feinmechanik & Optik, Flensburg, Germany)

Associated with the Elop Kamerawerk of Flensburg.

☐ **Ucaflex,** *c. 1950 35mm. SLR, Elolux f1.9/50mm. lens, focal plane shutter 1-1000.*
.... **175.00   225.00**

ULCA
(See Pittsburgh Camera Corporation)

ULTRA FEX

☐ **Ultra Fex,** *French post-war camera for 6 x 9cm. on 120 rollfilm, bakelite body, Fexar lens, simple shutter 25-100.*
.................**15.00   20.00**

ULTRIX
(See Ihagee)

UNA
(See Sinclair)

UNCA
(See Foitzik Trier)

UNDERWOOD
(E. T. Underwood, Birmingham, England)

☐ **Field camera,** *8 x 11cm., rear extension bellows, Underwood f11 brass barrel lens with iris diaphragm, Thornton-Picard shutter, square leather bellows, swing-out ground glass.*
.... **125.00   175.00**

UNETTE
(See Ernemann)

UNGER & HOFFMAN
(Dresden)

☐ **Verax,** *precision folding plate cameras, in 4.5 x 6cm. and 6.5 x 9cm. sizes, single extension bellows, f3.5 or 4.5 lens, Compound shutter 1-300, ground glass back.*
.................**45.00   60.00**

UNIFLASH
(See Universal Camera Corporation)

UNIFLEX
(See Schmitz & Thienemann, also Universal Camera Corporation)

UNION
(See Stockig)

UNITED STATES CAMERA COMPANY
(See Hetherington & Hibben)

UNITED STATES CAMERA CORPORATION
(Chicago)

☐ **Box & TLR cameras,** *cheap cameras such as Reflex, Rollex, Vagabond, etc.*
...................**8.00   10.00**

UNIVERSAL CAMERA CORPORATION
(N.Y.C.)

☐ **Buccaneer,** *c. 1945 35mm. RF camera, f3.5/50mm. Tricor lens, Chronomatic shutter 10-300, built-in extinction meter, flash synchronized, coupled rangefinder.*
.................**18.00   25.00**

☐ **Corsair I and II,** *c. 1941, for 24 x 36mm. exposures on perforated 35mm. film in special cartridges, Univex f4.5/50mm. lens in rimset shutter 25-200, flash synchronized, extinction meter.*
.................**20.00   25.00**

☐ **Iris,** *c. 1940, heavy cast-metal camera for 6 exposures 1⅛ x 1½" on Number 00 Universal film, Vitar f7.9/50mm., Ilex shutter.*
.................**15.00   20.00**

☐ **Mercury, Model CC,** *c. 1938, the first Mercury model, takes 18 x 24mm. vertical exposures on Universal Number 200 film, a special 35mm. wide film, Tricor f3.5/35mm. lens and rotating focal plane shutter 20-1000.*
.................**35.00   45.00**

☐ **Mercury II, Model CX,** *c. 1940, similar to Mercury CC, but for 65 exposures on standard 35mm. film, Tricor f2.7/35mm., rotary shutter 20-1000.*
.................30.00   40.00

☐ **Meteor,** *for 620 rollfilm.*
.................10.00   15.00

☐ **Minute 16,** *c. 1950's 16mm. subminiature, resembles a miniature movie camera, f6.3 meniscus lens, guillotine shutter.*
.................25.00   35.00

☐ **Norton,** *cheap black plastic camera for 6 exposures 1⅛ x 1½ on Number 00 rollfilm, similar to the Univex A, stamped metal viewfinder on back of body.*
.................10.00   15.00

☐ **Roamer I,** *folding camera for 8 exposures 2¼ x 3¼" on 620 film, f/11 coated lens, single speed shutter, flash synchronized.*
.................15.00   20.00

☐ **Roamer II,** *similar, f4.5 lens.*
.................10.00   15.00

☐ **Roamer 63,** *folding camera for 120 or 620 film, Universal Anastigmat Synchromatic f6.3/100mm. lens.*
.................12.00   15.00

☐ **Stere-all,** *c. 1954 for pairs of 24 x 24mm. exposures on 35mm. film, Tricor f3.5/35mm. lenses, single speed shutter.*
.................40.00   60.00

☐ **Twinflex,** *c. 1941, for 1⅛ x 1½", 29 x 38mm., on Number 00 rollfilm, plastic TLR, meniscus lens, simple shutter.*
.................15.00   20.00

☐ **Uniflash,** *cheap plastic camera for Number 00 rollfilm, f16/60mm. Vitar lens, with original flash and box.*
.................10.00   12.00

☐ **Uniflex, Models I and II,** *c. 1948 TLR for 120 or 620 rollfilm, Universal lens, f5.6 or 4.5/75mm., shutter to 200.*
.................15.00   20.00

☐ **Univex, Model A,** *c. 1936, the original small black plastic gem for Number 00 rollfilm, similar to the Norton, which is a later model, wire frame sportsfinder attached to front of camera, and molded plastic rear sight, cost $0.50 when new.*
.................12.00   15.00

☐ **Univex AF,** *c. late 1930's, a series of compact collapsing cameras for Number 00 rollfilm, cast metal body, various color combinations.*
.................20.00   25.00

UNIVERSAL JUWEL
(See Ica)

UNIVERSAL PALMOS
(See Zeiss)

UNIVERSAL RADIO MANUFACTURING COMPANY

246 / UNIVEX

☐ **Cameradio,** *late 1940's, 3 x 4cm. TLR box camera built into a portable tube radio, like the Tom Thumb listed under Automatic Radio Manufacturing Company.*
.... 125.00   150.00

UNIVEX
(See Universal Camera Corporation)

UNO
(See Seneca)

UR-LEICA
(See Leitz)

UTILITY MANUFACTURING COMPANY
(New York)

☐ **Miscellaneous cheap cameras,** *including Girl Scout Falcon, Falcon, Falcon Miniature, Carlton, Press Flash, etc.*
.... 10.00   12.00

VAG
(See Voigtlander)

VALSTS ELEKTRO TECHNISKA FABRIKA
(See Minox)

VANITY KODAK
(See Eastman)

VAUXHALL

☐ **Folding camera,** *for 120 film, styled like Zeiss Super Ikonta, for 12 or 16 exposures on 120 film, f2.9 lens, CRF.*
.... 35.00   45.00

VEGA
(Geneva, Switzerland)

☐ **Vega,** *c. 1900 folding book-style camera for plates, the camera opens like a book, the lens being in the "binding" position, and the bellows fanning out like pages, plate changing mechanism operates by opening and closing the camera.*
.... 750.00   800.00

VELOCIGRAPHE
(See Hermagis)

VELOX MAGAZINE CAMERA
(See Hurlburt)

VENA
(Amsterdam, Netherlands)

☐ **Venaret,** *telescoping camera for 6 x 6cm. exposures on 120 film, f7.7/75mm. doublet lens, simple shutter 25, 50, leather covered metal body, nickel trim.*
.... 15.00   20.00

VENTURA
(See Agfa)

VERASCOPE
(See Busch, Richard)

VERAX
(See Unger & Hoffmann)

VICTO
(England)

☐ **Folding field camera, full plate,** c. 1900, polished wood, black bellows, Thornton-Picard roller-blind shutter, brass barrel lens.
.... 150.00   200.00

☐ **Folding field camera, half plate,** "Triple Victo" c. 1890, triple extension, Taylor Hobson Cooke brass barrel lens, mahogany body.
.... 115.00   135.00

VIDEON
(See Stereocrafters)

VIEDEBOX

☐ **Metal box camera.**
.... 8.00   10.00

VIEW-MASTER
(See Sawyer)

VIFLEX

☐ **SLR box camera,** c. 1905, unusual, for 4 x 5" plates, or sheetfilm, when folded, viewing hood becomes carry case.
.... 225.00   250.00

VIGILANT
(See Eastman)

VIKING
(See Agfa, Ansco)

VINTEN
(W. Vinten, Ltd., London)

☐ **Aerial reconnaissance cameras,** for 95 exposures 55mm. square on 70mm. film.
.... 240.00   275.00

VIRTUS
(See Voigtlander)

VISCAWIDE
(Japan)

☐ **Viscawide 16 Panoramic,** c. 1961 for 10 exposures 10 x 52mm. on specially loaded 16mm. film, Ross f3.5/25mm. lens, shutter 60-300, angle of view, 120 degrees.
.... 165.00   185.00

VISCOUNT
(See Aires)

VITA-FLEX

☐ **TLR,** German 6 x 6cm. for 120 film, c. 1940, f4.5 lens.
.... 20.00   25.00

VITESSA
(See Voigtlander)

VITO
(See Voigtlander)

VITOMATIC
(See Voigtlander)

VITRONA
(See Voigtlander)

VIVE CAMERA COMPANY
(Chicago)

☐ **M.P.C., Mechanical Plate Changing,** magazine plate box cameras c. 1900, side crank advances plates, two sizes: for 4¼ x 4¼" or 4 x 5" plates.
.... 75.00   100.00

☐ **Vive No. 1,** c. 1897, the first U.S. camera to use the dark-sleeve to change plates in a camera, for 12 plates 4¼ x 4¼", simple lens and shutter.
.... 125.00   150.00

☐ **Vive No. 2,** c. 1897, an improved model of the Vive Number 1, with a self-capping shutter, and with viewfinder at the center front.
.... 100.00   150.00

☐ **Vive No. 4,** c. 1899, focusing model.
.... 85.00   95.00

248 / VIVID

- **Vive Tourist,** *c. 1897, like the Vive Number 1, but for 4 x 5" plates.*
  . . . . **100.00   150.00**
- **Vive Stereo,** *for stereo pairs on 3½ x 6" plates, similar to the Number 1, but stereo.*
  . . . . **675.00   735.00**

VIVID
(See Bell & Howell)

VOGUE
(See Coronet)

VOIGTLÄNDER & SON
(Braunschweig)

- **Alpin,** *c. 1910 folding plate camera for horizontal format 9 x 12cm. plates, Voigtländer Collinear f6.8/120mm. or Heliar f4.5/135mm. lens, Kolios, Compound, or Compur shutter, black tapered double-extension bellows, all metal body, black painted.*
  . . . . **125.00   175.00**
- **Avus,** *folding plate camera, 6 x 9cm., Skopar f4.5/105, Compur 1-250.*
  . . . . **25.00   35.00**
- **Same as above,** *9 x 12cm., Skopar f4.5/135, Compur.*
  . . . . **40.00   60.00**

Avus

- **Bergheil folding plate camera,** *4.5 x 6cm., Deluxe, brown leather, Heliar f4.5/75mm. lens.*
  . . . . **500.00   600.00**
- **Bergheil folding plate camera,** *6 x 9cm., c. 1930, Heliar f4.5/105, Compur 1-250.*
  . . . . **40.00   55.00**
- **Bergheil folding plate camera,** *6 x 9cm. Deluxe, green leathered body and green bellows, f3.5 or 4.5/105 Heliar, Compur 1-200, nickel trim.*
  . . . . **200.00   240.00**
- **Bergheil folding plate camera,** *9 x 12cm., c. 1925, Heliar f4.5/135mm., Compur shutter.*
  . . . . **40.00   55.00**
- **Bergheil folding plate camera,** *9 x 12cm. Deluxe, green leather and bellows.*
  . . . . **225.00   245.00**
- **Bergheil folding plate camera,** *10 x 15cm., c. 1924, Skopar f4.5/165 or Kollinear f6.3/165, Compur shutter.*
  . . . . **80.00   100.00**

VOIGTLÄNDER AND SON / 249

- [ ] **Bessa 6 x 6 "Baby Bessa,"** c. 1930, f3.5/75 Voigtar or Skopar, or f4.5 Vaskar.
  .... 40.00   50.00
- [ ] **Bessamatic,** 35mm., Skopar f2.8/50mm.
  .... 78.00   88.00

Berghell Folding Plate

- [ ] **Bessa folding rollfilm models,** c. 1936-1949, various shutter/lens combinations, including Voigtar, Vaskar, and Skopar lenses f3.5 to f7.7, Singlo, Prontor, or Compur shutters.
  .... 30.00   40.00
- [ ] **Bessa RF,** c. 1936, f3.5/105mm. Heliar, Helomar, or Skopar, Compur shutter.
  .... 100.00   115.00
- [ ] **Bessa I,** f3.5/105 Skopar or Helomar, or f4.5 Vaskar.
  .... 60.00   70.00
- [ ] **Bessa II,** c. 1950, CRF, with Skopar f3.5/105mm.
  .... 125.00   140.00
- [ ] **Same as above,** with Heliar f3.5.
  .... 325.00   375.00
- [ ] **Same as above,** with Apo-Lanthar f4.5, rare.
  .... 725.00   800.00

- [ ] **Brilliant,** c. 1933, cheap TLR camera, f6.3 or 7.7 Voigtar, f4.5 Skopar, or f3.5 Heliar lens,/75mm., quite common.
  .... 20.00   25.00
- [ ] **Daguerreotype "Cannon,"** reproduction of the original 1841 Voigtlander brass Daguerreotype camera, 31cm. long, 35cm. high, makes 80mm. diameter image.
  .... 3000.00   4000.00
- [ ] **Folding plate cameras, miscellaneous models.**
  .... 40.00   50.00
- [ ] **Folding rollfilms, miscellaneous models.**
  .... 15.00   25.00

250 / VOIGTLÄNDER AND SON

☐ **Inos II,** c. 1930's folding bed camera with self-erecting front, for 6 x 9cm. exposures on 120, Skopar f4.5/ 105mm., Compur to 250, or Embezet shutter to 100.
.... 50.00   65.00
☐ **Same as above,** with Heliar.
.... 75.00   95.00
☐ **Inos II, two format model,** for 6 x 9cm. or for 4.5 x 6cm. with reducing masks, Skopar f4.5/105mm., Compur 1-250.
.... 90.00   130.00
☐ **Jubilar,** folding camera for 6 x 9cm. on 120, Voigtar f9 lens.
.... 15.00   25.00
☐ **Perkeo, 3 x 4cm.,** c. 1938, folding camera with self-erecting front, for 16 exposures 3 x 4cm. on 127 film, camera can be focused before opening, via external knob, Heliar or Skopar f3.5 or 4.5/55mm. lens.
.... 75.00   100.00
☐ **Perkeo I,** c. 1960, folding camera for 6 x 6cm. exposures on 120 film, Prontor shutter, f4.5 Vaskar or f3.5 color Skopar lens.
.... 30.00   40.00
☐ **Perkeo II,** similar, but with Synchro-Compur shutter.
.... 35.00   45.00
☐ **Prominent,** c. 1932, folding camera for 6 x 9cm. on 120 film, or 4.5 x 6cm. with reducing masks, self-erecting front, coupled split-image rangefinder, extinction meter, Heliar f4.5/105mm. lens in Compur 1-250 shutter.
.... 750.00   875.00
☐ **Prominent 35mm.,** c. mid-1950's, price depends on lens, f3.5 Skopar.
.... 80.00   95.00
☐ **Same as above,** f2 Ultron.
.... 120.00   150.00
☐ **Same as above,** f1.5 Nokton.
.... 135.00   155.00

☐ **Stereflektoskop,** c. 1913 stereo cameras with plate changing magazine, 45 x 107mm. and 6 x 13cm. sizes, Heliar f4.5 lens, Compur shutter, this is a three-lens reflex, the center lens for 1:1 reflex viewing, this style was later used for the Heidoscop and Rolleidoscop cameras, 45 x 107mm. size.
.... 300.00   360.00
☐ **Same as above,** 6 x 13cm. size, less common.
.... 350.00   415.00
☐ **Superb,** c. 1933 TLR for 120 film, Skopar f3.5/75mm., a prism reflects the settings for easy visibility.
.... 120.00   160.00
☐ **Same as above,** with Heliar.
.... 150.00   200.00

☐ **Vag,** c. 1920's folding plate cameras, 6 x 9 and 9 x 12cm. sizes, f6.3 Voigtar or f4.5 Skopar in Ibsor or Embezet shutter.
.... 30.00   40.00

☐ **Virtus,** c. 1935, similar to the Prominent, but smaller, and more common, for 16 exposures on 120 film, automatically focuses to infinity upon opening, Heliar f3.5/75mm., Compur shutter 1-250.
.... **175.00   200.00**

☐ **Vitessa,** c. 1950, 35mm. camera, f2.8 Color Skopar or Ultron, Synchro Compur 1-500, coupled rangefinder.
.... **65.00   90.00**

☐ **Vitessa L,** c. 1955, Ultron f2/50mm., CRF, built-in meter.
.... **80.00   100.00**

☐ **Vitessa T,** f2.8/50 Color Skopar, synchronized Compur 1-500, CRF.
.... **85.00   115.00**

☐ **Vito,** c. 1950, 35mm. Skopar f3.5/50mm., Compur 1-300, folding style.
.... **20.00   40.00**

☐ **Vito II,** c. 1950, 35mm., Color Skopar f3.5, or Ultron f2, Prontor or Compur shutter.
.... **30.00   50.00**

☐ **Vito IIa.**
.... **40.00   50.00**

☐ **Vito III,** c. 1950, f2 Ultron, synchro Compur, 1-500, CRF, folding style.
.... **115.00   135.00**

☐ **Vito B,** f3.5 Skopar, Prontor SVS.
.... **30.00   45.00**

☐ **Vito C,** f2.8/45mm. Lanthar, Prontor.
.... **28.00   38.00**

☐ **Vito Automatic,** f2.8/50 Lanthar, Prontor Lux shutter.
.... **32.00   40.00**

☐ **Vitomatic,** f2.8 Skopar, Prontor.
.... **40.00   50.00**

☐ **Vitrona,** c. 1964, 35mm., f2.8/50 Lanthar, Prontor shutter 1-250, built-in electronic flash, never made in any large quantity, because they were novel and expensive.
.... **75.00   100.00**

VOKAR CORPORATION
(U.S.A.)

☐ **Vokar I,** c. 1946, 35mm. RF camera f2.8/50mm. Vokar Anastigmat lens in helical mount, leaf shutter 1-300.
.... **75.00   100.00**

VOLLENDA
(See Eastman, Nagel)

VOLTA
(See Zeiss-Ikon)

VOSS
(W. Voss, Ulm, Germany)

☐ **Diax II,** c. 1940's 35mm. RF camera, Xenon f2/45mm. lens in Synchro-Compur 1-500 shutter, coupled rangefinder.
.... **30.00   50.00**

WABASH PHOTO SUPPLY
(Terre Haute, IN)

☐ **Direct positive camera,** c. 1935, wood body, Ilex Universal f3.5/3" portrait lens, dimensions 5 x 8 x 20", with enlarger and dryer.
.... 175.00   200.00

WALKER MANUFACTURING COMPANY
(Palmyra, New York)

☐ **Takiv,** c. 1892, cardboard and leatherette construction, multiple exposures for 4 pictures, each 2½ x 2½" on dry plates, rotating shutter and lens assembly, septums for 4 exposures at rear.
.... 1150.00   1500.00

WALTAX

☐ **Folding camera,** Japanese, for 120 rollfilm, f3.5/75mm. lens, c. 1950's.
.................20.00   25.00

☐ **Waltax Jr.,** copy of Ikonta A, for 16 exposures 4.5 x 6cm. on 120, f4.5/75mm. lens, shutter 25-150.
..................15.00   20.00

WALZFLEX

☐ **Walzflex,** c. 1950's 6 x 6cm. TLR for 120 film, f3.5/75mm. Kominar lens in Copal shutter.
..................25.00   30.00

WALZ-WIDE

☐ **Walz-Wide,** 35mm., f2.8 Walzer lens.
..................35.00   45.00

WANAUS
(Josef Wanaus & Company, Vienna)

☐ **Full-plate view camera,** c. 1900, field-type camera for 13 x 18cm., 5 x 7", plates, light colored polished wood, nickel trim, Gustav-Rapp Universal Aplanat lens, waterhouse stops, geared focus, front and rear.
.... 185.00   230.00

WARA
(See Balda)

WARANETTE
(See Wauckosin)

WARDFLEX

☐ **Wardflex,** 6 x 6cm. TLR for 120 film, f3.5/80mm. lens, shutter 1-200.
..................25.00   30.00

WATCH CAMERAS
(See Expo, Houghton, Magic Introd. Co., Steineck, etc.)

WATERBURY
(See Scovill)

WATSON
(W. Watson & Sons, London)

☐ **Half-plate field camera,** c. 1885-1887, fine wood body, brass trim, Thornton-Picard roller blind shutter, Watson f8 brass barrel lens.
.... 200.00   250.00

WAUCKOSIN
(Frankfurt, Germany)

WELTA KAMERA WERKE / 253

☐ **Waranette,** *folding rollfilm camera for 5 x 8cm., f6.3/85mm. Polluxar lens in Vero shutter, 25-100.*
.................35.00   45.00

WEGA
(See Afiom)

WELMY
(See Taisei Koki)

WELTA KAMERA WERKE
(Waurich & Weber, Freital, Germany)

☐ **Welta 6 x 6cm.,** *on 120 film, f4.5 Weltar, or f2.8 Tessar/75mm., Compur shutter.*
.................20.00   25.00

☐ **Welta 6 x 9cm.,** *folding plate camera, Orion Rionar, Meyer Trioplan, Tessar, or Xenar f4.5/105mm. lens, Ibsor shutter, 1-125.*
.................30.00   40.00

☐ **Folding plate camera, 9 x 12cm.,** *f3.5 Rodenstock Eurynar, or f4.5 Doppel Anastigmat 135mm. lens, Compur shutter.*
.................30.00   40.00

☐ **Two-shuttered model, 10 x 14cm.,** *for plates, Goerz Dogmar f4.5/165mm. in Compur front shutter to 150, rear focal plane shutter, to 200.*
...............125.00   145.00

☐ **Welta Perfekta,** *c. 1934, folding TLR of unusual design for 6 x 6cm. exposures on 120, Meyer f3.5, or Tessar f3.8/75mm. lens, Compur shutter, 1-300.*
..............175.00   210.00

☐ **Welta Perle,** *folding camera for 16 exposures 4.5 x 6cm. on 120 film, f2.8 Xenar, or f2.9 Cassar lens.*
.................40.00   55.00

☐ **Welta Reflekta,** *6 x 6cm. TLR for 120 film, f3.5 or 4.5 Pololyt lens, Blitz shutter.*
.................18.00   25.00

☐ **Welta Superfekta,** *c. 1932, folding 6 x 9cm. TLR for 120 film, an unusual design, similar to the Perfekta, pivoting back for taking horizontal pictures, f3.8/105mm. Tessar or Trioplan lens, Compur shutter.*
...............365.00   410.00

☐ **Welta Trio,** *6 x 9cm. on 120, f4.5/105mm. in rimset Compur.*
.................16.00   20.00

☐ **Weltaflex,** *c. 1950 TLR for 6 x 6cm. on 120, Ludwig Meritar f3.5/75mm. in Prontor 1-300 shutter.*
.................25.00   35.00

☐ **Weltax, Weltax Jr.,** *c. 1939, 4.5 x 6 and 6 x 9cm. models for 120 film, Xenar or Tessar f2.8, or Trioplan f3.5/75mm. in Compur or Prontor shutter.*
.................25.00   35.00

☐ **Welti,** *c. 1935 folding 35mm., Tessar f2.8, or Xenar f3.5/50mm. in Vebur, Cludor, or Compur shutter.*
.................30.00   40.00

Weltur

- [ ] **Weltini,** *c. 1937 folding 35mm. with CRF, f2 Xenon, or f2.8 Tessar in Compur.*
  ....50.00   60.00
- [ ] **Weltix,** *folding 35mm., f2.9/50mm. Steinheil Cassar lens in Compur shutter.*
  ....25.00   35.00
- [ ] **Weltur,** *c. 1930's, for 16 exposures, 4.5 x 6cm. on 120 film, similar to the Super Ikonta, with coupled rangefinder, and one of the many available 75mm. lenses, f2.8 Xenar, f2.9 Trioplan, f2.8, 3.5, or 3.8 Tessar.*
  ....100.00   140.00

WENK
(Gebr, Wenk, Nürnberg, Germany)

- [ ] **Wenka,** *post-war 35mm. camera with interchangeable Leica-thread Xenar f2.8/50mm. lens, behind the lens shutter.*
  ....75.00   115.00

WENO
(See Eastman)

WERRA
(See Zeiss, Pentacon)

WESTAR
(See Nishida Optical)

WESTERN CAMERA MANUFACTURING COMPANY
(Chicago)

The Cyclone cameras listed here were made in 1898, before Western became a part of Rochester Optical & Camera Company in 1899. *(See Rochester for later models.)*

- [ ] **Cyclone Senior,** *4 x 5 plate box camera, not a magazine camera, a 4 x 5 size box camera with top rear door to insert plateholders.*
  ....35.00   50.00
- [ ] **Cyclone Junior,** $3\frac{1}{2}$ x $3\frac{1}{2}$" *plate box camera.*
  ....45.00   55.00
- [ ] **Magazine Cyclone No. 2.**
  ....50.00   60.00
- [ ] **Magazine Cyclone No. 3,** *4 x 5".*
  ....60.00   70.00
- [ ] **Magazine Cyclone No. 4,** $3\frac{1}{4}$ x $4\frac{1}{4}$.
  ....65.00   75.00
- [ ] **Magazine Cyclone No. 5,** *4 x 5".*
  ....60.00   70.00

WHITE
(David White Company, Milwaukee, Wis.)

- [ ] **Realist 35,** *not stereo, 35mm. camera made for David White by Iloca, identical to Iloca Rapid A, f3.5 or 2.8 Cassar lens.*
  ....30.00   40.00
- [ ] **Realist 45,** *stereo 35 made 1953-1957 for White by Iloca, f3.5 Cassar lenses.*
  ....100.00   125.00
- [ ] **Stereo Realist,** *35mm. stereo camera, c. 1950's, f3.5 lenses, case, flash.*
  ....125.00   155.00
- [ ] **Same as above,** *with f2.8 lenses, case, and flash.*
  ....275.00   325.00
- [ ] **Stereo Realist Macro.**
  ....400.00   475.00

WHITE HOUSE PRODUCTS
(Brooklyn, N.Y.)

- [ ] **Beacon,** *rollfilm camera for 127 film, plastic lens, simple spring shutter, black plastic body.*
  ....10.00   12.00
- [ ] **Same as above,** *colored models.*
  ....15.00   20.00
- [ ] **Beacon II.**
  ....10.00   12.00

WHITTAKER
(William R. Whittaker Company, Ltd., Los Angeles, California)

- **Micro 16,** *subminiature for 16mm. film in special cassettes, cartridge to cartridge feed, c. 1950's, meniscus lens, single speed shutter.*
  .... 35.00   45.00
- **Pixie,** *black plastic 16mm. subminiature wristwatch camera.*
  .... 40.00   50.00
- **Same as above,** *with flash etc.*
  .... 75.00   100.00

WILCA

- **Automatic,** *West German subminiature for 24 exposures 10 x 19mm. on 16mm. film in special cassettes, Wilcalux Filtra f2/16mm., synchronized Prontor shutter, coupled selenium meter, rare.*
  .... 475.00   535.00

WINDROW

- **Windrow,** *c. 1940's plastic 35mm. camera.*
  .... 10.00   15.00

WINDSOR

- **Windsor Stereo.**
  .... 100.00   135.00

WING
(Simon Wing, Charlestown, Mass.)

- **Multiplying View Camera,** *c. 1862, multiple images on single collodion plate 4 x 5" format, mahogany body, shifting front.*
  .... 950.00   1050.00
- **New Gem,** *c. 1901, for 15 exposures on 5 x 7" plates, sliding front lens panel.*
  .... 950.00   1100.00

WINKLER
(Dr. Winkler & Company, Berlin)
(See Roland)

WIPHOT
(See Reitzschel)

WIRGIN
(Gebr. Wirgin, Wiesbaden, Germany)

- **Edinex,** *c. 1930's compact 35mm. camera, almost identical to the Adox Adrette, telescoping front, film loads from bottom, early models, without rangefinder, with f4.5, 3.5, 2.8, or f2 lens.*
  .... 30.00   40.00

Klein-Edinex

- ☐ **Klein-Edinex,** *127 film, c. 1938, similar to the 35mm. model, but for 3 x 4cm. exposures on 127 film, Steinheil Cassar f2.9/50mm. lens.*
  . . . . .50.00   60.00
- ☐ **Edixa 16,** *c. 1960, for 12 x 16mm. exposures on 16mm. film, Schneider Xenar f2.8/25.*
  . . . . .55.00   65.00
- ☐ **Edixa Electronica,** *c. 1955 35mm. SLR, fully automatic with selenium meter, Culminar or Xenar f2.8/50mm. lens, Compur synchronized shutter, 1-500.*
  . . . . .70.00   80.00
- ☐ **Edixa Reflex,** *35mm. SLR, Exakta mount, c. 1960, f2.8 Isconar or Westanar, focal plane shutter to 1000.*
  . . . . .40.00   55.00
- ☐ **Edixa Stereo,** *35mm. stereo, Steinheil Cassar f3.5/35mm. lenses, Vario shutter.*
  . . . . 100.00   125.00
- ☐ **Gewirette,** *c. 1937, 3 x 4cm. exposures on 127 film, telescoping front, like the Edinex 127, film loads from the top.*
  . . . . .60.00   70.00
- ☐ **Wirgin folding camera, 6 x 9 rollfilm,** *for 120 film, Schneider Radionar f4.5, or Gewironar f8.8 or 6.3 lens.*
  . . . . .20.00   30.00
- ☐ **Wirgin 6 x 6cm. TLR,** *c. 1950, Rodenstock Trinar f2.8/75mm., built in extinction meter.*
  . . . . .30.00   40.00
- ☐ **Wirgin Stereo,** *35mm., Steinheil Cassar f3.5/35mm. lenses.*
  . . . . 100.00   150.00

WITT
(Wilhelm Witt, Hamburg, Germany)

- ☐ **Iloca I, Ia, II, IIa,** *c. 1930's to 1950's basic 35mm. camera, Models II and IIa have CRF, f3.5/45mm. Ilitar lens in Prontor shutter.*
  . . . . .20.00   30.00

- ☐ **Iloca Stereo,** *Models I and II, c. 1950's 35mm. stereo camera for 24 x 24mm. pairs, Ilitar f3.5 lenses, 35mm. or 45mm., Prontor-S shutter to 300.*
  . . . . .45.00   55.00

Tower
(See Tower.)

WITTNAUER

- ☐ **Scout,** *35mm., Chronox f2.8/45mm.*
  . . . . .50.00   70.00

WIZARD
(See Manhattan)

WOLLENSAK

- ☐ **Stereo camera,** *35mm., f2.7 lenses.*
  . . . . 155.00   175.00

WONDER AUTOMATIC CANNON
(See Chicago Ferrotype Company)

WONDER CAMERA

- ☐ **Magazine box camera,** *for 2½ x 3½" glass plates.*
  . . . . .80.00   125.00

WORLD'S FAIR CAMERA
(See Eastman)

WÜNSCHE
(Emil Wünsche, Reick b/Dresden)

- **Field camera,** *c. 1900, wood body, for 5 x 7", 13 x 18cm., plates, Wünsche Rectlinear Extra Rapid f8 brass barrel lens.*
  .... 140.00   160.00
- **Mars 99,** *c. 1895 box-plate camera for 9 x 12cm. plates, Aplanat f12/ 150mm. lens, rotating shutter.*
  .... 300.00   350.00
- **Reicka,** *c. 1912, folding plate camera for 9 x 12cm., double extension bellows, Rodenstock Heligonal f5.4/120mm. lens in Kolios 1-300 shutter, leather covered wood body.*
  .... 60.00   80.00

XIT
(See Shew)

YALE
(See Adams & Company)

YASHICA
(Japan)

- **Yashica 16,** *subminiature for 10 x 14mm. on 16mm. cassette film, c. 1958, f2.8 or 3.5/25mm. Yashinon lens.*
  .... 25.00   35.00
- **Yashica 44,** *c. 1956 TLR for 4 x 4cm. on 127 film, f3.5 lens.*
  .... 65.00   70.00
- **Yashica A,** *TLR.*
  .... 50.00   70.00
- **Yashica Atoron,** *subminiature for 9.5mm. film, Minox cassettes, f2.8 lens.*
  .... 40.00   70.00
- **Yashica Atoron Electro,** *with black finish.*
  .... 85.00   120.00
- **Same as above,** *with transparent body.*
  .... 90.00   110.00
- **Yashica D,** *6 x 6cm. TLR.*
  .... 70.00   110.00
- **Yashica Rapide,** *c. 1962, 35mm. half-frame, unusual style, stands vertically like a pocket-sized transistor radio, interchangeable Yashinon f2.8/28mm. lens in Copal 1-500 shutter, built-in meter.*
  .... 70.00   100.00
- **Yashica Sequelle,** *c. 1960, 35mm. half-frame for 18 x 24mm., styled like a movie camera, f2.8/28mm. Yashinon lens in Seikosha-L shutter, built-in meter.*
  .... 125.00   150.00
- **Yashica YF,** *Leica M3 copy, f1.8.*
  .... 115.00   135.00

ZECA
(See Zeh)

ZEDEL

- **Zedel,** *folding sheet film camera for 6.5 x 9cm. holders, Wallace Heaton Zedellax f4.5/120mm. lens in Compur shutter.*
  .... 30.00   50.00

ZEH
(Paul Zeh Kamerawerk, Dresden)

☐ **Zeca, 9 x 12cm.**, *folding sheet-film camera, 135mm. lenses, f6.3 Schneider Radionar, f6.8 Jena, f2.9 Zecanar or Xenar, leather covered wood body.*
.................25.00   35.00

☐ **Zeca, 6 x 9cm.**, *folding sheet-film camera, Steinheil f6.8 or Periskop f11 lens, Vario shutter, 25-100.*
.................20.00   30.00

☐ **Zeca-Flex**, *c. 1930's folding 6 x 6cm. TLR for 120 film, f3.5/75mm. Schneider Xenar lens, viewing lens is f2.9, the folding-style 6 x 6cm. reflex never became popular, so this model, along with the Perfekta and Superfekta from the neighboring suburb of Freital, was not made in large quantities.*
...............550.00   600.00

ZEISS, ZEISS-IKON

Before 1926, the Carl Zeiss Optical Company was located in Jena. In 1926, Contessa-Nettel, Ernemann, Goerz, Ica, and Carl Zeiss merged to form Zeiss-Ikon, and the headquarters became Dresden. After World War II, Zeiss-Ikon A.G. was located in Stuttgart, West Germany. Some camera models were still being made in the Jena and Dresden factories, but they were not really "Zeiss-Ikon" cameras, even though some bore the Zeiss-Ikon trademark. We have listed several of these models in the Zeiss section, since there really is no other place for them.

We have attempted to list Zeiss catalog numbers with these cameras whenever possible, to help in identification. Often, these numbers appear on the camera body. Sometimes, especially on U.S.A. models, they are not on the camera itself, but only in the catalog. Basically, the first half of the number designates the camera model. The second half of the number indicates negative size, and is standard from one model to another. A new or improved model usually changes only the last digit of the first number, generally increasing it by one. Hopefully, this information will help the user of this guide to locate his Zeiss camera by name, number, illustration, or a combination of the three.

☐ **Adoro**, *folding-plate camera, Tessar f4.5/105 in Compur shutter.*
.................25.00   35.00

☐ **Adoro, tropical model, 230/7**, *folding plate camera for 9 x 12cm., teak wood body, brown double extension bellows, f4.5/135 Double Anastigmat lens in Compur shutter.*
...............600.00   700.00

☐ **Baldur**, *metal box camera for 6 x 9cm. exposures on 120 film, Goerz Frontar lens, simple shutter, T, & I.*
.................20.00   25.00

☐ **Bebe**, *6 x 9cm. folding camera, Xenar f4.5/135 in Compur shutter.*
.................35.00   45.00

☐ **Bob, 510/2, 521/2,** *6 x 9cm. folding cameras Nettar f7.7/105mm., or Novar f4.5, Gauthier shutter 25-75, B, T.*
.................30.00   40.00

☐ **Bobette II, 548,** *c. 1927 folding camera for 22 x 33mm. on 35mm. film, Ernostar f2/42mm. lens, shutter ½-100, leather covered body, black bellows, the first miniature rollfilm camera with f2 lens.*
.................400.00   500.00

☐ **Same as above,** *with f3.5 or f4.5 lens.*
.................125.00   175.00

☐ **Box Tengor camera, "Baby Box," 54/18,** *for 3 x 4cm. exposures on 127 film, c. 1930, Goerz Frontar f11, or Novar f6.3/50mm., metal body, simple shutter.*
.................30.00   40.00

☐ **Box Tengor, 54/12,** *for 4 x 6.5cm. exposures on 127 film, all metal body, Goerz Frontar lens, simple shutter.*
.................40.00   50.00

☐ **Box Tengor, 54,** *for 4.5 x 6cm. exposures on 120 film, ½-frame 120, c. 1934, Goerz Frontar lens, adjustable focus by means of supplementary lens, single speed shutter, flash synchronized.*
.................40.00   50.00

☐ **Box Tengor, 54/2 pre-war, 56/2 post-war,** *for 6 x 9cm. exposures on 120 film, metal body, adjustable focus with supplementary lens, single speed shutter.*
.................25.00   30.00

☐ **Box Tengor, 54/15,** *6.5 x 11cm., 2½ x 4¼", on 116 rollfilm, all metal box, Goerz Frontar lens.*
.................30.00   40.00

☐ **Cocarette, 519/2,** *folding camera for 6 x 9cm. exposures on 120 film, f4.5 Tessar or Dominar Anastigmat, rimset Compur 1-250, focus via radial lever on bed.*
.................30.00   40.00

ZEISS, ZEISS-IKON / 259

☐ **Contaflex, 860/24,** *35mm. TLR, the original Contaflex model, c. 1935, f1.5 or f2 Sonnar, or f2.8 Tessar, metal focal plane shutter, 5-1000.*
.................775.00   825.00

☐ **Contaflex I, 861/24,** *c. 1950's, 35mm. SLR, Tessar f2.8 lens.*
.................50.00   75.00

☐ **Contaflex II, 862/24,** *c. 1954, similar to Contaflex I, but with built-in meter.*
.................45.00   55.00

☐ **Contaflex III, 863/24,** *c. 1958, Synchro-Compur 1-500.*
.................70.00   75.00

☐ **Contaflex IV, 864/24,** *interchangeable Tessar f2.8/50mm., Synchro Compur 1-500, built-in meter.*
.................75.00   100.00

☐ **Contaflex Super,** *35mm. SLR, f2.8/50mm. Tessar lens.*
.................100.00   135.00

260 / ZEISS, ZEISS-IKON

☐ **Contarex EE, nicknamed "Bullseye,"** f2/50mm. Planar lens.
.... 175.00   225.00

☐ **Contax I, 540/24,** c. 1932, 35mm., black body, f1.5 or f2 Sonnar, or f2.8 or 3.5 Tessar lens, focal plane shutter to 1000.
.... 375.00   450.00

☐ **Contax II, 543/24,** c. 1936, chrome body with black leather, focal plane shutter 2-1250.
.... 125.00   150.00

☐ **Contax III, 544/24,** c. 1936, Tessar f2.8, or Sonnar f1.5 or f2 lens, focal plane ½-1250.
.... 135.00   150.00

☐ **Contax IIa, 563/24,** early models.
.... 125.00   150.00
☐ **Same as above,** with MX synchronized.
.... 160.00   180.00

☐ **Contax IIIa, 564/24,** with f2, 1.5, or 1.2 Sonnar.
.... 150.00   160.00
☐ **Same as above,** with MX synchronized.
.... 175.00   200.00

☐ **Contax D,** c. 1953 35mm. SLR, made in the old Jena factory in USSR occupied East Germany, Zeiss Jena Biotar f2, Hexar f2.8, or Tessar f2.8, focal plane shutter to 1000.
.... 90.00   110.00

☐ **Contax "no name,"** manufactured in "USSR occupied Germany."
.... 135.00   150.00

☐ **Contax S,** c. 1950, made in East Germany, the first 35mm. prism SLR, Victor f2.9 or Biotar f2.
.... 180.00   200.00

☐ **Contessa, 533/24,** c. early 1950's folding 35mm. camera, Tessar f2.8/45mm. lens, synchronized Compur shutter 1-500, CRF, BIM.
.... 120.00   150.00

☐ **Contessa-Nettel folding plate cameras,** 6 x 9cm. or 9 x 12cm. sizes, after the merger which formed Zeiss-Ikon, the Contessa-Nettel plate cameras retained their own name in addition to the new corporate name during the period of change-over.
.... 50.00   70.00

☐ **Contina, 526/24,** 35mm. camera with CRF, Novar f3.5/45mm., Prontor SVS shutter.
.... 40.00   60.00

☐ **Contina,** folding types, Tessar lens.
.... 75.00   100.00

☐ **Donata, 227/7,** 9 x 12cm. double extension plate camera, Tessar f4.5/135mm. lens in Compur 1-200, leather bellows.
.... 40.00   60.00

ZEISS, ZEISS-IKON / 261

☐ **Ergo, 301,** c. 1926, monocular shaped disguised camera with right-angle viewing, a continuation of the Contessa Ergo and the Nettel Argus, f4.5/55mm. Tessar.
.... **1000.00   1200.00**

Ermanox
Although Zeiss-Ikon was the manufacturer after 1926, all Ermanox cameras are listed under Ernemann.

☐ **Folding plate cameras, folding rollfilm cameras,** miscellaneous unidentified models, rollfilm models.
..................**20.00   30.00**
☐ **Same as above,** plate models.
..................**30.00   40.00**
☐ **Hologon camera,** c. 1969, extreme wide angle 35mm. camera, non-interchangeable f8/15mm. Hologon lens, fixed f8 opening, focal plane shutter 1-500, changeable magazine, only 1,000 made.
...............**1000.00   1150.00**
☐ **Icarette, folding-bed rollfilm cameras,** various sizes.
..................**30.00   40.00**
☐ **Ideal folding-bed cameras,** 250/2, 6 x 9cm.
..................**50.00   60.00**
☐ **Same as above,** 250/7, 9 x 12cm.
..................**65.00   75.00**

Icarette, Folding-Bed Rollfilm

Ikoflex
6 x 6cm. TLR cameras for 120 film.

☐ **Ikoflex I, 850/16,** c. 1934, Novar f3.5 or 4.5/80mm. lens, shutter 25-100.
.... **100.00   110.00**
☐ **Ikoflex Ia, 854/16,** c. 1952, Tessar or Novar f3.5/75mm., Prontor 1-250.
..................**50.00   60.00**
☐ **Ikoflex Ic, 886/16,** c. 1956, f3.5 Tessar or Novar.
..................**70.00   80.00**
☐ **Ikoflex II, 851,** c. 1938, Tessar f3.5.
..................**60.00   75.00**
☐ **Ikoflex IIa, 855/16,** c. 1953, Tessar f3.5/75mm., Synchro Compur 1-500.
..................**70.00   80.00**
☐ **Ikoflex III, 853/16,** c. 1939, Tessar f2.8/75mm., Compur Rapid 1-200, Albada finder.
.... **120.00   150.00**

262 / ZEISS, ZEISS-IKON

Ikomat cameras
Re-named Ikonta after 1936.

☐ **Ikomat, 520,** c. 1935, folding camera for 4.5 x 6cm. exposures on 120 film, Nettar, Novar, or Tessar f4.5 lens in Derval shutter.
.... 50.00   60.00

☐ **Ikomat, 520/2,** c. 1930's folding camera for 6 x 9cm., 2¼ x 3¼", on 120 film, 105mm. lens in Derval shutter.
.... 50.00   60.00

☐ **Super Ikomat A, 530,** c. 1935 folding camera for 4.5 x 6cm. exposures on 120 rollfilm, Tessar f2.8, re-named Super Ikonta A after 1936.
.... 140.00   165.00

☐ **Ikonette, 504/12,** c. 1928, for 4 x 6.5cm. exposures on 127 film, full frame.
.... 40.00   50.00

☐ **Ikonette, 500/24,** blue-gray plastic 35mm. camera, f3.5/45mm. Novar Anastigmat lens, Pronto 15-200 shutter, front lens focus, unique lever around lens, one push winds film, second push fires shutter.
.... 40.00   50.00

☐ **Ikonta folding rollfilm camera, 520/18, 521/18,** for 16 exposures 3 x 4cm. on 127 rollfilm, Novar f4.5 or 6.3/50mm. lens, Derval shutter 25-75, T, B, front lens focusing, wire frame finder.
.... 100.00   125.00

Note: The 521 models were post-1936 and had double exposure prevention and body release.

☐ **Ikonta folding rollfilm camera, 520, 521,** for 4.5 x 6cm. exposures, half-frame, on 120 film, Novar f6.3, 4.5, or 3.5, Tessar f3.5 or 4.5, Telma, Compur, Compur Rapid, or Prontor shutter.
.... 60.00   75.00

☐ **Ikonta folding rollfilm camera, 6 x 6cm.,** 520/16, 521/16, 524/16, for 2¼ x 2¼" exposures on 120 film, Novar f3.5 or 4.5, Tessar f3.5, Pronto, Zeiss-Ikon, Klio, or Compur Rapid shutter.
.... 70.00   80.00

☐ **Ikonta folding rollfilm camera, 6 x 9cm.,** 515/2, 520/2, 521/2, 523/2, 524/2, for 8 exposures, 2¼ x 3¼ on 120, wide assortment of Tessar, Novar, Nettar and Dominar lenses, Compur, Prontor, Zeiss-Ikon, Klio, Gauthier, Derval, Telma shutter.
.... 75.00   85.00

☐ **Ikonta folding rollfilm camera, 35mm., 522/24,** for 24 x 36mm. exposures on standard 35mm. film, Novar or Xenar lens, Prontor, Derval, Zeiss, or Gauthier shutter.
.... 60.00   75.00

☐ **Super Ikonta A, 531,** c. 1950's, for 16 exposures 4.5 x 6cm. on 120 film, Tessar, Xenar, or Novar f3.5/75mm. lens, older models.
.... 155.00   180.00

☐ **Same as above,** with MX synchronized and Tessar.
.... 380.00   420.00

☐ **Super Ikonta B, 530/16,** for 11 exposures 6 x 6cm. on 120 film, f2.8/80mm. Tessar lens in Synchro Compur.
.... 100.00   120.00

☐ **Same as above,** with MX synchronized.
.... 125.00   200.00

☐ **Super Ikonta BX, 533/16,** similar to the "B," but with dual range meter.
.... 125.00   150.00

☐ **Same as above,** with MX synchronized and Tessar lens.
.... 225.00   275.00

☐ **Super Ikonta C, 531/2,** for 8 exposures 6 x 9cm., 2¼ x 3¼", on 120 film, Tessar or Novar f3.5/105mm., Compur shutter 1-500.
.... 125.00   150.00

☐ **Same as above,** *newer models with MX synchronized and Tessar.*
.... 400.00   450.00

☐ **Super Ikonta D, 530/15,** *for 6.5 x 11cm., 2½ x 4¼", exposures on 616 film, Tessar or Triotar f4.5/120mm., Compur Rapid or Klio shutter, coupled rangefinder, uncommon size.*
.... 325.00   375.00

☐ **Kolibri, 523/18,** *c. 1930, for 3 x 4cm. exposures, half-frame, on 127 film, telescoping front, Tessar f3.5/50mm. in Compur 1-300 shutter, made only a few years.*
.... 215.00   265.00

☐ **Night Kolibri,** *same as the Kolibri, but with f2/45mm. lens, rare.*
.... 625.00   725.00

☐ **Maximar A, 207/3,** *for 6.5 x 9cm. plates, c. 1940, Tessar f4.5/105mm., Compur shutter, double extension bellows.*
.... 65.00   85.00

☐ **Maximar B, 207/7,** *c. 1940, for 9 x 12cm. plates, double extension bellows, Tessar f4.5/135 lens in Compur 1-200 shutter.*
.... 50.00   65.00

Microflex
c. 1930's focal plane SLR.

☐ **Microflex, 6 x 9cm., 859/2,** *Tessar f3.5 or 4.5, focal plane shutter to 2000.*
.... 225.00   295.00

☐ **Microflex, 9 x 12cm., 859/7,** *Tessar f4.5/165mm. lens, focal plane shutter to 2000.*
.... 200.00   250.00

☐ **Nettar,** *folding cameras for 120 film, made in 2 sizes: 4.5 x 6cm., 512, and 6 x 9cm., 512/2, with Novar or Nettar f4.5 or 6.3 lens in Compur shutter 1-250.*
.... 30.00   40.00

☐ **Nettax, 538/24,** *c. 1937, 35mm. camera similar to the earlier Super Nettel, except that it has a collapsing lens mount rather than the bed and bellows, it is like a cross between the Super Nettel and the Contax, Novar f4.5 lens, focal plane shutter.*
.... 375.00   475.00

☐ **Nettax,** *6 x 6cm. on 120 rollfilm.*
.... 70.00   100.00

☐ **Nettel, Super, 536/24,** *folding-bed horizontal style 35mm., Tessar f3.5 or 2.8/50mm., focal plane shutter to 1000, self-erecting front via cross-struts and bellows.*
.... 275.00   375.00

☐ **Nettel, Tropical,** *fine wood folding camera with brown leather bellows and nickel trim, Tessar f4.5 lens and focal plane shutter to 2000, 6.5 x 9cm.,871/3.*
.... 700.00   800.00

☐ **Same as above,** *10 x 15cm., 871/9.*
.... 700.00   800.00

☐ **Nixe,** *folding cameras for rollfilm or plates various sizes from 2¼ x 3¼" through 3¼ x 5½", an interesting dual-purpose camera, well constructed.*
.... 65.00   85.00

264 / ZEISS, ZEISS-IKON

- ☐ **Onito,** c. 1927, 6 x 9cm. size, 126/2, and 9 x 12cm. size, 126/7, Novar Anastigmat f6.3, Derval shutter 1-100.
  . . . . 25.00   35.00
- ☐ **Orix, 306/9 and 308/9,** folding plate cameras for 10 x 15cm. plates, f6.8 Goerz, or f4.5 Tessar lens in Compur shutter.
  . . . . 120.00   150.00

Palmos cameras
Made by Carl Zeiss before the merger which formed Zeiss-Ikon.

- ☐ **Minimum Palmos,** c. 1902, wood bodied folding plate camera for 9 x 12 plates, Zeiss Tessar or Goerz Dagor lens, focal plane shutter, red leather bellows, black leather covered body.
  . . . . 100.00   125.00
- ☐ **Universal Palmos,** c. 1898 folding camera 9 x 12 or 10.5 x 16.5cm. size, with lens and shutter.
  . . . . 115.00   140.00
- ☐ **Stereo Palmos,** c. 1905, for stereo exposures on 6 x 13cm. plates, Tessar f4.5/75mm. lenses, variable speeds, black bellows.
  . . . . 300.00   340.00
- ☐ **Piccolette, 545/12,** c. 1927, for 4 x 6.5cm. exposures on 127 rollfilm, Tessar f4.5/75mm.
  . . . . 50.00   70.00
- ☐ **Sirene, 135/5,** folding sheet-film camera for 3¼ x 4¼" exposures, f6.3 or 4.5/135mm. lens.
  . . . . 20.00   40.00
- ☐ **Taxo, 122/3,** folding sheet film camera for 6.5 x 9cm. exposures.
  . . . . 20.00   40.00
- ☐ **Taxo, 122/7,** similar, for 9 x 12cm. films, Novar f6.3/135, Derval shutter.
  . . . . 20.00   25.00
- ☐ **Taxo, deluxe model, 126/7,** with radial focus lever on bed, 9 x 12cm. size.
  . . . . 50.00   75.00

- ☐ **Taxona,** c. 1950, the Taxona is the DDR successor to the pre-war Zeiss Tenax, for 24 x 24mm. exposures on 35mm. film, Novenar or Tessar f3.5 lens, Tempor 1-300 shutter.
  . . . . 35.00   45.00
- ☐ **Tenax I,** c. 1938, 35mm. camera for 24 x 24mm. exposures, Novar or Tessar f3.5 lens, Compur shutter 1-300.
  . . . . 60.00   75.00

- ☐ **Tenax II,** 24 x 24mm., interchangeable lens model, using the same bayonet system as the Nettax, and appearing much like it, f2 Sonnar or f2.8 Tessar, Compur Rapid shutter 1-400, coupled rangefinder.
  . . . . 200.00   245.00
- ☐ **Trix, 185/7,** 9 x 12cm. plate camera, double Anastigmat f6.8/135mm., dial Compur.
  . . . . 30.00   50.00
- ☐ **Trona folding plate camera, 6.5 x 9cm., 210/3,** f4.5/105 Tessar.
  . . . . 40.00   60.00
- ☐ **Trona folding plate camera, 9 x 12cm., 210/7,** f4.5/135 Dominar.
  . . . . 30.00   40.00
- ☐ **Volta folding plate camera, 6.5 x 9cm., 135/3,** f4.5/105 Dominar.
  . . . . 28.00   38.00
- ☐ **Volta folding plate camera, 9 x 12cm., 135/7,** f6.3/135 Novar.
  . . . . 25.00   30.00

- [ ] **Volta folding plate camera, deluxe model, 146/3, and 146/7,** with radial focus lever on bed.
  ....40.00   60.00
- [ ] **Werra,** c. 1955, 35mm. made in East Germany, Tessar f2.8/50mm., Compur Rapid 1-500, self-timer, olive green leather.
  ....45.00   60.00

ZENIT
(Russia)

- [ ] **Zenit 3, Zenit B,** 35mm. SLR cameras, including one of the various "normal" lenses.
  ....45.00   65.00

ZENITH EDELWEISS

- [ ] **Zenith Edelweiss,** folding 620 rollfilm camera.
  ....15.00   25.00

ZENITH KODAK
(See Eastman)

ZENOBIA
(See Daiichi Kogaku)

ZION
(Ed. Zion, Paris)

ZORKI / 265

- [ ] **Pocket Z,** folding camera for 6.5 x 9cm. plates, Rex Luxia or Boyer Sapphir lens, dial Compur shutter, leather bellows, metal body.
  ....85.00   115.00

ZORKI
(USSR)

35mm. cameras, copies of various Leicas.

- [ ] **Zorki,** c. 1952, Leica II copy, f3.5/50mm. Industar or f2/50 Jupiter.
  ....85.00   115.00
- [ ] **Zorki C,** Leica III copy.
  ....45.00   65.00
- [ ] **Zorki I,** Leica IIIa copy.
  .... 115.00   125.00
- [ ] **Zorki III,** f2.8, CRF.
  ....40.00   65.00
- [ ] **Zorki IV,** c. 1955, Jupiter f2/50mm. lens, focal plane shutter 1-1000, CRF, the most common model.
  ....55.00   75.00
- [ ] **Zorki V.**
  ....45.00   65.00

INDEX

INDEX A-E

ABC (Steineck): 215
Acma Sportshot: 57
Acro 127: 57
Adams Minex: 57
Adams Yale No. 2: 57
Adams & Westlake Adlake: 57
Adina: 57
Adlake: 57
Adoro: 31, 134, 91, 258
Adox 35: 57
Adox Adrette: 57
Adox Blitz: 57
Adox Golf: 58
Adox Sport: 58
Adrette: 57
Aerial Reconnaissance (Vinten): 247
Afiom Wega 11a: 58
Agfa (Folding Plate): 58
Agfa (Folding Rollfilm): 58
Agfa Ambi-Silette: 58
Agfa Antar: 58
Agfa Billy: 58
Agfa Billy Clack: 58
Agfa Billy Record: 58
Agfa Box: 58
Agfa Cadet: 58
Agfa Captain: 58
Agfa Clack: 58
Agfa Click: 58
Agfa Clipper PD-16: 58
Agfa Clipper Special: 58
Agfa Iso: 58
Agfa Isoflash: 58
Agfa Isolar: 58
Agfa Isolette: 58
Agfa Isolette I: 58
Agfa Isolette II: 58
Agfa Isolette III: 58
Agfa Isolette Super: 58
Agfa Isomat: 58
Agfa Karat 12: 58
Agfa Karat 36: 58

Agfa Karomat: 58
Agfa Major: 59
Agfa Memo: 59
Agfa Nitor: 59
Agfa Optima: 59
Agfa Plenax Hypar PB-20: 59
Agfa Plenax Hypar PD-16: 59
Agfa Readyset 1: 59
Agfa Readyset 1A: 59
Agfa Readyset PB-20: 59
Agfa Readyset Eagle: 59
Agfa Readyset Royal: 59
Agfa Readyset Special: 59
Agfa Readyset Traveler: 59
Agfa Schul-Prämie Box: 59
Agfa Selecta-M: 59
Agfa-Shur-Flash: 59
Agfa Shur-Shot: 59
Agfa Silette: 59
Agfa Silette Super: 59
Agfa Solinette: 59
Agfa Solinette II: 59
Agfa Solinette Super: 59
Agfa Speedex: 59
Agfa Standard (Plate): 59
Agfa Standard (Rollfilm): 59
Agfa Super Silette: 59
Agfa Super Solinette: 59
Agfa Synchro-Box: 60
Agfa Ventura: 60
Agfa Ventura Deluxe: 60
Agfa View: 60
Agfa Viking: 60
Aires 35 IIIC: 60
Aires 35 IIIL: 60
Aires 35 V: 60
Aires Airesflex: 60
Aires Penta 35: 60
Aires Viscount: 60
Airesflex: 60
AKA (Apparate & Kamerabau): 67
Akarelle: 67
Akarette: 67

Akarex: 67
Al-Vista Panoramic: 207, 208
Alethoscope (Joux): 187
All Distance Ensign: 178
Allied Carlton Reflex: 60
Alnea (Pignons): 215
Alpa (Pignons): 215, 216
Alpenflex: 38
Alpin (Voigtländer): 248
Alta (Reichenbach): 221
Altessa: 80
Altiflex: 60, 177
Altissa: 60, 177
Altissa Altiflex: 60
Altissa Altix: 60
Altix: 60
Altura: 92
Ambi-Silette: 58
Amerex: 61
American Advertising & Research Corp. Cub: 61
American Camera Mfg. Co. (Folding Plate): 61
American Camera Mfg. Co.
  Buckeye No. 2: 61
  Buckeye No. 3: 61
  Buckeye Tourist No. 1: 61
American Minute Photo Co.
  American Sleeve Machine: 61
American Optical Co. (Plate): 61
American Optical Co.
  Henry Clay: 61
American Optical Co. View: 62
American Safety Razor Corp.
  Foto-Disc: 62
American Sleeve Machine: 61
Ango (Goerz): 163
Animatic (Bencini): 74
Anniversary Kodak Camera: 100
Anniversary Speed Graphic: 172
Anschutz (Goerz): 66
Ansco (Box): 64
Ansco Anscoflex: 62

INDEX / 267

Ansco Anscoflex II: 62
Ansco Anscoset: 62
Ansco Automatic: 62
Ansco Automatic Reflex: 62
Ansco Buster Brown No. 2: 62
Ansco Buster Brown No. 2A: 62
Ansco Buster Brown No. 2C: 62
Ansco Buster Brown No. 3: 62
Ansco Buster Brown
  Folding No. 1 Model B: 62
Ansco Buster Brown
  Folding No. 2A: 62
Ansco Buster Brown
  Folding No. 3: 62
Ansco Buster Brown
  Folding No. 3A: 62
Ansco Buster Brown Junior: 62
Ansco Cadet Flash: 62
Ansco Cadet Model B-2: 62
Ansco Clipper: 62
Ansco Clipper Flash: 62
Ansco Clipper Special: 62
Ansco Commander: 62
Ansco Craftsman: 62
Ansco Dollar: 62
Ansco Flash Clipper: 62
Ansco Folding No. 1: 65
Ansco Folding No. 1A: 65
Ansco Folding No. 3: 65
Ansco Folding No. 3A: 65
Ansco Folding No. 4 Model C: 65
Ansco Folding No. 4 Model D: 65
Ansco Folding No. 6: 65
Ansco Folding No. 7: 65
Ansco Folding No. 9 Model B: 65
Ansco Folding No. 10: 65
Ansco Folding Buster Brown: 62
Ansco Folding Deluxe No. 1: 64
Ansco Folding Junior No. 1A: 65
Ansco Folding Junior No. 2C: 65
Ansco Folding Junior No. 3: 65
Ansco Folding Pocket No. 5: 65
Ansco Folding Special No. 1: 65

268 / INDEX

Ansco Goodwin (Box) No. 2: 63
Ansco Goodwin (Box) No. 3: 63
Ansco Goodwin Jr. No. 1: 63
Ansco Karomat: 63
Ansco Lancer: 63
Ansco Memo: 63
Ansco Official Boy Scout Memo: 63
Ansco Panda: 63
Ansco Photo Vanity: 63
Ansco Pioneer: 63
Ansco Plenax PD-16: 63
Ansco Readyflash: 63
Ansco Readyset No. 1: 63
Ansco Readyset No. 1A: 63
Ansco Readyset Royal: 63
Ansco Readyset Viking: 63
Ansco Rediflex: 63
Ansco Regent: 63
Ansco Regent Super: 63
Ansco Semi-Automatic: 63
Ansco Shur-Flash: 64
Ansco Shur-Shot: 64
Ansco Speedex: 64
Ansco Speedex No. 1A: 64
Ansco Speedex No. 3A: 64
Ansco Speedex Special: 64
Ansco Super Regent: 63
Ansco Vest Pocket Model A: 64
Ansco Vest Pocket No. 0: 64
Ansco Vest Pocket No. 1: 64
Ansco Vest Pocket No. 2: 64
Ansco Vest Pocket Junior: 64
Ansco View: 65
Ansco Viking: 64
Ansco Viking Readyset: 63
Anscoflex: 62
Anscoset: 62
Antar: 58
Anthony (Box): 66
Anthony Ascot Cycle No. 1: 66
Anthony Ascot Folding No. 25: 66
Anthony Ascot Folding No. 29: 66
Anthony Ascot Folding No. 30: 66
Anthony Buckeye: 66
Anthony Daylight Enlarging Camera: 66
Anthony Klondike: 66
Anthony Normandie: 66
Anthony Novelette: 66
Anthony Patent Novelette: 66
Anthony PDQ: 67
Anthony Stereo Plate Camera: 67
Anthony View: 67
Antique Oak (Scovill): 229
Apollo: 67
Apparate & Kamerabau Akarelle: 67
Apparate & Kamerabau Akarette I: 67
Apparate & Kamerabau Akarette II: 67
Apparate & Kamerabau Akarex: 67
Aptus Ferrotype (Moore): 207
Arette: 67
Argoflash (Argus AA): 68
Argoflex: 69
Argus (Nettel): 209
Argus 21 Markfinder: 69
Argus A: 67
Argus A2: 68
Argus A2B: 68
Argus A2F: 68
Argus A3: 68
Argus A4: 68
Argus AA (Argoflash): 68
Argus AF: 67
Argus Argoflash (AA): 68
Argus Argoflex: 69
Argus Argoflex Model 40: 69
Argus Argoflex Model 75 Black: 69
Argus Argoflex Model 75 Brown: 69
Argus Argoflex Model 75 Super: 69
Argus Argoflex Model E: 69
Argus Argoflex Model EF: 69
Argus Argoflex Model EM: 69
Argus Autronic 35: 69
Argus Autronic C 3: 69
Argus C: 68
Argus C2: 68
Argus C3: 68

INDEX / 269

Argus C3 Autronic: 69
Argus C3 Match-Matic: 68
Argus C4: 68
Argus C4R: 69
Argus C20: 69
Argus C33: 69
Argus C44: 69
Argus C44R: 69
Argus CC (Colorcamera): 68
Argus FA: 68
Argus K: 68
Argus Markfinder (21): 69
Arnold Karma: 69
Arnold Karmaflex: 69
Arrow: 69
Artist's Reflex (Ica): 183
Ascot: 66
ASR Foto-Disc: 62
Astraflex: 70, 156
Atom (Hüttig): 180
Atom (Ica): 180
Atoron (Yashica): 257
Atoron Electro (Yashica): 257
Auto Graflex: 168
Auto Ultrix: 186
Autocord (Minolta): 205
Autoflex (Kiyabashi): 70, 190
Autographic Brownie: 109, 110
Autographic Kodak Camera: 101, 102
Automatic Radio Tom Thumb
  Camera Radio: 70
Automatica (Durst): 98
Autorange Ensign: 78
Autronic (Argus): 69
Avus (Voightlander): 248
Baby Bessa: 249
Baby Box (Zeiss): 259
Baby Brownie: 107
Baby Hawkeye: 76
Baby Sibyl (Newman & Guardia): 210
Balda Baldalette: 70
Balda Baldarette: 70
Balda Baldax: 70

Balda Baldaxette I: 70
Balda Baldaxette II: 71
Balda Baldessa Ib: 71
Balda Baldi: 71
Balda Baldina: 71
Balda Baldina Super: 71
Balda Baldinette: 71
Balda Baldinette Super: 71
Balda Beltica: 71
Balda Jubilette: 71
Balda Juwella: 71
Balda Piccochic: 71
Balda Poka: 71
Balda Pontura Super: 71
Balda Rigona: 71
Balda Rollbox 120: 71
Balda Super Baldina: 71
Balda Super Baldinette: 71
Balda Super Pontura: 71
Balda Wara: 71
Baldalette: 70
Baldarette: 70
Baldax: 70
Baldaxette: 70
Baldessa: 71
Baldi: 71
Baldina: 71
Baldinette: 71
Baldur Box (Zeiss): 258
Bantam: 104, 105
Bauer: 71
Bausch & Lomb Camera Obscura: 72
Bazin & Leroy Stereocycle: 72
Beacon (Whitehouse Products): 254
Beau Brownie: 102
Beauty (Taiyodo): 239
Beautycord (Taiyodo): 239
Beautyflex (Taiyodo): 239
Bebe: 181, 258
Beck Frena: 72
Beck Frena Deluxe: 72
Beica: 72
Beier (Folding Plate): 72

Beier Beira: 72
Beier Beirax: 72
Beier Beirette: 72
Beier Precisa: 72
Beier Rifax: 72
Beil & Freund (Folding Plate): 73
Beira: 72
Beirax: 72
Beirette: 72
Belca Belfoca: 73
Belca Belplasca: 73
Belca Beltica: 73
Belfoca: 73
Bell-14: 73
Bell & Howell Dial 35: 73
Bell & Howell Foton: 73
Bell & Howell TDC Stereo Colorist: 73
Bell & Howell TDC Stereo Vivid: 73
Bell Camera Co. Straight-Working Panorama: 73
Bell Kamera Model KTC-62: 73
Bella (Kurbi & Niggeloh): 194
Bellieni Jumelle: 74
Bellieni Jumelle Stereo: 74
Belplasca: 73
Beltax: 74
Beltica (Balda): 71
Beltica (Belca): 73
Ben Akiba (Lehmann): 195
Bencini Animatic 600: 74
Benetfink Lightning Detective: 74
Benson Street: 74
Bentzin Planovista: 74
Bentzin Primar: 74
Bentzin Primar Folding Reflex: 75
Bentzin Primar Reflex: 74
Bentzin Primarflex: 75
Bentzin Stereo Reflex: 75
Bergheil (Voigtländer): 248
Berning Robot I: 75
Berning Robot II: 75
Berning Robot Junior: 75
Berning Robot Luftwaffe: 75
Berning Robot Royal 36: 75
Berning Robot Star: 75
Berning Robot Star II: 75
Bessa (Voigtländer): 249
Bessamatic (Voigtländer): 249
Bettax: 75
Billy (Agfa): 58
Billy Clack (Agfa): 58
Billy Record (Agfa): 58
Bilora Bella 44: 194
Bilora Blitz Boy: 194
Bilora Boy: 194
Bilora Radix: 194
Bioflex: 75
Bischoff Detective: 76
Blair Hawkeye Baby: 76
Blair Hawkeye Combination: 76
Blair Hawkeye Combination No. 3: 76
Blair Hawkeye Detective All wood: 76
Blair Hawkeye Detective & Combination: 76
Blair Hawkeye Folding: 77
Blair Hawkeye Folding No. 3 Model 3: 77
Blair Hawkeye Folding No. 4 Model 3: 77
Blair Hawkeye Folding No. 4 Model 4: 77
Blair Hawkeye Junior: 76
Blair Hawkeye Stereo: 77
Blair Hawkeye Tool-Box style: 76
Blair Hawkeye Tourist: 77
Blair Hawkeye Weno No. 2: 77
Blair Hawkeye Weno No. 3: 77
Blair Hawkeye Weno No. 4: 78
Blair Hawkeye Weno No. 6: 78
Blair Hawkeye Weno No. 7: 78
Blair Kamaret: 78
Blair Lucidograph No. 1: 78

INDEX / 271

Blair Lucidograph No. 2: 78
Blair Lucidograph No. 3: 78
Blair Premier: 76
Blair Stereo Hawkeye: 77
Blair Stereo Weno: 77
Blair View: 78
Blitz Boy (Kurbi & Niggeloh): 194
Block-Notes (Gaumont): 161
Bo-Peep (Manhattan): 202
Bob: 152, 259
Bobette: 152, 259
Bolsey (Pignons): 216
Bolsey 8: 79
Bolsey B: 79
Bolsey B2: 79
Bolsey B22 Set-O-Matic: 79
Bolsey Bolseyflex: 79
Bolsey C: 79
Bolsey C22 Set-O-Matic: 79
Bolsey Explorer: 79
Bolsey Jubilee: 79
Bolsey Reflex: 79
Bolseyflex: 79
Bolta Photavit: 79
Borsum Reflex: 79
Borsum Reflex New Model: 80
Boston Bulls-Eye: 80
Boston Hawkeye Detective (All wood): 80
Boston Hawkeye Detective Leather covered): 80
Bower Jr. (Schleissner): 228
Bower X (Schleissner): 228
Box Tengor (Goerz): 165
Box Tengor (Zeiss): 259
Boy Scout (Herco): 176
Boy Scout Kodak: 105
Boy Scout Memo (Ansco): 63
Boyer (plastic cameras): 25
Boyer Altessa: 80
Brack Field: 80
Braun Colorette Super: 80
Braun Gloriette: 80

Braun Pax Model M2: 81
Braun Pax Model M3: 81
Braun Pax Model M4: 81
Braun Paxette I: 81
Braun Paxette Automatic III: 81
Braun Paxette Super: 81
Braun Paxina II: 81
Brilliant (Voigtlander): 249
Brooklyn: 81
Brownell Stereo: 81
Brownie: 105-113
Brownie Scout (Herco): 176
Buccaneer (Universal): 125
Buckeye (American Camera Mfg.): 61
Buckeye (Anthony): 66
Buckeye (Eastman): 113
Buess Multiprint: 81
Bullard (Folding Plate): 81
Bullard (Magazine): 81
Bullet (Brownie): 107
Bullet (Eastman): 114
Bulls-Eye (Boston): 80
Bulls-Eye (Brownie): 107
Bulls-Eye (Eastman): 114-116
Burke & James Grover: 81
Burke & James Ideal: 81
Burke & James Ingento Folding 3A-Model 3: 81, 82
Burke & James Ingento Jr. 1A: 81
Burke & James Ingento Jr. 3A: 82
Burke & James Press: 82
Burke & James Rexo 1A: 82
Burke & James Rexo 3: 82
Burke & James Rexo (Box): 82
Burke & James Rexo Junior 1A: 82
Burke & James Rexo Junior 2C: 82
Burke & James Rexo Junior 3: 82
Burke & James Rexo Vest Pocket: 82
Burke & James Rexoette: 82
Burke & James View: 82
Burke & James Watson-Holmes Fingerprint: 82
Busch Pressman: 82

Busch Verascope F40: 82
Buster Brown: 62
Busy Bee (Seneca): 231
Butcher Cameo: 82
Butcher Carbine No. 2: 83
Butcher Carbine
 (Folding Rollfilm): 82
Butcher Carbine Reflex: 83
Butcher Carbine Watch Pocket: 83
Butcher Klimax: 83
Butcher Midg No. 0: 83
Butcher Midg No. 00: 83
Butcher Midg No. 1: 83
Butcher Midg No. 1a:83
Butcher Midg No. 2: 83
Butcher Midg No. 3: 83
Butcher Midg No. 4: 83
Butcher Midg No. 4a: 83
Butcher Midg No. 4b: 83
Button Tintype (Talbot): 239
Cadet (Agfa): 58
Cadet (Ansco): 62
Cadot Scenographe Panoramique: 83
Cam-O: 83
Cambinox: 206
Camel Model II: 83
Cameo (Butcher): 82
Cameo (Ica): 181
Cameo Ultrix (Ihagee): 186
Camera-Lite: 83
Camera Obscura
 (Bausch & Lomb): 72
Camera Radio (Tom Thumb): 70
Camera-scope: 83
Cameradio (Universal): 246
Candid Perfex Fifty-Five: 84
Candid Perfex Forty-Four: 84
Candid Perfex One-O-One: 84
Candid Perfex One-O-Two: 84
Candid Perfex Speed Candid: 84
Candid Perfex Thirty-Three: 84
Cane handle camera (Lehmann): 195
Canon 7: 84
Canon 7-S: 84
Canon Canonet: 84

Canon Demi: 84
Canon Dial-35: 84
Canon II: 84
Canon II-B: 84
Canon II-F: 84
Canon II-S: 84
Canon III: 84
Canon III-A: 84
Canon IV: 84
Canon IV-F: 84
Canon IV-S: 84
Canon IV-S2: 84
Canon L-1: 84
Canon P: 84
Canon VT: 84
Canonet: 84
Captain (Agfa): 58
Carbine (Butcher): 82, 83
Carlton (Utility): 246
Carlton Reflex (Allied): 60
Carmen Pygmee: 85
Carpentier Photo-Jumelle: 85
Cartridge Hawkeye: 125
Cartridge Kodak: 116
Cartridge Premo: 136
Casca (Steinheil): 237
Caspa (Demaria): 96
Century 35: 167
Century Field camera: 85
Century Graphic: 172
Century Universal View: 167
Certo Certonet: 86
Certo Certosix: 86
Certo Certosport: 86
Certo Certotrop: 86
Certo Dollina: 86
Certo Dollina II: 86
Certo Dollina Super: 86
Certo Dolly: 86
Certo Dolly Supersport: 87
Certo Dolly Supersport
 Rangefinder: 87
Certo Doppel Box: 87

Certo Folding Plate: 87
Certonet: 86
Certosix: 86
Certosport: 86
Certotrop: 86
Challenge (Lizars): 199
Chase Magazine: 87
Chautauqua (Seneca): 231
Chevron: 116
Chicago Camera Co. Photake: 87
Chicago Ferrotype Co.
 Mandel PDQ: 87
Chicago Ferrotype Co. Mandel
 Post Card Machine No. 2: 87
Chicago Ferrotype Co.
 Mandelette: 87
Chicago Ferrotype Co.
 Wonder Automatic Cannon Photo
 Button Machine: 87
Chief (Seneca): 231
Chiyodo Chiyoko: 87
Chiyodo Konan Automat 16: 87
Chiyoko: 87
Cirkut Camera: 117
Cirkut Outfit: 117
Ciro 35 (Graflex): 167
Ciro 35 Model R: 88
Ciro 35 Model S: 88
Ciro 35 Model T: 88
Ciro Ciro-flex Model A: 88
Ciro Ciro-flex Model B: 88
Ciro Ciro-flex Model C: 88
Ciro Ciro-flex Model D: 88
Ciro Ciro-flex Model E: 88
Ciro Ciro-flex Model F: 88
Ciro-flex: 88
Citoskop (Contessa): 92
Clack (Agfa): 58
Clack (Rietzschel): 221
Clarissa (Contessa): 92
Clarovid (Rodenstock): 226
Clarus MS-35: 88
Click (Agfa): 58

Clipper (Agfa): 58
Clipper (Ansco): 62
Clix 120: 88
Close & Cone Quad: 88
CMC: 88
Coat Pocket Tenax (Goerz): 164
Cocarette: 92, 259
Colly: 88
Color Camera (Devin): 97
Color Camera (Fotochrome): 158
Color Camera (Hess-Ives): 176
Color Camera (Jos-Pe): 187
Color Camera (Mikut): 204
Color Camera
 (National Photocolor): 209
Colorcamera (Argus CC): 68
Colorette (Braun): 80
Colorist (Bell & Howell): 73
Columbia Pecto No. 1A: 89
Columbia Pecto No. 5: 89
Combat Graphic: 172
Combination Hawkeye: 76
Commander (Ansco): 62
Compact Graflex: 168
Compagnie Francaise de
 Photographie Photosphere: 89
Compass: 89
Competitor View (Seneca): 231
Concealed Vest Camera (Stirn): 238
Condor (Galileo): 160
Conley Folding Plate Camera: 90
Conley Folding Rollfilm: 91
Conley Junior: 91
Conley Kewpie No. 2: 90
Conley Kewpie No. 2A: 90
Conley Kewpie No. 3: 90
Conley Kewpie No. 3A: 90
Conley Magazine: 91
Conley Stereo Box: 91
Conley View: 91
Contaflex: 259
Contarex: 260
Contax: 260
Contax FB (Pentacon): 213

Contessa (Zeiss): 260
Contessa Adoro: 91
Contessa Altura: 92
Contessa Citoskop: 92
Contessa Clarissa Tropical: 92
Contessa Cocarette: 92
Contessa Deckrullo-Nettel: 92
Contessa Deckrullo-Nettel Stereo: 92
Contessa Deckrullo-Nettel Tropical: 92
Contessa Deckrullo-Nettel Stereo Tropical: 92
Contessa Donata: 92
Contessa Duchessa: 92
Contessa Ergo: 92
Contessa Folding Plate Tropical Camera: 92
Contessa Miroflex: 92
Contessa Nic 63: 93
Contessa Onito: 93
Contessa Piccolette 201: 93
Contessa Sonnar: 93
Contessa Sonnet: 93
Contessa Stereax: 93
Contessa Steroco: 93
Contessa Taxo: 93
Contessa Tessco: 93
Contessa Tropical Folding Plate Camera: 93
Contessa-Nettel (Zeiss): 260
Contina: 136
Corfield Periflex: 93
Cornu Ontobloc: 93
Cornu Ontoflex: 93
Cornu Reyna II: 94
Cornu Reyna Cross III: 94
Coronet 3-D Stereo: 94
Coronet Midget: 94
Coronet Vogue: 94
Corsair (Universal): 125
Cosmic 35: 94
Craftex Hollywood Reflex: 34
Craftsman: 62
Crown Graphic: 172
Crystar: 94
Cub (American Advertising): 61
Cub Scout (Herco): 176
Cupid (Houghton): 178
Cupido (Ica): 181
Cycle Graphic: 172
Cycle Poco (Rochester): 224
Cyclone (Rochester): 224
Cyclone (Western): 254
Cyclops (16mm binocular camera): 94
Daci: 95
Daguerreotype camera: 95
Daguerreotype camera (Palmer & Longking): 213
Daguerreotype camera (Voightländer): 249
Daiichi Kogaku Zenobia: 95
Dallmeyer Speed: 95
Dan-35: 95
Dancer Stereo: 95
Dangelmaier Decora I: 95
Darling 16: 95
Day-Xit (Shew): 234
Daydark Photo Postcard: 95
Daydark Tintype: 95
Daylight Enlarging Camera (Anthony): 66
Daylight Kodak Camera: 117, 118
Dayspool (Lizars): 199, 200
Debrie Sept: 96
Deckrullo (Nettel): 209
Deckrullo-Nettel (Contessa): 92
Decora (Dangelmaier): 95
Dehel: 96
Dejur Reflex: 96
Delmar (Seroco): 233
Delta (Krugener): 193
Delta Stereo: 96
Demaria Jumelle Caspa: 96
Demaria Stereo: 96
Derby (Foth): 158
Derlux: 96
Derogy (Plate): 96
Detective Hawkeye: 76
Detrola 400: 97

Detrola Model B: 97
Detrola Model D: 97
Detrola Model E: 97
Detrola Model GW: 97
Detrola Model HW: 97
Detrola Model KW: 97
Devin Tri-Color: 97
Devry QRS Kamra: 97
Dial 35 (Bell & Howell): 73
Dial 35 (Canon): 84
Diax (Voss): 251
Dick Tracy: 97
Diplomat: 97
Direct Positive Camera
 (Wabash): 252
Direct Positive Street Camera
 (Thompson): 240
Diva (Phoba): 214
Dollar Box (Ansco): 62
Dollina (Certo): 86
Dolly (Certo): 86
Donald Duck (Herco): 176
Donata: 92, 260
Doppel Box (Certo): 87
Doris: 97
Dossert Detective: 98
Dover 620A: 98
Dreivier (Mentor): 166
Duaflex: 118
Dubroni Photographe de Poche: 98
Duca (Durst): 98
Ducati: 98
Duchess: 98
Duchessa (Contessa): 92
Duex: 118
Duo-620: 118
Duplex (Ihagee): 184
Duplex (Iso): 187
Duplex (Joux): 187
Duplex (Thornton-Pickard Ruby): 241
Durst 66: 98
Durst Automatica: 98
Durst Duca: 98
Eagle (Agfa Readyset Eagle): 59
Earl Products Co. Scenex: 228

EASTMAN KODAK CO.
Anniversary Camera: 100
Autographic Kodak No. 1A: 101
Autographic Kodak No. 3: 101
Autographic Kodak No. 3A: 102
Autographic Kodak Junior No. 1: 102
Autographic Kodak
 Junior No. 1A: 102
Autographic Kodak
 Junior No. 2C: 102
Autographic Kodak
 Junior No. 3A: 102
Autographic Kodak
 Special No. 1: 103
Autographic Kodak
 Special No. 1A: 103
Autographic Kodak
 Special No. 1A (RF): 103
Autographic Kodak
 Special No. 2C: 103
Autographic Kodak
 Special No. 3: 103
Autographic Kodak
 Special No. 3A: 103
Autographic Kodak Special No. 3A
 Model B: 103
Automatic 35: 146
Baby Brownie: 107
Bantam f3.9 RF: 105
Bantam f4.5: 105
Bantam f5.6: 105
Bantam f6.3: 104
Bantam f8: 104
Bantam Flash: 105
Bantam RF f3.9: 105
Bantam Special Compur Rapid: 105
Bantam Special Supermatic: 105
Beau Brownie: 107
Bou Scout Kodak: 105
Brownie (Box) No. 0: 105
Brownie (Box) No. 1 (Original): 106
Brownie (Box) No. 1 Improved: 106
Brownie (Box) No. 2: 106
Brownie (Box) No. 2A: 106
Brownie (Box) No. 2C: 107
Brownie (Box) No. 3: 107
Brownie Baby: 107
Brownie Beau: 107
Brownie Bull's-Eye: 107

276 / INDEX

Brownie Bullet: 107
Brownie Fiesta: 108
Brownie Flash Six-20: 112
Brownie Flash 20: 112
Brownie Flashmite 20: 112
Brownie Folding No. 2: 108
Brownie Folding No. 3: 108
Brownie Folding No. 3A: 108
Brownie Folding Autographic No. 1A: 109
Brownie Folding Autographic No. 2: 109
Brownie Folding Autographic No. 2A: 109
Brownie Folding Autographic No. 2C: 109
Brownie Folding Autographic No. 3A: 111
Brownie Folding Pocket No. 2: 111
Brownie Folding Pocket No. 2A: 111
Brownie Folding Pocket No. 3: 111
Brownie Folding Pocket No. 3A: 111
Brownie Hawkeye: 111
Brownie Holiday: 111
Brownie Junior: 112
Brownie Reflex 20: 112
Brownie Six-16: 112
Brownie Six-16 Junior: 112
Brownie Six -16 Special: 112
Brownie Six-20: 112
Brownie Six-20 Junior: 112
Brownie Six-20 Special: 112
Brownie Special: 112
Brownie Starflex: 112
Brownie Starlet: 112
Brownie Starmatic: 112
Brownie Stereo No. 2: 113
Brownie Target Six-16: 113
Brownie Target Six-20: 113
Brownie Twin 20: 113
Buckeye: 113
Bullet: 114
Bullet No. 2: 114
Bullet No. 2 Improved: 114
Bullet No. 2 Special: 114
Bullet No. 4: 114
Bullet No. 4 Special: 114
Bulls-Eye Folding No. 2: 115
Bulls-Eye No. 2: 115
Bulls-Eye No. 2 Special: 116
Bulls-Eye No. 3: 115
Bulls-Eye No. 4 (Improved): 115
Bulls-Eye No. 4 Special: 116
Cartridge Hawkeye: 125
Cartridge Kodak No. 3: 116
Cartridge Kodak No. 4: 116
Cartridge Kodak No. 5: 116
Cartridge Premo: 136
Chevron: 116
Cirkut Camera No. 5: 117
Cirkut Camera No. 6: 117
Cirkut Camera No. 10: 117
Cirkut Camera No. 16: 117
Cirkut Outfit No. 6: 117
Cirkut Outfit No. 8: 117
Daylight Kodak A: 117
Daylight Kodak B: 118
Daylight Kodak C: 118
Duaflex: 118
Duaflex II: 118
Duaflex III: 118
Duaflex IV: 118
Duex: 118
Duo Six-20: 118
Duo Six-20 Series II: 119
Ektra: 119
Eureka No. 2: 119
Eureka No. 4: 119
Eureka Junior No. 2: 119
Falcon No. 2: 120
Fiftieth Anniversary Box Camera: 100, 101
Film Pack Hawkeye: 125
Film Pack Premo: 136
Film Plate Premo: 136
Film Premo: 136
Flat Folding Kodak: 120
Flexo No. 2: 120
Flush Back Kodak No. 3: 120
Folding Autographic Brownie: 109
Folding Brownie: 108
Folding Cartridge Hawkeye: 125

INDEX / 277

Folding Cartridge Premo: 136
Folding Film Pack Hawkeye: 125
Folding Hawkeye: 125
Folding Kodak No. 4A: 121
Folding Kodak (Satchel-style)
 No. 4: 120
Folding Kodak (Stachel-style) No. 4
 Improved: 120
Folding Kodak (Satchel-style)
 No. 5: 121
Folding Kodak (Satchel-style)
 No. 6: 121
Folding Kodet: 128
Folding Pocket Brownie: 111
Folding Pocket Kodak (Original): 121
Folding Pocket Kodak No. 0: 121
Folding Pocket Kodak No. 1 (dual
 finders) Model C: 122
Folding Pocket Kodak No. 1
 (reversible finder) Model D: 122
Folding Pocket Kodak No. 1A: 122
Folding Pocket Kodak No. 1A
 Special: 124
Folding Pocket Kodak No. 2: 122
Folding Pocket Kodak No. 3
 (concealed shutter): 122
Folding Pocket Kodak No. 3
 (concealed shutter) Model A: 123
Folding Pocket Kodak No. 3
 (concealed shutter) Model AB: 122
Folding Pocket Kodak No. 3
 (exposed shutter): 123
Folding Pocket Kodak No. 3A: 123
Folding Pocket Kodak No. 3
 Special: 124
Folding Rainbow Hawkeye: 126
Gift Kodak: 124
Girl Scout Kodak: 125
Hawkette No. 2: 125
Hawkeye No. 2 Special: 126
Hawkeye No. 2A Special: 126
Hawkeye Cartridge No. 2: 125
Hawkeye Cartridge No. 2A: 125
Hawkeye Film Pack No. 2: 125
Hawkeye Folding No. 1: 125
Hawkeye Folding No. 1A: 125

Hawkeye Folding No. 2: 125
Hawkeye Folding No. 2A: 125
Hawkeye Folding No. 3: 125
Hawkeye Folding No. 3A: 125
Hawkeye Folding Six-16: 125
Hawkeye Folding Six-20: 125
Hawkeye Folding Cartridge
 No. 2: 125
Hawkeye Folding Cartridge
 No. 2A: 125
Hawkeye Folding Cartridge
 No. 3A: 125
Hawkeye Folding Film Pack
 No. 2: 125
Hawkeye Folding Special: 125
Hawkeye Rainbow No. 2: 126
Hawkeye Rainbow No. 2A: 126
Hawkeye Rainbow Folding
 No. 2: 126
Hawkeye Rainbow Folding No. 2
 Special: 126
Hawkeye Rainbow Folding
 No. 2A: 126
Hawkeye Rainbow Folding No. 2A
 Special: 126
Hawkeye Stereo: 126
Hawkeye Target No. 2: 126
Hawkeye Target No. 2A: 126
Hawkeye Target Six-16: 126
Hawkeye Target Six-20: 126
Hawkeye Vest Pocket: 126
Hawkeye Weno No. 2: 126
Hawkeye Weno No. 4: 126
Hawkeye Weno No. 5: 126
Hawkeye Weno No. 7: 126
Jiffy Kodak Six-16: 126
Jiffy Kodak Six-20: 126
Jiffy Kodak Vest Pocket: 126
Kodak (Original Model): 99
Kodak No. 1: 99
Kodak No. 2: 99
Kodak No. 3: 99
Kodak No. 3 Junior: 100
Kodak No. 4: 100
Kodak No. 4 Junior: 100
Kodak Automatic 35: 146
Kodak Junior No. 1: 127
Kodak Junior No. 1A: 127
Kodak Junior Six-16: 143

278 / INDEX

Kodak Junior Six-20: 144
Kodak Senior Six-16: 143
Kodak Senior Six-20: 144
Kodak Six-16: 143
Kodak Six-16 Special: 143
Kodak Six-20 144
Kodak Six-20 Special: 144
Kodak 35: 146
Kodak 35 Rangefinder: 146
Kodak Reflex (Model I): 138
Kodak Reflex (Model II): 138
Kodak Stereo: 145, 146
Kodak Super Six-20: 146
Kodet No. 4: 127
Kodet Folding No. 4: 128
Medalist I: 128
Medalist II: 128
Monitor Six-16: 128
Monitor Six-20: 129
Motormatic 35: 129
Nagel Junior: 129
Nagel Pupille: 129
Ordinary Kodak A: 130
Ordinary Kodak B: 130
Ordinary Kodak C: 130
Panoram Kodak No. 1 (Model A): 130
Panoram Kodak No. 1 (Model B): 130
Panoram Kodak No. 1 (Model C): 130
Panoram Kodak No. 1 (Model D): 130
Panoram Kodak No. 3A: 130
Panoram Kodak No. 4 (Model A): 130
Panoram Kodak No. 4 (Model B): 131
Panoram Kodak No. 4 (Model C): 131
Panoram Kodak No. 4 (Model D): 131
Petite: 131
Plate Camera No. 4 Series D: 119
Pocket Kodak Model 1895: 131
Pocket Kodak Model 1896: 131
Pocket Kodak No. 1: 132
Pocket Kodak No. 1 Junior: 134
Pocket Kodak No. 1 Junior (Colored): 134
Pocket Kodak No. 1 Series II: 132
Pocket Kodak No. 1A: 132
Pocket Kodak No. 1A (Colored): 132
Pocket Kodak No. 1A Junior: 134
Pocket Kodak No. 1A Series II: 132
Pocket Kodak No. 1A Special: 134
Pocket Kodak No. 2C: 133
Pocket Kodak No. 3: 133
Pocket Kodak No. 3 Special: 134
Pocket Kodak No. 3A: 133
Pocket Premo: 136
Pony 135: 135
Pony 135 Model B: 135
Pony 135 Model C: 135
Pony 828: 135
Pony II: 135
Pony IV: 135
Pony Premo: 137
Premo No. 1: 136
Premo No. 8: 136
Premo No. 9: 136
Premo No. 12: 135
Premo Cartridge No. 00: 136
Premo Cartridge No. 2: 136
Premo Cartridge No. 2A: 136
Premo Film No. 1: 136
Premo Film-Pack: 136
Premo Film Plate: 136
Premo Film Plate Special: 136
Premo Folding Cartridge No. 2: 136
Premo Folding Cartridge No. 2A: 136
Premo Folding Cartridge No. 2C: 136
Premo Folding Cartridge No. 3: 136
Premo Folding Cartridge No. 3A: 136
Premo Junior No. 0: 136
Premo Junior No. 1: 136
Premo Junior No. 3: 136
Premo Junior No. 4: 136
Premo Pocket: 136
Premo Pocket C: 136
Premo Pony Model A: 137
Premo Pony Model C: 137
Premo Pony Model D: 137
Premo Pony Model E: 137

Premo Pony No. 1: 137
Premo Pony No. 2: 137
Premo Pony No. 3: 137
Premo Pony No. 4: 137
Premo Pony No. 5: 137
Premo Pony No. 6: 137
Premo Pony No. 7: 137
Premo Senior: 137
Premo Senior Special: 136
Premo Star: 137
Premoette No. 1: 137
Premoette No. 1A: 137
Premoette Junior: 137
Premoette Junior No. 1: 137
Premoette Junior No. 1 Special: 137
Premoette Junior No. 1A: 137
Premoette Junior No. 1A Special: 137
Premoette Senior: 137
Pupille: 138
Quick Focus Kodak No. 3B: 138
Rainbow Hawkeye: 126
Recomar No. 18: 138
Recomar No. 33: 138
Reflex: 138
Regent: 139
Retina: 140
Retina I: 140
Retina IA: 140
Retina IB: 140
Retina II: 140
Retina II a: 140
Retina II c: 140
Retina III c: 140
Retina III C: 140
Retina III S: 141
Retina Automatic I: 141
Retina Automatic III: 141
Retina Reflex: 141
Retina Reflex III: 141
Retina Reflex IV: 141
Retina Reflex S: 141
Retinette: 141
Retinette: IA: 141
Retinette II: 141
Screen Focus Kodak No. 4: 142
Signet 30: 142
Signet 35: 142
Signet 35 (military model): 142
Signet 40: 142
Signet 50: 143
Signet 80: 143
Special Kodak No. 1A: 144
Special Kodak No. 3: 144
Special Kodak No. 3A: 144
Speed Kodak No. 1A: 145
Speed Kodak No. 4A: 145
Star Premo: 137
Stereo Brownie: 113
Stereo Hawkeye: 126
Stereo Kodak Model 1: 146
Stereo Kodak No. 2: 146
Stereo Kodak (35mm): 146
Super Kodak Six-20: 146
Target Hawkeye: 126
Tourist: 147
Tourist II: 147
Vanity Kodak: 148
Vanity Kodak Ensemble: 148
Vest Pocket Hawkeye: 126
Vest Pocket Jiffy: 126
Vest Pocket Kodak: 148
Vest Pocket Kodak Autographic: 148
Vest Pocket Kodak Autographic Special: 148
Vest Pocket Kodak Model B: 148
Vest Pocket Kodak Model B Autographic: 148
Vest Pocket Kodak Model B Autographic Special: 148
Vest Pocket Kodak Model B Series III: 148
Vest Pocket Kodak Model B Series III Autographic: 148
View: 149
Vigilant Six-16: 149
Vigilant Six-20: 149

280 / INDEX

Vigilant Junior Six-16: 149
Vigilant Junior Six-20: 149
Vollenda: 150
Vollenda Six-16: 150
Vollenda Six-20: 150
Vollenda Junior Six-20: 150
Weno Hawkeye: 126
World's Fair Flash Camera
 1964-1965: 150
Zenith Kodak No. 3: 150

INDEX E-Z
Easy-Load: 155
Ebner: 151
Ebony (Hoei): 177
Echo 8: 151
Eclipse (Horsman): 178
Eclipse (Shew): 234
Edelweiss (Zenith): 265
Edinex (Wirgin): 255
Edixa (Wirgin): 256
Eho-Altmann Juwel Altissa
 (Hofert): 177
Eho Altiflex (Hofert): 177
Eho Altiscop (Hofert): 177
Eho Box (Hofert): 177
Eho Stereo Box: 177
Eka (Krauss): 192
Ektra: 119
Elaner: 151
Elca (Elop): 151
Electronica (Wirgin Edixa): 256
Elega: 151
Elf (Spiegel): 366
Eljy (Lumiere): 201
Elop Elca: 151
Emmerling & Richter
 Field Camera: 151
Emson: 151
Encore Deluxe: 152
Enolde: 152
Ensemble (Vanity Kodak): 148
Ensign (Houghton): 178
Ensignette (Houghton): 178
Ergo: 92, 261

Erko: 152
Ermanox (Ernemann): 152
Ernemann (Box): 152
Ernemann (Stereo Box): 152
Ernemann Bob O: 152
Ernemann Bob I: 152
Ernemann Bob IV: 152
Ernemann Bobette I: 152
Ernemann Ermanox (Folding): 152
Ernemann Ermanox
 (Non-folding): 152
Ernemann Ernoflex (Folding): 152
Ernemann Ernoflex Simplex
 Stereo: 152
Ernemann Globus: 153
Ernemann Heag Tropical: 153
Ernemann Heag O: 153
Ernemann Heag I: 153
Ernemann Heag II-Series II: 153
Ernemann Heag VII: 153
Ernemann Heag XIV: 153
Ernemann Heag XV: 153
Ernemann Klapp: 153
Ernemann Klapp (Bed-type)
 Tropical: 153
Ernemann Klapp (swing struts)
 Tropical: 154
Ernemann Liliput: 153
Ernemann Liliput Stereo: 153
Ernemann Reflex: 153
Ernemann Reporter: 153
Ernemann Reporter Tropical: 155
Ernemann Rolf: 153
Ernemann Simplex Stereo: 154
Ernemann Tropical Heag: 154
Ernemann Tropical Klapp: 154
Ernemann Tropical Reporter: 155
Ernemann Two-Shuttered: 155
Ernemann Unette: 155
Ernoflex: 152
Errtee (Talbot): 239
Essem: 155
Eulitz Grisette: 155
Euming Eumigetta: 155
Eureka (Eastman): 119

Exa (Ihagee): 185
Exakta (Ihagee): 185
Exco: 155
Explorer (Bolsey): 79
Expo Easy-Load: 155
Expo Police: 155
Expo Watch: 155
Express (Murer): 208
Extra (Sida): 235
Eye-Matic (Revere): 222
Falcon (Eastman): 120
Falcon (Utility): 246
Favorit (Ica): 181
Favorite (Rochester): 224
Feca: 156
Fed No. 1: 156
Fed No. 2: 156
Fed No. 3: 156
Fed No. 4: 156
Fed-Flash: 156
Feinak-Werke (Folding Plate): 156
Feinoptische Astraflex II: 156
Feinwerk Mec 16: 156
Feinwrek Mec 16 SB: 156
Felica: 156
Ferrania Rondine: 157
Fertsch Feca: 156
Fex Ultra: 244
Fiesta (Brownie): 108
Film Pack Hawkeye: 125
Film Pack Premo: 136
Film Plate Premo: 136
Film Premo: 136
Filmet (Seneca): 231
Finetta: 157
Finette: 157
Fingerprint (Burke & James): 82
Fingerprint (Graflex): 170
Firstflex: 157
Flash 20 (Brownie): 108
Flash Bantam: 105
Flash Cadet (Ansco): 62
Flash Clipper (Ansco): 62
Flash Six-20 (Brownie): 108

Flashmite 20 (Brownie): 112
Flat Folding Kodak: 120
Flektar: 157
Flexaret (Meopta): 204
Flexo (Eastman): 120
Flush Back Kodak: 120
Focal Plane Ticka (Houghton): 179
Foinix: 157
Foitzik Trier Foinix: 157
Foitzik Trier Unca: 157
Foldex (Photak): 214
Folding Ansco: 65
Folding Ascot: 66
Folding Autographic Brownie: 109
Folding Brownie: 108
Folding Bulls-Eye: 115
Folding Buster Brown: 62
Folding Cartridge Hawkeye: 125
Folding Cartridge Premo: 136
Folding Film Pack Hawkeye: 125
Folding Hawkeye (Blair): 77
Folding Hawkeye (Eastman): 125
Folding Klito: 178
Folding Kodak: 120
Folding Kodak
   (Satchel-style): 120-121
Folding Kodet: 127
Folding Montauk: 162
Folding Pocket Ansco: 65
Folding Pocket Brownie: 108
Folding Pocket Kodak: 132
Folding Rainbow Hawkeye: 126
Folmer & Schwing: 157
Fornidar (Nagel 30): 209
Foth Derby Model I: 158
Foth Derby Model II: 158
Foth Folding Rollfilm 1A: 158
Foth-Flex: 158
Foto-Disc (ASR): 62
Foto-Flex: 158
Fotochrome Color Camera: 158
Foton (Bell & Howell): 73
Fotron (Traid): 243

Francia (Mackenstein): 201
Franka Rolfix: 158
Franka Solida: 158
Franke & Heidecke Heidoscop: 158
Franke & Heidecke Rollei 16: 158
Franke & Heidecke Rollei 35: 159
Franke & Heidecke Rolleicord I: 159
Franke & Heidecke Rolleicord Ia: 159
Franke & Heidecke Rolleicord II: 159
Franke & Heidecke Rolleicord III: 159
Franke & Heidecke Rolleicord IV: 159
Franke & Heidecke Rolleicord V: 159
Franke & Heidecke Rolleidoscop: 159
Franke & Heidecke Rolleiflex 4x4: 159
Franke & Heidecke Rolleiflex (Original): 159
Franke & Heidecke Rolleiflex Sport: 160
Franke & Heidecke Rolleiflex Standard: 159
Franke & Heidecke Rolleimagic: 160
Franke & Heidecke Rolleimagic II: 160
Frena (Beck): 72
FT-2: 160
Fuji Lyra: 160
Fuji Lyra Semi: 160
Fuji Mini: 160
Futura S: 160
Galileo Condor I: 160
Galileo Gami-16: 160
Gallus: 160
Galter Hopalong Cassidy: 161
Gamma: 161
Gami: 161
Garland (Wet Plate): 161
Gaumont Block-Notes: 161
Gaumont Block-Notes Stereo: 161
Gaumont Spido Stereo: 161
Gaumont Stereo: 61
Gelto (Takahashi): 239
Gem (Wing): 255
Gem Poco (Rochester): 225
Gemflex: 161
Genie: 161
Gennert Montauk (Detective plate box): 161
Gennert Montauk (Rollfilm): 162

Gennery Montauk Folding: 162
Gennert Penny Picture: 162
Genos Rapid: 162
Gevabox: 162
Gevaert: 162
Gewirette (Wirgin): 256
Gift Kodak: 124
Gilles-Faller Studio camera: 162
Girl Scout (Herco): 176
Girl Scout (Utility): 246
Girl Scout Kodak: 124
Global: 162
Globus (Ernemann): 153
Gloriette (Braun): 80
Glunz (Folding Plate): 163
Glunz (Folding Rollfilm): 163
Glyphoscope (Richard): 223
Goeker Field camera: 163
Goerz (Folding Rollfilm): 164
Goerz Ango: 163
Goerz Ango Stereo: 163
Goerz Anschutz: 163
Goerz Anschutz Stereo: 163
Goerz Folding Reflex: 164
Goerz Minicord: 164
Goerz Minicord III: 164
Goerz Minicord IV: 164
Goerz Stereo Photo Binocle: 164
Goerz Tenax (Folding Plate): 165
Goerz Tenax (Rollfilm): 165
Goerz Tenax Coat Pocket: 164
Goerz Tenax Manufok: 165
Goerz Tenax Stereo: 165
Goerz Tenax Vest Pocket (Plates): 164
Goerz Tenax Vest Pocket (Rollfilm): 164
Goerz Tengor: 165
Goldeck-16: 165
Golden Ricoh 16 (Riken): 223
Golden Steky (Riken): 223
Goldi: 165
Goldmann Field: 165
Goldmann Press: 165
Golf (Adox): 58
Golz & Breutmann Mentor II: 166

Golz & Breutmann Mentor Compur Reflex: 166
Goltz & Breutmann Mentor Dreivier: 166
Goltz & Breutmann Mentor Folding Reflex: 166
Goltz & Breutmann Mentor Klein: 167
Goltz & Breutmann Mentor Reflex: 166
Goltz & Breutmann Mentor Stereo Reflex: 166
Goltz & Breutmann Mentorett: 167
Goodwin (Ansco): 63
Graflex IA: 167
Graflex 3A: 167
Graflex 22: 167
Graflex Auto: 168
Graflex Auto Junior: 168
Graflex Auto R.B.: 168
Graflex Auto Stereo: 170
Graflex Century 35: 167
Graflex Century Graphic: 172
Graflex Century Universal View: 167
Graflex Ciro 35: 167
Graflex Compact: 168
Graflex Fingerprint: 170
Graflex Graphic No. 0: 171
Graflex Graphic 35: 173
Graflex Graphic Century: 167
Graflex Graphic Combat: 168
Graflex Graphic Crown Pacemaker: 172
Graflex Graphic R.B. Cycle: 168
Graflex Graphic Speed (pre-anniversary): 172
Graflex Graphic Speed Anniversary: 172
Graflex Graphic Speed Pacemaker: 172
Graflex Graphic Stereo: 172
Graflex Graphic Stereo (35mm): 172
Graflex Graphic Super: 122
Graflex Graphic View: 172
Graflex Home Portrait R.B.: 170
Graflex Inspectograph Fingerprint: 170
Graflex National Series I: 170
Graflex National Series II: 170
Graflex Naturalist's: 170
Graflex Pacemaker Crown Graphic: 172
Graflex Pacemaker Speed Graphic: 172
Graflex Press: 170
Graflex R.B. Auto: 168
Graflex R.B. Cycle Graphic: 171
Graflex R.B. Home Portrait: 170
Graflex R.B. Series B: 169
Graflex R.B. Series C: 169
Graflex R.B. Series D: 169
Graflex R.B. Super D: 169
Graflex Series B: 168
Graflex Speed Graphic: 172
Graflex Stereo Auto: 170
Graflex Stereo Graphic: 172
Graflex Super Graphic: 172
Graflex Tele-Graflex: 171
Graphic: 171, 172, 173
Gray: 173
Griffiths (Magazine): 173
Grisette (Eulitz): 155
Grover (Burke & James): 81
Gundlach Korona: 173
Gundlach Korona Banquet: 173
Gundlach Korona Petit: 173
Gundlach Korona Stereo: 173
Gundlach Korona View: 173
Guthe & Thorsch (Folding Plate): 174
Guthe & Thorsch Kawee: 174
Guthe & Thorsch Patent Etui: 173
Guthe & Thorsch Patent Etui Deluxe: 173
Guthe & Thorsch Pilot 6: 174
Guthe & Thorsch Pilot Reflex: 174
Guthe & Thorsch Pilot Super: 174
Guthe & Thorsch Prakti: 174
Guthe & Throsch Praktica: 174
Guthe & Throsch Praktica FX: 174
Guthe & Throsch Praktica Nova: 174
Guthe & Throsch Praktiflex: 174
Guthe & Throsch Praktiflex FX: 174
Guthe & Throsch Praktiflex II: 174
Guthe & Throsch Praktina IIa: 174
Guthe & Throsch Praktisix: 174
Guthe & Throsch Reflex Box: 174
Guthe & Throsch Rival Reflex: 174
Hadds Mfg. Co. Foto-Flex: 158
Haking Halina: 174
Halina: 174

Halloh (Ica): 181
Hamco: 175
Handy (Rochester): 224
Haneel Tri-Vision Stereo: 175
Hapo (Photo-Porst): 215
Happi-Time: 175
Happy: 175
Harboe: 175
Hare Stereo: 175
Hare Tourist: 175
Harmony: 175
Harvard (Mason): 203
Hawkette: 125
Hawkeye (Blair): 76, 77, 78
Hawkeye (Boston): 80
Hawkeye (Brownie): 111
Hawkeye (Eastman): 125, 126
Heag (Ernemann): 153, 154
Heidoscop (Franke & Heidecke): 158
Heli-Clack (Rietzschel): 221
Helios (Hüttig): 180
Hemax: 176
Henry Clay (American Optical Co.) 61
Herbert-George Co. (Herco): 176
Herco Boy Scout: 176
Herco Brownie Scout: 176
Herco Cub Scout: 176
Herco Donald Duck: 176
Herco Girl Scout: 176
Herco Imperial: 176
Herco Imperial Reflex: 176
Herco Imperial Satellite Flash: 176
Herco Official Boy Scout: 176
Herco Official Brownie Scout: 176
Herco Official Cub Scout: 176
Herco Official Girl Scout: 176
Herco Roy Rogers & Trigger: 176
Herlango: 176
Hermagis Velocigraphe: 176
Hess-Ives Hicro Color Camera: 176
Hetherington & Hibben
   Magazine: 177
Hexacon: 177
Hicro Color Camera: 176
Highlander (Polaroid 80): 217
Hit: 177
Hit Stereo: 177
Hoei Ebony 35: 177

Hofert Eho Altiflex: 177
Hofert Eho-Altmann Juwel
   Altissa: 177
Hofert Eho Box: 177
Hofert Eho Stereo Box: 177
Holiday (Brownie): 111
Hollywood Reflex: 173
Hollywood: 177
Hologon (Zeiss): 261
Home Portrait Graflex: 170
Homeos (Richard): 223
Homer 16: 178
Hopalong Cassidy (Galter): 161
Horizont: 178
Horsman Eclipse No. 3: 178
Houghton Cupid: 178
Houghton Ensign (Box): 178
Houghton Ensign Folding
   Rollfilm: 178
Houghton Ensign All-Distance: 178
Houghton Ensign Autorange 220: 178
Houghton Ensign Popular Reflex: 179
Houghton Ensign Reflex: 179
Houghton Ensign Roll Film
   Reflex: 179
Houghton Ensignette No. 1: 178
Houghton Ensignette No. 2: 178
Houghton Klito: 178
Houghton Klito Folding: 178
Houghton May Fair: 178
Houghton Midget: 178
Houghton Selfix 16-20: 179
Houghton Ticka: 179
Houghton Ticka Focal Plane: 179
Houghton Ticka Enlarger: 179
Huckelberry Hound: 179
Hunter Purma Special: 179
Hurlbut Velox Magazine: 180
Hüttig (Folding Plate): 180
Hüttig (Magazine): 180
Hüttig Atom: 180
Hüttig Helios: 180
Hüttig Ideal: 180
Hüttig Ideal Stereo: 180
Hüttig Lloyd: 180
Hüttig Monopol: 180
Hüttig Record Stereo: 180

INDEX / 285

Hüttig Stereolette: 180
Hüttig Tropical Plate: 180
Ica (Folding Plate): 181
Ica Artist's Reflex: 183
Ica Atom Horizontal format: 180
Ica Atom Vertical format: 181
Ica Bebe: 181
Ica Cameo Stereo: 181
Ica Cupido: 181
Ica Favorit 425: 181
Ica Halloh 505: 181
Ica Halloh 510: 181
Ica Halloh 511: 181
Ica Icar: 181
Ica Icarette A: 181
Ica Icarette C: 181
Ica Icarette D: 181
Ica Icarette L: 181
Ica Ideal: 182
Ica Ideal Stereo 651: 183
Ica Ideal Stereo 660: 183
Ica Juwel Universal: 182
Ica Lloyd Stereo: 182
Ica Maximar: 182
Ica Minimal: 182
Ica Minimum Palmos: 182
Ica Nelson 225: 182
Ica Nero: 182
Ica Niklas: 182
Ica Nixe: 182
Ica Palmos Minimum: 182
Ica Periscop: 183
Ica Plascop: 183
Ica Polyscop: 183
Ica Reflex: 183
Ica Sirene: 183
Ica Stereo 610: 183
Ica Stereo Ideal 651: 183
Ica Stereo Ideal 660: 183
Ica Stereolette: 183
Ica Stereolette Cupido 620: 183
Ica Teddy: 183
Ica Toska: 184
Ica Trilby 18: 184
Ica Trix: 184
Ica Trona: 184
Ica Tropica 285: 184
Ica Tudor Reflex: 183
Ica Universal Juwel: 182
Ica Victrix 48: 184
Icar: 181
Icarette: 181, 261
Ideal (Burke & James): 81
Ideal (Huttig): 180
Ideal (Ica): 182
Ideal (Rochester): 224
Ideal (Zeiss): 261
Ideal Kookie Kamera: 184
Ideal Sibyl (Newman & Guardia): 210
Ihagee Auto Ultrix: 186
Ihagee Cameo Ultrix: 186
Ihagee Duplex: 184
Ihagee Duplex Two-Shuttered: 184
Ihagee Exa I: 185
Ihagee Exa I a: 185
Ihagee Exa II: 185
Ihagee Exa II a: 185
Ihagee Exa II b: 185
Ihagee Exakta 66
  (Horizontal): 185, 186
Ihagee Exakta 66 (Vertical): 186
Ihagee Exakta A: 185
Ihagee Exakta B: 185
Ihagee Exakta C: 185
Ihagee Exakta II: 185
Ihagee Exakta V: 185
Ihagee Exakta VX: 185
Ihagee Exakta VX IIA: 185
Ihagee Exakta Junior: 185
Ihagee Exakta Night: 185
Ihagee Folding Plate Camera: 186
Ihagee Folding Rollfilm Camera: 186
Ihagee Kine Exakta: 185
Ihagee Night Exakta: 185
Ihagee Paff: 186
Ihagee Parvola: 186
Ihagee Patent Klapp Reflex: 186
Ihagee Stereo: 186
Ihagee Ultrix Auto: 186
Ihagee Ultrix Cameo: 186
Ihagee Ultrix Weeny: 186
Ikko-Sha Start-35: 186
Ikoflex (Zeiss): 261

286 / INDEX

Ikomat (Zeiss): 262
Ikonette (Zeiss): 262
Ikonta (Zeiss): 262
Iloca (Witt): 256
Imperial (Herco): 176
Ingento (Burke & James): 81
Inos (Voigtländer): 250
Inspectograph (Graflex): 170
Instantograph (Lancaster): 194
Iris (Universal): 244
Irwin Kandor: 187
Irwin Reflex: 187
Iso (Agfa): 58
Iso Duplex: 187
Isoflash (Agfa): 58
Isolar (Agfa): 58
Isolette (Agfa): 58
Isomat (Agfa): 58
J33 (Polaroid): 217
J66 (Polaroid): 217
Japy Pascal: 187
Jeanneret Monobloc: 187
Jem Jr.: 187
Jiffy Kodak: 126
Jos-Pe Tri-Color: 187
Joux Alethoscope: 187
Joux Ortho Jumelle Duplex: 187
Jubilar (Voigtländer): 250
Jubilee (Bolsey): 79
Jubilette (Balda): 71
Jumelle (Bellieni): 74
Jumelle (Carpentier): 85
Jumelle (Demaria): 96
Jumelle (Gallus): 160
Jumelle (Joux): 187
Jumelle (Krugener): 193
Jumelle (Mackenstein): 201
Jumelle (Papigny): 213
Jumelle (Roussel): 227
Juwel (Ica): 182
Juwella (Balda): 71
Kalart Press: 188
Kalimar A: 188
Kalloflex (Kowa): 191
Kamaret (Blair): 78
Kameret Jr. No. 2: 188
Kamrex (Lancaster): 194
Kandor (Irwin): 187
Karat (Agfa): 58
Kardon (Premier): 218
Karma (Arnold): 69
Karmaflex (Arnold): 69
Karomat (Agfa): 58
Karomat (Ansco): 63
Kawee (Guthe): 174
Kemper Kombi: 188
Kenflex: 188
Kenngott (Plate): 188
Kenngott (Plate) Tropical: 189
Kent: 189
Kewpie (Conley): 90
Key Stereo Products Trivision: 189
Keystone Street Camera: 189
Kiev: 189
Kilfitt Mecaflex: 189
Kinax: 190
Kinder Kindar Stereo: 189
Kine Exakta (Ihagee): 185
King Camera (Japan): 190
King Camera (Metropolitan Supply Co.): 204
King Poco (Rochester): 225
King Regula: 189
King Regula B: 189
King Regula I: 189
King Regula IIID: 189
King Regula KG: 189
King Regula PD: 189
Kinn Kinax: 190
Kirk Stereo Model 33: 190
Kiyabashi Autoflex: 190
Klapp (Ernemann): 153
Klapp-Reflex (Ihagee Patent): 186
Kleffel Field: 190
Klein-Edinex (Wirgin): 256
Klein-Mentor (Goltz & Breutmann): 167
Klimax (Butcher): 83
Klito (Houghton): 178
Klondike (Anthony): 66
Knack (Scovill): 229
Kochmann Korelle K: 190
Kochmann Korelle P: 191

Kochmann Korelle (Rollfilm): 191
Kochmann Korelle Master: 191
Kochmann Korelle Meister: 191
Kochmann Korelle Reflex: 191
Kodak (Eastman): 99-150
Kodak (Original): 99
Kodak-35: 146
Kodak Reflex: 138
Kodak Six-16: 143
Kodak Six-20: 144
Kodet: 127, 128
Kola: 191
Kolibri (Zeiss): 263
Komaflex: 191
Kombi (Kemper): 188
Konan (Chiyodo): 87
Konica:
Konishiroku Konica: 191
Konishiroku Konica II: 191
Konishiroku Konica III: 191
Konishiroku Pearl Baby: 191
Konishiroku Pearl II: 191
Konishiroku Pearlette: 192
Konishiroku Semi-Pearl: 192
Kookie Kamera (Ideal): 184
Korelle (Kochmann): 190, 191
Korona (Gundlach): 173
Kosmo-Clack (Rietzschel): 222
Kowa Kalloflex: 192
Krauss Eka: 192
Krauss Peggy I: 192
Krauss Peggy II: 193
Krauss Photo Revolver: 193
Krauss Polyscop: 193
Krauss Rollette: 193
Krauss Takyr: 193
Krugener Delta (Folding Plate): 193
Krugener Delta (magazine): 193
Krugener Delta Periskop: 193
Krugener Jumelle-style Magazine
 camera: 193
Krugener Simplex Magazine: 193
Kullenberg Field: 194
Kunick Petie: 194
Kunick Tuxi: 194
Kunick Tuximat: 194

INDEX / 287

KW (Folding Plate): 174
KW Kawee: 174
KW Patent Etui: 173
KW Patent Etui Deluxe: 173
KW Pilot 6: 174
KW Pilot Reflex: 174
KW Pilot Super: 174
KW Prakti: 174
KW Praktica: 174
KW Praktica FX: 174
KW Praktica Nova: 174
KW Praktiflex: 174
KW Praktiflex FX: 174
KW Praktiflex II: 174
KW Praktina IIa: 174
KW Praktisix: 174
KW Reflex Box: 174
KW Rival Reflex: 223
Kurbi & Niggeloh Bilora Bella: 194
Kurbi & Niggeloh Bilora Blitz Boy: 194
Kurbi & Niggeloh Bilora Boy: 194
Kurbi & Niggeloh Bilora Radix: 194
Laack Padie: 194
Ladies Camera (Lancaster): 194
Lamperti & Garbagnati (Detective): 194
Lancaster Instantograph: 194
Lancaster Kamrex: 194
Lancaster Ladies Camera: 194
Lancaster Merveilleux: 194
Lancer (Ansco): 63
Lehmann Ben Akiba (cane handle
 camera): 195
Leica (Leitz): 195-198
Leidolf Leidox II: 195
Leidolf Lordomat: 195
Leidolf Lordomatic: 195
Leidolf Lordox: 195
Leidox: 195
Leitz Leica 250 Reporter (FF): 196
Leitz Leica 250 Reporter (GG): 196
Leitz Leica I (A) Anastigmat lens: 195
Leitz Leica I (A) Elmar lens: 195
Leitz Leica I (A) Elmax lens: 195
Leitz Leica I (A) Luxus: 198
Leitz Leica I (A) Luxus Replica: 198
Leitz Leica I (B) Dial-set Compur: 195

Leitz Leica I (B) Rim-set Compur: 195
Leitz Leica I (C) Non-standard
 mount: 196
Leitz Leica I (C) Standard mount: 196
Leitz Leica I c: 197
Leitz Leica I f: 197
Leitz Leica I g: 198
Leitz Leica II (D) Black Body: 196
Leitz Leica II (D) Chrome Body: 196
Leitz Leica II c: 197
Leitz Leica II f Black Dial: 197
Leitz Leica II f Red Dial: 197
Leitz Leica III (F) Black Body: 196
Leitz Leica III (F) Chrome Body; 196
Leitz Leica III a (G): 196
Leitz Leica III a (G)
 Monte en Sarre: 197
Leitz Leica III b (G): 197
Leitz Leica III c: 197
Leitz Leica III c K-Model: 197
Leitz Leica III C. Luftwaffe: 197
Leitz Leica III c Wehrmacht: 197
Leitz Leica III f Black Dial: 197
Leitz Leica III f Red Dial: 197
Leitz Leica III f Red Dial
 w/self-timer: 197
Leitz Leica III g: 197
Leitz Leica III g Swedish
 Crown Model: 197
Leitz Leica M2: 198
Leitz Leica M3 Double-
 stroke advance: 198
Leitz Leica M3 Single-
 stroke advance: 198
Leitz Leica Single-Shot: 198
Leitz Leica Standard (E): 196
Leitz Ur-Leica (Replica): 195
Leningrad: 198
Lenz: 198
Leonar: 198
Leotax (Showa): 234
Lerochrome (National Photocolor): 209
Leroy-Minimus: 198
Leroy Stereo Panoramique: 198
Leullier Summum Special: 198
Levy-Roth Minigraph: 198
Lewis Wet Plate camera: 198

Liebe Monobloc: 199
Life-O-Rama III: 199
Lightning (Benetfink): 199
Liliput (Ernemann): 153
Lilliput Detective: 199
Linex (Lionel): 199
Linhof Silar: 199
Linhof Stereo Panorama: 199
Linhof Technika I: 199
Lionel Linex Stereo: 199
Lipca Rollop: 199
Little Wonder: 199
Lizars Challenge: 199
Lizars Challenge Dayspool: 199
Lizars Challenge Dayspool
 Tropical: 200
Lizars Challenge Stereo Model I-B: 200
Lizars Challenge Stereo Model B: 200
Lloyd (Hüttig): 180
Lloyd (Ica): 182
Lloyd (Andrew J. & Co.)
 Box camera: 200
Loeber (Folding Plate): 200
Loisir: 200
London Stereoscopic Tailboard
 Stereo: 200
London Stereoscopic Wet Plate
 camera: 200
Long Focus Premo (Rochester): 226
Lordomat (Leidolf): 195
Lordomatic (Leidolf): 195
Lordox (Leidolf): 195
Lubitel: 200
Lucidograph (Blair): 78
Lumiere Box No. 49: 201
Lumiere Eljy: 201
Lumiere Luminor: 201
Lumiere Lumix F: 201
Lumiere Sinox: 201
Lumiere Sterelux: 201
Luminor: 201
Lumix: 201
Lundelius Magazine camera: 201
Lure: 201
Luttke & Arndt Folding Plate: 201
Luttke & Arndt Folding Rollfilm: 201
Lynx (Pontiac): 218

Lyra (Fuji): 160
Mackenstein Francia: 201
Mackenstein Stereo Jumelle: 201
Macris-Boucher Nil Melior: 201
Madison I: 201
Magic Introduction Co. Photoret Watch: 202
Major (Agfa): 59
Makina (Plaubel): 216
Mamiya 6: 202
Mamiya 16: 202
Mamiyaflex: 202
Mandel (Chicago Ferrotyp Co.): 87
Mandelette (Chicago Ferrotype Co.): 87
Manhattan Bo-Peep: 202
Manhattan Bo-Peep B: 202
Manhattan Night-Hawk Detective: 202
Manhattan Wizard A: 202
Manhattan Wizard B: 202
Manhattan Wizard Baby: 202
Manhattan Wizard Cycle: 202
Manhattan Wizard Cycle Long Focus: 202
Manhattan Wizard Junior: 202
Manhattan Wizard Senior: 202
Manhattan Wizard Senior Long-Focus: 202
Manhattan Wizard Wide Angle: 202
Manufok Tenax: 165
Marion Perfection: 202
Marion Soho Reflex: 202
Marion Soho Reflex Tropical: 203
Mark II Stereo (Sawyers): 228
Mark IV (Sawyers): 228
Markfinder (Argus): 69
Mars (Wunsche): 257
Marvel (Putnam): 219
Marvelflex: 203
Mascot (Scovill): 229
Mason Harvard: 203
Master Korelle: 191
Match-Matic (Argus C3): 68
Maximar: 182, 263
May Fair (Houghton): 178
Mazo Field Camera: 203
McBean Stereo Tourist: 203
Mec (Feinwerk Technik): 156

Mecaflex (Kilfitt): 189
Medalist (Eastman): 128
Meister Korelle: 191
Meisuppii: 203
Memo (Agfa): 59
Memo (Ansco): 63
Mendel (Detective): 203
Mentor (Goltz): 166
Mentorett (Goltz): 167
Meopta Flexaret: 204
Meopta Mikroma: 204
Meopta Mikroma II: 204
Meopta Mikroma Stereo: 204
Mercury (Universal): 244, 245
Meridian: 204
Merit: 204
Merveilleux (Lancaster): 194
Meteor (Universal): 245
Metropolitan Supply Co. King: 204
Metropolitan Supply Co. MF Stereo: 204
MF Stereo: 204
Mick-A-Matic: 204
Micro: 204
Micro 16 (Whittaker): 255
Midas: 204
Midg (Butcher): 83
Midget (Coronet): 94
Midget (Houghton): 178
Mighty (Tokyo Shashin): 242
Mikado: 204
Mikroma (Meopta): 204
Mikut Color Camera: 204
Mimosa I: 205
Mimosa II: 205
Minetta: 205
Minex (Adams): 57
Mini (Fuji): 160
Minicord (Goerz): 164
Minigraph (Levy-Roth): 198
Minimal (Ica): 182
Minimum Palmos: 182, 264
Minimus (Leroy): 198
Minolta 16: 205
Minolta 16-EE: 205
Minolta 16-EE-II: 205

290 / INDEX

Minolta 16-11: 205
Minolta 16-MG: 205
Minolta 16-P: 205
Minolta 16-PS: 205
Minolta 16-QT: 205
Minolta 35: 205
Minolta 35 Model F: 205
Minolta 35 Model I: 205
Minolta 35 Model II: 205
Minolta 35 Model IIB: 205
Minolta A: 205
Minolta A2: 205
Minolta A5: 205
Minolta Auto Semi-Minolta: 205
Minolta Autocord: 205
Minolta Semi-Minolta: 205
Minolta Semi-Minolta Auto: 205
Minolta Six: 205
Minoltacord: 205
Minox (Original): 206
Minox (Made in USSR): 206
Minox A: 206
Minox B: 206
Minox II: 206
Minox III: 206
Minox III Gold Plated: 206
Minox III-S: 206
Minute 16 (Universal): 245
Miranda G: 206
Miroflex: 92, 260
Mirror Reflex (Hall): 174
Mitsukoshi Picny: 206
Moller Cambinox: 206
Momehm (Moment): 206
Moment: 206
Monitor (Eastman): 128, 129
Monobloc (Jeanneret): 187
Monobloc (Liebe): 199
Monopol (Hüttig): 180
Monroe Model 7: 207
Monroe Pocket: 207
Monroe Pocket Poco A: 207
Monroe Vest Pocket: 207
Montanus Montiflex: 207
Montauk (Gennert): 161
Monte (Monti): 207

Monte Carlo (Monti): 207
Montgomery Ward Model B: 207
Montgomery Ward Wardflex: 207
Monti Monte-35: 207
Monti Monte Carlo: 207
Montiflex (Montanus): 207
Moore Aptus Ferrotype: 207
Moscow-4: 207
Moscow-5: 207
Motormatic (Eastman): 129
Multiplying View (Wing): 255
Multiprint (Buess): 81
Multiscope & Film Co. Al-Vista
 Panoramic Model 4B: 207, 208
Multiscope & Film Co. Al-Vista
 Panoramic Model 5B: 208
Multiscope & Film Co. Al-Vista
 Panoramic Model 5D: 208
Multiscope & Film Co. Al-Vista
 Panoramic Model 5F: 208
Murer (Folding Plate): 208
Murer Express: 208
Murer Reflex: 208
Murer Stereo: 208
Muro (Suter): 239
Mycro (Sugaya): 238
Myracle (Sugaya): 238
Negel 18 (Recomar): 208
Nagel 30 (Fornidar): 209
Nagel 33 (Recomar): 209
Nagel Junior: 129
Nagel Pupille: 138, 209
Nagel Ranca: 209
Nagel Recomar 33: 209
Nagel Regent: 209
Nagel Vollenda: 209
National Camera Folding Field
 camera: 209
National Graflex: 170
National Photocolor One-Shot
 (Lerochrome): 209
Naturalist's Graflex: 170
Nelson (Ica): 182
Nero (Ica): 182
Nescon-35: 209
Nettar (Zeiss): 263

Nettax (Zeiss): 263
Nettel (Zeiss): 263
Nettel (Folding Plate): 210
Nettel Argus: 209
Nettel Deckrullo: 209
Nettel Sonnet Tropical: 210
New Gem (Wing): 255
New Ideal Sibyl (Newman
 & Guardia): 210
New Ideas (Magazine): 210
New Special Sibyl (Newman
 & Guardia): 210
New York Ferrotype Co. (Tintype): 210
Newman & Guardia (Magazine): 210
Newman & Guardia Folding
 Reflex: 210
Newman & Guardia Sibyl: 210
Newman & Guardia Sibyl Baby: 210
Newman & Guardia
 Sibyl Deluxe: 210
Newman & Guardia
 Sibyl New Ideal: 210
Newman & Guardia Sibyl
 New Special: 210
Newman & Guardia Special
 (Magazine Box): 211
Nic (Contessa): 93
Nicca III: 211
Nicca IIIS: 211
Night Exakta (Ihagee): 185
Night-Hawk (Manhattan): 202
Night Kolibri (Zeiss): 263
Nikkorex: 211
Niklas (Ica): 182
Nil Melior (Macris): 201
Nikon F: 211
Nikon Nikkorex: 211
Nikon S: 211
Nikon S2: 211
Nikon S3: 211
Nikon SP: 211
Nishida Westar: 211
Nitor (Agfa): 59
Nixe: 182, 263
Nodark Tintype (Popular
 Photograph Co.): 218
Nomar No. I: 211
Normandie (Anthony): 66

Norris: 211
Norton (Universal): 245
Novelette (Anthony): 66
Noviflex: 211
Official Boy Scout (Herco): 176
Official Brownie Scout (Herco): 176
Official Cub Scout (Herco): 176
Official Girl Scout (Herco): 176
Official Boy Scout Memo: 63
Okam: 211
Olympus Olympus 35: 212
Olympus Pen: 212
Olympus Pen D: 212
Olympus Pen F: 212
Olympus Pen FT: 212
Omega (Simmon): 235
Ompex-16: 212
Onito: 93, 264
Ontobloc (Cornu): 93
Ontoflex (Cornu): 93
Opema: 212
Optima (Agfa): 59
Ordinary Kodak: 130
Orion (Box): 212
Orion (Folding Plate): 212
Orion Rio Tropical: 212
Orix (Zeiss): 264
Ortho Jumelle Duplex (Joux): 187
Owla Stereo: 212
Pacemaker Crown Graphic: 172
Pacemaker Speed Graphic: 172
Padie (Laack): 194
Paff (Ihagee): 186
Palmer & Longking Daguerreotype
 camera (bellows type): 213
Palmos: 182, 264
Panda (Ansco): 63
Panoram Kodak: 130
Papigny Jumelle Stereo: 213
Parvola (Ihagee): 186
Pascal (Japy): 187
Patent (Magazine box camera): 213
Patent Etui (Guthe): 173
Patent Klapp Reflex (Ihagee): 186
Patent Novelette (Anthony): 66
Patent Reflex Hand Camera
 (Reflex Camera Co.): 221

Pathfinder (Polaroid 110): 217
Pax (Braun): 81
Paxette (Braun): 81
Paxina (Braun): 81
PD-16 (Agfa): 59
PDQ (Anthony): 67
PDQ (Chicago Ferrotype Co.): 87
Pearl (Konishiroku): 191, 192
Pearlette (Konishiroku): 192
Pecto (Columbia): 89
Peerflekta: 213
Peggy (Krauss): 192, 193
Pen (Olympus): 212
Penny Picture (Gennert): 162
Pentacon: 213
Pentacon Contax FB: 213
Pentacon F: 213
Pentacon FB: 213
Pentacon FBM: 213
Pentacon Penti: 213
Pentcon Werra: 214
Penti: 213
Perfection (Marion): 202
Perfekta (Welta): 253
Perfex (Candid): 84
Periflex (Corfield): 93
Periscop (Krugener): 193
Periskop (Ica): 183
Perka: 214
Perken (Studio): 214
Perkeo (Voigtländer): 251
Perle (Welta): 253
Petal (Sakura): 228
Petie (Kunick): 194
Petit Korona (Gundlach): 173
Petitax: 214
Petite (Eastman): 131
Petri: 214
Photak Foldex: 214
Phoba Diva: 214
Photak (Chicago Camera Co.): 87
Photavit: 79, 214
Photina: 215
Photo Binocle (Goerz): 164
Photo Button Machine (Chicago Ferrotype Co.): 87
Photo Master: 215

Photo Postcard (Daydark): 95
Photo Revolver (Krauss): 193
Photo See: 215
Photo Vanity (Ansco): 63
Photo-Jumelle (Carpentier): 85
Photo-Porst Hapo 35: 215
Photo-Porst Hapo 36: 215
Photo-Porst Hapo 66: 215
Photographe de Poche (Dubroni): 98
Photolet: 215
Photoret (Magic Introduction Co.): 202
Photoscopic: 215
Photosphere (Compagnie Francaise): 89
Photrix Quick B: 215
Piccochic (Balda): 71
Piccolette: 93, 264
Picny (Mitsukoshi): 206
Pignons Alpa 6: 216
Pignons Alpa 9d: 216
Pignons Alpa Alnea 7: 215
Pignons Alpa Reflex (Original): 216
Pignons Bolsey: 216
Pilot (Guthe): 174
Pinetta: 216
Pioneer (Ansco): 63
Pipon (Magazine): 216
Pipon Self-Worker: 216
Pittsburgh Camera Corp. Ulca: 216
Pixie (Whittaker): 255
Planovista (Bentzin): 74
Plascop (Ica): 183
Plasmat Roland: 226
Platos Pocket: 216
Plaubel (Folding Plate): 216
Plaubel Makina: 216
Plaubel Makina II: 216
Plaubel Makina III: 217
Plaubel Makina Stereo: 217
Plaubel Rollop: 217
Plenax (Agfa): 59
Plenax (Ansco): 63
Pocket Kodak: 131
Pocket Monroe: 207
Pocket Platos: 216
Pocket Poco (Monroe): 207

Pocket Poco (Rochester): 224
Pocket Premo (Kodak): 136
Pocket Z (Zion): 265
Pockette (Simplex): 235
Poco (Rochester): 224, 225
Poka (Balda): 71
Polaroid J33: 217
Polaroid J66: 217
Polaroid Model 80 (Highlander): 217
Polaroid Model 80 A (Highlander): 217
Polaroid Model 80 B: 217
Polaroid Model 95 (Speedliner): 217
Polaroid Model 95 A (Speedliner): 217
Polaroid Model 95 B (Speedliner): 217
Polaroid Model 100: 217
Polaroid Model 110 (Pathfinder): 217
Polaroid Model 110 A (Pathfinder): 217
Polaroid Model 110 B (Pathfinder): 217
Polaroid Model 150: 217
Polaroid Model 180: 217
Polaroid Model 210: 217
Polaroid Model 800: 218
Polaroid Model 900: 218
Polaroid SX-70 Deluxe (Original): 217
Police Camera: 155
Polyscop (Ica): 183
Polyscop (Krauss): 193
Pontiac Folding: 218
Pontiac Lnyx: 218
Pontura (Balda): 71
Pony (Eastman): 135
Pony Premo (Eastman): 137
Pony Premo (Rochester): 225
Popular Photograph Co. Nodark Tintype: 218
Popular Pressman (SLR); 218
Post Card Machine (Chicago Ferrotype Co.): 87
Pouva Start: 218
Prakti (Guthe): 174
Praktica (Guthe): 174
Praktiflex (Guthe): 174
Praktina (Guthe): 174
Praktisix (Guthe): 174
Precisa (Beier): 72
Premier (Blair): 78
Premier (Rochester): 225
Premier Kardon Civilian Model: 218
Premier Kardon Military Model: 218
Premium (Plate Box): 218
Premo (Eastman): 135, 136, 137
Premo (Rochester): 225, 226
Premoette (Eastman): 137
Press Graflex: 170
Pressman (Busch): 82
Primar (Bentzin): 74
Primarflex: 75
Primo (Tokyo Kogaku): 242
Prominent (Voigtländer): 250
Puck (Thornton-Pickard): 241
Pupille: 138, 209
Purma Special: 179
Putnam Marvel: 219
Pygmee (Carmen): 85
Q.P.: 219
QRS Kamra: 97
Quad (Close & Cone): 88
Quick B (Photrix): 215
Quick Focus Kodak: 138
Raaco: 219
Radix (Kurbi & Niggeloh): 194
Rainbow Hawkeye: 126
Rajar No. 6: 219
Ranca (Nagel): 209
Rapide (Yashica): 257
Ray (Box): 220
Ray Ray No. 1: 219
Ray Ray No. 2: 219
Ray Ray Jr.: 219
RB Auto Graflex: 168
RB Cycle Graphic: 171
RB Graflex Series B: 169
RB Graflex Series C. 169
RB Graflex Series D: 169
RB Graflex Super D: 169
Readyflash (Ansco): 63
Readyset (Agfa): 59
Readyset (Ansco): 63
Readyset Eagle (Agfa): 59
Readyset Royal (Agfa): 59
Readyset Royal (Ansco): 59
Readyset Traveler (Agfa): 59

Realist (White): 254
Recomar: 138, 209
Record (Agfa): 58
Record (Hüttig): 180
Rectaflex Standard: 220
Rediflex (Ansco): 63
Reflekta (Welta): 253
Reflex Camera Co. Focal Plane Postcard Camera: 220
Reflex Camera Co. Junior Reflex: 221
Reflex Camera Co. Patent Reflex Hand Camera: 221
Reflex Camera Co. Reflex: 221
Reflex Kodak: 138
Reflex Meteor (Schmitz & Thienemann): 229
Regal Miniature: 221
Regent (Ansco): 63
Regent (Nagel): 209, 221
Regent (Japan): 221
Regula (King): 189
Reichenbach Alta D: 221
Reicka (Wunsche): 257
Reid & Sigrist Reid III: 221
Reporter (Ernemann): 153
Reporter 250 (Leitz): 196
Retina (Eastman): 140, 141
Retinette (Eastman): 141
Reve: 222
Revere Eye-Matic EE 127: 222
Revere Stereo-33: 222
Reversible Back Premo: 226
Rex Kayson: 222
Rex Magazine Camera Co. Rex Magazine: 222
Rexo (Burke & James): 82
Rexoette (Burke & James): 82
Reygonaud: 222
Reyna (Cornu): 94
Reyonlds & Branson (Field): 222
Richard Glyphoscope: 223
Richard Homeos: 223
Richard Verascope: 223
Ricoh-35: 223
Ricoh Golden-16: 223
Ricohflex: 223
Rietzschel (Folding Plate): 222
Rietzschel Clack: 222
Rietzschel Heli-Clack: 221
Rietzschel Cosmo-Clack: 222
Rietzschel Special-Wiphot: 222
Rifax (Beier): 72
Rigona (Balda): 71
Riken Steky: 223
Riken Steky II: 223
Riken Steky III: 223
Riken Steky IIIa: 223
Riken Steky IIIb: 223
Riken Steky Golden: 223
Rilex: 223
Riley: 223
Rio (Orion): 212
Rival Reflex: 223
Roamer (Universal): 245
Robot (Berning): 75
Robra: 223
Rochester Cycle Poco: 224
Rochester Cyclone Junior: 224
Rochester Cyclone Magazine No. 2: 224
Rochester Cyclone Magazine No. 4: 224
Rochester Cyclone Magazine No. 5: 224
Rochester Cyclone Senior: 224
Rochester Favorite: 224
Rochester Gem Poco: 225
Rochester Handy: 224
Rochester Ideal: 224
Rochester King Poco: 225
Rochester Pocket Poco: 224
Rochester Poco: 224, 225
Rochester Poco Cycle: 224
Rochester Poco Gem (Box): 225
Rochester Poco Gem (Folding): 225
Rochester Poco King: 225
Rochester Poco Pocket: 224
Rochester Poco Telephoto: 225
Rochester Premier (Detective Box): 225
Rochester Premier (Folding): 225
Rochester Premo A: 225
Rochester Premo B: 225
Rochester Premo C: 225
Rochester Premo D: 225
Rochester Premo E: 225

Rochester Premo No. 3B: 225
Rochester Premo No. 4: 225
Rochester Premo No. 6: 225
Rochester Premo No. 7: 225
Rochester Premo Long Focus: 226
Rochester Premo Pony: 225
Rochester Premo Pony Sr.: 225
Rochester Premo
  Reversible Back: 226
Rochester Premo Star: 225
Rochester Stereo: 226
Rochester Telephoto Poco: 225
Rochester View: 226
Rodenstock (Folding Plate): 226
Rodenstock (Folding Rollfilm): 226
Rodenstock Clarovid: 226
Roland: 226
Rolf (Ernemann): 153
Rolifix (Franka): 158
Rollbox (Balda): 71
Rollei (Franke & Heidecke): 158, 159
Rolleicord (Franke & Heidecke): 159
Rolleidoscop
  (Franke & Heidecke): 159
Rolleiflex
  (Franke & Heidecke): 159-160
Rolleimagic
  (Franke & Heidecke): 160
Rollette (Krauss): 193
Rollex 20
  (United States Camera Corp.): 177
Rollop (Lipca): 199
Roll-Op (Plaubel): 217
Rom Scat: 227
Rondine (Ferrania): 157
Rorox: 227
Ross Sutton Panoramic: 227
Roussel Stella Jumelle: 227
Roy Rogers & Trigger (Herco): 176
Royal (Agfa Readyset Royal): 59
Royal (Ansco Readyset Royal): 63
Royal (Berning Robot Royal): 75
Royer Savoyflex: 227
Royet Reyna Cross III: 94
Rubix 16: 227
Ruby (Thornton-Pickard): 241
Ruthine: 227
Sabre: 227
Saint Louis: 227

Sakura Petal (Octagonal): 228
Sakura Petal (Round): 228
Samoca Samoca 35: 228
Samoca Samoca 35 II: 228
Samoca Samoca 35 III: 228
Samoca Samoca Super: 228
Sanderson Sanderson De Luxe: 228
Sanderson Sanderson Regular: 228
Satellite Flash (Herco): 176
Savoyflex (Royer): 227
Sawyers Mark IV: 228
Sawyers Primo Jr.: 228
Sawyers View-Master
  Mark II Stereo: 228
Sawyers View-Master
  Personal Stereo: 228
Sawyers View-Master
  Stereo Color: 228
Scat (Rom): 227
Scenex: 228
Scenographe Panoramique
  (Cadot): 83
Schiansky Universal Studio: 228
Schleissner Bower: 228
Schleissner Bower Jr.: 228
Schleissner Bower X: 228
Schmitz & Thienemann
  Uniflex Reflex Meteor: 229
Schul-Pramie (Agfa): 59
Scout (Seneca): 232
Scout (Wittnauer): 256
Scovill Antique Oak Detective: 229
Scovill Detective: 229
Scovill Field: 230
Scovill Knack: 229
Scovill Mascot: 229
Scovill Stereo: 230
Scovill Stereo Solograph: 230
Scovill Triad Detective: 229
Scovill Waterbury Detective: 229
Scovill Waterbury View: 230
Screen Focus Kodak: 142
Seagull No. 203: 230
Sears Delmar: 233
Sears Marvel-Flex: 203
Sears Seroco
  (Folding Plate): 233, 234
Sears Seroco Stereo: 234
Sears Tower 35 Type 3: 242

Sears Tower Stereo: 242
Secam Stereophot: 230
Secam Stylophot Luxe: 230
Secam Stylophot Standard: 230
Selecta (Agfa): 59
Self-Worker (Pipon): 216
Selfix (Houghton): 179
Semi-Automatic Ansco: 63
Semi-Leotax (Showa): 234
Semi-Lyra: 160
Semi-Minolta: 205
Semi-Pearl (Konishiroku): 192
Seneca (Box Plate): 231
Seneca (Folding Plate): 231
Seneca (Folding Plate) No. 9: 231
Seneca Busy Bee: 231
Seneca Chautauqua: 231
Seneca Chief 1A: 231
Seneca Competitor View: 231
Seneca Filmet: 231
Seneca Pocket No. 3A: 232
Seneca Pocket No. 29: 232
Seneca Pocket Jr. No. 1: 232
Seneca Scout (Box) No. 2: 232
Seneca Scout (Box) No. 2A: 232
Seneca Scout (Box) No. 3: 232
Seneca Scout (Box) No. 3A: 232
Seneca Scout Folding No. 2A: 232
Seneca Scout Folding No. 3: 232
Seneca Scout Folding No. 3A: 232
Seneca Stereo View: 232
Seneca Trio No. 1A: 232
Seneca Uno: 232
Seneca Vest Pocket: 232
Seneca View: 233
Seneca View Improved Model: 233
Sept (Debrie): 96
Sequelle (Yashica): 257
Seroco Delmar: 233
Seroco Folding Plate: 233
Seroco Stereo: 234
Set-O-Matic (Bolsey B22 & C22): 79
Shalco: 234
Shew Day-Xit: 234
Shew Eclipse: 234
Shew Xit: 234

Showa Gemflex: 161
Showa Leotax: 234
Showa Semi-Leotax: 234
Shur-Flash (Agfa): 59
Shur-Flash (Ansco): 64
Shur-Shot (Agfa): 59
Shur-Shot (Ansco): 64
Shur-Shot (early box plate camera): 234
Sibyl (Newman & Guardia): 210
Sico (Simons): 235
Sida Extra: 235
Signal Corps Signet-35: 142
Signet (Eastman): 142
Silar (Linhof): 199
Silette: 59
Simda Stereo: 235
Simmon Omega 120: 235
Simons Sico: 235
Simplex (Krugener): 193
Simplex Pockette: 235
Simplex Stereo (Ernemann): 154
Simplex Stereo (Ernoflex): 154
Sinclair Una: 235
Single-lens Stereoscope: 176
Singlo: 235
Sinox (Lumiere): 201
Sirene: 183, 264
Smyth (John M.) View: 236
Soennecken (Folding camera): 236
Soho (Marion): 202
Solida (Franka): 158
Soligor I: 236
Soligor II: 236
Silinette: 59
Solograph (Scovill): 230
SOM: 236
Sonnar (Contessa): 93
Sonnet (Contessa): 93
Sonnet (Nettel): 210
Spartaflex: 236
Spartus 35: 236
Spartus 35F: 236
Spartus 120: 236
Spartus Folding: 236
Spartus Spartaflex: 236

Special Kodak: 144
Special Wiphot (Rietzschel): 222
Speed Candid Perfex: 84
Speed Graphic: 172
Speed Kodak: 145
Speed-O-Matic: 236
Speed-O-Matic
 Salesman's Demo: 236
Speedex (Agfa): 59
Speedex (Ansco): 64
Speedliner (Polaroid 95): 217
Spido (Gaumont): 161
Spiegel Elf: 236
Sport (Adox): 58
Sportshot (Acma): 57
Sputnik Stereo: 237
St. Louis: 227
Standard (Agfa): 59, 60
Star (Berning Robot Star): 75
Star Premo (Eastman): 137
Star Premo (Rochester): 225
Star-Lite: 237
Starflex (Brownie): 112
Starlet (Brownie): 112
Starmatic (Brownie): 112
Start (Ikko Sha): 186
Start (Pouva): 218
Stegemann (Field camera): 237
Steineck ABC: 237
Steinheil Casca I: 237
Steinheil Detective: 237
Steinheil Tropical: 237
Steky (Riken): 223
Stella Jumelle (Roussel): 227
Stere-All (Universal): 245
Stereax (Contessa): 93
Stereflektoscop (Voightländer): 250
Sterelux (Lumiere): 291
Stereo Ango (Goerz): 163
Stereo Anschutz (Goerz): 163
Stereo Auto Graflex: 170
Stereo Brownie: 113
Stereo Cameo (Ica): 181
Stereo Challenge (Lizars): 200
Stereo Colorist (Bell &
 Howell): 73
Stereo Delta: 96

INDEX / 297

Stereo Edixa (Wirgin): 256
Stereo Eho (Hofert): 177
Stereo Ernoflex: 152
Stereo Exco: 155
Stereo Graphic: 172
Stereo Haneel: 175
Stereo Hare: 175
Stereo Hawkeye (Blair): 77
Stereo Hawkeye (Eastman): 126
Stereo Hit: 177
Stereo Ica: 183
Stereo Ideal: 81, 180, 183, 261
Stereo Ihagee: 186
Stereo Iloca (Witt): 256
Stereo Jumelle (Bellieni): 74
Stereo Jumelle (Mackenstein): 201
Stereo Jumelle (Papigny): 213
Stereo Kodak: 145, 146
Stereo Korona (Gundlach): 173
Stereo Liliput (Ernemann): 153
Stereo Lloyd (Ica): 182
Stereo Makina (Plaubel): 217
Stereo Mikroma (Meopta): 204
Stereo Murer: 208
Stereo Muro (Suter): 239
Stereo Nil-Melior (Macris): 201
Stereo Palmos: 264
Stereo Panoramique (Leroy): 198
Stereo Photo Binocle (Goerz): 164
Stereo Plate Camera (Anthony): 67
Stereo Puck (Thornton-Pickard): 241
Stereo Realist (White): 254
Stereo Record (Hüttig): 180
Stereo Rochester: 226
Stereo Scovill: 230
Stereo Seneca View: 232
Stereo Simda: 235
Stereo Simplex: 152
Stereo Solograph (Scovill): 230
Stereo Spido (Gaumont): 161
Stereo Sputnik: 237
Stereo Sumner: 238
Stereo Tenax (Goerz): 165
Stereo Tourist (McBean): 203
Stereo Tower: 242
Stereo Tri-Vision: 189

298 / INDEX

Stereo Viewmaster (Sawyers): 228
Stereo Vive: 248
Stereo Vivid (Bell & Howell): 73
Stereo Weno: 77
Stereo Windsor: 255
Stereo Wirgin: 256
Stereo Wollensak: 256
Stereocrafters Videon: 238
Stereocycle (Bazin & Leroy): 72
Stereolette (Hüttig): 180
Stereolette (Ica): 183
Stereolette Cupido (Ica): 183
Stereophot (Secam): 230
Stereoscopic Graphic: 172
Steroco (Contessa): 93
Stirn Concealed Vest Camera No. 1: 238
Stöckig Union: 238
Straight-Working Panorama: 73
Street camera (Benson): 74
Street camera (Chicago Ferrotype Co.): 87
Street camera (Daydark): 95
Street camera (Keystone): 189
Street camera (Thompson): 24
Stylophot (Secam): 230
Sugaya Mycro Myracle Model II: 238
Summum (Leullier): 198
Sumner Stereo: 238
Sunart Folding View: 238
Sunart Junior: 238
Super 75 (Argoflex): 69
Super Baldina: 71
Super Baldinette: 71
Super Colorette (Braun): 80
Super Contaflex (Zeiss): 259
Super Dollina (Certo): 86
Super Graphic: 172
Super Ikomat (Zeiss): 262
Super Ikonta (Zeiss): 262
Super Kodak Six-20: 144
Super Nettel (Zeiss): 263
Super Paxette (Braun): 81
Super Pontura (Balda): 71
Super Regent (Ansco): 63
Super Silette (Agfa): 59
Super Solinette (Agfa): 59
Superb (Voigtländer): 250
Superfekta (Welta): 253
Supersport Dolly (Certo): 87
Suter Detective Magazine: 239
Suter Muro Stereo: 239
Sutton Panoramic (Ross): 227
SX-70: 217
Synchro-Box (Agfa): 60
Taisei Koki Welmy 35: 239
Taisei Koki Welmy Six: 239
Taisei Koki Welmy Wide: 239
Taiyodo Koki Beauty Super L: 239
Taiyodo Koki Beautycord: 239
Taiyodo Koki Beautyflex: 239
Taiyokoki Viscawide-16: 247
Takahashi Gelto D III: 239
Takiv (Walker): 252
Takyr (Krauss): 193
Talbot Errtee (Button Tintype): 239
Talbot Errtee (Folding Plate): 239
Talbot Errtee (Folding Rollfilm): 240
Tanack: 240
Tanaka Tanack IV-S: 240
Target (Brownie): 113
Target (Hawkeye): 126
Tauber: 240
Taxo: 93
Taxona (Zeiss): 264
TDC Stereo Colorist: 73
TDC Stereo Vivid: 73
Technika (Linhof): 199
Teddy (Ica): 183
Tele-Graflex: 171
Teleca: 240
Telephoto Poco: 225
Tenax (Goerz): 164, 165
Tenax (Zeiss): 264
Tengor (Goerz): 165
Tengor (Zeiss): 259
Tennar: 240
Tessco (Contessa): 93
Tessina: 240
Thompson (W.J. & Co.) Direct Positive Street Camera: 240
Thornton-Pickard (Folding Plate): 241
Thornton-Pickard (Reflex): 241

Thornton-Pickard Puck Special: 241
Thornton-Pickard Puck Stereo: 241
Thornton-Pickard Ruby Deluxe: 241
Thornton-Pickard Ruby
 Duplex Reflex: 241
Thornton-Pickard Ruby Folding: 241
Thornton-Pickard Ruby Special: 241
Thornward Dandy: 241
Thowe Field: 241
Thowe Folding Plate: 241
3-D Stereo (Coronet): 94
Ticka (Houghton): 179
Tintype camera (Daydark): 94
Tintype camera
 New York Ferrotype): 210
Tintype camera (Popular
 Photograph Co.): 218
Tintype camera (Talbot): 239
Tisdell T&W Detective: 242
Tisdell Hand: 242
Tivoli: 242
Togodo Toyoca 35: 242
Tokyo Kogaku Primo Jr.: 242
Tokyo Shashin Mighty: 242
Tom Thumb Camera Radio: 70
Tone: 242
Top: 242
Toska (Ica): 184
Tourist (Eastman): 147
Tourist (Hare): 175
Tourist (McBean): 203
Tourist (Vive): 248
Tourist Buckeye: 61
Tourist Hawkeye: 77
Tower: 242
Tower Stereo: 242
Toyoca: 242
Traid Fotron: 243
Traid Fotron III: 243
Trambouze: 242
Traveler (Agfa Readyset
 Traveler): 59
Traveler (Japan): 243
Traveler Reflex: 243
Tri-Color (Devin): 97
Tri-Color (Jos-Pe): 187
Tri-Color (National Photocolor): 209

Tri-Vision: 189
Triad (Scovill): 229
Trilby (Ica): 184
Trio (Seneca): 232
Trio (Welta): 253
Trivision (Keys): 189
Trix: 184, 264
Trona: 184, 264
Tropica (Ica): 184
Tropical Challenge Dayspool
 (Lizars): 200
Tropical Clarissa: 92
Tropical Deckrullo-Nettel: 92
Tropical Heag: 154
Tropical Hüttig: 180
Tropical Klapp (&Ernemann): 154
Tropical Nettel (Zeiss): 263
Tropical Reporter (Ernemann): 155
Tropical Steinheil: 237
Trumpfreflex: 243
Tudor Reflex (Ica): 183
Turret Panoramic: 243
Tuxi (Kunick): 194
Tuximat (Kunick): 194
T&W (Tisdell and Whittelsey): 242
Twin 20 (Brownie): 112
Twinflex (Universal): 245
Two-Shuttered Camera
 (Ernemann): 155
Two-Shuttered Camera
 (Ihagee Duplex): 184
Two-Shuttered Camera (Welta): 253
Tynar: 243
Uca: 243
Ucaflex: 244
Ulca (Pittsburgh Camera Corp.): 216
Ultra Fex: 244
Ultrix (Ihagee): 186
Una (Sinclair): 235
Unca (Foitzik): 157
Underwood Field camera: 244
Unette (Ernemann): 155
Unger & Hoffman Verax: 244
Uniflash (Universal): 245
Uniflex (Schmitz & Thienemann): 229
Uniflex (Universal): 245
Union (Stockig): 238

300 / INDEX

United States Cam-O Corp.
　Camo-O:83
United States Camera Corp.
　Reflex: 244
United States Camera Corp.
　Rollex 20: 244
United States Camera Corp.
　Vagabond: 244
Universal Buccaneer: 244
Universal Corsair I: 244
Universal Corsair II: 244
Universal Iris: 244
Universal Mercury Model CC: 244
Universal Mercury II Model CX: 245
Universal Meteor: 245
Universal Minute 16: 245
Universal Norton: 245
Universal Roamer 63: 245
Universal Roamer I: 245
Universal Roamer II: 245
Universal Stere-All: 245
Universal Twinflex: 245
Universal Uniflash: 245
Universal Uniflex I: 245
Universal Uniflex II: 245
Universal Univex Model A: 245
Universal Univex Model AF: 245
Universal Palmos (Zeiss): 264
Universal Radio Cameradio: 246
Univex (Universal): 245
Uno (Seneca): 232
Ur-Leica Replica: 195
Utility Carlton: 246
Utility Falcon: 246
Utility Falcon Girl Scout: 246
Utility Falcon Miniature: 246
Utility Press Flash: 246
Vag (Voigtländer): 250
Vagabond (United States
　Camera Corp.): 244
Vanity Kodak: 148
Vauxhall: 246
Vega: 246
Velocigraphe (Hermagis): 176
Velox (Hurlbut): 180
Vena: 246
Venaret: 246

Ventura (Agfa): 60
Verascope (Busch): 82
Verascope (Richard): 223
Verax (Unger & Hoffman): 244
Vest Pocket Ansco: 64
Vest Pocket Hawkeye: 126
Vest Pocket Jiffy: 126
Vest Pocket Kodak: 148
Vest Pocket Monroe: 206
Vest Pocket Rexo: 82
Vest Pocket Seneca: 232
Vest Pocket Tenax: 164
Victo Field camera: 247
Victrix (Ica): 184
Videon (Stereocrafters): 238
View-Master (Sawyers): 228
Viflex: 247
Vigilant (Eastman): 149
Viking (Agfa): 60
Viking (Ansco): 64
Viking Readyset: 63
Vinten (Aeria Reconnaissance: 247
Virtus (Voightländer): 251
Viscawide-16: 247
Viscount (Aires): 60
Vitaflex: 247
Vitessa (Voigtländer): 251
Vito (Voightländer): 251
Vitomatic (Voigtländer): 251
Vitrona (Voigtlander): 251
Vive No. 1: 247
Vive No. 2: 247
Vive No. 4: 247
Vive M.P.C.: 247
Vive Stereo: 248
Vive Tourist: 248
Vivid (Bell & Howell): 73
Vogue (Coronet): 94
Voigtländer (Folding Plate): 248
Voigtländer (Folding Rollfilm): 249
Voigtländer Alpin: 248
Voigtländer Avus: 248
Voigtländer Bergheil: 248
Voigtländer Bergheil Deluxe: 248
Voigtländer Bessa: 249
Voigtländer Bessa RF: 249

Voigtländer Bessa I: 249
Voigtländer Bessa II: 249
Voigtländer Bessa Baby: 249
Voigtländer Bessamatic: 249
Voigtländer Brilliant: 249
Voigtländer Daguerreotype Cannon: 249
Voigtländer Inos II: 250
Voigtländer Inos II Two-Format: 250
Voigtländer Jubilar: 250
Voigtländer Perkeo: 250
Voigtländer Perkeo I: 250
Voigtländer Perkeo II: 250
Voigtländer Prominent (35mm): 250
Voigtländer Prominent (Folding Rollfilm): 250
Voigtländer Stereflextoskop: 250
Voigtländer Superb: 250
Voigtländer Vag: 250
Voigtländer Virtus: 251
Voigtländer Vitessa: 251
Voigtländer Vitessa L: 251
Voigtländer Vitessa T: 251
Voigtländer Vito: 251
Voigtländer Vito B: 251
Voigtländer Vito C: 251
Voigtländer Vito II: 251
Voigtländer Vito II a: 251
Voigtländer Vito III: 251
Voigtländer Vito Automatic: 251
Voigtländer Vitomatic: 251
Voigtländer Vitrona: 251
Vokar I: 251
Vollenda: 150, 209
Volta (Zeiss): 264, 265
Voss Diax II: 251
Wabash Direct Positive Camera: 252
Walker Takiv: 252
Waltax: 252
Waltax Jr.: 252
Walz-Wide: 252
Walzflex: 252
Wanaus View: 252
Wara (Balda): 71
Waranette (Wauckosin): 253
Wardflex: 252
Watch Camera (Expo): 155
Watch Camera (Houghton Ticka): 179

Watch Camera (Magic Introduction Co. Photoret): 202
Watch Camera (Steineck ABC): 237
Watch Pocket Carbine (Butcher): 83
Waterbury (Scovill): 229, 230
Watson & Sons field: 252
Watson-Holmes Fingerprint (Burke & James): 82
Waucksin Waranette: 253
Weeny Ultrix: 186
Wega (Afiom): 58
Welmy (Taisei Koki): 239
Welta (Folding Plate): 253
Welta (Folding Rollfilm): 253
Welta Perfekta: 253
Welta Perle: 253
Welta Reflekta: 253
Welta Superflekta: 253
Welta Trio: 253
Welta Two-Shuttered camera: 253
Welta Weltaflex: 253
Welta Weltax: 253
Welta Weltax Jr.: 253
Welta Welti: 253
Welta Weltini: 254
Welta Weltix: 254
Welta Weltur: 254
Weltaflex: 253
Weltax: 253
Welti: 253
Weltini: 254
Weltix: 254
Weltur: 254
Wenk: 254
Wenka: 254
Weno Hawkeye (Blair): 77, 78
Weno Hawkeye (Eastman): 126
Werra: 214, 265
Westar (Nishida): 211
Western Cyclone Jr.: 254
Western Cyclone Magazine No. 2: 254
Western Cyclone Magazine No. 3: 254
Western Cyclone Magazine No. 4: 254
Western Cyclone Magazine No. 5: 254

302 / INDEX

Western Cyclone Sr.: 254
Wet Plate camera (Garland): 161
Wet Plate camera (Lewis): 198
Wet Plate camera
 (London Stereoscopic): 200
White Realist: 254
White Realist 45: 254
White Realist Stereo: 254
White Realist Stereo Macro: 254
Whitehouse Products Beacon: 254
Whitehouse Products Beacon II: 254
Whittaker Micro-16: 255
Whittaker Pixie: 255
Wilca Automatic: 255
Windrow: 255
Windsor Stereo: 255
Wing Multiplying View: 255
Wing New Gem: 255
Wiphot (Rietzschel): 222
Wirgin (Folding Rollfilm): 256
Wirgin Edinex: 255
Wirgin Edixa-16: 256
Wirgin Edixa Electronica: 256
Wirgin Edixa Reflex: 256
Wirgin Edixa Stereo: 256
Wirgin Gewirette: 256
Wirgin Klein-Edinex: 256
Wirgin Reflex: 256
Wirgin Stereo: 256
Witt Iloca I: 256
Witt Iloca II: 256
Witt Iloca II a: 256
Witt Iloca Stereo I: 256
Witt Iloca Stereo II: 256
Wittnauer Scout: 256
Wizard (Manhattan): 202
Wollensak Stereo: 256
Wonder (magazine box camera): 256
Wonder Automatic Cannon: 87
World's Fair Flash Camera: 150
Wünsche (Field): 257
Wünsche Mars-99: 257
Wünsche Reicka: 257
Xit (Shew): 234
Yale (Adams): 57
Yashica-16: 257

Yashica-44: 257
Yashica A: 257
Yashica Atoron: 257
Yashica Atoron Electro: 257
Yashica D: 257
Yashica Rapide: 257
Yashica Sequelle: 257
Yashica YF: 257
Zeca: 258
Zeca-Flex: 258
Zedel: 257
Zeh Zeca: 258
Zeh Zeca-Flex: 258
Zeiss (Folding Plate): 260
Zeiss (Folding Rollfilm): 260
Zeiss Adoro: 258
Zeiss Adoro Tropical: 258
Zeiss Baby Box: 259
Zeiss Baldur Box: 258
Zeiss Bebe: 258
Zeiss Bob: 259
Zeiss Bobette II: 259
Zeiss Box Tengor: 259
Zeiss Cocarette: 259
Zeiss Contaflex: 259
Zeiss Contaflex I: 259
Zeiss Contaflex II: 259
Zeiss Contaflex III: 259
Zeiss Contaflex III: 259
Zeiss Contaflex IV: 135
Zeiss Contaflex Super: 259
Zeiss Contarex EE: 260
Zeiss Contax D: 260
Zeiss Contax No-Name: 260
Zeiss Contax S: 260
Zeiss Contax I: 260
Zeiss Contax II: 260
Zeiss Contax IIa: 260
Zeiss Contax III: 260
Zeiss Contax IIIa: 260
Zeiss Contessa 35: 260
Zeiss Contessa-Nettel
 (Folding Plate): 260
Zeiss Contina: 260
Zeiss Donata: 260
Zeiss Ergo: 261

Zeiss Hologon: 261
Zeiss Icarette: 261
Zeiss Ideal A: 261
Zeiss Ideal B: 261
Zeiss Ikoflex I: 261
Zeiss Ikoflex Ia: 261
Zeiss Ikoflex Ic: 261
Zeiss Ikoflex II: 261
Zeiss Ikoflex IIa: 261
Zeiss Ikoflex III: 261
Zeiss Ikomat: 262
Zeiss Ikomat Super A: 262
Zeiss Ikonette: 262
Zeiss Ikonta: 262
Zeiss Ikonta A: 262
Zeiss Ikonta B: 262
Zeiss Ikonta C: 262
Zeiss Ikonta Super A: 262
Zeiss Ikonta Super B: 262
Zeiss Ikonta Super BX: 262
Zeiss Ikonta Super C: 262
Zeiss Ikonta Super D: 263
Zeiss Ikonta 35: 262
Zeiss Kolibri: 263
Zeiss Kolibri Night: 263
Zeiss Maximar A: 263
Zeiss Maximar B: 263
Zeiss Minimum Palmos: 264
Zeiss Micoflex: 263
Zeiss Nettar A: 263
Zeiss Nettar C: 263
Zeiss Nettax: 263
Zeiss Nettel Tropical: 263
Zeiss Nettel Super: 263
Zeiss Nixe: 263
Zeiss Onito: 264

Zeiss Orix: 264
Zeiss Palmos Minimum: 264
Zeiss Palmos Stereo: 264
Zeiss Palmos Universal: 264
Zeiss Piccolette: 264
Zeiss Sirene: 264
Zeiss Super Ikomat A: 262
Zeiss Super Ikonta A: 262
Zeiss Super Ikonta B: 262
Zeiss Super Ikonta BX: 262
Zeiss Super Ikonta C: 262
Zeiss Super Ikonta D: 263
Zeiss Taxo: 264
Zeiss Taxo Luxus: 264
Zeiss Taxona: 264
Zeiss Tenax I: 264
Zeiss Tenax II: 264
Zeiss Trix: 264
Zeiss Trona: 264
Zeiss Universal Palmos: 264
Zeiss Volta: 264
Zeiss Volta Luxus: 265
Zeiss Werra: 265
Zenit-3: 265
Zenit-B: 265
Zenith Edelweiss: 265
Zenith Kodak: 150
Zenobia (Daiichi): 95
Zion Pocket Z: 265
Zorki: 265
Zorki C: 265
Zorki I: 265
Zorki III: 265
Zorki IV: 265
Zorki V: 265

DESCRIPTION	DATE PURCHASED	COST	DATE SOLD	PRICE	CONDITION

For More Information...

PRICE GUIDE TO ANTIQUE & CLASSIC STILL CAMERAS
Fourth Edition 1983-1984 — By James M. & Joan C. McKeown

Recognized worldwide as the leading reference work on antique cameras, this perennial bestseller has been completely revised and greatly expanded. The entire compilation is alphabetical by manufacturer, with full cross-referencing and a complete index.

Descriptions for the cameras include a wide variety of historical and technical information, identification features, original prices and much more. The variety of cameras ranges from the rare and exotic to the common box and novelty cameras.

Current values are listed for all entries.
360 pp. 5½" x 8½" Paperback. — *Over 1000 illustrations.* $15.95

OFFICIAL DEALER BLUE BOOK OF CAMERAS — By James M. & Joan C. McKeown

This all new guide takes over where the *Price Guide to Antique Cameras* leaves off. It includes about 2500 cameras right up to the most current models which are still rolling off the line. Entries include camera and lens name, dates of production, list price, discount price, and trade-in allowance. The alphabetical format and pocket size make it especially handy.
64 pp. 4½" x 6½" Paperback. — *Illustrated.* $8.95

COLLECTORS GUIDE TO KODAK CAMERAS — By James M. & Joan C. McKeown

The first and only illustrated identification guide to Kodak, Brownie, and Instamatic cameras from 1886-1980. The well-indexed chronological listing includes model identification, characteristics, lens, shutter, film type, image size, camera size, weight and dates.
176 pp. 5½" x 8½" Paperback. — *372 Illustrations.* $12.95

CATALOG OF PREMO CAMERAS — By Joan C. McKeown

This chronology of nearly 100 Premo models traces the camera's history from the Rochester Optical Company in 1893 through the Eastman Kodak Company in 1922. It includes information about the lens, shutter, film size, dates of manufacture, and original price for each of over 1200 variations of this important American camera line.
64 pp. 8¼" x 11" Paperback. — *Illustrated.* $9.95

Available at your local bookseller or direct from:

CENTENNIAL PHOTO SERVICE
ROUTE 3, P.O. BOX 1125
GRANTSBURG, WI 54840

Get In The Collecting Picture at...

INTERNATIONAL CAMERA CORP.

460 East Highway 436
Suite 101
Casselberry, Florida 32707

THE *CAMERA COLLECTOR'S SHOWPLACE* OF CENTRAL FLORIDA...

You'll **Always** find the **Rarities**... the **Hard-To-Get** and **Desirable Collector Models,** that you may have searched for in vain elsewhere. In a shop that's deservedly called the **HEADQUARTERS** for all serious cam-era collectors and connoisseurs ... as well as professional and amateur photographers. Nationwide contacts plus **YEARS OF EXPERIENCE** in the collector market enable us to present one of the largest and finest selections to be found anywhere in America... at realistic prices.

ALSO... a full line of **CURRENT MAKES AND MODELS, IN ALL PRICE RANGES AND ACCESSORIES**
- **PROJECTORS • BINOCULARS**
- **SCIENTIFIC INSTRUMENTS**

and **EXPERT *REPAIR SERVICE*** for cameras of all ages and types!!

Imagine... **ALL** your collecting and photo-hobby needs under one roof... backed by a reputation for integrity and fair dealing at **INTERNATIONA CAMERA CORP.**

How did your plates do?

Reco's "Little Boy Blue" by John McClelland
UP 214% in 1 Year

Some limited edition plates gained more in the same year, some less, and some not at all . . . But Plate Collector readers were able to follow the price changes, step by step, in Plate Price Trends, a copyrighted feature appearing in each issue of the magazine.

Because The Plate Collector is your best source guide . . . has more on limited editions than all other publications combined . . . and gives you insight into every facet of your collecting . . . you too will rate it

Your No. 1. Investment
In Limited Editions.

In 1972, Plate Collector was the first to feature limited editions only. It's expanded, adding figurines, bells and prints, earning reader raves like you see below.

To bring you the latest, most valuable information, our editors crisscross the continent. Sometimes stories lead them to the smaller Hawaiian Islands, or to the porcelain manufacturers of Europe.

Their personal contact with artisans, hobby leaders, collectors, artists and dealers lets you share an intimate view of limited editions.

Each fat, colorful issue brings you new insight, helps you enjoy collecting more.

You'll find Plate Collector a complete source guide. Consider new issue information and new issue announcements, often in full color. Use the ratings of new releases and wide array of dealer ads to help you pick and choose the best.

Read regular columns, including one on Hummels, and check current market values in Plate Price Trends to add to your storehouse of knowledge.

You'll profit from tips on insurance, decorating, taxes . . . just a sample of recurring feature subjects.

Read Plate Collector magazine to become a true limited edition art insider. Order now. See new and old plates in sparkling color. Enjoy 2 issues every month, delivered to your home at savings up to 37% from newsstand price.

12 issues (6 months) $17.50
24 issues (year) $30
The PLATE COLLECTOR
P.O. Box 1041-HC   Kermit, TX 79745

To use VISA and MasterCard, include all raised information on your card.

Here is Plate Collector, as viewed by our readers in unsolicited quotes . . .

"Objective and Impartial," has "great research," yet is warm and personal . . . "I am delighted in 'our' magazine." A New York couple says flatly, "It is the best collector magazine on the market."

"Quality printing is valuable to me because there are no stores near me where I can view and decide," says an Arizona reader. It is "a major guide to the plates I buy," says a Massachusetts reader, while "It is the best investment in a magazine I ever made," comes from Illinois.

"I enjoy your articles on artists," "The full-color pictures are great," "Your staff was most helpful," "I depend on Plate Collector," and "I look forward to receiving it twice a month," are other reader reactions.

A California reader said simply, "I am glad there is a Plate Collector."

Members report
SAVINGS of $1,000.00 and more
as a result
of
American Collector Club
membership

American Collector Club
Membership Number | Expiration Date
0110MSM0110 | 10/87

MARY M MCSMITH
0110 EAST ANYWHERE
TIMBUCKTOO US 01110

is an Associate in good standing and entitled to all Associate benefits and opportunities through the expiration date shown above.

James K. Barker
Associate Director

Watch for this emblem

10

in shops offering automatic discounts to members.

This card can save you money too!

Members receive
American Collector each month

Featuring collectables of the last 100 years, special American Collector editions spotlight
* Roseville   * Americana   * Paper
* Modern Dolls   * Porcelain   * Glass
* Clocks & Watches   * Political   * Pottery
* Antique Dolls   * Patriotic   * Toys
* Limited Editions   * Advertising   * Jewelry

There are regular columns for collectors of:
* Books   * Bottles   * Photographica   * Dolls
* Records   * Nippon   * Barberiana   * Jars
* Stoneware   * Glass   * Stocks & Bonds   * Paper

Questions are answered in "Readers Ask." "What Is It?" challenges. It's helpful, fun and informative!
American Collector is just one of many ACC member Benefits!

Your member-only newsletter

brings you news reference info, book discounts up to 70%, other special money-savers, FREE member bonuses several times a year.

NEWSLETTER

* Book Discounts
* Barter through ACE
* Discounts on Collectables
* FREE bonus gifts
* Publication Discounts
* A sample of Member Benefits

Members often save more than annual dues in the first month of membership.

For buyers of this Official Guide, 5-month trial membership, $9.95; 12 months, $20.

Send your application to:

American Collector Club
P.O. Drawer C (HC), Kermit, TX 79745

There is only one...
OFFICIAL
PRICE GUIDE

THE <u>MULTIPURPOSE</u> REFERENCE GUIDE!!

THE OFFICIAL PRICE GUIDE SERIES has gained the reputation as <u>the standard barometer of values</u> on collectors' items. When you need to check the market price of a collectible, turn first to the OFFICIAL PRICE GUIDES . . . for impartial, unbiased, current information that is presented in an easy-to-follow format.

• **CURRENT VALUES FOR BUYING AND SELLING.** ACTUAL SALES that have occurred in all parts of the country are CAREFULLY EVALUATED and COMPUTERIZED to arrive at the most ACCURATE PRICES AVAILABLE.

• **CONCISE REFERENCES.** Each OFFICIAL PRICE GUIDE is designed primarily as a *guide to current market values.* They also include a useful summary of the information most readers are seeking: a history of the item; how it's manufactured; how to begin and maintain a collection; how and where to sell; addresses of periodicals and clubs.

• **INDEXED FORMAT.** The novice as well as the seasoned collector will appreciate the unique alphabetically *indexed format* that provides *fast retrieval* of information and prices.

• **FULLY ILLUSTRATED.** All the OFFICIAL PRICE GUIDES are richly illustrated. Many feature COLOR SECTIONS as well as black and white photos.

Over 21 years of experience has made
THE HOUSE OF COLLECTIBLES
the most respected price guide authority!

PRICE GUIDE SERIES

American Silver & Silver Plate
Today's silver market offers excellent opportunities *to gain big profits* — if you are well informed. *Over 15,000 current market values* are listed for 19th and 20th century American made Sterling, Coin and Silverplated flatware and holloware. Special souvenir spoon section. *ILLUSTRATED.*
$9.95-2nd Edition, 576 pgs., 5⅜" x 8", paperback, Order #: 184-5

Antique & Classic Still Cameras
More than *3,000 up-to-the-minute selling prices* for all types of popular collector cameras. An encyclopedia of American and foreign camera brands and models. Advice on buying and building a collection. *ILLUSTRATED.*
$9.95-1st Edition, 532 pgs., 5⅜" x 8", paperback, Order #: 383-X

Antique Clocks
A pictorial price reference for all types of American made clocks. Over *10,000 detailed listings* insure positive identification. *Includes company histories. ILLUSTRATED.*
$9.95-1st Edition, 576 pgs., 5⅜" x 8", paperback, Order #: 364-3

Antique & Modern Dolls
More than *6,000 current retail selling prices* for antique dolls in wax, carved wood, china and bisque; modern and semi-modern dolls in celluloid, chalk, plastic, composition, and cloth. Advice on where and how to buy, care and display, and selling dolls. *ILLUSTRATED.*
$9.95-1st Edition, 544 pgs., 5⅜" x 8", paperback, Order #: 381-3

Antique & Modern Firearms
This unique book is an encyclopedia of gun lore featuring over *20,500 listings with histories* of American and foreign manufacturers *plus a special section on collector cartridge values. ILLUSTRATED.*
$9.95-3rd Edition, 544 pgs., 5⅜" x 8", paperback, Order #: 363-5

Antique Jewelry
Over *8,200 current collector values* for the most extensive listing of antique jewelry ever published, Georgian, Victorian, Art Nouveau, Art Deco. *Plus a special full color gem identification guide. ILLUSTRATED.*
$9.95-2nd Edition, 672 pgs., 5⅜" x 8", paperback, Order #: 354-6

Antiques & Other Collectibles
Introduces TODAY'S world of antiques with *over 100,000 current market values* for the most complete listing of antiques and collectibles IN PRINT! In this *new — 832 PAGE edition, many new categories have been added to keep fully up-to-date with the latest collecting trends. ILLUSTRATED.*
$9.95-4th Edition, 832 pgs., 5⅜" x 8", paperback, Order #: 374-0

Bottles Old & New
Over *22,000 current buying and selling prices* of both common and rare collectible bottles . . . ale, soda, bitters, flasks, medicine, perfume, poison, milk and more. *Plus expanded sections on Avon and Jim Beam. ILLUSTRATED.*
$9.95-6th Edition, 672 pgs., 5⅜" x 8", paperback, Order #: 350-3

Collectible Toys
Over *25,000 current values* for trains, windups, autos, soldiers, boats, banks, guns, musical toys, Disneyana, comic characters, Star Trek, Star Wars, and more. Valuable collecting tips. *ILLUSTRATED.*
$9.95-1st Edition, 540 pgs., 5⅜" x 8", paperback, Order #: 384-8

Collector Cars
Over *37,000 actual current prices* for 4000 models of antique and classic automobiles — U.S. and foreign. Complete with engine specifications. *Special sections on auto memorabilia values and restoration techniques. ILLUSTRATED.*
$9.95-4th Edition, 544 pgs., 5⅜" x 8", paperback, Order #: 357-0

For your convenience use the handy order form.

PRICE GUIDE SERIES

Collector Handguns
Over *10,000 current values* for antique and modern handguns. Plus the most up-to-date listing of current production handguns. *ILLUSTRATED.*
$9.95-1st Edition, 544 pgs., 5⅜" x 8", paperback, Order #: 367-8

Collector Knives
Over *13,000 buying and selling prices* on U.S. and foreign pocket and sheath knives. *Special sections on bicentennial, commemorative, limited edition, and handmade knives.* By J. Parker & B. Voyles. *ILLUSTRATED.*
$9.95-5th Edition, 704 pgs., 5⅜" x 8", paperback, Order #: 324-4

Collector Plates
Destined to become the "PLATE COLLECTORS' BIBLE." This unique price guide offers the most comprehensive listing of collector plate values — *in Print! Special information includes: the histories of companies; artists' backgrounds; and helpful tips on buying, selling and storing a collection. ILLUSTRATED.*
$9.95-1st Edition, 672 pgs., 5⅜" x 8", paperback, Order #: 349-X

Collector Prints
Over *14,750 detailed listings* representing over 400 of the most famous collector print artists from Audubon and Currier & Ives, to modern day artists. *Special feature includes gallery/artist reference chart. ILLUSTRATED.*
$9.95-4th Edition, 544 pgs., 5⅜" x 8", paperback, Order #: 189-6

Comic & Science Fiction Books
Over *31,000 listings with current values* for comic and science fiction publications *from 1903-to-date. Special sections on Tarzan, Big Little Books, Science Fiction publications and paperbacks. ILLUSTRATED.*
$9.95-6th Edition, 544 pgs., 5⅜" x 8", paperback, Order #: 353-8

Glassware
Over *60,000 listings* for all types of American-made glassware, pressed and pattern, depression, cut, carnival and more. *ILLUSTRATED.*
$9.95-1st Edition, 544 pgs., 5⅜" x 8", paperback, Order #: 125-X

Hummel Figurines & Plates
The most complete guide ever published on every type of Hummel — including the most recent trademarks and size variations, with *6,100 up-to-date prices. Plus tips on buying, selling and investing. ILLUSTRATED.*
$9.95-3rd Edition, 448 pgs., 5⅜" x 8", paperback, Order #: 352-X

Kitchen Collectibles
This beautiful pictorial guide has *hundreds of illustrations* — truly a MASTERPIECE of reference. This first really complete *History of America in the Kitchen* describes hundreds of implements and lists *28,000 current market values. ILLUSTRATED.*
$9.95-1st Edition, 544 pgs., 5⅜" x 8", paperback, Order #: 371-6

Military Collectibles
This detailed historical reference price guide covers the largest accumulation of military objects — 15th century-to-date — listing over *12,000 accurate prices. Special expanded Samurai sword and headdress sections. ILLUSTRATED.*
$9.95-2nd Edition, 576 pgs., 5⅜" x 8", paperback, Order #: 191-8

Music Machines
Virtually every music-related collectible is included in this guide — over *11,000 current prices. 78 recordings, mechanical musical machines, and instruments. ILLUSTRATED.*
$9.95-2nd Edition, 544 pgs., 5⅜" x 8", paperback, Order #: 187-X

For your convenience use the handy order form.

PRICE GUIDE SERIES

Old Books & Autographs
Descriptions of the finest literary collectibles available, with over **11,000 prices for all types of books:** Americana, bibles, medicine, cookbooks and more. **Plus an updated autograph section.** *ILLUSTRATED.*
$9.95-4th Edition, 512 pgs., 5⅜" x 8", paperback, Order #: 351-1

Oriental Collectibles
Over **10,000 detailed listings and values** for all types of Chinese & Japanese collectibles, pottery, rugs, statues, porcelain, cloisonne, metalware. *ILLUSTRATED.*
$9.95-1st Edition, 544 pgs., 5⅜" x 8", paperback, Order #: 375-9

Paper Collectibles
Old Checks, Invoices, Books, Magazines, Newspapers, Ticket Stubs and even Matchbooks — any paper items that reflects America's past — are gaining collector value. This book contains **over 26,000 current values** and descriptions for all types of paper collectibles. *ILLUSTRATED.*
$9.95-2nd Edition, 608 pgs., 5⅜" x 8", paperback, Order #: 186-1

Pottery & Porcelain
Over **10,000 current prices and listings** of fine pottery and porcelain, plus an extensive Lenox china section. **Special sections on the histories of companies and on identifying china trademarks.** *ILLUSTRATED.*
$9.95-2nd Edition, 576 pgs., 5⅜" x 8", paperback, Order #: 188-8

Records
Over **31,000 current prices** of collectible singles, EPs, albums, plus 20,000 memorable song titles recorded by over 1100 artists. **Rare biographies and photos are provided for many well-known artists.** *ILLUSTRATED.*
$9.95-4th Edition, 544 pgs., 5⅜" x 8", paperback, Order #: 356-2

Royal Doulton
This authoritative guide to Royal Doulton porcelains contains over **5,500 detailed listings** on figurines, plates and Toby jugs. Includes tips on buying, selling and displaying. **Plus an exclusive numerical reference index.** *ILLUSTRATED.*
$9.95-2nd Edition, 544 pgs., 5⅜" x 8", paperback, Order #: 355-4

Wicker
You could be sitting on a **fortune!** Decorators and collectors are driving wicker values to unbelievable highs! This pictorial price guide **positively identifies all types** of Victorian, Turn of the Century and Art Deco wicker furniture. **A special illustrated section on wicker repair is included.** *ILLUSTRATED.*
$9.95-1st Edition, 416 pgs., 5⅜" x 8", paperback, Order #: 348-1

Encyclopedia of Antiques
A total of more than **10,000 definitions, explanations, concise factual summaries of names, dates, histories, confusing terminology** . . . for every popular field of collecting. An exclusive appendix includes many trademark and pattern charts as well as a categorized list of museums and reference publications.
$9.95-1st Edition, 704 pgs., 5⅜" x 8", paperback, Order #: 365-1

Buying & Selling Guide to Antiques
Covers every phase of collecting, from beginning a collection to its ultimate sale . . . examines in detail the collecting potential of **over 200 different catagories of items in all price ranges. Special features include a dealer directory, a condition grading report, list of museums and reference publications, plus a discussion of buying and selling techniques.** *ILLUSTRATED.*
$9.95-1st Edition, 608 pgs., 5⅜" x 8", paperback, Order #: 369-4

For your convenience use the handy order form.

MINI PRICE GUIDE SERIES

Antiques & Flea Markets
Discover the fun and profit of collecting antiques with this handy pocket reference to **over 15,000 types of collectibles.** Avoid counterfeits and learn the secrets to successful buying and selling. *ILLUSTRATED.*
$2.50-1st Edition, 240 pgs., 4" x 5½", paperback, Order #: 308-2

Antique Jewelry
A handy pocket-sized update to the larger *Official Price Guide to Antique Jewelry*, lists **thousands of values** for bracelets, brooches, chains, earrings, necklaces and more. **Special sections on gold, silver and diamond identification.**
$2.95-1st Edition, 240 pgs., 4" x 5½", paperback, Order #: 373-2

Baseball Cards
This guide lists **over 100,000 current market values** for baseball cards – Bowman, Burger King, Donruss, Fleer, O-Pee-Chee and Topps. *ILLUSTRATED.*
$2.95-3rd Edition, 332 pgs., 4" x 5½", paperback, Order #: 376-7

Beer Cans
The first pocket-sized guide to list **thousands of values** for cone and flat top beer cans produced since the mid 1930's. Each listing is graphically detailed for positive identification. *ILLUSTRATED.*
$2.95-1st Edition, 240 pgs., 4" x 5½", paperback, Order #: 377-5

Cars
Over **5,000 current auction and dealer prices** for all popular U.S. and foreign made antique, classic and collector cars. **Learn how to evaluate** the condition of a collector car the way the professionals do! *ILLUSTRATED.*
$2.95-1st Edition, 240 pgs., 4" x 5½", paperback, Order #: 391-0

Comic Books
Young and Old are collecting old comic books for fun *and Profit!* This handy pocket-sized price guide lists current market values and detailed descriptions for the most sought-after collectible comic books. **Buying, selling and storing tips are provided for the beginning collector.** *ILLUSTRATED.*
$2.50-1st Edition, 240 pgs., 4" x 5½", paperback, Order #: 345-7

Dolls
Doll collecting is one of America's favorite hobbies and this guide lists **over 3,000 actual market values** for all the manufacturers! Kewpies, Howdy Doody, Shirley Temple, GI Joe plus comprehensive listings of Barbies. *ILLUSTRATED.*
$2.95-1st Edition, 240 pgs., 4" x 5½", paperback, Order #: 316-3

O.J. Simpson Football Cards
The world famous O.J. Simpson highlights this comprehensive guide to football card values. **Over 21,000 current collector prices** are listed for: Topps, Bowman, Fleer, Philadelphia and O-Pee-Chee. **Includes a full color O.J. SIMPSON limited edition collector card.** *ILLUSTRATED.*
$2.50-2nd Edition, 256 pgs., 4" x 5½", paperback, Order #: 323-6

Guns
Over **3,000 dealer prices** compiled from nationwide sales records for handguns, rifles, and shotguns. Covers American and foreign manufacturers. Information on the history of firearms, and collecting techniques! *ILLUSTRATED.*
$2.95-1st Edition, 240 pgs., 4" x 5½", paperback, Order #: 396-1

For your convenience use the handy order form.

MINI PRICE GUIDE SERIES

Hummels
How much are your Hummels worth? You can become an expert on these lovely figurines with this guide, *FULLY ILLUSTRATED*, with a handy numerical index that puts descriptions and **3,000 market prices** at your fingertips. Learn why the slightest variation could mean hundreds in value.
$2.95-1st Edition, 240 pgs., 4" x 5½", paperback, Order #:318-X

Military Collectibles
Over **4,000 current prices** for a wide assortment of military objects from all over the world — 19th century to World War II. Valuable collecting tips — How to build a collection, grading condition, and displaying your collection. *ILLUSTRATED.*
$2.95-1st Edition, 240 pgs., 4" x 5½", paperback, Order #: 378-3

Paperbacks & Magazines
Old discarded paperbacks and magazines could be worth 50-100 times their original cover price. Learn how to identify them. *Thousands* of descriptions and prices show which issues are rare. *ILLUSTRATED.*
$2.50-1st Edition, 240 pgs., 4" x 5½", paperback, Order #: 315-5

Pocket Knives
This mid-season update to the larger *Official Price Guide to Collector Knives* lists **over 4,000 collector values** for Case, Kabar, Cattaraugus, Remington, Winchester and more. **Special sections on buying and selling plus a list of limited edition pocket knives.**
$2.95-1st Edition, 240 pgs., 4" x 5½", paperback, Order #: 372-4

Records
Over **5,000 current market prices** for Rock and Country recordings. A chronological listing of discs from 1953 to date. How to begin a collection . . . how and where to buy and sell . . . and how to grade condition. *ILLUSTRATED.*
$2.95-1st Edition, 240 pgs., 4" x 5½", paperback, Order #: 400-3

Scouting Collectibles
Discover the colorful history behind scouting, relive childhood memories and profit from those old family heirlooms. *Thousands of prices* are listed for all types of Boy and Girl Scout memorabilia. *ILLUSTRATED.*
$2.50-1st Edition, 240 pgs., 4" x 5½", paperback, Order #: 314-7

Sports Collectibles
Over **12,000 current prices** for all the popular collectibles of baseball, football, basketball, hockey, boxing, hunting, fishing, horse racing and other top sports. Inside facts on buying from dealers and selling your sports collectibles. *ILLUSTRATED.*
$2.95-1st Edition, 240 pgs., 4" x 5½", paperback, Order #: 379-1

Star Trek / Star Wars Collectibles
The most startling phenomena in decades! Star Trek and Star Wars fans have created a space age world of collectibles. *Thousands of current values* for book, posters, photos, costumes, models, jewelry and more . . . **Plus tips on buying, selling and trading.** *ILLUSTRATED.*
$2.95-1st Edition, 240 pgs., 4" x 5½", paperback, Order #: 319-8

Toys
Kids from eight to eighty enjoy collecting toys and this comprehensive guide has them all! Trains, trucks, comic and movie characters, space toys, boats and **MORE**. *Over 8,000 current market values* of toys, old and new, plus investment tips and histories. *ILLUSTRATED.*
$2.95-1st Edition, 240 pgs., 4" x 5½", paperback, Order #: 317-1

For your convenience use the handy order form.

NUMISMATIC SERIES

THE BLACKBOOKS are more than just informative books, they are the most highly-regarded authority on the nation's most popular hobbies.

1984 Blackbook Price Guide of United States Coins
A coin collector's guide to current market values for all U.S. coins from 1616 to date—over **16,500 prices**. **THE OFFICIAL BLACKBOOK OF COINS** has gained the reputation as the most reliable, up-to-date guide to U.S. Coin values. This new edition features, an exclusive gold and silver identification guide. Learn how to test, weigh and calculate the value of any item made of gold or silver. Proven professional techniques revealed for the first time. Take advantage of the current 'BUYERS' MARKET'' in gold and silver. *ILLUSTRATED.*
$2.95-22nd Edition, 288 pgs., 4" x 5½", paperback, Order #: 385-6

1984 Blackbook Price Guide of United States Paper Money
Over **9,000 buying and selling prices** covering U.S. currency from 1861 to date. Every note issued by the U.S. government is listed and priced including many Confederate States notes. Error Notes are described and priced, and there are detailed articles on many phases of the hobby for beginners and advanced collectors alike. *ILLUSTRATED.*
$2.95-16th Edition, 240 pgs., 4" x 5½", paperback, Order #: 387-2

1984 Blackbook Price Guide of United States Postage Stamps
Featuring all U.S. stamps from 1847 to date pictured in full color. Over **19,000 current selling prices** You will find new listings for the most current commemorative and regular issue stamps, a feature not offered in any other price guide, at any price! There were numerous important developments in the fast moving stamp market during the past year and they are all included in this **NEW REVISED EDITION**. *ILLUSTRATED.*
$2.95-6th Edition, 240 pgs., 4" x 5½", paperback, Order #: 386-4

INVESTORS SERIES

The Official Investors Guide Series shows you, *step-by-step,* how to select the right items for your investment program, how to avoid the many pitfalls that can foil new investors, with full instructions on when to sell and **How And Where To Sell** in order to realize the **Highest Possible Profit.**

Investors Guide to Gold, Silver, Diamonds
All you need to know about making money trading in the precious metals and diamond markets. This practical, easy-to-read investment guide is for everyone in all income brackets. *ILLUSTRATED.*
$6.95-1st Edition, 208 pgs., 5³⁻₈" x 8", paperback, Order #: 171-3

Investors Guide to Gold Coins
The first complete book on investing in gold coins. Exclusive price performance charts trace all U.S. gold coin values from **1955 to date**. *ILLUSTRATED.*
$6.95-1st Edition, 288 pgs., 5⅜" x 8", paperback, Order #: 300-7

Investors Guide to Silver Coins
The most extensive listing of all U.S. silver coins. Detailed price performance charts trace actual sales figures from **1955 to date**. *ILLUSTRATED.*
$6.95-1st Edition, 288 pgs., 5⅜" x 8", paperback, Order #: 301-5

Investors Guide to Silver Dollars
Regardless of your income, you can **become a successful silver dollar investor**. Actual sales figures for every U.S. silver dollar **1955 to date**. *ILLUSTRATED.*
$6.95-1st Edition, 192 pgs., 5⅜" x 8", paperback, Order #: 302-3

— *For your convenience use the handy order form.* —

FOR IMMEDIATE DELIVERY

VISA & MASTERCARD CUSTOMERS
ORDER TOLL FREE!
1-800-327-1384

This number is for orders only, it is not tied into the customer service or business office. Customers not using charge cards must use mail for ordering since payment is required with the order — sorry no C.O.D.'s. Florida residents call (305) 857-9095 — ask for order department.

OR SEND ORDERS TO

THE HOUSE OF COLLECTIBLES, ORLANDO CENTRAL PARK
1900 PREMIER ROW, ORLANDO, FL 32809   PHONE (305) 857-9095

☐ Please send me the following price guides—(don't forget to add postage & handling):
☐ I would like the most current edition of the books checked below.

☐ 184-5 @ 9.95	☐ 324-4 @ 9.95	☐ 186-1 @ 9.95	☐ 391-0 @ 2.95	☐ 379-1 @ 2.95
☐ 383-X @ 9.95	☐ 349-X @ 9.95	☐ 188-8 @ 9.95	☐ 345-7 @ 2.50	☐ 319-8 @ 2.95
☐ 364-3 @ 9.95	☐ 189-6 @ 9.95	☐ 356-2 @ 9.95	☐ 316-3 @ 2.95	☐ 317-1 @ 2.95
☐ 381-3 @ 9.95	☐ 353-8 @ 9.95	☐ 355-4 @ 9.95	☐ 323-6 @ 2.50	☐ 385-6 @ 2.95
☐ 363-5 @ 9.95	☐ 125-X @ 9.95	☐ 348-1 @ 9.95	☐ 396-1 @ 2.95	☐ 387-2 @ 2.95
☐ 374-0 @ 9.95	☐ 352-X @ 9.95	☐ 365-1 @ 9.95	☐ 318-X @ 2.95	☐ 386-4 @ 2.95
☐ 354-6 @ 9.95	☐ 371-6 @ 9.95	☐ 369-4 @ 9.95	☐ 378-3 @ 2.95	☐ 171-3 @ 6.95
☐ 350-3 @ 9.95	☐ 191-8 @ 9.95	☐ 308-2 @ 2.50	☐ 315-5 @ 2.50	☐ 300-7 @ 6.95
☐ 384-8 @ 9.95	☐ 187-X @ 9.95	☐ 373-2 @ 2.95	☐ 372-4 @ 2.95	☐ 301-5 @ 6.95
☐ 357-0 @ 9.95	☐ 351-1 @ 9.95	☐ 376-7 @ 2.95	☐ 400-3 @ 2.95	☐ 302-3 @ 6.95
☐ 367-8 @ 9.95	☐ 375-9 @ 9.95	☐ 377-5 @ 2.95	☐ 314-7 @ 2.50	

Add $1.50 postage and handling for the first book and 50¢ for each additional book. Add $2.50 to each order for insurance and special handling. Florida residents add 5% sales tax.

☐ Check or money order enclosed $_____ (include postage and handling)

☐ Please charge $_____ to my: ☐ MASTERCARD   ☐ VISA

Charge Card Customers Not Using Our Toll Free Number Please Fill Out The Information Below.

Account No. (All Digits) _____ Expiration Date _____

Signature _____

NAME (please print) _____ PHONE _____

ADDRESS _____ APT. # _____

CITY _____ STATE _____ ZIP _____

⑩